Driving Towards Socialism

POLISH STUDIES – TRANSDISCIPLINARY PERSPECTIVES

Edited by Jarosław Fazan and Krzysztof Zajas

VOLUME 50

Hubert Wilk

Driving Towards Socialism

Society, Power, and Cars in Poland 1945–1970

PETER LANG
Berlin · Bruxelles · Chennai · Lausanne · New York · Oxford

Bibliographic Information published by the Deutsche Nationalbibliothek
The Deutsche Nationalbibliothek lists this publication in the Deutsche Nationalbibliografie; detailed bibliographic data is available online at http://dnb.d-nb.de.

Library of Congress Cataloging-in-Publication Data
A CIP catalog record for this book has been applied for at the Library of Congress.

This Publication is co-financed from the state budget as part of a program implemented by the Minister of Science and Higher Education under the name "National Program for the Development of Humanities, project no. NPRH/U21/SP/496332/2021/10, amount of co-financing PLN 68 455," total value of the project PLN 68 455.

NATIONAL PROGRAMME FOR THE DEVELOPMENT OF HUMANITIES

Cover image: National Digital Archives, Zbyszko Siemaszko, 3/51/0/6.21/206/1

Translation of H. Wilk, *Między pragmatyzmem a oczekiwaniami. Społeczeństwo, władza i samochody w Polsce 1945-1970*, Warszawa 2017

ISSN 2191-3293
ISBN 978-3-631-94951-1 (Print)
ISBN 978-3-631-94952-8 (ePDF)
ISBN 978-3-631-95270-2 (ePUB)
DOI 10.3726/b23769

Published by Peter Lang GmbH, Berlin, Germany

info@peterlang.com

This publication has been peer reviewed.

www.peterlang.com

Contact for General Product Safety Regulation (GPSR): gpsr@peterlang.com

Contents

Figures

Tables

Introduction

> A car is unlike any other piece of equipment. Many people pray to it, experience erotic thrills at the sight of it, believe that it has a soul, call it a secret name and, when no one is listening, talk to it. A car is the key to freedom, and maybe that is why it stimulates the acquisition gland so strongly through the human imagination. With a car, you gain the desired, if somewhat illusory, independence: you can be where you want, when you want.[1]

The above words are those of Andrzej Krzysztof Wróblewski, a columnist and journalist associated with the *Polityka* weekly, writing in the late 1980s. Krzysztof Pomian treated the car as a civilisational achievement that could easily be filled with meaning; it symbolised material status, a lifestyle. The car carried within itself the idea of rebellion and freedom, but also comfort and safety.[2] Henri Lefebvre called it a "Leading-Object" that promotes hierarchisation in various ways. The French sociologist wrote: "Today the greater part of everyday life is accompanied by the noise of engines."[3] Roland Barthes went even further when, in his classic collection of essays *Mythologies*, he deified the latest model of the Citroën DS 19 by way of a play on words, calling it a "Goddess" (*déesse*), and stated that cars are "almost the exact equivalent of

---

1 A. K. Wróblewski, *Polska na kółkach*, Warszawa 1989, p. 5.

2 J. Jaworska, "Samochód dla każdego," in: *Obyczaje polskie. Wiek XX w krótkich hasłach*, ed. M. Szpakowska, Warszawa 2008, p. 300.

3 H. Lefebvre, *Everyday Life in the Modern World*, New York 2016, pp. 86–88.

the great Gothic cathedrals."[4] Fascinated by speed, Italian futurists reached deeper into the past, writing in their Manifesto about "a roaring car ... more beautiful than the Nike of Samothrace."[5] In his famous essay "Life Behind the Wheel," sociologist John Urry noted the importance of the car as an article of individual consumption.[6] Jean Baudrillard, on the other hand, observed that the car is "one of the main foci of daily and long-term waste, both private and collective."[7] Many such opinions and statements point to the vital role played by the car in the last century.[8] For the twentieth century, it was what the railroad and the steam engine had been a hundred years earlier, central as they were to the nineteenth-century transportation revolution.[9] Roberto Salvadori placed the car on the same level as another revolutionary invention of the preceding century—the cinema. Together, they constituted a synthesis and symbol of the process by which individual and social life were mechanised.[10]

Modernity, speed and progress were especially important to communism. They perfectly corresponded to Marxism's demand for modernisation and fascination with technology, which can be seen, for example, in the Soviet

4 R. Barthes, "The New Citroën," in: *idem*, *Mythologies*, trans. Annette Lavers, London: Vintage, 1993, p. 88.

5 The creator of the Futurist Manifesto, Filippo Tommaso Marinetti, once suffered a serious car accident and, according to Giovanni Lista, this fact "achieved the rank of a miracle of rebirth, a resurrection to another life." See G. Lista, *Futuryzm*, Warszawa 2002, p. 29; T. Miczka, *Czas przyszły niedokonany. O włoskiej sztuce futurystycznej*, Katowice 1994, pp. 40–41.

6 J. Urry, "Życie za kółkiem," in: *Socjologia codzienności*, ed. P. Sztompka i M. Bogunia-Borowska, Kraków 2008, p. 412.

7 J. Baudrillard, *The Consumer Society: Myths and Structures*, London: SAGE Publications, 1998, p. 47.

8 Cf. M. Fałkowski, "Życie codzienne w samochodzie. Schematy interakcji i wzajemnego postrzegania się kierowców z perspektywy socjologii życia codziennego," *Kultura i Społeczeństwo*, 2010, vol. 54, no. 1, pp. 163–164.

9 W. Reinhard, *Życie po europejsku. Od czasów najdawniejszych do współczesności*, Warszawa 2009, pp. 371–372.

10 R. Salvadori, "Sceny pierwotne," in: *Mitologia codzienności*, Warszawa 2004, pp. 39–40.

obsession with the conquest of space[11] and of the air,[12] but also with the automotive industry.[13] The development of industries responsible for the production of automobiles offered an opportunity for the technological modernisation of the entire economy. However, socialist vehicles were not to be passenger cars—a potentially destabilising factor due to their association with the values of individualism—but rather tractors, trucks, and buses, to serve the collective.[14] Hence the primacy, in almost all socialist economies, of truck production over passenger cars and of collective transport over individual motorisation. Exceptions were Czechoslovakia and the German Democratic Republic (GDR, East Germany), whose automotive traditions dated back to the turn of the twentieth century. Nevertheless, despite serious attempts to eliminate some of the problematic meanings and symbols associated with the passenger car and to turn it into a mere means of transport, the perception of individual motorisation in countries ruled by communists after 1945 did not differ significantly from that of their neighbours on the western side of the Iron Curtain. As early as 1957, Stanisław Lem wrote in *Przekrój* that the car was used primarily "to shine, to spread the peacock's tail, to stab a knife into the heart of friends and to twist it slowly. … The car thus becomes more of an object of worship than an object of use; it is not so much a means of transport from place to place as a wonderful device, transporting its owner from the gray crowd into the sphere of the Refined Elite." In one of his commentaries broadcast by the Polish Radio, Andrzej Szczypiorski stated: "In the current stage of civilisation, the automobile has ceased to be a means of transportation and became a means of expression for the psyche of an individual living in the society. Instead of an object, it has

---

11 See e.g.: H. Wilk, "Od Sputnika do selenautów. Kosmiczny wyścig w świetle oficjalnej propagandy PRL (1957–1969)," in: *Yesterday. Studia z historii najnowszej. Księga dedykowana prof. Jerzemu Eislerowi w 65. rocznicę urodzin*, ed. J. Olaszek, A. Dudek, Ł. Kamiński, K. Kosiński, M. Przeperski, K. Rokicki, P. Sasanka, R. Spałek, and S. Stępień, Warszawa 2017, p. 375.

12 S. Fitzpatrick, *Życie codzienne pod rządami Stalina. Rosja radziecka w latach trzydziestych XX wieku*, Kraków 2012, p. 103ff.

13 N. Nettleton, "Driving towards communist consumerism. AvtoVAZ," *Cahiers du monde russe* 2006, vol. 47, no. 1–2, pp. 131–151, here p. 132.

14 L. Gatejel, "The Common Heritage of the Socialist Car Culture," in: *The Socialist Car: Automobility in the Eastern Bloc*, ed. L. H. Siegelbaum, New York 2011, p. 145.

become a goal."[15] These sentiments were echoed by Waldemar Hanasz, who believed that the development of individual motorisation was the beginning of the end of the communist system.[16]

For a number of years, the history of the automobile and of the automotive industry has been an object of growing interest for scholars in various parts of the academia, including the humanities.[17] There are definitely more publications concerned with the development of the automotive industry in Western Europe[18] and in the United States[19] than in countries that, after World War II, found themselves within the sphere of influence of the Union of Soviet Socialist Republics or within Soviet borders themselves. One author who deserves to be mentioned here is Lewis H. Siegelbaum, whose history of "cars for comrades" set the direction for further research on motorisation in the people's republics.[20] He also edited a volume of studies devoted to motorisation in the Eastern Bloc.[21] There is a relatively large amount of studies about motorisation in East Germany.[22] Among the most important authors in this area are Jonathan Zatlin and Peter Kirchberg.[23] Luminita Gatejel compared

---

15 Quoted in: W. Tobis, "Uwaga apokalipsa, *Motor* 1963, no. 4, p. 3.

16 W. Hanasz, *Engines of liberty. Cars and the Collapse of Communism in Eastern Europe. A personal essay*, p. 15 (http://www.cei.org/pdf/1755.pdf, accessed: March 15, 2014).

17 See: M. Jastrząb, "Historia motoryzacji i przemysłu motoryzacyjnego. Stan i cele badań," in: *Przegląd badań nad historią gospodarczą w XXI wieku*, ed. R. Matera and A. Pieczewski, Łódź 2011, pp. 161–173.

18 See e.g.: L. J. K. Setright, *Drive On! A Social History of the Motor Car*, London 2003; A. Marvick, *The Sixties: Cultural revolution in Britain, France, Italy and the United States, c. 1958–1974*, New York 1998; *The Economic and Social Effects of the Spread of Motor Vehicles*, ed. T. Barker, London 1987; S. Gunn, "People and the car: The expansion of automobility in urban Britain, 1955–1970," *Social History* 2013, vol. 38, no. 2, pp. 220–237.

19 See e.g.: C. McShane, *Down the Asphalt Path: The Automobile and the American City*, New York 1994; J. A. Heitmann, *The automobile and American Life*, Jefferson 2009. Books on the history of Henry Ford's empire alone have been published by the dozen.

20 L. H. Siegelbaum, *Cars for Comrades: The Life of the Soviet Automobile*, Cornell University Press 2008.

21 *The Socialist Car: Automobility in the Eastern Bloc*, ed. L. H. Siegelbaum, New York 2011.

22 See e.g.: S. Friedrich, *Autos bauen im Sozialismus. Arbeit und Organisationskultur in der Zwickauer Automobilindustrie nach 1945*, Leipzig 2008.

23 P. Kirchberg, *Plaste, Blech und Planwirtschaft. Die Geschichte des Automobilbaus in der DDR*, Berlin 2000.

the situation in three countries: the USSR, East Germany, and Romania.[24] In turn, the case of Czechoslovakia has been studied by Valentina Fava, who was primarily interested in the history of the local automotive industry.[25] The differences and similarities between Eastern and Western Europe were addressed by the authors of an edited collection entitled *Towards Mobility: Varieties of Automobilism in East and West*.[26]

Meanwhile, the history of the Polish automobile and Poland's automotive industry has so far not been the subject of broader interest for historians.[27] As far as the People's Republic of Poland (PRL) is concerned, Mariusz Jastrząb has published the most on the subject.[28] The only monograph on the history of the automotive industry in the PRL is a book about the Syrena car by Karol J. Mórawski.[29] Jakub de Mezer has written about Polish motorcycles.[30] Tomasz

---

24 L. Gatejel, *Warten, hoffen und endlich fahren. Auto und Sozialismus in der Sowjetunion, in Rumänien und der DDR, 1956–1989/91*, Frankfurt am Main 2014.

25 V. Fava, *The Socialist People's Car: Automobiles, Shortages, and Consent on the Czechoslovak Road to Mass Production (1918–1964)*, Amsterdam 2013.

26 *Towards mobility. Varieties of Automobilism in East and West*, ed. D. Schlinkert, M. Grieger, and U. Gutzmann, Wolfsburg 2009.

27 A study by Mariusz W. Majewski, published in 2016, discusses the development of the automotive industry in the Second Polish Republic: *idem*, *Rozwój motoryzacji w Drugiej Rzeczpospolitej*, Kraków 2016.

28 M. Jastrząb, "Fiat's small cars for Polish mass motorisation: The Small Engine Car Factory in Bielsko-Biała and Tychy, 1971–1980," *Journal of Transport History* 2017, vol. 38, no. 1, pp. 37–52; *idem*, "Zajazdy dla zmotoryzowanych w Polsce lat siedemdziesiątych," *Przegląd Historyczny* 2013, no. 2, pp. 325–348; *idem*, "Socjalistyczna praworządność i egalitaryzm. Nadużycia władzy w epoce gierkowskiej i walka z nimi. Przykład talonów samochodowych," in: *Społeczeństwo polskie w latach 1980–1989*, ed. N. Jarska and J. Olaszek, Warszawa–Kraków 2015, pp. 70–86; M. Jastrząb and E. Jastrząb, "Edukacja w zakresie bezpieczeństwa ruchu drogowego w polskich szkołach. Historia inercji instytucjonalnej," in: *Na lądzie, w wodzie i w powietrzu… Z dziejów transportu i komunikacji na ziemiach polskich na przestrzeni wieków*, ed. T. Głowiński and R. Klementowski, Wrocław 2014, pp. 279–288; *idem*, "Nadzór nad wielką inwestycją przemysłową: budowa Fabryki Samochodów Małolitrażowych i wdrożenie produkcji Fiata 126p," in: *Z dziejów przemysłu na ziemiach polskich*, ed. R. Klementowski and E. Kościk, Wrocław 2012, pp. 113–122; M. Jastrząb and J. Wawrzyniak, "Dwie nowoczesności polskiego przemysłu motoryzacyjnego. O rozwoju zależnym Fabryki Samochodów Osobowych, *Acta Poloniae Historica* (w druku).

29 K. J. Mórawski, *Syrena. Samochód PRL*, Warszawa 2005.

30 J. de Mezer, *Cywilizacja motocyklowa. Motoryzacja motocyklowa w Polsce 1945–1965*, Warszawa 2011.

Szczerbicki authored a popular monograph on the Syrena and other cars from the PRL era, but these works are mostly comprised of trivia amassed by an author driven by a deep passion for automobiles.[31] Another volume by this author, on the history of the Mercedes in Poland, is similar in character.[32] Paweł Sowiński noted the impact that motorisation had on tourism on the margins of his work on the subject.[33] Błażej Brzostek's study about everyday life in Warsaw devoted a great deal of space to motorisation and its impact on the life of the city's inhabitants.[34] A great deal has been written about the history of the production of individual models; among the most important of such contributions are works by Aleksander Rummel[35] and Andrzej Zieliński[36] devoted to Polish car production. Representatives of other fields in the humanities, such as sociology, psychology, and anthropology, have referred somewhat more often to issues related to the automotive industry.[37]

The development of the automotive industry in Poland was closely associated with political breakthroughs—a fact noted by Jacek Kuroń, who said in an interview with Jacek Żakowski: "The final victory of the new [communist] order gave Poland the Warszawa car—a copy of the M-20 Pobeda built on Soviet license … The child of the thaw [in 1956] was the Syrena …. In 1968, production of Polish Fiat 125p began."[38] If we add to this the change of power in 1970, when Władysław Gomułka was replaced as first secretary by Edward Gierek (who, unlike his predecessor, adopted the "car for everyone"

---

31 T. Szczerbicki, *Syrena*, Poznań 2016; *idem*, *Samochody w PRL. Rzecz o motoryzacji i nie tylko…*, Poznań 2010.

32 T. Szczerbicki and J. Tarczyński, *Mercedes a sprawa polska*, Warszawa 2006.

33 P. Sowiński, *Wakacje w Polsce Ludowej. Polityka władz i ruch turystyczny (1945–1989)*, Warszawa 2005.

34 B. Brzostek, *Za progiem. Codzienność w przestrzeni publicznej Warszawy lat 1955–1970*, Warszawa 2007.

35 A. Rummel, *Polskie konstrukcje i licencje motoryzacyjne w latach 1922–1980*, Warszawa 1985.

36 A. Zieliński, *Rozwój koncepcji samochodu osobowego w XX wieku*, Warszawa 2005.

37 E.g. J. Jaworska, "Samochód dla każdego"; R. Sulima, *Antropologia codzienności*, Kraków 2000; R. Bugowski, "Polski Fiat jako 'miejsce pamięci'. Rola i obraz marki polskiej drugiej połowy XX wieku. Refleksje wokół koncepcji," *Klio* 2011, no. 1, pp. 123–140; T. Komornicki, *Przemiany mobilności codziennej Polaków na tle rozwoju motoryzacji*, Warszawa 2011; M. Falkowski, "Życie codzienne w samochodzie."

38 J. Kuroń and J. Żakowski, *PRL dla początkujących*, Wrocław 1995, pp. 140–141.

policy), we obtain the timespan, from 1945 to 1970, which encompasses the main parts of this book. Roch Sulima writes that with the departure of the Syrena—the last Syrena rolled off the assembly lines in 1983—"the heroic episode of the Polish socialist automotive industry came to an end."[39] Certainly, it is worth pondering the words of this cultural anthropologist for a moment. An analysis of the postwar quarter century tends to suggest a slightly different chronology of this "heroic period," one which coincides exactly with the years 1945–1970, especially if one takes into account the growth of individual motorisation. In my opinion, this period ends with the appearance of "Maluch"—more precisely, with the announcement by Edward Gierek's administration of its plans for development in this area—rather than a decade later. Thus, I limited the chronology of my book to the years 1945–1970. This decision was prompted by the fact that during this period, Polish society first encountered private cars on a large scale. Never before and never after did the number of cars increase so rapidly (though only in relative numbers) as when Władysław Gomułka was First Secretary. Even if it was not until the 1970s that a real automotive boom came to Poland, several phenomena in the thus far under-examined period of 1956–1970 related to the constantly increasing presence of the passenger car on Polish roads. It was in this period that important social attitudes and behaviours towards the automotive industry were shaped, that Polish society "learned" about cars, and that cars exerted influence on Poles. Hence the chronological framework of this book.

An account of the development of the Polish automotive industry would be incomplete without reference to the beginning of the twentieth century and the Second Polish Republic, when cars first appeared on Polish roads. State policy towards motorists during that period, along with the devastating effects of World War II, were decisive for the later fate of the industry. The first chapter is devoted to these issues. The second chapter covers the years 1945–1955, when the Polish state rebuilt its automobile fleet with great difficulty and practically from scratch. It contains information about the institutions responsible for the development of the automotive industry, about plans established for the industry, and about the ways in which motor vehicles

39 R. Sulima, *Antropologia codzienności*, p. 50.

were obtained. This was also the period when the production of passenger cars began in Żerań, the popular name for the Passenger Car Factory (FSO), which was located in Żerań, a district of Warsaw.

The difficulties associated with obtaining licences for cars are also discussed in this chapter, which closes with a description of the "automotive everyday" in the face of deepening Stalinisation, manifested, among others, in restrictive legislation on vehicle registration, but also on automobile traffic. The following chapter describes the quarter century of Władysław Gomułka's rule. Gomułka, colloquially known as comrade "Wiesław," the First Secretary of the Central Committee of the Polish United Workers' Party, governed Poland from October 1956 to December 1970. The fourth chapter is devoted entirely to "Poles on the road to the automobile." It discusses the possibilities of buying one's own car, both through official sales channels (Motozbyt, internal export, redundant company vehicles) and through non-official distribution systems (maritime import, car exchanges). This chapter also presents privileged groups, which had easier access to passenger cars compared to the broader society. A separate subchapter is devoted to miners and to the irregularities in the allocation of vouchers and shares in the foreign exchange fund. The last chapter focuses on the everyday concerns of Poles who had their own automobiles. It discusses what are, in my opinion, the most important phenomena and problems experienced by the motorised segment of the society in the 1950s and 1960s: the condition and size of vehicle fleet, issues of road safety, legislation and crime related to motorisation, problems with fuel, service stations, parking lots and garages. Separate sub-chapters present case studies of sorts, often reaching beyond the period of Władysław Gomułka's era; this is necessary in order to demonstrate the sources of particular problems.

The main assumptions and the course of the development of the automotive industry in Poland, including the role of automobile manufacturing and its place in the country's economy, are therefore well within the purview of my study. Of particular interest are the following questions: What kind of pragmatism characterised the actions taken by authorities, and to what degree had it hindered or catalysed developments? Did the authorities see privately owned passenger cars as a manifestation of "Western fashion," a real threat undermining the regime's ideological foundations, or rather as a modernising impulse that could help increase the expansion of the economy?

(Such was the case with countries on the western side of the Iron Curtain.) Could a passenger car become an export commodity that generated significant profit and thus attracted the much-needed foreign currency? In the socialist economy and its realities, the plans of the authorities were one thing, and their implementation was something quite different. So, did the expansion of the necessary infrastructure—roads, service stations, gas stations, a sufficient number of garages and parking spaces—keep up with developments within the automotive industry? The picture would be incomplete if an attempt were not made to reconstruct the impact these developments had on the Polish society—for instance, due to safety concerns in connection with the increase in the number of motor vehicles travelling on the roads.

The catalogue of problems is long and naturally, for my purposes here, had to be limited. Thus, even interesting questions—such as changes in the way Poles spent their free time, the presence of vehicles in culture, or the impact of automobiles on environmental pollution and the landscape, which changed irreversibly under the influence of the expanding automotive industry—were beyond the scope of this work. Apart from sketching the postwar history of the Polish Automobile Club (Automobilklub Polski, AP), it does not discuss the various social organisations that interacted with the automotive industry broadly understood. In practice, each of these subjects deserves a separate study. Two-wheeled vehicles, which were extremely popular in Poland at the time, rarely appear in these pages. Omitting this subject was one of the more difficult choices I faced while writing. Nevertheless, I decided that focusing on passenger cars would simplify the narrative, making it clearer and more accessible to the reader.

Looking for answers to these research questions, I analysed various sources, the core of which were the documents created by state institutions in the period under discussion. The query covered primarily the files stored in the Archiwum Akt Nowych (Central Archives of Modern Records) and the Archiwum Instytutu Pamięci Narodowej (Archive of the Institute of National Remembrance). Several interesting sources were also found in the State Archives in Kielce, Lublin, and Gdańsk. The query in the Archives of the Ministry of Foreign Affairs, where I sought information on trade agreements between Poland and other countries, yielded unsatisfactory results. I found highly interesting materials in the Central Archives of Bank Pekao S.A. News dailies (e.g. *Trybuna Ludu*), socio-cultural periodicals (mainly *Polityka* and

Życie Gospodarcze), and industry magazines (*Motor* and *Motoryzacja*) proved to be extremely valuable. Personal testimonies were also an important category of sources; I used journals, diaries, and memoirs, as well. At the same time, due to problems with establishing a sufficient sample of respondents, I abandoned the idea of pursuing eye-witness interviews, aware though I was of the potential value of materials of this kind, especially when analysing the social aspects of the development of the automotive industry in Poland. Reports published both in the press and in standalone form turned out to be interesting from the point of view of methodology. Letters that Poles wrote to institutions—e.g. the Polish Radio or the Central Committee of the Polish United Workers' Party—were extremely important in establishing the source base. A query of audiovisual materials was carried out in the Archives of Polish Radio and Television, the National Digital Archives, the Polish Press Agency, the Forum Polish Photographers Agency, and on the Internet, where a complete collection of episodes of the *Polska Kronika Filmowa* (Polish Film Chronicle) is available. Source material also included published statistical data gathered by the Central Statistical Office (GUS) and public opinion polls conducted by the Center for Public Opinion Research and Program Studies (OBOPiSP), currently available in the digital archive of TNS Polska. Materials of great value were culled from research carried out in the late 1960s and early 1970s by a team led by Zdzisław Krasiński, published in volumes entitled *Czynniki ekonomiczno-społeczne rozwoju motoryzacji indywidualnej w Polsce w świetle badań ankietowych* (Socioeconomic factors in the development of individual motorisation in Poland in the light of survey data, Poznań 1972) and *Handel i usługi na tle rozwoju motoryzacji indywidualnej* (Trade and services in the context of the development of individual motorisation, Warsaw 1977). An important complement to the greater whole are satirical drawings on automotive topics, published in the Polish press in the years 1955–1970, particular those printed in the weekly *Szpilki*.

* * *

This book would not have been written without the help of my colleagues in the Department of Research on the History of Poland after 1945 at the Tadeusz Manteuffel Institute of History of the Polish Academy of Science. I would also like to thank those who kindly reviewed the manuscript: Dr Jarosław

Dulewicz and Dr Mariusz Jastrząb, whose comments and suggestions allowed me to avoid various errors and mistakes. During work on the book, many people shared their findings with me, which greatly facilitated my work on the subject of Polish motorisation: Professor Dariusz Jarosz, Professor Jerzy Kochanowski, Drs. Ewelina Szpak, Michał Przeperski and Edyta Wróbel, to whom I also express my gratitude. Finally, I want to thank Maciej Wilmański, Director of the Central Archives of Bank Pekao S.A., whose assistance facilitated my query in the bank archives.

Starting Point

1.1 The beginnings of motorisation in polish lands

The beginnings of the Polish automotive industry date back to the turn of the twentieth century. Under the partitions, Poland was as if removed from events that gave rise to mass motorisation in Europe and the United States. It was not until the last decade of the nineteenth century that the industrial capacity necessary for the production of internal combustion engines—powered by gasoline and diesel fuel—was developed, first at Rajmund Machczyński's Gas and Oil Motor Factory at Skierniewicka Street 4 in Warsaw. Machczyński was a pioneer of automotive industry in the Polish territories. Subsequent, similar factories were established in Warsaw: the Ursus Fittings and Motor Factory and the Perkun Motor Factory. However, companies involved in this type of production were definitely less numerous than those building various types of carriages. According to Mariusz W. Majewski, in the years 1850–1914, there were over a hundred of the latter in Poland, only some of which could smoothly switch to more complicated type of production involving the construction of automobile bodies for chassis imported from abroad.[40] As Aleksander Rummel has noted, there was practically no automotive industry in the entire territory of the future Polish state because plans for the erection of an automobile factory in Kraków in 1911–1912 and of the Automotor plant in Lviv in 1917 were not implemented beyond craftsmanship tests involving

40 M. W. Majewski, "Powstanie przemysłu motoryzacyjnego w II Rzeczypospolitej 1919–1928," in: *Z dziejów przemysłu przed 1945 rokiem*, ed. J. Chumiński and M. Zawadzki, Wrocław 2012, p. 207.

an eight-seat "omnibus," produced in Warsaw in 1904 by Henryk Brzeski and Wincenty Schindler, and the three-wheeler from 1906.[41]

Backwardness in this respect affected the degree to which society was motorised. The first automobiles in Poland were to be purchased in 1897 by Stanisław Grodzki, later president of the Polish Automobile Club, and Karol Raczyński. Grodzki, co-owner of the Agricultural Machinery and Tools Depot in Warsaw, held the first documented automobile "show" by driving a 3.5-horsepower Peugeot along the routes Senatorska Street—Plac Bankowy—Senatorska Street and Senatorska Street—Plac Trzech Krzyży—Senatorska Street. More vehicles appeared soon thereafter; for example, in Galicia, there were 40 automobiles in 1907; meanwhile, in Kraków, there were 12, but by mid-1913, the number increased to 113. Similar numbers were recorded in Warsaw, with 28 automobiles in 1902, 62 in 1909, and 217 in 1913. At the forefront was Poznań, and Greater Poland more generally, where 834 passenger cars were registered in 1912.[42] It is not possible to determine more precisely the shape of automobile ownership in other parts of the country.

For military purposes, the partition authorities confiscated these privately owned cars, regardless of their small number. Estimates from 1914, prepared by Department II of the General Staff of the Polish Army, stated that there were about 1,500 motor vehicles registered in the Kingdom of Poland, an autonomous administrative unit within the Russian Empire. Later estimates prepared by the Motorised Section of the Department II of the Ministry of Military Affairs indicate that in November 1920, there were already over 10,000 automobiles within the borders of the Second Polish Republic. These were primarily vehicles taken from Austrian and German troops, which were usually in poor technical condition and of little value; included in this number was a negligible amount of privately imported cars. A slight improvement came with the return of the army of General Józef Haller from France, which after playing significant role on the Western Front, brought along some motor vehicles (926 passenger cars and trucks and 70 motorcycles) along with American vehicles from French demobilisation depots (1,700 cars and

---

41 A. Rummel, *Polskie konstrukcje*, p. 13; J. Tarczyński and W. Jeleń, *Początki polskiej motoryzacji. Samochody CWS*, Warszawa 1991, p. 9.

42 J. M., *Zmotoryzujmy Polskę*, Warszawa 1939, p. 6; S. Szelichowski, *Dzieje polskiej motoryzacji*, Łódź 2012, p. 10.

281 motorcycles). A number of vehicles were also provided by institutions organising charity aid for Poland.[43]

The first new automobiles reached Poland in 1919, when 300 Fiat trucks were purchased for the army. At that time, a small number of passenger Fords were also imported, intended for civilian use.[44] Larger imports were halted when the Polish-Soviet War (February 1919–March 1921) broke out and customs borders were closed, remaining so until 1922.[45] One should also mention the imposition of an extraordinary state duty from the beginning of October to the end of December 1921. Pursuant to this regulation, listed vehicle owners had to pay a certain fee, which in the case of a passenger car with a 15-horsepower engine came to one million marks, and in the case of less powerful vehicles amounted to 750,000 marks.[46] It represented an expenditure equivalent to at least several months' salary of a qualified worker. In addition, owners of private cars were again forced to hand their vehicles over to the army for the duration of the war.[47]

The increase in the size of the vehicle fleet also broadened the number of makes and models, which translated into difficulties in providing these vehicles with maintenance facilities. Some makes were available in only a few units, which made the importation of spare parts unprofitable. It is thus not surprising that in subsequent years, the number of vehicles in Poland decreased as a result of wear and tear and as they were gradually

---

43 T. Wójcik, "Centralne Warsztaty Samochodowe w Warszawie w latach 1918–1928. Przyczynek do genezy polskiej motoryzacji," *Przegląd Historyczno-Wojskowy* 2013, no. 2, pp. 187–188; *idem*, "Wybrane aspekty działalności wojska w rozwoju motoryzacji II Rzeczypospolitej," in: *Z dziejów przemysłu przed 1945 rokiem*, pp. 304–305; A. Rostocki and J. Tarczyński, *Automobilizm w Warszawie do 1939 r.*, Warszawa 1988, p. 152. Kazimierz Groniewski mentions the following brands of passenger cars left behind by the armies of both partitioning powers: NAG, Stoever, Opel, Dixi, Horch, Wanderer, and Adler. From France came: Delage, Renault, Chenard-Walker, Delahay, and Delaunay-Belleville. On the other hand, American surplus consisted mainly of Dodge, Cadillac, and Ford Model T cars; see *idem*, *Technika motoryzacyjna w Polsce międzywojennej*, Warszawa 1965, p. 43.

44 J. Kaliński, "Motoryzacja a infrastruktura drogowa w Polsce po 1918 r.," in: *Na lądzie, w wodzie i w powietrzu…*, p. 139.

45 M. W. Majewski, "Powstanie przemysłu motoryzacyjnego," p. 208.

46 "Dziennik Urzędowy" (hereafter: Dz. Urz.) 1922, no. 1, pos. 1.

47 A. Rostocki and J. Tarczyński, *Automobilizm w Warszawie*, p. 152.

decommissioned. The French magazine *L'Auto* reported that in 1922 there were about 5,000 automobiles in Poland. The first nationwide data on the ownership of cars presented by the Ministry of Public Works come from 1924, when the obligation to register them was introduced. At that time, there were 7,500 vehicles in Poland, of which 27% were trucks (Table 1). Inflation in the first half of the 1920s made the automobile a quite safe investment, one that lost value only slowly. Hence, there was a fairly significant, though still small, increase in the number of cars.[48]

Table 1. The state of motorisation in the Second Polish Republic

Year	Automobiles						Motorcycles
	General	Passenger			Trucks	Per 10,000 Inhabitants	
		Together	Including				
			Taxis	Buses			
1922	5000	–	–	–	–	–	–
1924	7547	–	–	–	–	–	934
1925	9789	–	–	–	–	–	–
1926	14670	11807	2283	756	2811	4.9	2481
1927	16633	13588	2970	1012	2966	5.5	3022
1928	21922	18316	3973	1544	3494	7.2	3734
1929	29701	24527	6016	2841	4896	9.6	4597
1930	37418	30258	7332	4048	6738	11.8	5901
1931	39391	31320	7140	4293	7440	12.1	7940
1932	28690	22163	5152	3047	5801	8.9	7940
1933	26015	19643	5426	2545	5623	7.7	8182
1934	26969	20667	4941	2160	5466	7.9	8322
1935	25868	19876	4578	1542	4945	7.8	8305
1936	25734	19659	4298	1499	5000	7.7	8395
1937	28570	21881	4453	1543	5545	8.4	8898

48 J. Kaliński, "Motoryzacja a infrastruktura drogowa," p. 139.

Year	Automobiles						Motorcycles
	General	Passenger			Trucks	Per 10,000 Inhabitants	
		Together	Including				
			Taxis	Buses			
1938	34324	26248	4946	1754	6843	9.9	9876
1939	41948	31804	5216	2038	8609	12.1	12061

Source: Mały Rocznik Statystyczny GUS 1939, Warszawa 1939, p. 199; M. W. Nestorowicz, Sprawa drogowa w Polsce, Warszawa 1923, p. 3; J. Makłowicz, Zmotoryzujmy Polskę, Warszawa 1933, pp. 6–8.

—No data

Only when the economic situation improved in 1926 was there growth in this regard, mainly thanks to imports. However, as historians studying this matter have emphasised, this growth was not regulated by any state policy and basically took into account neither the economic nor military needs of the country.[49] When in 1932 military leaders issued the *Alfabetyczny spis istniejących marek samochodów i motocykli* (Alphabetical List of Existing Makes of Cars and Motorcycles), it turned out that there were over 500 different makes of automobiles and over 300 different makes of motorcycles on Polish roads.[50] Apart from the above-mentioned problems with providing mechanical facilities for these vehicles, this situation was particularly worrisome for the military, which sought to unify the automotive fleet in case of an armed conflict.[51] In 1921, the army "organised" the types and brands of vehicles, mandating the use of the following truck brands: US, Packard, Pierce Arrow, and White, as well as Cadillac V8, Dodge, and Ford Model T. The remaining makes were sold to civilians.[52] Interestingly, buyers often purchased several cars of a given model—of course, if there was such a possibility—in order to ensure access to spare parts, at least for a while.[53]

49 Ibid.

50 M. Relich, "Załamanie motoryzacji w Polsce na skutek tzw. demotoryzacji kraju w latach 1931–1935 i próby jej odbudowy w drugiej połowie lat 30. XX wieku," in: *Na lądzie, w wodzie i w powietrzu…*, p. 201.

51 M. W. Majewski, "Powstanie przemysłu motoryzacyjnego," p. 208.

52 A. Rostocki and J. Tarczyński, *Automobilizm w Warszawie*, p. 152.

53 K. Groniewski, *Technika motoryzacyjna w Polsce*, p. 36.

The first attempts to start Polish automobile production were made two years after Poland regained independence in November 1918. At that time, Warsaw car specialists Stefan Kozłowski and Antoni Frączkowski, who had established themselves still under the partitions, decided to open a small car factory producing the make S.K.A.F. This little vehicle was supposed to reach a speed of 40 km/h. The manufacturers intended to provide each car with a free toolkit containing a pump, a wrench and the tools needed to replace a punctured tyre. In addition, buyers would receive instructions for building a garage: a padlocked box. However, no S.K.A.F. has probably ever left the factory halls.[54] Two other models—the Polonia, designed by engineer Mikołaj Karpowski and presented to the general public in early June 1924, and Stefan Tysziewicz's Ralf-Stetysz, dating from around the same time—also failed to become fixtures on Polish roads. While in the case of the former, the production run ended with a single vehicle, Ralf-Statysz was successfully produced in Boulogne in France, and then at the Warsaw-based factory of the Count Stefan Tyszkiewicz Agricultural-Automobile Factory, Joint-Stock Company (Towarzystwo Akcyjne "Rolniczo-Automobilowa Fabryka Hr. Stefan Tyszkiewicz"). A total of two hundred units were made, but the entire project was stopped by a fire in the factory, which the constructor subsequently failed to convince shareholders to rebuild.[55]

The beginning of the Polish automotive industry after regained independence is generally associated with the start of operations by the Centralne Warsztaty Samochodowe (Central Automotive Works, CWS). Located on Terespolska Street in Warsaw, these German military workshops were taken over by Poles in November 1918. Due to the above-mentioned terrible technical condition of the automobile fleet during the first years of its operation, CWS dealt mainly with repairs; in 1920, it began the production of car bodies, and five years later, it produced the first passenger car, designed by engineer Tadeusz Tański—the CWS T 1.[56] In 1928, the plant was reorganised. CWS was renamed as National Automobile Factory (Państwowa

54 W. Rychter, *Dzieje samochodu*, Warszawa 1979, p. 341.

55 Ibid., pp. 341–343.

56 For more on the history of CWS plants, see e.g.: J. Tarczyński and W. Jeleń, *Początki polskiej motoryzacji*; T. Wójcik, "Centralne Warsztaty Samochodowe w Warszawie."

Wytwórnia Samochodów) and—along with, among other entities, the Ursus Mechanical Works, after the latter was taken over by the state in the wake of bankruptcy proceedings—was incorporated into the Państwowe Zakłady Inżynierii (National Engineering Works, PZInż), which would focus solely on the production of automobiles.[57] On September 21, 1931, an agreement was concluded with Italian carmaker Fiat on the production of passenger cars, pursuant to which work began at PZInż on Polish Fiats 508 and 518.[58]

As early as 1924, representative offices of leading automotive companies appeared in Poland, with Ford, General Motors, and Austro-Deimler opening local branches. However, subject to extremely high taxes (including a 10% luxury tax), their cars found few buyers. The duty could be circumvented by importing chassis into Poland, which were then built on site. According to Mariusz W. Majewski, there were over eighty Polish companies involved in body construction.[59] The economic boom of the second half of the 1920s, which was a derivative of "The Roaring Twenties" and ended with the Great Depression, impelled foreign automotive giants to again look favourably upon the Polish automobile market. More assembly plants began to appear. The L.J. Borkowski Commercial-Industrial Joint-Stock Company, owner of the Elibor Plant, who had initially cooperated with Ford, launched a Chevrolet assembly plant in 1928 at Wolska Street in Warsaw, in effect creating the ninth GMC branch in the world. The Polish Citroën Car Society, located on Górnośląska Street in Warsaw, the official Polish sales and assembly subsidiary of the French car manufacturer, had a car assembly plant of this French brand, as well as a parts shop.[60] Fiat, Ford, and Czechoslovak Kolben-Denek assembly plants were also established.[61]

---

57 T. Wójcik, "Wybrane aspekty działalności wojska," p. 307; J. Kaliński, "Motoryzacja a infrastruktura drogowa," p. 140; M. W. Majewski, "Powstanie przemysłu motoryzacyjnego," p. 215.

58 J. Tarczyński and T. Szczerbicki, *Samochody osobowe Polski Fiat 508 i 518*, Warszawa 2003, pp. 10, 16–17; *Rynek motoryzacyjny*, ed. Z. Krasiński, Warszawa 1980, p. 41.

59 M. W. Majewski, "Powstanie przemysłu motoryzacyjnego," p. 208.

60 A. Rostocki and J. Tarczyński, *Automobilizm w Warszawie*, p. 198ff

61 M. W. Majewski, "Powstanie przemysłu motoryzacyjnego," p. 208; J. Kaliński, "Motoryzacja a infrastruktura drogowa," pp. 139–140.

In this situation, in order to maintain the privileged position of PZInż, which was slowly starting the production of Fiats, the government imposed a high duty on imported vehicles, and state institutions were still obliged to purchase cars produced by CWS.[62] Two legal acts created an additional fiscal burden for car owners; indeed, as it turned out later, especially in the face of the great economic crisis, they represented the final nail in the coffin of the Polish automotive industry, which was still in its infancy. The first was the Act on the State Road Fund, introduced in February 1931. This so-called *Lex Neugebauer* (named after the Minister of Public Works, General Mieczysław Norwid-Neugebauer) required that each owner of a car or a car trailer paid a tax of "40 [Polish] zlotys for every 100 kg of weight" of the vehicle. Even higher fees were to be paid by people engaged in the business of commercial passenger transport—here, each seat in the vehicle intended for a traveller was taxed. Funds collected in this way were to be used for the maintenance, construction, and strengthening of state and local government roads.[63] The second legal act that further complicated the already difficult situation of car owners involved an increase in the fuel tax. Natural gas and oil products went up by 12 groszys per kilogram. As a result, prices per litre of gasoline increased, reaching as high as 68 groszys in Warsaw, placing them among the highest in Europe; only Berlin, Zurich, and Paris had more expensive fuel.[64] Revenues from this increase were also intended for the State Road Fund. Ultimately, by late 1937 and early 1938, this fund transferred 282 million zlotys for its statutory purpose[65]—which was certainly not the result that the authorities hoped for because many car owners (as much as one in five, according to estimates) de-registered their vehicles from September to May, thus avoiding quarterly fees.

All of this meant that the first half of the 1930s was a time of serious regression for the Polish automotive industry. While in 1931, the total number of

---

62 M. Relich, "Załamanie motoryzacji w Polsce," p. 202.

63 Dz. Urz. 1931, no. 138, pos. 81; M. Relich, "Załamanie motoryzacji w Polsce," pp. 202–203.

64 W. M. Majewski, "Poszukiwania złóż ropy naftowej i gazu w Polsce (1919–1939)," *Annales Universitatis Pedagogicae Cracoviensis. Studia Historica* 2009, vol. 8, p. 146.

65 *Mały Rocznik Statystyczny 1938*, Warszawa 1939, p. 198.

cars reached a peak of 39,400, as many as 31,000 of which were passenger cars, over the next few years, this number systematically decreased; in 1936, the total was only 25,700 vehicles, 19,600 of which were passenger cars (see Table 1). This dramatic situation provoked opposition against the state's automotive indolence. Even before the economic crisis, critical voices emerged primarily among private car owners, but also among those who understood that the automotive industry was not concerned solely with private ownership of a vehicle. As the brochure *Zmotoryzujmy Polskę* (Let's Motorise Poland), the first (of three) issue of which appeared in 1931, proclaims: "The 'age without horses' has begun; we live under the sign of motorised transport. … The car has become an excellent modern means of transport; it has become an indispensable factor in everyday life, both private and public, just as the railway, telephone, electric light had become indispensable before it …. The world has understood what the car is for today's life …." The author of the brochure drew attention to what was increasingly passing Poland by: the motorisation of not only Europe, but also the rest of the world: "The motorisation of vehicular traffic has become so popular all over the world that even savage tribes are eagerly seeking cars, for example on the islands of Fiji, in the Negro Republic of Liberia …. In Arabia, pilgrims are tired of dragging their camels through the hot sands of the desert for weeks on end, so they are making the pilgrimage to Mecca and Medina by car."[66]

In June 1934, at a conference organised by the Polish Automobile Club, Ryszard Hereget, one of the co-founders and directors of the Polish Citroën Car Society in Warsaw, delivered a paper on the impact of automotive policy on the development of automobilism. The speech was interesting because it contained a description of the situation in twenty-five countries around the world—the increase in the number of cars, and the impact that increase had on the economy and infrastructure. Hereget devoted the most space to Germany, Italy, and Russia, which, in his opinion, were model examples of how motorisation could help raise a country's economic level. The Polish government's policy was not left unscathed because by taxing road transport, it placed the railway in a privileged position, which generated losses instead

66 J. Makłowicz, *Zmotoryzujmy Polskę*, Warszawa 1931, p. 3.

of bringing profits. "This is a portrait of the automotive world—terrible for us, as well as for you and for individual citizens," said Hereget. "The reasons for the de-motorisation of Poland lie simply in the artificial inhibition of the normal development of motoring through bad policy, exceptionally high tariffs, excessive taxation, and the State's monopoly on the market. As a result of such policies, the basic conditions for the dissemination of the car—low price and cheap operation—cannot be achieved."[67]

Two small brochures published in the first half of 1934 by the Circle of Merchants and Industrialists at the Association of Polish Merchants shared an almost identical message. They contained reprints of articles from the contemporaneous press offering sharp criticism of official automotive policy.[68] The first of them also contained the *Memoriał kupiectwa samochodowego w sprawie motoryzacji kraju* (Statement of Automobile Merchants on the Motorisation of the Country)—a kind of "promotional" manifesto that made a strong case for the decisive importance of motorisation in the development of a modern state. Once again, Germany was cited as an example: the authors of the *Memoriał* pointed out that just in one month, Poland's western neighbour, which was also—they emphasised—strongly affected by the economic crisis, registered about 5,000 new cars. Meanwhile, in Poland, the number of cars continued to fall: in the second half of 1933, over 5,000 cars were taken off the roads. Despite these negative phenomena, expressed in dramatic statistics, the *Memoriał* proclaims: "… we believe that there is a natural healthy push towards the country's motorisation and that the needs in this area are democratising, which is extremely valuable and should become a signpost for all basic policy actions aimed at the motorisation of the country." The solution to Poland's situation was "cheap motor vehicles," because the Polish market "will not be able to consume other cars in mass." However, cheap cars were only one element of the overall solution proposed by the merchants. A much greater role was to be played by a special commission that would

---

67 A. F. Augustynowicz, *Walka o samochód w Polsce*, Warszawa 1934, pp. 15, 24.

68 The topics of the reprinted texts are divided between thematic chapters—part one: "Co mówią cyfry statystyczne?" "Problem motoryzacji," "Umowy licencyjne PZI," "Nowa taryfa celna"; part two: "Jak rozstrzygnąć problem motoryzacji?" "O polityce motoryzacyjnej," and "Problem drogowy." See: *Motoryzacja Polski w świetle opinii publicznej część pierwsza*, n.p., 1934; Motoryzacja Polski w świetle opinii publicznej część druga, n.p., 1934.

exercise complete control over the automotive policy. This commission would be assisted by a specially appointed "Council of Automobile Enthusiasts, which would involve all organised parties interested in the motorisation of the country."[69]

The idea of establishing such a body responsible for the motorisation of Poland was included in Hereget's speech quoted above: "Let's imagine an ideal state: a responsible player steps forward—thus earning the right to take risky decisions—who specifies the problems of motorisation and road network in the following way (having overseen this matter comprehensively, consulted many minds, and with the help of 4 to 6 various official commissions, working no longer than 3 weeks in total). First the car—then the roads. Time for both—three years."[70]

Such an organisation did actually emerge. At the end of 1934, the Economic Committee of Ministers appointed the Inter-Ministerial Commission for National Motorisation within the Ministry of Transportation, composed of representatives of the Praesidium of the Council of Ministers and of the ministries of Military Affairs, Treasury, and Industry and Trade, as well as of the General Staff. It was headed by Deputy Prime Minister Juliusz Piasecki. The creation of the commission coincided with a change in the Polish government's stance toward the automotive industry. A redefinition of automotive policy was being pushed by the military, whose leaders, were afraid that, as the international situation worsened, Poland would become too economically disadvantaged compared to its eastern and western neighbours, especially in the field of automotive technology.[71] To them, the Second Polish Republic was inferior not just in terms of the size of its vehicle fleet, which was over sixty-two times smaller than that of Nazi Germany, but more importantly, in terms of production. While in 1935 alone, factories and assembly plants in Poland produced a total of approximately 2,000 cars, as many as 169,000 were produced in Germany in that same year, while Soviet Union, whose

69 *Motoryzacja w świetle opinii publicznej część pierwsza*, pp. 5–7, 9–10.

70 A. F. Augustynowicz, *Walka o samochód w Polsce*, p. 24.

71 As early as 1932, regulations were issued regarding the promotion of a specific category of motor vehicles, including cars that met the requirements of national defence. A bonus was issued in the shape of a 60% discount on the fee that had to be paid to the Road Fund. See M. Pyter, "Prawne zasady użytkowania pojazdów mechanicznych," *Czasopismo Prawno-Historyczne* 2011, vol. 63, no. 2, p. 107.

automotive industry had even less of a tradition than that of Poland, produced as many as 72,000 vehicles.[72]

The Polish government practically reversed its automobile policy by taking actions aimed at levelling the differences between the Polish and Western automotive industries, and—as it turned out—that of its Eastern neighbour, as well. First of all, customs duties on imported cars were lowered; then, PZInż gave up its privileges, which meant that private companies were allowed to produce cars. The aforementioned Inter-Ministerial Commission was responsible for granting concessions for production. The first of them was granted in 1936 to plants belonging to Lilpop, Rau, and Loewenstein SA, which began production of American cars and trucks under a GMC licence. The next two concessions were granted to the Zakłady Samochodowe Wspólnoty Interesów SA (Automotive Works of Shared Interest), which would produce German cars in Radom, and the Wytwórnia Samochodów i Wyrobów Metalowych Fablok SA (Automobile and Metallurgical Works Fablok), producing vehicles under a French licence from Renault.[73] A concession for the production of Radwan passenger cars was also granted to Stanisław Pragłowski.[74]

Further actions taken by the Commission focused primarily on easing the fiscal burden on car owners. Payments made to the Road Fund by users of trucks and commercial passenger cars, as well as fees on motor oils, were reduced, thus slightly lowering the price of petrol.[75] In order to promote motorisation in eastern voivodeships (*Nowogrodzkie*, *Poleskie*, *Stanisławowskie*, *Tarnopolskie*, *Wileńskie*, and *Wołyńskie*)—that is, the most backward areas in terms of motorisation—fees charged locally for the Fund were also reduced.[76] A debt forgiveness action concerning missing payments for the Road Fund was also widespread; this action affected, among others, taxi and truck drivers.[77] The government also facilitated instalment sales with the Act of April 28,1938 on registered real rights over motor vehicles.[78]

---

72 T. Wójcik, "Wybrane aspekty działalności wojska," p. 313.
73 Ibid., p. 313.
74 M. Relich, "Załamanie motoryzacji w Polsce," p. 209.
75 Dz. Urz. 1935, no. 65, pos. 405; Dz. Urz. 1936, no. 58, pos. 428.
76 M. Pyter, "Prawne zasady użytkowania," p. 107.
77 Dz. Urz. 1936, no. 54, pos. 392.
78 Dz. Urz. 1938, no. 36, pos. 302.

However, the regulations of May and July 1936 were of the greatest importance. At that time, a presidential decree established income tax relief for all those who purchased new cars, motorcycles, and tractors between April 1, 1936 and January 1, 1938 from sellers "professionally engaged in the sale, assembly or production" of vehicles in the Republic of Poland. Thus, such relief did not apply to imports.[79] This nearly two-year period was extended through the end of 1939 by the Act of April 9, 1938 on investment relief.[80] Although these efforts yielded actual results, since the number of cars began to slowly grow, gradually making up for the losses incurred in the mid-1930s, the fact is that for the vast majority of the Polish society, car ownership remained a distant dream, mostly because of high costs. Tadeusz Grabowski, editor-in-chief of the magazine *ATS Auto i Technika Samochodowa*, wrote: "A potential car buyer could easily choose an automobile suitable for his needs and taste. And yet the average well-to-do citizen could not choose a car that suited his wallet. The Poznań Motor Show revealed how expensive middle-class cars still are in Poland."[81]

This portrait of motorised Poland would be incomplete without mentioning the problem of roads. The lands of the three partitions that came within the borders of the new Polish state after World War I constituted a patchwork of three different road systems. From the Prussian partition, the Second Polish Republic inherited a fairly dense network of good hard-surfaced roads, which were still in good condition despite the war. Most of the lands belonging to the Austrian partition possessed a satisfactory road infrastructure. Eastern Galicia was in the worst shape; its road system suffered a great deal as a result of war. The situation was similar in the former Congress Kingdom of Poland, which belonged to the Russian partition; in the first years of the war, the front line moved eastward across it, leading to the destruction of most bridges and damage to road surfaces. Nevertheless, during the German and Austrian occupation, damaged roads were partially repaired, especially in the northern regions of the kingdom, as required by logistical activities carried out behind the front lines. The eastern regions of the Russian partition suffered the most, due to the fact that they were the site of military operations practically throughout the entire war. In

79 Dz. Urz. 1936, no. 39, pos. 294; M. Pyter, "Prawne zasady użytkowania," p. 108.
80 Dz. Urz. 1936, no. 26, pos. 224.
81 and T. Szczerbicki and J. Tarczyński, *Mercedes a sprawa polska*, 95.

addition to direct damage as a result of the fighting along a shifting front line, World War I also saw the partitioning powers fail to pursue a consistent road policy—that is, maintain existing routes in good condition. This meant that hardened road surfaces were allowed to slowly degrade, and their repair became a priority once hostilities ended.[82]

After Poland regained independence and the Polish-Soviet War ended, there were only about 44,000 km of paved roads within Poland's borders, a density of approximately 0.1 km per 1 km^2.[83] In this respect, the voivodeships of the former Austrian and Prussian partitions ranked the best; there, the density of paved and cobbled roads was two to three times higher than the national average. The Eastern Borderlands fared the worst, with the density of hard roads not exceeding 0.02 km.

Table 2. Road density in the territory of the Second Polish Republic (as of 1922)

Regions	Area (km^2)	Total length of paved and cobbled roads	National Roads			Voivodeship Roads			Length of paved and cobbled roads per 1 km^2
			Total	Paved and cobbled	Dirt	Total	Paved and Cobbled	Dirt	
Prussian Partition	47166	14200	2110	21100	–	–	–	–	0.299
Galicia	79080	16300	3636	3382	254	3132	2830	302	0.206
Congress Poland	137879	11600	5838	5211	627	5193	3419	1774	0.084
Eastern Border-lands	109536	1800	4804	1625	3179	2541	145	2396	0.017
Central Lithuania area	14721	100	–	–	–	–	–	–	0.007
Total	388442	44000	16388	12328	4060	10886	6394	4472	0.113

Source: based on M. W. Nestorowicz, Sprawa drogowa w Polsce…, p. 66.

[82] M. W. Nestorowicz, *Stan dróg kołowych Królestwa Polskiego*, Warszawa 1913, pp. 3–6; *idem*, *Sprawa drogowa w Polsce. Zagadnienie gospodarcze*, Warszawa 1924, pp. 46–49, 51–52, 54–58.

[83] *Mały Rocznik Statystyczny GUS 1939*, Warszawa 1939, pp. 197–198.

The east-west road orientation dominated, a remnant of the trade routes between Prussia and Russia; the new geopolitical situation required a transformation toward a south-north orientation.[84] Contemporary calculations indicated that the unification of the road system in Poland required the construction of about 75,000 km of new roads, due to the fact that, as already mentioned, different parts of the country differed greatly in terms of road density. Only a small percentage of those new roads would be completed: in the years 1924–1938, 17,600 km of new roads were built and a further 2,600 were modernised. This pace of construction was determined by the country's economic situation. In the first years of peace, owing to financial problems, only about 800 km of roads were built each year, and in the second half of the 1930s, that number increased to about 1,700 km per year. Between 1927 and 1938, a total of 979 million zlotys were spent on the construction and extension of national and local roads, which was only enough for 63,000 km of hard-surface roads. Perhaps it was the condition of the road infrastructure (or, more precisely, Poland's lack of roads) that determined the state of Polish motorisation in the interwar period.

To conclude considerations on this subject, one more fact deserves mention. Despite the involvement of many actors in the promotion and development of the automotive industry in the Second Polish Republic, the results were far from the "European average" (however imprecisely measured), although it should be remembered that the starting point was very low. In 1922, Poland had one car per 6,015 people. In the same year, in other European countries, this figure was 136 (in Great Britain), 161 (France), 260 (Czechoslovakia), and even 2,640 (Italy). At the end of 1938, there was one car per 1,420 inhabitants in Poland, meaning that, despite a tenfold increase in the number of cars, the ratio was ten times worse than in Germany and Italy (148), not to mention countries such as Czechoslovakia and Belgium (54), France (23) and the United Kingdom (24).[85] In addition, if one considers the geographical distribution of the number of registered cars by province, over a quarter of all passenger cars were registered in Warsaw and the Warsaw Voivodeship. In the capital city, there were eighty-three cars per 10,000 residents. The rest of the country

---

84 J. Kaliński, "Motoryzacja a infrastruktura drogowa," p. 137.

85 J. Purš, "The Internal Combustion Engine and the Revolution in Transport: The Case of Czechoslovakia with some European Comparisons," in: *The Economic and Social Effects of the Spread of Motor Vehicles*, ed. T. Barker, London 1987, p. 204.

could not even dream of approaching these numbers. Only some voivodeships—*Poznańskie, Pomorskie, Śląskie, Krakowskie, Lubelskie, Lwowskie, Łódzkie,* and *Kieleckie*—could boast of possessing cars in the thousands. Elsewhere, the values were dramatically lower. In the *Wołyńskie* and *Poleskie* voivodeships, there were 3.2 and 2.7 cars per 10,000 inhabitants, respectively.[86] The same applies to hard-surfaced roads—here, too, the disparities were great. In 1938, in the two voivodeships most disadvantaged in this respect—*Poleskie* and *Wołyńskie*—there were only 1,087 and 1,492 km of hard-surface roads, respectively, which translates into 2.9 km and 4.1 km per 100 km², respectively, of the kind of road network most suitable for automobile traffic. In this regard, the western and central voivodeships fared the best.[87]

Table 3. Transportation network in Poland (as of 1938)

Voivodeship	Total	per 100 km²	per 10 000 inhabitants
Poland	63169	16.2	19.6
Warszawskie	6024	24.1	28.4
Łódzkie	3134	24.6	15.5
Kieleckie	4777	18.6	16.3
Lubelskie	3846	11.2	22.2
Białostockie	3642	11.2	22.2
Wileńskie	2067	7.1	16.1
Nowogrodzkie	2214	9.6	20.8
Poleskie	1087	2.9	9.6
Wołyńskie	9085	32.3	38.8
Poznańskie	9085	32.3	38.8
Pomorskie	6463	25.1	34.3
Śląskie	5181	29.7	22.5
Krakowskie	5181	29.7	22.5
Lwowskie	5396	19.0	17.2
Stanisławowskie	3010	17.8	20.3
Tarnopolskie	3493	21.1	21.8

Source: Mały Rocznik Statystyczny 1939, Warszawa 1939, p. 188

86 *Mały rocznik statystyczny GUS 1939*, p. 199.
87 Ibid., p. 188.

Despite ambitious attempts to move the country into the "age without horses," the Second Polish Republic remained stuck in the third world of motorisation; Lithuania, Latvia, Estonia, Romania and—among non-European countries—Egypt, Ceylon, and Brazil all had more cars.[88] The outbreak of World War II and the occupation, along with the social and economic effects of the war, pushed back the dream of a motorised Poland even further.

1.2 The second world war

In almost all European countries under German occupation, drastic restrictions on the movement of motor vehicles were introduced. In his sketches about occupied capitals, Polish historian Tomasz Szarota notes that only a handful of vehicle owners received permits to continue using them. In Paris, which had 350,000 registered automobiles before the war, such permits were granted to only 4,500 Frenchmen. In Brussels, a ban on the use of private passenger cars was issued, and soon only one in ten motor vehicle owners were allowed to drive.[89]

In Poland, occupation authorities confiscated most cars and trucks for military needs. In addition, they introduced a ban on the movement of vehicles in Warsaw, from which only certain companies and institutions were exempt. The situation became even worse after the assassination of Franz Kutschera; in light of the fact that three cars (an Opel Kapitän, a Mercedes 170 V and an Adler Trumpf Junior) driven by Poles were involved in the incident, a regulation was issued completely prohibiting "non-Germans" from driving passenger cars and motorcycles. It is difficult to estimate how many cars were destroyed in the first month of the war, before the capitulation of Warsaw. It seems that those that survived were few and far between. Most were destroyed in the first weeks of the war.[90]

---

88 In terms of the number of cars, Poland surpassed only Bulgaria and Yugoslavia per capita: Z. Landau and J. Tomaszewski, *Zarys historii gospodarczej Polski 1918–1939*, Warszawa 1999, pp. 307–308.

89 T. Szarota, *Życie codzienne w stolicach okupowanej Europy. Szkice historyczne. kronika wydarzeń*, Warszawa 1995, p. 87.

90 Ibid., p. 88; T. Szarota, *Okupowanej Warszawy dzień powszedni. Studium historyczne*, Warszawa 1988, p. 292; T. Szczerbicki, *Samochody w PRL. Rzecz o motoryzacji i nie tylko…*, Poznań 2010, p. 13.

Nevertheless, as they prepared for war against the Soviet Union, the Germans initiated limited investments in the transport network on Polish territory. Plans were made for the construction of new roads and railway lines and modernisation of existing ones within the *Generalgouvernement*. In subsequent years, 790 bridges that were destroyed in the first months of the war were rebuilt and 3,400 paved roads were repaired. However, particular emphasis was placed on the modernisation and construction of railway lines in the territories incorporated into the Reich and in the *Generalgouvernement*, a German-occupied administrative zone established in Central Poland after the successful invasion in 1939; after the outbreak of war with the Soviet Union, 90% in the former and 60% in the latter would serve the eastern front.[91]

Wartheland, a German administrative district created from the western parts of occupied Poland, would also become an important link in the Third Reich's transport system. Almost immediately after cessation of hostilities in September 1939, the occupation authorities started repairing damaged rolling stock, clearing waterways, and rebuilding roads. By the end of 1940, passage had been cleared over a total of 170 bridges and several hundred kilometres of railway track. A significant part of the damaged road surfaces and several railway stations had also been rebuilt. In order to increase and improve the capacity of the system, expansion works began on the road and transport networks in Wartheland. Plans included the construction of "Polish sections" of the motorways Frankfurt (Oder)—Poznań—Łódź; Gdańsk—Poznań—Wrocław; Königsberg—Upper Silesia—Wieluń; and Grudziądz—Toruń—Łódź. Some of these were successfully implemented in the years 1940–1942, before the course of the war turned against Germany in 1943. As was the case in the *Generalgouvernement*, German preparations for war with the Soviet Union resulted in the modernisation of local roads in Wartheland, which the German army would use to move east. By the fall of 1941, about 1,000 km of roads had been rebuilt.[92]

The outbreak of World War II led to the near-complete liquidation of the Polish automotive industry. Already in the first days of September 1939, bombing raids destroyed the Państwowe Zakłady Inżynierii facilities in

---

91 J. Skodlarski, *Zarys historii gospodarczej Polski do 1945 roku*, Warszawa–Łódź 1997, p. 308.

92 C. Łuczak, *Pod niemieckim jarzmem (Kraj Warty 1939–1945)*, Poznań 1996, pp. 114–115.

Warsaw between Mińska, Terespolska, and Podskarbińska streets. Remaining machinery from other factories within this plant was removed almost entirely to the Reich. The same fate befell the still unfinished Lilpop automobile factory in Lublin.[93]

1.3 Wartime damage

Apart from enormous human losses, military operations during World War II brought severe material losses. The European transportation system came out of the conflict badly damaged.[94] Many major European routes were impassable due to devastated road surfaces, and their continuity was interrupted because of damaged bridges. On German territory, more than 1,700 bridges over ten metres in length were destroyed.[95] In Italy, 60% of the main roads, along with 20% of local roads and over 8,000 bridges were destroyed. All the bridges connecting Buda and Pest were destroyed. Railway networks were particularly hard hit. In Italy alone, almost 90% of the electrified railway lines had been rendered useless.[96] Of the two million train cars that ran on European tracks before the outbreak of World War II, 300,000 were completely destroyed and 800,000 damaged. Yugoslavia lost half of its high-seas fleet, all of its cars, and 40% of its peasant carts. The effects of this devastation were felt for years to come. It was estimated that World War II meant seventy years of regression for the infrastructure of Central and Eastern European countries.[97] The situation was better in Western Europe, though in the summer of 1947 the railway system was able to transport only about 20% of the daily hard coal extraction from mines in the Ruhr area. During the harsh winter of 1947 and 1948, the lack of coal was acute.[98]

---

93 A. Rummel, *Polskie konstrukcje*, p. 66.

94 See J. Kaliński, *Historia gospodarcza XIX i XX w.*, Warszawa 2008, p. 230.

95 F. Busch, "Transportation in Postwar Germany," *Annals of the American Academy of Political and Social Science* 1948, vol. 260, p. 87.

96 P. Duignan and L. H. Gann, *The Rebirth of the Democratic World 1945–1958*, Cambridge 1992, p. 26; I. T. Berendt, *Central and Eastern Europe 1944–1993: Detour from the periphery to the periphery*, Cambridge 1996, p. 6.

97 I. T. Berendt, *Central and Eastern Europe*, p. 6.

98 F. Schipper, "Changing the face of Europe: European road mobility during the Marshall Plan years," *Journal of Transport History* 2007, vol. 28, no. 2, p. 213.

The aforementioned actions taken by the German occupiers (vehicle requisitions, restrictions, and bans on traffic) led to an almost complete halt, even a retreat, in the development of individual motorisation among Europeans. Between 1937 and 1948, the number of private cars in France decreased from 2.02 million to 1.5 million, and in Italy from 270,000 to 219,000, while the largest drop, understandably, was felt in Germany, where only 283,000 of the over 1.1 million prewar cars remained after the war. Only Great Britain recorded an increase; there, the number of private cars grew from 1.8 million to 2.02 million.[99] After the war, there was a deep hunger for automobiles that could not be satisfied by surplus equipment left on the European continent by American troops. Tyres, spare parts, and fuel were also in short supply. Against this already very unappealing background, Poland's situation seemed even worse

After the war, under the Yalta and Potsdam agreements, Poland lost 20% of its territory. Its prewar area decreased from 389,000 km^2 to 312,000 km^2. In exchange for lands lost east of the Curzon line, Poland was granted the western and northern territories that had been part of the Third Reich before the war. In addition to territorial and population losses, Poland suffered substantial material losses, estimated at approximately $20 billion, which was more than the corresponding values for Germany, Yugoslavia, the USSR or France per capita ($840 in 1938 prices).[100] Slightly different estimates are presented by Andrzej Karpiński and Jan Szpak; using data from the War Reparations Bureau, Karpiński calculated Poland's per capita loss to be $703, while Szpak estimated it at $621, Regardless of these differences, Poland's losses were the highest among all European countries.[101]

The transportation infrastructure suffered greatly. Janusz Kaliński reports that losses in the value of transport equipment amounted to as much as half, which meant that they were even higher than losses in industry or agriculture.[102] As a result of the war, 63% of bridges, 29% of hard-surface

---

99 P. Duignan and L. H. Gann, *The Rebirth of the West*, p. 26.

100 A. Zawistowski, "Polska Ludowa. Wzrost podporządkowany doktrynie politycznej," in: *Polskie osiągnięcia gospodarcze. Perspektywa historyczna*, ed. J. Kaliński, Warszawa 2010, pp. 185–196.

101 A. Karpiński, "PRL a uprzemysłowienie i urbanizacja Polski," in: *Zrozumieć PRL*, ed. W. Żółtkowski, Warszawa 2012, p. 35.

102 J. Kaliński, *Plan odbudowy gospodarczej 1947–1949*, Warszawa 1977, p. 168.

roads, and 33% of railway tracks were destroyed. Most paved road surfaces required immediate repairs. According to estimates put forward by the Ministry of Transport in 1946, the damage to roads within Poland's new borders amounted to 1.6 billion zlotys, most of which was associated with road surfaces, bridges, and viaducts. Of this amount, destruction of infrastructure in the area within Poland's prewar borders was estimated at just over a billion zlotys, while the remaining 581 million zlotys related to the newly acquired western and northern territories.[103] Losses stemming from the moving of the eastern border were estimated at over 800 million zlotys—this sum mainly accounted for hard-surface roads (17,800 km), valued at 746 million zlotys; 32,000 metres of bridge structures, valued at 35.5 million zlotys; and road equipment worth 8.9 million zlotys. Interestingly, in documents, this last category was called "equipment sent to the USSR."[104] The War Compensation Bureau calculated that the total losses to the vehicle fleet and the road transportation infrastructure amounted to 10 billion zlotys.[105] The technical documentation held by construction offices and by drawing and draft archives spoke of an irreparable loss; as a result of war, the achievements of years of hard work by Polish engineers and constructors were almost completely destroyed.[106]

The prewar automotive industry suffered extensive damage.[107] Losses of equipment and buildings belonging to such factories as the Państwowe Zakłady Inżynierii, Lilpop, Rau and Loewenstein, and Fiat, were estimated at 565 million zlotys. In addition, damage caused to garages and petrol stations

---

103 Archiwum Akt Nowych (hereafter: AAN), Ministerstwo Komunikacji (hereafter: MK), sygn. 628, Wykaz strat wojennych na drogach kołowych wg województw, 12 III 1946, unnumbered pages; J. Kaliński and B. Liberadzki, *Transport w Polsce w latach 1918–1978. Zarys historii*, Warszawa 1986, p. 68.

104 AAN, MK, sygn. 628, Straty wojenne na drogach, [8 XI 1946], unnumbered pages; ibid., [Straty w sprzęcie drogowym], 6 XI 1946, unnumbered pages.

105 J. Skodlarski, Zarys historii gospodarczej Polski, p. 348.

106 AAN, Centralny Urząd Planowania (hereafter: CUP), sygn. 2921, Motoryzacja w Trzyletnim Planie Odbudowy, grudzień 1946, p. 7.

107 See: A. Rostocki and J. Tarczyński, *Automobilizm w Warszawie*, pp. 198–259; S. Misztal, "Branże wiodące stołecznego przemysłu w latach 1945–1976," in: *Wielkie zakłady przemysłowe Warszawy*, Warszawa 1974, pp. 113–115.

was valued at 54 million zlotys.[108] The fleet of vehicles was almost completely obliterated, the losses being estimated at over 550 million zlotys. The Polish refining industry was levelled nearly to the ground; such was the fate of refineries in Glinik, Trzebinia, and Czechowice. Starting on July 1, 1944, as the front approached, the Germans began the planned dismantling and removal of products, warehouses, technical materials, and equipment. After the armies of the 1st Ukrainian Front entered the area, production began with substantial assistance from the Soviets, who provided transportation, ensured the supply of equipment and materials, and secured technical assistance. At the same time, however, practically all production went to the Red Army, and all the material that the Germans could not take with them—fuel and lubricants—was taken as loot.

It is impossible to determine how many of the nearly 30,000 passenger cars that rode on Polish roads before the war survived military operations. We can certainly assume that most of them were destroyed. According to various estimates, at the end of the war, there were between 3,000 and 7,000 vehicles on Polish territory, mainly formerly German vehicles in very poor technical condition.[109] Official estimates published by the Ministry of Public Administration in December 1945 spoke of 19,000 motor vehicles, of which the majority (11,900) were trucks.[110]

It has to be said that the westward shift of Poland's borders in 1945 represented a net gain for the country; the road network within the new borders was almost twice as extensive as in the prewar borders.[111] Nevertheless, it was still just a drop in the bucket of Polish needs.

---

108 AAN, Urząd Rady Ministrów (hereafter: URM), sygn. 5/468, Zarys programu polityki motoryzacyjnej. Uwagi Państwowego Urzędu Samochodowego do ankiety M[inisterstwa] K[omunikacji], [luty 1946], p. 36.

109 T. Szczerbicki, *Samochody w PRL*, p. 13; AAN, URM, sygn. 5/468, Zarys programu polityki motoryzacyjnej. Uwagi Państwowego Urzędu Samochodowego do ankiety MK, [luty 1946], p. 36.

110 AAN, Ministerstwo Administracji Publicznej (hereafter: MAP), sygn. 488 (mf B-1473), [Pismo Informacyjne] Do Ob. Ministra Administracji Publicznej, Warszawa, [grudzień 1945], p. 12.

111 A. Zawistowski, "Wzrost podporządkowany doktrynie politycznej," pp. 185–186.

The Automotive Rubicon

2.1 Institutions

War damage to the Polish automotive industry opened up opportunities for the creation of new rules of operation, whereby the mistakes of the interwar period could be avoided. Decision-makers in the wartime Polish Underground State were convinced of this fact; while preparing plans for the reconstruction of postwar Poland, they argued that the interwar Polish automotive industry had been handled by a "lay tinker" who added extensions to the automotive "manor house" without rhyme or reason. After the war, engineer Zygmunt Okołów, an engine designer before the war and later head of the Central Design Office of the Automotive Industry (BKPM), wrote: "When rebuilding the country, we will face a vacuum in this field of economy [the automotive industry] and we will need to approach it as a completely new task. On the other hand, the question of the automotive industry will be a blank page from the very beginning; we will have to begin planning its development right away, unburdened by the heredity of old diseases."[112] The first order of business was the creation of institutions that would be responsible for the renewed motorisation of Poland.

2.1.1 The Ministerial Level

The Decree of January 8, 1946 on the organisation of the automotive administration and economy in the postwar Republic of Poland entrusted all issues

112 AAN, Komitet Centralny Polskiej Partii Robotniczej (hereafter: KC PPR), sygn. 295/XI-277 (mf 2334/16), W sprawie motoryzacji kraju, [no date], p. 239.

related to the administration and management of motor vehicles to the Minister of Transportation (MK). From November 4, 1944, this post was held by Jan Rabanowski from the Alliance of Democrats party. The Ministry of Transportation itself had been established on December 31, 1944, with the transformation of the Polish Committee of National Liberation (PKWN) into the Provisional Government. Earlier, as of July 1944, the Department of Transportation, Posts, and Telegraphs was headed by Jan Michał Grubecki from the Peasant Party, who was replaced in early November by Rabanowski. On December 1, 1944, two departments were created on the basis of the above-mentioned department: the Department of Transportation and the Department of Posts and Telegraphs, which from December 5 was headed by Tadeusz Kapeliński, member of the Peasant Party. Rabanowski held his position until March 14, 1951, when the Ministry of Transportation was transformed into the Ministry of Railways (headed by Rabanowski) and the Ministry of Road and Air Transport, with Jan Rustecki from the Polish United Workers' Party (Polska Zjednoczona Partia Robotnicza PZPR, formed through the forced merger of the Polish Workers' Party (Polska Partia Robotnicza PPR) and the Polish Socialist Party (Polska Partia Socjalistyczna PPS)) as head. The two ministries were reunited in March 1957. Rustecki remained in office throughout the existence of this ministry.[113]

2.1.2 State Automobile Office

Following the Red Army's push to the West, the new communist authorities immediately started organising state structures, including for transport and communication. Still in Chełm in Lublin Voivodeship, the Autotransport state enterprise was established, headed by Major Ignacy Wrzos. After more than six months of operation, this unit was transformed into the State Automobile Office (Państwowy Urząd Samochodowy PUS), also headed by Wrzos. PUS's broad responsibilities included setting general automotive policy, managing state-owned enterprises in the automotive and transport economy, planning the scope of repairs, and organising technical supplies for motor vehicles. In addition, PUS maintained vehicle registrations, trained and examined future drivers, issued driver's licences, and performed tasks

---

[113] A. Kochański and Jan Rustecki, *Polski Słownik Biograficzny* (hereafter: PSB), vol. 33, 1991, no. 1, p. 160.

related to the popularisation of the automotive idea. District and Regional Automobile Offices were established at lower administrative levels.[114] As would become clear, in practice, PUS grasped all issues related to the automotive industry within its own hands.

At the same time as PUS, an enterprise called the State Workshops and Automobile Works was established, intended to oversee eighty-four plants ensuring the technical efficiency of the state automobile fleet. It was an urgent necessity to bring vehicles that had been left in the country as the spoils of war back to running condition.[115]

PUS was a rather mysterious state administrative office. It was impossible to find the exact date the office was established (probably March or May 1945) and the decision that created it. Only draft resolutions survive, and some sources suggest that the existence of PUS was never fully sanctioned.[116] The remaining documentation of the activities of the office is also far from complete—only fragmentary sources have been found.[117] Nevertheless, even these few remnants give us insights into the mechanisms by which the state automobile administration functioned.

Critics repeatedly emphasised (and complained) that PUS strove to be a kind of "sovereign power" in terms of not only the conduct of automotive policy, but also the use of vehicles belonging to commercial, industrial, and agricultural enterprises,[118] which meant that PUS officials would often allow themselves to act beyond the bounds of their powers, and repeatedly also beyond the bounds of the law. One example is the dispute between PUS and the Orbis travel agency over the organisation of transport and the inclusion of private initiative within the latter organisation; this case is interesting in part because we can detect Bolesław Bierut's, the chairman of the State

114 AAN, KC PPR, sygn. 295/XI-278 (mf 2334/16), Struktura organizacyjna i zakres działalności Państwowego Urzędu Samochodowego, jego agend terytorialnych oraz podległych przedsiębiorstw, [no date], pp. 75–77.

115 Ibid., p. 79.

116 See e.g.: AAN, Urząd Rady Ministrów (hereafter: URM), sygn. 5/463.

117 The Archives of Modern Records does not contain a separate collection under the title "Państwowy Urząd Samochodowy."

118 AAN, Ministerstwo Przemysłu i Handlu (hereafter: MPiH), sygn 789, [Centralny Zarząd Przemysłu Paliw Płynnych] Do Biura Prawnego Prezydium Rady Ministrów, 29 I 1946 r., p. 32.

National Council (Krajowa Rada Narodowa KRN), who de facto served as the Head of State, personal involvement. In September 1945, KRN, this pro-Soviet, communist-dominated quasi-parliament served as the de facto legislature and highest state authority, received a request from representatives of the company that reported a need to legalise the registration of private cars. As it turned out, due to an insufficient number of vehicles of its own, Orbis was forced to secure its operations by hiring subcontractors, usually private individuals with their own cars, to perform certain transport tasks. This action was opposed by PUS, which refused several times to register these vehicles. Neither assurances given by "Orbis" representatives about the transparency of the entire undertaking, which was supervised by the Supreme Audit Office, nor the proposal that owners of private cars cooperating with Orbis pay a certain sum of money during registration helped. PUS's attitude was unwavering. Thus, Orbis complained to the President of the KRN about the actions of the state officials. The complaint read, in part:

> Orbis has gotten down to work ... with full determination, investing a great deal of energy and organisational skill, and it believes it has done well in improving the country's difficult transportation situation. [...] in addition to people, Orbis transports newspapers, magazines, and brochures by regular mail in bags, as well as press materials for Polpress and Czytelnik. Besides, it always provides buses for the Ministry of Information and Propaganda for the transportation of foreign guests, correspondents, and others on sightseeing tours of Pomerania, Silesia, Majdanek, Wilanów, etc. ... .

According to Orbis representatives, PUS had failed to fulfil its task of developing car transport in the country, and its fears that the use of cars belonging to private persons violated the state monopoly were unfounded because vehicles used for these purposes were wartime leftovers with all the associated problems, mainly technical: "Cars [are] exclusively former German and there are no parts for them, and they are assembled from several machines into one whole, so that, after several months, they wear out completely and are withdrawn. They are now operational because they are operated by owners who are chauffeurs and mechanics and look after their cars in their own well-understood interest."

While decreeing the *Orbis* magazine into existence, Bierut wrote on the margin: "I believe that the interest of a private initiative in an appropriate form to launch cars for public purposes is *desirable* while maintaining control and leadership in the hands of competent state authorities. Strictly suburban transport should be handed over to cities."[119] As this case shows, in the initial period, difficulties in the automotive fleet led state officials to accept the possibility of using private carriers and their services, with certain exceptions.

In response, PUS focused primarily on the origin, use, and technical condition of private cars. It posed rhetorical questions concerning the origin of the fuel, oils, and lubricants used by these vehicles because Orbis did not apply for such allocations, and "there are no other sources for purchase, apart from theft of state property." According to PUS, this private fleet was to be made up of cars that were either the result of "looting of former German property, and thus state-owned property," or "had been cobbled from spare parts in a random way" without appropriate technical oversight, and were fuel-demanding, and thus not able to guarantee safety and punctuality. Furthermore—and here they made direct reference to Bierut's decree—Orbis was tasked with transferring suburban transport to private carriers and concentrate on more profitable long-distance routes. Allegations that tasks related to passenger transport were not being fulfilled were overshadowed by the hierarchy of needs, given that the transport of goods was considered a priority, especially in light of scarcity within the state fleet. In their summary, PUS officials wrote that the policy advanced by Orbis was "simply destructive," especially as Poland was "fighting for fuel and an automobile fleet that can fulfill such basic, but important tasks as providing supplies, securing repatriation, and supporting agricultural campaigns."[120]

The existence of a single state body dealing with the automotive industry, even if (or perhaps because) it lacked a legal basis, did not prevent the inter-ministerial consultations that began in late 1945 with the purpose of formulating a decree for the organisation of the administration and management of automobiles in Poland. The resulting project proposed that all issues related to the automotive industry be entrusted with the Ministry of

---

119 AAN, URM, sygn. 5/463, [Informative document] Do Ob. Dyrektora Biura Prezydialnego Rady Ministrów Dr Jana Zuniaka, Warszawa, 24 IX 1945 r., p. 1; ibid., Notatka dla Ob. Prezydenta Krajowej Rady Narodowej o sytuacji na rynku krajowym, Warszawa, [17 IX 1945 r.], p. 2.

120 AAN, URM, sygn. 5/463, [PUS response], pp. 7–11.

Transportation, which would establish a Central Motorisation Authority (CZM) assigning to it this responsibility.[121] These regulations were adopted on January 8, 1946.[122] In addition to issues related to transportation, automobile fleet management and car traffic broadly understood, the responsibilities of the ministry and the newly appointed authority also included issuing regulations on vehicle registration, driver training, and the establishment of automotive policy rules.

The scope of its activities meant that, for a certain period, PUS's existing responsibilities were duplicated. The Legal Office of the Ministry of Industry and Trade (Ministerstwo Przemysłu i Handlu MPiH) took an unequivocally critical stance towards the January decree, which drew attention to the fact that it offered only a vague description of the scope of activities of the Central Motorisation Authority, and that the needs of industry and trade and already existing bodies (a reference to PUS, since MPiH officials wrote: "nowhere is it stated what the relationship between the two institutions is supposed to be") were completely overlooked.[123] Another object of criticism was the inclusion of the matters of purchase and distribution of fuels within the scope of CZM's activities. This provoked a reaction of the leadership of the Central Office of Petroleum Products (Centrala Przemysłu Naftowego, CPN), assigned since early January 1945 by a resolution of the Economic Committee of the Council of Ministers (Komitet Ekonomiczny Rady Ministrów KERM) with the exclusive right to distribute fuel, as well as to supervise petroleum depots, tanks, bases, and stations.[124] Moreover, another decree, establishing the State Motor Transport (Państwoa Komunikacja Samochodowa PKS), the nationalised road transport monopoly also appropriated some of the CPN's powers, giving PKS supervision over the "organisation and operation of petrol pump stations, fuel tanks."[125]

---

121 AAN, MPiH, sygn. 789, Do wszystkich ministerstw oraz Centralnego Urzędu Planowania, Warszawa, 17 XII 1945 r., pp. 1–10.

122 "Dziennik Ustaw" (hereafter: Dz. U.) 1946, no. 7, pos. 58.

123 AAN, MPiH, sygn 789, Projekty 3-ch dekretów w sprawie administracji gospodarki samochodowej, Warszawa, 17 I 1946 r., pp. 59–60.

124 Ibid., Dotyczy: stacji benzynowych, Warszawa, 7 III 1946 r., p. 71.

125 Moreover, PKS's responsibilities coincided with those of the CZM, since the decree stated that the supervision of all vehicles owned by the State would be carried out by PKS: ibid., Uwagi PPT do projektu dekretu o utworzeniu przedsiębiorstwa

This overlapping of responsibilities would be a characteristic feature of Poland's early postwar years, when automotive policy was conducted by individual administrative institutions—a fact which is particularly visible, for example, in the matter of foreign purchases. Citing the January decree, the Ministry of Transportation demanded compliance with the rules of automotive policy, especially regarding importation. As it turned out, many institutions had not consulted with CZM in that regard; prominent among them were foreign trade establishments belonging to the Ministry of Shipping and Foreign Trade (MŻiHZ).[126] The Transportation Department of the Central Committee of the Polish Workers' Party (KC PPR) took up the matter, calling this state of affairs "anarchy" in an internal study. To prevent further disputes over responsibility, authorities established the Varimex State Society for Foreign Trade (PTHZ), which was given power over, and eventually monopolised, automotive imports.[127] PPR representatives also criticised the lack of continuity in leadership at CZM; on average, the position of CZM managing director changed hands every quarter.[128]

Representatives of the Provincial National Council (Wojewódzka Rada Narodowa WRN) of Dąbrowa Silesia also reacted to the January decree, sending a memorandum to the KRN Transportation Commission in which they criticised the regulations introduced in early 1946, emphasising their general and provisional character. Moreover, according to the authors of the memorandum, the decree repealed all previous laws and regulations: "Any citizen who owns a car can drive it without registration, without a driver's licence, etc. and cannot be punished because the correct regulations

---

państwowego "Państwowa Komunikacja Samochodowa" z 25 X 1945 r., pp. 23–26; Dz. U. 1946, no. 4, pos. 31.

126 Ibid., Centralny Urząd Planowania (hereafter: CUP), sygn. 1937, Do Ministerstwa Żeglugi i Handlu Zagranicznego, Warszawa, 20 XI 1946 r., p. 7475.

127 Ibid., KC PPR, sygn. 295/XI-81 (mf 2315/15), Sprawozdanie z działalności Wydziału Komunikacyjnego KC PPR za miesiąc wrzesień–listopad 1946 r., 4 XII 1946 r., p. 11. Finally, an Automotive Department was established within the structures of Varimex, dealing exclusively with the importation of automotive products: cars, motorcycles, trolleybuses, tractors, special trailers, tyres, accessories, and spare parts, along with service stations and their equipment. Varimex was also involved in exports—bicycles were the main exported commodity; ibid., sygn. 295/XI-381 (mf 2354/4), Varimex [struktura], p. 67.

128 Ibid.

have not been published." Councillors proposed that powers of regulation of "automotive matters" should be removed from the central authorities and transferred to the voivodes. Deputies who comprised the commission responded negatively to some of the opinions and ideas contained in the memorandum. In particular, they regarded the idea of delegating decisions concerning motor vehicles to voivodes as contrary to the principles behind the state's automotive policy. The legal interpretation of the decree that councillors from the Śląsko-Dąbrowskie Voivodeship proposed was also not well received. The discussion of the memorandum provided an opportunity for criticism of the actions of the Ministry of Transportation. In fact, not only were there frequent changes in the position of the CZM director, but the statute of the management board (also provisional) was also only established by the ministry in April 1946. The decree on the organisation of administration and management of automobiles was deemed vague and inaccurate, leaving room for interpretation. It was clear to deputies in the KRN that the constitution of decision-making bodies in automotive matters was transitional in nature. They emphasised that "a solution to this issue"—i.e. the question of responsibility for automotive policy and the final shape of the relevant governing body—"is being pursued by almost all decision-making agents within the State at various levels, [seeking to establish] a regular department within the current Ministry of Transportation, or rather of the Railways with add-ons—road, water, air, and more recently, motor—from the Central Automotive Office, in the reconstituted Ministry of Transportation, or even of the Ministry of Motorisation."[129] Evidently, the plan was to improve the profile of the body managing motorisation, even to the point of establishing a separate ministry. Meanwhile, direct criticism of the CZM led to its liquidation, which likely occurred in early 1947, and its responsibilities were taken over by the newly created Automobile Department within the Ministry of Transportation.[130]

---

[129] AAN, Krajowa Rada Narodowa (hereafter: KRN), sygn. 27, Protokół z 41 posiedzenia Komisji Komunikacyjnej, Warszawa, 20 XII 1946 r., pp. 743–744; ibid., Do Komisji Komunikacyjnej przy Krajowej Radzie Narodowej w Warszawie, Katowice, 16 IX 1946 r., pp. 783–786; ibid., [Omówienie memoriału Śląsko-Dąbrowskiej Wojewódzkiej Rady Narodowej], pp. 791–1795.

[130] AAN, KC PPR, sygn. 295/XI-3, Wytyczne aktywu PPR motoryzacji z 17 VII 1947 r., pp. 51–53.

Almost two years after the establishment of PUS, *Motoryzacja* magazine published a highly interesting article assessing the office's actions from the perspective of several years of operation of the administrative body dealing with automobiles in Poland. The assessment was ambiguous. On the one hand, the author wrote that "the undeniable merit of this Office was and still is the very fact that ... it was established and that it operated," as well as the fact that it collected all enthusiasts of automotive matters in one place. However, this was not enough to warrant a completely positive assessment of its activities because "[PUS] mobilised ...[,] almost from the very first day of its existence, vast numbers of motorists 'on the opposite side'" of the issue, leading the author of the text to observe the almost universal opposition to the conduct of the officials.[131] Furthermore, it was this opposition (referred to in the text as "public opinion") who were deemed responsible for the liquidation of the office led by General Ignacy Wrzos.

2.1.3 The Commission for National Motorisation

Confusion during the development of formal management of the nascent Polish automobilism did not prevent growth, albeit slow, in the number of vehicles on Polish roads. The specific causes of this increase will be discussed later. At this point, suffice it to say that it was created by vehicles with a wartime past, delivered to Poland by sea and rail convoys organised by the United Nations Relief and Rehabilitation Administration (UNRRA) and coming from military surplus. New vehicles, mainly imported, accounted for a small percentage of the total. As the number of vehicles increased, the variety of makes and models increased also, which gave rise to serious challenges of ensuring effective maintenance for a diverse fleet of machines. Given the simultaneous lack of a single institution that would concentrate all automotive matters in its hands, the spectre of total chaos on Polish roads was looming on the horizon.

Two concepts were advanced to control this disorder. The first called for the appointment of a Government Plenipotentiary for Motorisation, bestowed with all relevant prerogatives. The plenipotentiary himself would have the appropriate qualifications to perform his duties and would be equipped

---

131 Inż. O. U., "CZM. Departament motoryzacyjny czy urząd motoryzacyjny," *Motoryzacja* 1947, no. 1, p. 210.

with the "necessary executive powers." The second concept proposed the establishment of an Automotive Commission (Komisja Motoryzacyjna KM) at the Central Planning Office (Centralny Urząd Planowania CUP). Decision-makers resisted the first concept, writing that "[it] does not yet express the opinions of the important players."[132] They therefore decided to pursue the second concept.

Draft projects stipulated that the commission would be "small in number" and conduct systematic meetings; that it would "have an executive body overseeing matters that do not require KERM resolutions"; and that it would drum up popular support from the beginning by "positively and quickly settling at least a few specific and urgent matters."[133] Locating the planned commission within the structures of the administrative offices responsible for economic planning seemed an obvious choice, since that would provide opportunities to include issues related to automobiles at a very early stage of planning.

In January 1947, it was decided that this project would be implemented. By decision of CUP President Czesław Bobrowski, the Automotive Commission was set up as an advisory and opinion-forming body. Aside from representatives of the CUP, its membership included envoys of ministries keenly interested in the problem of automobile use: the Ministries of Industry, Transportation, National Defence, Agriculture and Agrarian Reform, and of the General Staff. The commission was headed by Stefan Askanas. The newly established body was to handle the development of state automotive policy, coordinate the work of individual ministries in the area of motorisation, and oversee its development. All this was to take place within the framework of the Three-Year Economic Reconstruction Plan, or the Three-Year Plan (officially the Economic Reconstruction Plan, the first major economic programme implemented in Poland after World War II). Subcommittees were established within the KM to address specific issues: foreign purchases, fuel procurement, mechanical issues, and coordination.[134]

---

132 AAN, KC PPR, sygn. 295/XI-277 (mf 2334/16), W sprawie motoryzacji kraju, [no date], p. 24.

133 AAN, Komitet Ekonomiczny Rady Ministrów (hereafter: KERM), sygn. 210, p. 11.

134 Ibid., Zarządzenie no. 2 Prezesa Centralnego Urzędu Planowania z 26 I 1947 r. w sprawie powołania Komisji Motoryzacyjnej przy Centralnym Urzędzie Planowania, pp. 2–3;

Despite high-profile announcements, the new body quickly adapted to the atmosphere in the sphere of automobilism. The commission's activities yielded limited results, although it should be said that the fault did lay entirely with it. Those who participated in its work lamented that "recently, it has been observed that a certain number of automotive topics have begun to pass on to various other bodies, leading to dispersion and the lack of a guiding idea."[135] Furthermore, the imprecisely defined role assigned to the commission meant that the effects of its work were very limited, and their actual impact on the development of automobilism in the country was negligible. The previously quoted Okołów, who was a member of the commission, said in October 1947: "The issue of automotive policy in our country is in limbo. … Today, the Automotive Commission is closer to an internal body of the CUP. I do not know how conclusive and authoritative the Commission's resolutions are. We pass important things, but we do not feel that the rulings are one step away from being approved by the Economic Committee [of the Council of Ministers]."[136] Okołów's words perfectly describe the fate of the coordinating subcommittee operating as part of the Automotive Commission. Its responsibilities included streamlining and facilitating cooperation between individual ministries interested in automotive issues.[137] At the same time, its members repeatedly emphasised that they were encountering "fundamental difficulties" in their work, given that there was as yet no legal basis for the commission's existence and no official competencies to justify its existence to the ministries.[138] In truth, the shape of Polish automotive policy was actually defined only by the Subcommittee on Foreign Purchases, which consulted, and then approved, each purchase of motor vehicles from abroad.[139]

Despite internal doubts as to the viability of its existence and the effectiveness of its work, the commission continued to operate for several months. Among its achievements were the "Automotive Theses," to which I will return later. However, this did not significantly improve the atmosphere

---

ibid., Regulamin Komisji Motoryzacyjnej przy Centralnym Urzędzie Planowania, p. 4.

135 Ibid., Komisja Motoryzacyjna. Protokół 10-go posiedzenia 2 IX 1947 r., p. 112.

136 Ibid., Komisja Motoryzacyjna. Protokół 11-go posiedzenia 2 X 1947 r., p. 131.

137 AAN, KERM, sygn. 216, Regulamin Podkomisji Koordynacyjnej, [no date], p. 1.

138 Ibid., Sprawozdanie z działalności za okres od 9 XII 1946 do 9 I 1947 r., p. 76.

139 E.g. AAN, KERM, sygn. 214—this item includes the minutes of individual meetings of the Subcommittee on Foreign Purchases.

around KM, which quietly ended its work as early as July 1948, although the aforementioned Subcommittee on Foreign Purchases continued to function for some time after. It is not possible to unequivocally state who decided that the commission had to be disbanded and why it had to happen. Perhaps the decisive factors were political issues and the darkening atmosphere around the CUP. As we will see, a new body was established almost immediately, one with a structure and powers closely resembling those of the Automotive Commission. Perhaps, however, the commission's demise was the result of its slow pace of work and decision-makers' dissatisfaction with its results. Unfortunately, no clear answer is possible, nor an unambiguous assessment of its activities. On the one hand, this experiment seems not to have been entirely successful because the impact of the decisions the members of the commissions made about the shape of the policy pursued by the authorities in the field of motorisation was very limited. On the other hand, the effects of the work of two subcommittees—the aforementioned Subcommittee on Foreign Purchases and the Fuel Subcommittee—did not go unnoticed.[140] It is also worth mentioning here that members of the commission prepared a number of plans and forecasts which would later form the basis for long-term economic plans in the field of motorisation.

2.1.4 The Motorisation Subcommittee

The tasks of the Automotive Commission were taken over by the newly established Motorisation Subcommittee (PM) of the KERM, established in the resolution of August 27, 1948. Its tasks included "putting the automotive sector in order," developing planning guidelines in matters related to the nation's motorisation, and overseeing the implementation of automotive

140 The military was very interested in the meetings of the Fuel Subcommittee, and its representatives actively participated in the subcommittee's work. The main effort was focused primarily on developing a demand plan for petroleum products and on accelerating the quality improvement of domestic oils and lubricants and the use of alternative fuels for engines: see AAN, KERM, sygn. 212, Program pracy Podkomisji Paliwowej, p. 4 ff; ibid., Sprawozdanie z prac Podkomisji Paliwowej, Warszawa, 29 IV 1947 r., p. 8; AAN, KERM, sygn. 213, Notatka, Warszawa, 11 XI 1947, unnumbered pages.

plans.[141] The subcommittee's responsibilities were therefore identical to those of its predecessor, as was its structure. In addition, even as the Automotive Commission ceased operations, its subcommittee managing foreign purchases continued to function and was incorporated into the structures of the newly established Motorisation Subcommittee—. Thus, the subcommittee would ensure continuity in activities related to the finalisation of trade agreements. It was headed by Piotr Jaroszewicz, the then-Deputy Minister of Ministry of National Defence (Ministerstwo Obrony Narodowej, MON).[142] This is a fact worth emphasising because it meant the subcommittee's activities were more closely tied to military interests in automotive matters; representatives of the military (including the above-mentioned Wrzos and even Paweł Solski) held important positions in all administrative bodies responsible for questions related to automobilism.

However, that a new structure was established did not mean that its work was of new and higher quality. Many doubts as to the scope of the subcommittee's activities emerged in the initial phase, during inter-ministerial consultations regarding its statute.[143] Already the first meeting, during which the composition of the subcommittee was established, revealed many issues that could not be resolved. It was difficult to reconcile the interests of several ministries whose representatives comprised the subcommittee and who were keenly interested in automotive issues, especially given the desire to influence the shape of state automotive policy on the part of the military.[144] Representative for the Ministry of Defence in the Motorisation Subcommittee, Colonel Paweł Solski, noted that despite the existence of the

---

141 AAN, KERM, sygn. 217, Uchwała Komitetu Ekonomicznego Rady Ministrów w sprawie Podkomitetu Motoryzacyjnego, pp. 1–2; ibid., Protokół z pierwszego posiedzenia Podkomitetu Motoryzacyjnego z 1 X 1948 r., p. 5.

142 The Subcommittee also included Colonel Paweł Solski, who had previously worked on the Automotive Commission.

143 See e.g. AAN, KERM, sygn. 221, Uwagi Departamentu Komunikacji i Łączności CUP do projektu uchwały Komitetu Ekonomicznego Rady Ministrów w sprawie utworzenia Podkomitetu Motoryzacyjnego, [no date], p. 32.

144 In addition to representatives of MON and the General Staff, the Motorisation Subcommittee was made up of delegates of the following ministries: Industry and Trade, Public Security, Transportation, Agriculture and Agricultural Reform, and the CUP; AAN, KERM, sygn. 217, Uchwała Komitetu Ekonomicznego Rady Ministrów w sprawie powołania Podkomitetu Motoryzacyjnego, p. 2.

Automotive Commission, many issues related to automobilism were still within the purview of different ministries. "There is not a single ministry," he said, "that would not be interested in automotive issues." In turn, Karol Rojek from the MPiH stated:

> ... to be honest, we do not yet know what CUP has done in this area [automobilism], what its practical actions have been. ... The Ministry of Industry and Trade has certain ambitions and pursues a number of projects, but without any legal basis. The main feature of all these activities is that whoever feels stronger takes up some of the work. There has to be regulation, or there will be a lot of bureaucracy.

Kazimierz Sokołowski, vice-chairman of CUP, also chimed in, explaining that his institution had thus far been dealing with a large number of different issues outside the scope of its tasks because there were no one else would take them up. Once again, there was a conflict of responsibilities in connection with the idea of establishing a Fuel Commission within the Motorisation Subcommittee, which Deputy Minister of Transportation Wincenty Jastrzębski vehemently opposed out of the conviction that the existence of such a commission would interfere with the activities of the CPN.[145] Moreover, the advisability of creating a commission within a subcommittee was questioned, and it was suggested that important issues be explored within the ministries that were most interested in solving them, while the commissions, if they were created, would only deal with "fragmentary problems. "Two views of the role of the PM were at odds here. The first one, pushed by the military (primarily Solski), expected the new body to deal with a broad range of issues. Representatives of individual ministries were against such a solution because they feared that the subcommittee would be too dispersed in its executive work, which would indirectly translate into bureaucratic overgrowth. Further doubts were caused by the development of the automotive plan that was to be included in the rapidly approaching Six-Year Plan, second economic programme. Eventually, an order of business was agreed: preliminary work was to be performed by the CUP, preparing

[145] However, W. Jastrzębski would only assent to the appointment of such a commission if it dealt with scientific and research work; AAN, KERM, sygn. 217, Protokół z pierwszego posiedzenia Podkomitetu Motoryzacyjnego z 1 X 1947 r., p. 13ff

guidelines for the plan, which would then be approved by the PM. After approval, the CUP would develop a final version of the plan.[146]

The subcommittee was dissolved by the resolution of the KERM of May 15, 1949. Its functions were taken over by the Division of Automobile Management within the Department of Transportation and Communications in the newly established State Commission for Economic Planning (Państwowa Komisja Planowania Gospodarcego PKPG) the body responsible for all economic activities.[147] Though the Division had the power to adopt directive resolutions that specific ministries had to implement, the impact of its actions was limited. The subcommittee met a total of thirteen times. During these meetings, guidelines for the Six-Year Plan were approved and the scope of imports of automotive equipment for 1949 was set.[148] However, no agreement was reached on who was to manage motorisation in Poland and how. It is impossible to avoid the impression that the Motorisation Subcommittee's activities were the last act of Stalinisation within automobilism, especially if we take a closer look at the place of private car users and the fate of private initiative within the newly drafted plans.

2.2 Planning

The importance of setting the right course for the development of Polish automobilism after World War II was clear from the very beginning. As early as 1946, Jan Śmigielski from the Department of Transportation and Communications of the CUP lucidly explained the importance of a proper plan within Polish realities: "If the shortest path between two points in space is a straight line, then within the problem of motorisation, the straight line from the current state of affairs to the specific goal leads through an automotive plan."[149] It was therefore clear that, in order not to repeat the mistakes of the Second Polish Republic, the development of automobilism

146 Ibid.

147 M. P. 1949, no. 59, pos. 799; A. Rostocki, "Transport samochodowy a rozwój motoryzacji," in: *Transport samochodowy w Polsce ludowej*, Warszawa 1977, p. 20.

148 AAN, KERM, sygn. 217, Sprawozdanie z działalności Podkomitetu Motoryzacyjnego, [no date], pp. 288–289.

149 AAN, Ministerstwo Komunikacji (hereafter: MK), sygn. 219, Jan Śmigielski, Wytyczne polityki…, unnumbered pages.

had to be properly managed. This would be achieved by a well-developed plan. The postwar decade abounded in documents of this type, formulated in various circles, both governmental and expert. This subchapter is devoted to ideas for the development of automobilism advanced between 1945 and 1955.

2.2.1 The First Plans for the Development of the Automobilism

One of the first comprehensive plans for the future development of automobilism in Poland, concerning both its institutional shape and the role it was to play in economic and political life, as well as social life, came from the milieu of the PUS. These were the "Issues of Automotive Economy," developed in early 1946 and addressed to Prime Minister Edward Osóbka-Morawski. The document was signed by Ignacy Wrzos, but it is doubtful that he authored the entire document; most likely, he acted as head of the PUS, signing a document prepared by his subordinates.

The "Issues" attempted to answer the following questions: "What must be done for this branch of the economy to keep pace with the general expansion of the national economy and catch up at least with the last-place countries, if not the first-place country?" and: "How should we conceive of the transport authorities so as to give the motorisation of the country a proper start?"[150] It should be noted that motorisation and transport were not considered separately here, in the belief that they constituted a larger whole. Poland was to follow the model developed in the USSR, where—unlike in the prewar Western ("capitalist" or "fascist") states—the problem of motorisation was developed "in the most classical, planned way." Motorisation in the Soviet sense involved not only questions related to transportation, but also "universal-economic and political" matters, which is why it was decided to create a separate ministry to manage it in the USSR. As the "Issue" states, this approach allowed for "the full expression of the development of motorisation according to the needs of the whole, and not according to the power and whims of the initiators. The investment of the necessary national capital was ensured according to the hierarchy of common needs, achieving independence from undirected individual aspirations. "However,

---

150 AAN, URM, sygn. 5/468, Do premiera Rządu Jedności Narodowej ob. Osóbka-Morawskiego, 16 II 1946 r., p. 1.

according to the assessment of PUS officials, it was still too early for such a separate ministry to be established in Poland: "We are not currently pursuing classic planning solutions to the degree that we demand an automotive ministry today." The greatest strength by far of Polish automobilism was the "large personnel legacy (staff)," which had to be included in the work of the new administration of automobilism. This administrative body, whose working name was the "Main Office for Motorisation," was to be incorporated into the structures of the Ministry of Transportation, which would perform a supervisory function. The CUP was to cooperate with the ministry, which would be responsible for coordinating partial plans with national plans through its departments (automotive and transport). The scope of activities of the planned office included management of automotive issues at the central level and the development of guidelines for the management of state-owned enterprises. However, one of its main tasks was to "carry out automotive policy" understood as "legislative and personnel policy, matters of traffic, transport, and rolling stock, the development of its own ... budget, accounting, financial and economic plans, and reports of subordinate enterprises, ... licensing, tariff, fuel, and investment policy, road traffic control, standardisation, vehicle management oversight, training and educating automotive staff." Nevertheless, it was accepted that this wide scope "requires, on the one hand, a fairly extensive apparatus, and on the other, its manager must receive special prerogative to communicate with other ministries." At the voivodeship and county level, offices were to be excluded from the control of local authorities and "remain dependent in symbolic, purely personal terms on the voivode, without his interference in the core issues." PUS also envisioned that, "in addition to the planning element, two other elements: of scientific and social cooperation" would be formed, taking the shape of a Research-Transportation Institute (Instytut Badawczo-Komunikacyjny). As is evident, the new administration dealing with automotive issues was being tailored to fit the new times, an attempt to create a new organisation "in a Poland destroyed and unmotorised," but rich in experience from the interwar period, an innovative organisation that took into account "planning, coordination, and entrepreneurship on the part of the modern state." The authors of "Issues" proclaimed: "It [modern administration of automotive matters] does not require many more people, but provides for the proper distribution of work and functions among them, separating planning, coordination, and supervision."[151]

Despite their broad scope, "Issues" did not take into account many key subjects, such as the development of the automotive industry or matters tied to individual motoring; it focused primarily on the institutional side of things. Perhaps the document was created in response to the adoption of regulations on the Central Motorisation Authority in early 1946. In this light, PUS' "Issues" fit perfectly into the discussion about the shape and scope of responsibilities of the new entity that was to manage Polish automobilism.

Much more detailed and complex was the document prepared by Jan Śmigielski bearing the telling title: "Guidelines for Automotive Policy and Economy." Śmigielski did not hesitate to criticise the current authorities and their inaction with regard to motorisation; he compared them with the leadership of the Second Polish Republic, in which the lack of planning was "a cause of tragic mistakes." Śmigielski wrote: "This lack of a plan makes itself felt to the highest degree in the favoring of expanding incompetence and stillborn ideas." The main goals for motorisation included: the development of a rational transportation network that would eliminate the substantial differences between the Recovered Territories newly incorporated into the country's borders and the rest of the country; the creation of a market of automobiles for requisition in consultation with the military intended to relieve the State Treasury; the increase of social income through the establishment of new industries and transportation enterprises; the raising of the standard of living of the working masses "by placing several million horsepower at their service"; and the facilitating of temporary work by the enabling of the registration of vehicles. All of these goals were to be met with the achievement of the level of 115,000 vehicles in the country by 1947 (about 4.5 per 1,000 inhabitants), of which 35,000 were to be the passenger cars. At the same time, the most important guidelines for future automotive policy included: the creation of a favourable atmosphere and appropriate conditions in which "the spread of motor vehicles as a means of transport and communication would not encounter difficulties"; the ensuring of the supply of an appropriate number of new vehicles to the market "in sizes

---

151 AAN, URM, sygn. 5/465, Zagadnienia gospodarki motoryzacyjnej w Polsce, luty 1946, pp. 4–9.

corresponding to demand"; the expansion of the existing service network; the ending of "car looting and privateering"; and the acceptance of the needs of automobile traffic in the design of new urban centres. In order to achieve these goals, it was necessary to establish the State Automotive Council under KERM, which was to include "eminent experts in automotive issues." An Institute of Motorisation dealing with scientific research was also to function within the council. At voivodeship level, Automobile Commissions attached to national councils would serve as advisory bodies. The State Automotive Council would also issue its own publication devoted exclusively to motorisation. The question of preparing an automotive plan also figured prominently in Śmigielski's document. To ensure coordination with the national plan, it was to be drawn up under the auspices of the CUP, which would also monitor its implementation—a task delegated to the relevant ministries, the entire process taking place under the supervision of the KERM. Śmigielski also devoted space to private entrepreneurs, seeing a place for them in the new reality, provided that the private initiative be "healthy and coordinated with the state plan." Only then could such an initiative "merit the support and protection of the State." Finally, the "Guidelines" presented a detailed enumeration of the types of cars that were to be included in the domestic production programme: trucks, agricultural tractors, buses and specialised cars, ambulances, motorcycles, and passenger cars. The latter were to take the shape of a "popular 4-seat, 2-door vehicle" and a "large, 6-seat, 4-door vehicle." Passenger cars were to be modelled after the German DKW because of its simple construction, low operating costs, and the fact that it had "passed the final trail in Polish conditions and on Polish roads."[152]

Even a cursory glance at these two documents—"Issues of Automotive Economy" prepared by PUS and "Guidelines for Automotive Policy and Economy"—reveals significant differences in perceptions of the future role of motorisation. The key problem was the proper approach to individual car owners. While the first document envisaged no place for them, Śmigielski allowed for their presence in the postwar reality, with certain limitations. Moreover, the "Guidelines" treated car ownership not as a luxury, but as a common means of enabling representatives of certain professions to perform

[152] AAN, MK, sygn. 219, Jan Śmigielski, Wytyczne polityki..., unnumbered pages.

their duties. This fact is worth emphasising because, as would later turn out to be the case, it was members of the "freelance workers" who would be the first to enjoy the ability to own private cars.

2.2.2 The Three-Year Plan

The Three-Year Economic Reconstruction Plan (1947–1949) was the first of the long-term economic plans that set the direction and pace of development, both economic and social, in the People's Republic of Poland. Guidelines for the plan, prepared by a team headed by Czesław Bobrowski, were adopted by the KRN on September 21, 1946, and the Sejm passed an act concerning the plan on July 2, 1947.[153] Among the most important tasks in the plan, apart from the "economic reconstruction" referred to in its title, was raising the standard of living of the working population above the prewar level.[154] The development of motorisation was understood primarily as the expansion of wheeled transport, which was to supplement the transportation of goods and people carried out by the dominant player in this respect—the railways. The act explicitly mentions passenger cars, setting out the goal of achieving 80% of the number for 1938 in 1949 (see Table 1), meaning that in the last year of the Three-Year Plan, there would be fewer than 21,000 passenger vehicles on Polish roads. On the other hand, trucks were the clear priority, with an expected sixfold increase compared to the prewar period. The number of motorcycles was to double. These amounts were considered sufficient to meet needs of rebuilding the country, streamlining the administration, ensuring an even distribution of goods and food, managing territorial acquisitions in the west, "reviving the economic life of the eastern borderlands," and "facilitating the work of free professionals—a general acceleration of economic processes and thereby an increase in social income." The potential of the automotive industry was also mentioned, the development of which was said to require a coordinated cooperation with other branches of industry. "These features and this goal put the automotive industry at the forefront

[153] Dz. U., 1947, no. 53, pos. 285.

[154] For more on this topic, see: J. Kaliński, *Plan odbudowy gospodarczej 1947–1949*, Warszawa 1977.

of economic needs," the act proclaimed.[155] However, given the realities of economic recovery and the fact that individual industries were in the initial stages of the relaunch, the time perspective had to be longer than three years. It was therefore decided to adopt a period of one decade.

It was anticipated that a decade would suffice for Poland to develop its automotive industry to the level of that in Czechoslovakia. This meant that in the plan's tenth year, there would be 350,000 vehicles in Poland: 140,000 trucks, 200,000 passenger cars and 10,000 buses. Such a significant increase in the number of passenger cars was supposed to be followed by a rise in wealth in the society. Since it was assumed that the standard of living would first rise among the poor, the number of potential buyers in the initial period of the ten-year plan was to be small. Only "with favorable economic development and a planned increase in social income ... will the passenger car become highly sought after, at the end of the first five years." Then, there was the question of motorcycles. The authors of the plan believed that the motorcycle was an object with "little economic justification." Therefore, as an "intermediate link between a bicycle and a car," it was useful to a limited degree, mainly for meeting the needs of the militia, post office, and army. It was predicted that in the plan's last year, the number of motorcycles would equal the number of cars.[156] The level of 200,000 passenger cars would be reached by the end of the decade thanks to own production; importation was to be reserved only for special cars, missing resources, and necessary parts for the domestic automotive industry.

However, the ambitious tasks set in the plan were revised by Poland's post-war realities. It soon turned out that the planned expansion of the automotive industry required a doubling of the financial expenditures. Achieving the 20,900 passenger cars by 1949 would prove impossible. Ultimately, however, the results of the Three-Year Plan showed that it was precisely the number of cars that rose beyond expectations (by over 16,000 units), while the planned number of trucks could not be reached—the shortage amounted to 5,000

155 AAN, CUP, sygn. 2921, Motoryzacja w Trzyletnim Planie Odbudowy. Referat zgłoszony na Kongres Techników polskich w Katowicach 1–4 XII 1946 r., pp. 13–14.

156 Ibid., p. 15.

vehicles.[157] As one author commented regarding the numbers, "life itself motorised us."[158]

The person behind the goals of the ten-year development plan for the Polish automotive industry was the aforementioned Zygmunt Okołów. He notably raised two additional problems: human resources and the role of private initiative. As he noted, it was people who constituted the greatest potential for the Polish automotive industry, and their "work and experience will have to be put to full use in order to solve the problem [of the automotive industry]." In the new political and economic reality, the state would play an important role, intervening to stimulate private initiative and tailor its activities to the general interest.[159] At the time, the issue of private entrepreneurs, especially those whose primary focus was the production of spare parts (which were scarce goods), and their participation in the creation of the automotive industry, was raised repeatedly. Communist authorities believed that access to products offered by private entrepreneurs was an indispensable condition for the proper functioning of the technical base, although a careful reading of the documents shows that the focus was, in fact, primarily on extending wider control over "privateers." The "Guidelines for PPR Activists" proclaim:

> … the development of a small private automotive industry should be supported, particularly in the production of spare parts, which cannot be performed by state industry now or is not worthwhile for state industry (non-series), while striving to draw capital away from speculative trading and the exploitation of the industrial potential that exists in private hands. On the other hand, authorities need to be vigilant and create a system of control over private industry so that it does not siphon off state capital and machinery for itself, does not cheat on prices, etc.[160]

CZM representatives investigated the production capacity of private entrepreneurs, for example those associated with the Chamber of Commerce and Industry (IPH), and their possible involvement in future automotive

157 "Rocznik Statystyczny Transportu", 1967, p. XXVIII.

158 AAN, CUP, sygn. 2921, Motoryzacja w Planie Trzyletnim, p. 7.

159 AAN, KC PPR, sygn. 295/XI-277 (mf 2334/16), W sprawie motoryzacji, [no date], pp. 238–244.

160 AAN, KC PPR, sygn. 295/XI-17, Wytyczne narady aktywu PPR motoryzacji z 17 VII 1947 r., p. 52.

production, especially of spare parts.[161] Plans were even made to hold a joint conference to discuss this issue. Priority in the supply of the necessary raw materials and machinery was given to private entrepreneurs who would eventually cooperate. The Ministry of Industry finally obtained a declaration of acceptance for the proposal under the condition that information would be provided sufficiently in advance about the types and number of necessary spare parts, the reason being that "so far, no one was ever fully informed about what was needed."[162]

The papers and proposals cited above never really resulted in specific implementations. Why was this so? It seems that a major reason is that the authorities lacked a real determination to motorise Poland. However, this does not change the fact that ideas were put forward that were designed to serve as a catalyst for the development of motorisation, and many people truly believed that Poland's rulers would give it the green light. Nevertheless, the relatively low influence of the people and institutions behind these ideas, as well as the institutional chaos that fed a blurring of responsibilities, meant that the matter of the development of motorisation came to a dead end.

Let us return to the Three-Year Plan. The guidelines prepared by the CUP focused primarily on Poland's postwar recovery and unification of the country's new western territories. Road infrastructure took precedence, with a drive to increase the use of road transport at the expense of rail transport. Spending for this purpose amounted to 27% of all expenditures planned in 1947–1949. Only industry was allocated more money (35% of the total). However, in the plan's last two years, expenditures on transport development were significantly reduced (to 24.9% and 17.8%, respectively), as funds were redirected to industrial development (36.2% and 40.7%). This naturally had a negative impact on development of the automotive industry.

As mentioned above, one of the results of the work of the Automotive Commission operating at CUP were documents outlining plans to develop motorisation, among which were the previously mentioned "Automotive Theses" drawn up by Jan Śmigielski. In a systematic way (in 15 points) Śmigielski enumerated the steps to be taken in order to motorise Poland,

161 Ibid., Izba Przemysłowo-Handlowa, sygn. 1196, [Pismo Zjednoczenia Przemysłu Motoryzacyjnego do Izby Przemysłowej], Warszawa, 28 VI 1946 r., unnumbered pages.

162 Ibid., Protokół, [after 19 II 1947], unnumbered pages.

which, by and large, replicated Śmigielski's earlier "Guidelines for Automotive Policy and Economy."[163] However, there were some differences. Most significantly, the theses emphasised the relationship between the development of motorisation and the defence of the country (thesis 10). This was probably the result of both pressure from the military, which wanted at all costs to exert greater control over the development of motorisation, and the international situation. Greater emphasis was also placed on the development of engineering staff related to motorisation (thesis 12). In the future, Śmigielski's theses would form the basis of the "Long-term General Automotive Plan."

However, before that happened, Śmigielski produced another paper, entitled "The Polish State Automotive Plan." Several dozen pages in length, this document repeated the essential points from the author's earlier pronouncements. Poland's motorisation would be based on domestic production, which would, at the same time, form the basis for the country's defence, though domestic production would be supplemented by imports. This broader cooperation with foreign carmakers would involve mainly Slavic countries. Transport would be transferred "from rails to motor vehicles" by way of a network of modern roads. Śmigielski placed great emphasis on the mechanisation of agriculture, especially on providing the Polish countryside with an appropriate number of tractors. On the one hand, this was supposed to help develop Polish agriculture, while on the other hand, it would release more people to work in the industry. All activities in the field of motorisation were to be supervised by well-prepared cadres of specialists. The "Polish State Automotive Plan" also provides for individual motorisation and passenger cars. Once again, Śmigielski criticised the conduct of automotive policy, from its lack of a specific action plan to personnel matters: "If there were an automotive plan, then work in the field would be different, management appointments would be more appropriate, efforts would be coordinated, and the whole work … would seem more appealing. If a sailor sets out to sea without knowing his port of call, then no favourable wind is ever favourable to him. "He emphasised the paradox "… that under a system of planned

[163] AAN, KERM, sygn. 210, Tezy Motoryzacyjne opracowane przez inż. Śmigielskiego, [listopad 1948 r.], pp. 32–34; there is an even earlier (thirteen-point) version of this document, which, however, does not differ in essential points from the final, fifteen-point version; ibid., Tezy motoryzacyjne, grudzień 1947, pp. 30–31.

economy, which is our system, we do not have a plan for the motorisation of the country." The "Polish State Automotive Plan" foresaw that within a decade, 500,000 vehicles would be on Polish roads—vehicles produced almost exclusively by the Polish industry. After the first five years, however, slightly less than half of that number of vehicles was expected to exist—200,000, which meant a ratio of 4.2 cars per 1,000 inhabitants in 1952, and 7.0 in 1957.

The Polish automotive industry was intended to produce, for instance, medium-capacity passenger cars under a contract being negotiated at that time with the Italian Fiat. However, the plan did not specify who, and on what terms, would produce the smallest cars, which were to become the basis of Poland's motorisation. Śmigielski criticised the current situation, opining that automotive matters were being handled "haphazardly ... by ad hoc foreign purchases" and put off "to an unspecified future." In his view, the import policy lacked a coherent perspective on the future of this branch of the automotive industry. An important role here was to be played by the agreement with Fiat, for which Śmigielski had much hope. At the same time, he added that, though the signing of the contract represented a promising beginning, it could not guarantee success.[164]

The plan prepared by Jan Śmigielski was probably the most complex and complete study on the development of the automotive industry in postwar Poland in the period. The engineer himself was aware of the importance of the matter, writing: "This time, the Rubicon in the automotive problem has been crossed, ... there is no return to the gloomy past, and ... in 1948 Poland will have an automotive plan."[165] However, reality showed that even if the plan was a step in the right direction, there was still a long way to go to implementing even some of Śmigielski's goals, which is evidenced, for example, by the reactions to his papers preserved in sources: a discussion that did not add much of substance, and remnants of a dispute between the engineer and the vice-president of the CUP regarding the fee for preparing the plan.[166]

---

164 AAN, KERM, sygn. 211, Polski Państwowy Plan Motoryzacyjny, pp. 20–89.

165 Ibid., Dotyczy: Planu Motoryzacji, Warszawa, 30 VI 1948 r., p. 2.

166 Ibid., pp. 1–3.

2.2.3 The Six-Year Plan

As mentioned, the Automotive Commission's successor, which took the shape of the Motorisation Subcommittee, was to be primarily responsible for preparing guidelines for the planned motorisation of Poland and for overseeing their implementation. The final plan was to be based on studies prepared by CUP and previously approved by the subcommittee. For this purpose, in September 1948, a special commission was established for matters related to the preparation of the country's motorisation plans in the office headed by Czesław Bobrowski.[167] As a result of its work, several preliminary projects were created that ultimately combined into the "Guidelines for the 6-year Automotive Plan 1950–1955, Excluding the Needs of the MON and the Ministry of Security." One of the projects was entitled "Detailed Elements for the Guidelines of the 6-year Automotive Plan." It justifies interest because it includes a section on the shape of the automobile fleet during the Six-Year Plan, which would be based on domestically produced trucks with a carrying capacity of 1.5 to 4 tons and imported 7-to-8 ton trucks, along with agricultural tractors and motorcycles produced in Poland. The latter were to be "a popular means of movement, communication, inspection, and sport." The automobile fleet was to be supplemented with three types of passenger cars: medium-engine automobiles with a displacement of 1.35–1.7 litres, produced domestically for the needs of state and economic administration; imported small-engine (0.7–1 litre) automobiles "designed for city driving and suburban trips"; and foreign large-engine (over 1.7 litres) vehicles for representative and special purposes.[168] Vehicles for private use could be sold only after the most urgent needs of communication and transportation of goods had been satisfied. The necessity of ownership of a car for both individuals and

---

[167] AAN, CUP, sygn. 2994, Zarządzenie no. 51 Prezesa CUP, [wrzesień 1948], pp. 8–9. The guidelines would concern: production plans for the automotive industry (types and kinds of vehicles); road transport and road management plans; the question of motorisation; importation and sale of motor vehicles and fuel; see AAN, CUP, sygn. 2994, Wstępny projekt wytycznych do planu motoryzacyjnego w latach 1950–1955, p. 60; ibid., Szczegółowe elementy do wytycznych 6-cioletniego planu motoryzacji, pp. 61–65.

[168] AAN, CUP, sygn. 2994, Szczegółowe elementy do wytycznych 6-cio letniego planu motoryzacji, p. 61; compare AAN, KERM, sygn. 217, Sprzęt motoryzacyjny przewidziany do importu w planie 6-letnim, pp. 130–131.

private enterprises was to be approved on a case-by-case basis by chambers of industry and commerce and of crafts.[169] Before it was accepted for further elaboration, the document was consulted with individual ministries.[170] At the end, Śmigielski himself responded to many comments. It soon turned out that the point referring to individual car owners had attracted controversy. Śmigielski protested quite strongly against the inclusion of the following sentence in the final version of the document: "the use of passenger cars and motorcycles in individual journeys may only be undertaken by certain and authorised groups of citizen"; in his view, "this amounts to creating an automobile 'elite', or even a 'caste', which is contrary to the principles of a people's democracy and of a socialist country. The state strives to raise the standard of living of all working citizens, and everyone should thus have equal opportunities to use a motorcycle or passenger car, if it is at all possible."[171]

In turn, officials at the Automobile Department of the Ministry of Transportation noticed another very important and thus far overlooked issue involved in privately owned cars: car maintenance costs: "The 6-year plan cannot yet include a private car for personal needs because maintenance of a small-engine passenger car valued at 80,000 zlotys without a driver costs about 400,000 zlotys at an annual mileage of 15,000 km, which is not proportional to the increase in social income during the period of the 6-year plan."[172]

In their final guise, the "Guidelines" prepared by the CUP commission resembled preceding documents discussed above both in terms of layout and the issues they raised. They were comprised of ten parts devoted to the following issues: the scope, needs, and purpose of an automotive plan; the tasks of motorisation; the organisation of its authorities; the hierarchy of needs; the demand for services and equipment; the repairs and operation;

169 AAN, CUP, sygn. 2994, Szczegółowe elementy do wytycznych 6-cio letniego planu motoryzacji, p. 63.

170 Ibid., p. 93ff

171 Ibid., Uwagi do wytycznych 6-cio letniego Planu Motoryzacyjnego, opracowanego przez Dep[artament] Kom[unikacji] i Łączn[ości]—W[ydzia]ł Motoryzacyjny, Warszawa, 25 XI 1948 r., pp. 164–165.

172 AAN, KERM, sygn. 217, [Opinia Departamentu Samochodowego Ministerstwa Komunikacji], p. 85.

the road network; fuel issues; and the so-called human factor.[173] Individual car users were in the fifth (last) place in the hierarchy of automotive needs, behind tractors, trucks, public passenger vehicles, and personal cars intended for the state administrative apparatus. They were to be sold production surpluses or "worn out" state-owned cars. As in previous studies, there was a proposed solution to the question of automotive management through the CUP, individual ministries, and local administration. The Polish automotive industry was also supposed to be autarkic. In the hierarchy of automotive needs, motorisation of agriculture remained in the lead. The greatest change concerned the role of vehicles in transport—the primacy of rail and inland waterway transport was to be maintained, and the motor vehicle was designated as an "auxiliary means of transporting people and goods." Given the political realities, the "Guidelines" no longer mentioned private entrepreneurs, who in earlier studies were supposed to significantly supplement state automotive production.

As can be seen, the guidelines for the six-year automotive plan ultimately directed the Polish automotive industry towards a particular form of development, understood primarily as the development of transport. Private car users were treated as marginal, while private initiative was to disappear completely.

The final shape of the guidelines, which would serve as the basis for the final plan, including in the field of motorisation, was decided personally by the most important people in the country: members of the Politburo of the Central Committee of the PZPR. During the discussion on elements of the Six-Year Plan, presented by a specially appointed commission,[174] participants decided to modify the guidelines presented to them for the preparation of the "Six-Year Plan for the Development and Economic Reconstruction of Poland." Point 18, dealing with the development of the automotive industry,[175]

---

[173] Ibid., Wytyczne do 6-cioletniego Planu Motoryzacyjnego 1950–1955 r., 17 XII 1948 r., pp. 95–101.

[174] The commission was made up of Hilary Minc (chair), Eugeniusz Szyr, Stefan Jędrychowski, Julian Kole, Franciszek Blinowski, Hilary Chełchowski, Stanisław Tkaczow, Jerzy Tepicht, Mieczysław Popiel, Leon Kasman, Piotr Jaroszewicz, Jerzy Albrecht, Edward Ochab, Ryszard Strzelecki, Adam Wang, and Stanisław Strzeszewski.

[175] "For the development of road transport, the decisive factor will be the launch of the automotive industry within the Six-Year Plan, as a result of which we should produce

was appended with the following paragraph: "The development of the automotive industry will help meet the growing needs in the field of freight transport and equip state and economic administration bodies with means of personal transport, especially in the health services, post office, and rural cooperatives."[176]

These guidelines were then submitted and approved during the 1st Congress of the PZPR. At the time, it was assumed that the annual growth rate of the entire industrial production would reach 11–12%. However, already half a year later, in a resolution passed by the Council of Ministers on May 30, 1949, this indicator was increased. Finally, the third, corrected draft of the Six-Year Plan was presented at the 5th Plenum of the Central Committee of the PZPR, which took place in mid-July 1950, and the Act on the Six-Year Plan for Economic Development and Building the Foundations of Socialism for the years 1950–1955 was adopted on July 21, 1950. The predicted increase in industrial production would amount to 158.3%.[177] Indicators regarding the development of motorisation also evolved. The volume of production of trucks in the last year of the plan increased from 15,000 units (in the guidelines adopted in December 1948) up to 25,000 units (in the Act of July 21, 1950), and of passenger cars, from 7,000 up to 12,000 units.[178] The plan for branches concentrated in the Central Board of the Metal Industry (CZPM) also assumed that in the plan's last year, 35,000 passenger cars produced in

---

about 20,000 trucks and 10,000 passenger cars in 1955. At the same time, a great expansion of the car tyre industry in Poland should be envisaged"; AAN, Komitet Centralny Polskiej Zjednoczonej Partii Robotniczej (hereafter: KC PZPR), sygn. 1635 (mf 2819), Wytyczne dla sporządzenia 6-letniego planu rozwoju i przebudowy gospodarczej Polski, p. 175.

176 AAN, KC PPR, sygn. 295/V/3 (mf 2090/1), Poprawki do wytycznych do sporządzenia 6-letniego planu rozwoju i przebudowy gospodarczej Polski, [no date: September 1948?], p. 74.

177 J. Kaliński, Polityka gospodarcza Polski w latach 1948–1955, Warszawa 1987, pp. 60–62.

178 Ibid., p. 69; AAN, Centralny Zarząd Przemysłu Metalowego (hereafter: CZPM), sygn. 2, Plan Sześcioletni II, [lipiec 1949 r.], unnumbered pages. In 1949, during a discussion on the guidelines for the Six-Year Plan at one of the meetings of the Automotive Subcommittee, Minister Adam Wang argued that the production of passenger cars in the period 1950–1955 would amount to 18,000; AAN, KERM, sygn. 218, Protokół z piątego posiedzenia Podkomitetu Motoryzacyjnego z 5 I 1949 r., p. 258.

Poland would be riding on Polish roads. Planners predicted that only 5,000 of them would be privately owned.[179]

These cars were to be produced by one of the flagship investments of the Six-Year Plan, the Passenger Car Factory (FSO) in Żerań. Initially built under Italian licence, the factory was eventually constructed almost entirely with Soviet assistance—as will be discussed later in this chapter. Trucks were to be produced by the Load-carrying Vehicle Factory in Starachowice, the Load-carrying Vehicle Factory in Lublin, and the Automobile Works in Jelcz. In addition to them, vehicles were to be produced in the Motorcycle Factory in Warsaw, the Delivery Car Factory in Nysa, and the Bus Factory in Sanok.[180]

The pace of industrialisation soon began to encounter considerable difficulties. The complicated international situation (the Korean War) resulted in increased expenditures on armaments and heavy industry at the expense of industries producing consumer goods. At the same time, there were problems with raw materials, and the list of delayed investments was growing longer. The armaments industry, intended to be one of the motors of the Polish economy over the course of the Six-Year Plan, failed to reach the planned pace of development. Slower-than-expected development in metallurgical production—especially rolled products and stainless steel, resulting from, among other things, a shortage of raw materials and delays in the construction of steelworks combine in Nowa Huta and of the Warszawa Foundry—led to problems in other industrial sectors. This applied primarily to the aviation, defence, and automotive industries, which were unable to achieve full production capacity. Suffice it to say that even the machine industry was able to produce only at half capacity.[181]

In early 1953—that is, at the halfway point of the Six-Year Plan—enterprises under the supervision of the Ministry of Mechanical Industry registered shortages of working capital totalling over 365 million zlotys. The largest shortage was recorded in sectors responsible for transport and communication: shipbuilding, rolling stock, and automobiles, accounting for (respectively) 144, 112 and 49 million zlotys. Such high totals were the result of a

---

179 AAN, CZPM, sygn. 1, Plan 6-letni 1950–1955, 25 VII 1949 r., p. 386.
180 W. Morawski, *Dzieje gospodarcze Polski*, Warszawa 2010, p. 284.
181 J. Kaliński, *Polityka gospodarcza Polski*, pp. 80–82, 108.

failure to meet production plans, as well as excessive increases in wages and production costs.[182] In other words, too little was produced at too high a price.

The year 1955 was the deadline for the completion of tasks set out in the plan. According to official data (later questioned), the output of the socialised industry reached a level above that of 1949 by almost 185%. At the same time, however, the assumed production volumes of most industrial products called for in the plan could not be achieved. This also applied to automobiles. In 1955, 10,500 Star trucks were produced, accounting for only 80% of what was anticipated in the last year of the plan. Over the entire six years, the factory in Starachowice delivered less than 37,000 vehicles, reaching 86.5% of the planned 42,500. In the case of passenger cars, production was even lower. The FSO in Żerań produced 8,789 Warszawa cars over the course of six years—less than 40% of what had been planned. The result would have been even worse had it not been for the landmark achievement of the workers in 1955, when 4,000 cars rolled off the Żerań factory assembly lines. Previously, production remained at a level of 1,500 cars per year.[183]

The Six-Year Plan's last year was a good moment to draw conclusions about the effects of the changes that had been introduced into the Polish economy. A similar accounting process was applied to the field of motorisation, and the results were not positive:

> The automotive industry in Poland is one of the branches of industry that does not have a long-term development plan. This is not accidental because the importance of the automotive industry in the modern society can be seen to be underestimated at every step. However, it should be noted that no branch of production has the strong impact on the formation of a wide range of social activities that the automotive industry has. … The automotive industry's requirements are increased by cooperating industries and demand a higher technical level. The growing amount of automotive equipment in use results in greater work efficiency, and presents demands on

182 AAN, KERM, sygn. 218/24, Uchwała no. 300/53 Prezydium Rządu z 18 IV 1953 r. w sprawie zaliczkowego pokrycia niedoboru środków obrotowych na 1 I 1953 r. wynikłych wskutek poniesienia w roku 1952 nieplanowanych lub ponadplanowych strat względnie nieosiągnięcia planowanego zysku w przedsiębiorstwach podległych nadzorowi Ministra Przemysłu Maszynowego, pp. 72–74.

183 AAN, Państwowa Komisja Planowania Gospodarczego (hereafter: PKPG), sygn. 781, Prowizoryczne obliczenia wykonania planu 6-letniego w zakresie przemysłu, rolnictwa, transportu, inwestycji, budownictwa, obrotu towarowego, skupu, realnej płacy ludności, p. 7; J. Kaliński, *Polityka gospodarcza Polski*, p. 95.

> urban planning and road construction. The lack of a long-term development plan is already evident in short-sighted industrial investments, faulty urban planning, and road construction. The location of FSO precludes further expansion in the future. The arbitrary division into cooperating factories and non-ministerial factories providing only for short-term needs has caused frequent transfers of production and the associated additional costs and disturbances. Despite the small number of cars, there is already a shortage of planned garages and car parks in the urban development plan for Warsaw, as well as traffic jams at key intersections during peak hours. … It remains, therefore, to ask: what are the development prospects for automobilism in Poland, and thus for transportation and automotive industries?[184]

The authors of this document were certain that decision-makers had disregarded virtually all aspects of motorisation in Poland. If one considers the first ten years of People's Poland and the real opportunity for the country to be put on the path of faster automotive development, it becomes clear that it was a wasted decade.

2.3 Acquiring motor vehicles

The first official data on the vehicle fleet from December 1945 listed 19,000 motor vehicles, of which over 7,000 were passenger cars. If we compare these numbers with estimates from the end of the war, it turns out that in just a few months the number of cars on Polish roads had almost tripled. The causes of this increase were various: UNRRA deliveries, military appropriation, repatriation and reclamation, and, to a small extent, imports.

2.3.1 "From El Alenai to Tunis"— The UNRRA, Surplus, and Reclamations

UNRRA was established on November 9, 1943 in Washington by the United States, Great Britain, the USSR, and China. Its activities, which lasted until the end of 1946, focused on providing material assistance to Allied countries most severely affected by the war.[185]

---

[184] AAN, KC PZPR, sygn. 237/IX-105, Perspektywy rozwoju motoryzacji w Polsce, 1955, pp. 76–77.

[185] J. Reinisch, "'We shall Rebuild Anew a Powerful Nation': UNRRA, Internationalism and National Reconstruction in Poland," *Journal of Contemporary History* 43, 2008, no. 3, p. 460.

The first contacts between UNRRA and Poland were established by the government-in-exile in the summer of 1944. The founding of the PKWN significantly influenced negotiations on future material assistance. For several months, two-way talks took place. The situation changed with the establishment of the Provisional Government of National Unity and its recognition by the USA and Great Britain on July 5, 1945.[186] Negotiations were concluded almost immediately, and on September 14, an agreement was signed regulating the principles of providing assistance to Poland. The Office of UNRRA, Military Surplus, and Relief at the Ministry of Industry and Trade was to supervise deliveries and surplus purchases by the Poles.[187]

Initially, small transports reached Poland by land from the USSR.[188] The next batch of shipments, which were delivered before the end of the war, in April 1945, arrived by sea to Constanţa, Romania, from where they were sent to Poland by rail.[189] The port of Gdynia received its first deliveries in September 1945 and continued to do so until 1949. Aid provided under the auspices of UNRRA consisted mainly of food, medicine, clothing, and technical equipment, though a number of vehicles were also included. The total value of goods donated by UNRRA amounted to approximately US $470 million, of which 38% (approximately US $180 million) was food.[190] Funds provided for rebuilding industry amounted to over US $95 million. Of this amount, the funds allocated to transportation and communications amounted to US $27.5 million. According to data from the Ministry of Foreign Trade, 18,900 vehicles were sent to Poland as part of UNRRA assistance, the vast majority of them being lorries and small trucks (86%). The remaining

---

186 On behalf of the UNRRA, negotiations with Poland were conducted by Mikhail Sergeyevich Menshikov, a representative of the USSR who was assigned this task by UNRRA Director General Herbert H. Lehman; J. Reinisch, "'We shall Rebuild Anew a Powerful Nation'," pp. 460–461.

187 A. Juźwik, "Zagraniczna pomoc charytatywna dla dzieci i młodzieży w Polsce w latach 1945–1950," *Polska 1944/45–1989. Studia i Materiały* 2013, no. 11, p. 95.

188 AAN, KRN, sygn. 27, Protokół z 37 posiedzenia Komisji Komunikacyjnej oraz 12 [posiedzenia Komisji] Morskiej i Handlu Zagranicznego, 25 X 1946 r., p. 633.

189 J. Reinisch, "'We shall Rebuild Anew a Powerful Nation'," p. 461.

190 AAN, Ministerstwo Skarbu (hereafter: MS), sygn. 1533, Notatka z działalności w 1949 r. Działu UNRRA Wydziału Rozrachunków Zagranicznych NBP, Warszawa, 7 I 1950 r., p. 9.

several hundred cars were off-road vehicles of American brands—Jeeps, Ford GPWs, and Dodge WCs—totalling 856 in number.[191]

The distribution of vehicles from UNRRA deliveries was initially handled by PUS (transports from the USSR), then by KERM and CUP.[192] The technical side of the entire project was overseen by PUS. In order to collect a vehicle, a buyer had to pay the amount due according to a price list prepared by KERM. The first price lists did not adjust vehicle prices depending on their technical condition or whether they were new or used, which often caused confusion and concern for buyers who believed they had paid for new vehicles. It was also a common practice to dismantle the most damaged and battered vehicles to obtain parts for those in a better technical condition.[193] Of one transport in October 1945, consisting mainly of Canadian surplus Fords and Chevrolets, only 20% were deemed "fit for further immediate use," while the remaining 80% were considered "moderately and heavily damaged." The damage ranged from insignificant to serious, often requiring expensive repairs:

> ... broken windows, broken bumpers, bent car bodies, damaged furnishings, broken starters, generators, and petrol pumps, leaky radiators (coolers—water leaks), damaged electrical systems, etc. All batteries must be supplied with acid and distilled water and charged. About 40% of the batteries are completely discharged, and half of them are not suitable for re-use. Furnishings are usually missing; about 80% of the surplus is without tarpaulins, while the tarpaulins still on the cars were rolled up wet and are moldy, and we are thus forced to hang them in the attics immediately after receiving them, clean them of mold, and dry them in order to prevent their complete destruction. ... All vehicles, apart from completely new ones, have tires damaged by around 20%, in some cases reaching up to 50%, of which about 10% have fresh threads. All cars except new Fords lack spare wheels.

---

191 T. Szczerbicki, *Samochody w PRL*, p. 13; AAN, MPiH, sygn. 2151, Wykaz samochodów odebranych z dostaw UNRRA, Warszawa, 2 IX 1946 r., p. 23; AAN, Ministerstwo Handlu Zagranicznego (hereafter: MHZ), sygn. 2/1, Sprawozdanie z akcji UNRRA w Polsce 1945–1949, grudzień 1949 r., p. 82. Slightly different data on the number of passenger cars are provided in the study "Części zamienne dla pojazdów samochodowych," prepared for PKPG (Warsaw 1949), according to which more than 1,300 passenger cars (mainly Jeeps) were included in UNRRA transports.

192 AAN, KRN, sygn. 27, Protokół z 37. posiedzenia Komisji Komunikacyjnej oraz 12. [posiedzenia Komisji] Morskiej i Handlu Zagranicznego, 25 X 1946 r., p. 633.

193 AAN, MHZ, sygn. 2/1, Sprawozdanie z akcji UNRRA w Polsce 1945–1949, grudzień 1949, p. 133.

As noted by a member of the Division of Vehicle Inspection and Reception at PUS, "[t]hese vehicles … passed through the African campaign from El Alenai [El Alamein] to Tunis" and the Italian campaign, and their odometers ran up to 35,000 miles.[194]

The UNRRA statute of November 9, 1943 clearly defined the rules for the distribution of goods. They were to be sold "for local currency," and funds obtained in this way were to be used to help the population. During a KERM Praesidium meeting in October 1945, fees for motor vehicles supplied by UNRRA were increased (from 5,000 to 150,000 zlotys, depending on the type of vehicle), and access to discounts depending on the condition of the vehicle was introduced.[195] The president of the CUP, Czesław Bobrowski, reminded Prime Minister Osóbka-Morawski of these conditions when Osóbka-Morawski ordered the free release of vehicles financed by UNRRA. Bobrowski explained that Poland had accepted the terms by which goods from UNRRA would be sold in an agreement from July 1945. Moreover, to give away these goods would mean a de facto reduction in the overall amount of aid granted to Poland. Bobrowski also mentioned the possibility that the Minister of Treasure could cover the payments.[196] Osóbka-Morawski did not change his mind: "I do not consider these contract provisions to be right," he wrote in a note on the document containing Bobrowski's opinion. "After all, when we give cars—we give them to *help those in need*. Do what you want, but don't make it so absurd that the cars are parked [and] the ministries cannot buy them because they don't have funds. What's the economic benefit of cars just sitting around?"[197]

In early February 1946, in order to improve the distribution of cars, KERM issued two resolutions: the first established the Automobile Sales Centre, which was to take over the collection and distribution of vehicles from foreign deliveries. Pursuant to the second resolution, fee amounts for vehicles and associated discounts due would be determined depending on the

---

194 AAN, URM, sygn. 5/464/ [Pismo informacyjne PZS no. 6 w Gdyni do Biura Kontroli przy Prezydium KRN], Gdynia, 13 X 1945 r., p. 1.

195 AAN, KERM, sygn. 1, Protokół Posiedzenia Prezydium Komitetu Ekonomicznego Rady Ministrów z 23 X 1945 r., p. 167.

196 AAN, URM, sygn. 5/467, Notatka dla Obywatela Premiera w sprawie uregulowania należności za samochody, Warszawa, 17 XII 1945, p. 3.

197 Ibid., Dekretacja Ob. Premiera, 31 XII 1945 r., p. 4 (my italics—HW).

motor vehicle's condition.[198] The activity of the new entity in the form of the Automobile Sales Centre was subject to control by a special subcommittee established at the Transportation Commission within the State National Council. However, the establishment of the Sales Centre did not improve car distribution in any way. The vehicles that reached Poland were garaged in terrible conditions. Parked in a muddy area in Gdynia-Orłowo, they stood "axle-deep in mud, having to be pulled out by tractors." The square where the car park was located was unfenced and poorly guarded. People coming for cars moved around the park at will, choosing the best (i.e. least damaged) vehicles for themselves. Cases in which missing or damaged components were removed from other cars were common. KRN inspectors observed that missing spare parts were the object of looting, in which practically everyone participated, including employees of the Centre.

In addition to vehicles, large amounts of spare parts were delivered to Poland as part of the UNRRA aid programme. They were sent in crates with no description in terms of their contents or purpose, which made it very difficult to identify and make use of them. Post-inspection documents drew attention to one more very important detail. As calculated, UNRRA transports included several dozen different car brands, most of which were represented by a few, perhaps a dozen, automobiles.[199] Meanwhile, PUS highlighted a "leaky" vehicle distribution system. In practice, though some of those vehicles went to state offices or workplaces, they did so through third parties who came into their possession illegally. PUS officials warned: "Events and beliefs that before the war seemed unthinkable outside the world of conveyors of stolen goods are now commonplace." Cars, motorcycles, and spare parts stolen from UNRRA shipments were also purchased by private individuals: "honest workers, or in some cases demobilised soldiers, lose their savings by purchasing motor vehicles unknowingly from fences or even thieves, the ownership of which will not be recognised by the State."[200]

---

198 AAN, MHZ, sygn. 2/1, Sprawozdanie z akcji UNRRA w Polsce 1944–1949, grudzień 1949, p. 133.

199 AAN, KRN, sygn. 27, Protokół 25 posiedzenia Komisji Komunikacyjnej Krajowej Rady Narodowej w dniach 24 i 25 X 1946 r., pp. 184–191.

200 AAN, Ministerstwo Administracji Publicznej (hereafter: MAP), sygn. 488 (mf B-1473), Ostrzeżenie, 5 XII 1945 r., p. 16.

In addition to UNRRA deliveries, vehicles from surplus, war reparations, and property reclamations arrived in Poland. Out of these three sources, the most important were vehicles from redundant military equipment. Poland bought both American equipment (in the so-called A-50 programme) and British equipment (in the B-6 programme). American surplus items were purchased on the basis of a loan agreement concluded between Polish and American governments on April 22, 1946 for the amount of US $50 million.[201] The Polish Mission for the Purchase of American Surplus, which was responsible for purchases, was located in Paris. Its first chairman was Zygmunt Modzelewski, who held this position until February 1947, when he was appointed Minister of Foreign Affairs. Modzelewski was succeeded by Wincenty Piekarc.[202] By mid-1947, a variety of motor vehicles had been purchased for a total of $29 million, including several thousand cars, lorries, and fire trucks of various makes and models for over $3.6 million.[203] However, the funds derived from the loan agreement, which continued through 1947, were not used in entirety. At the end of August of that year, the Paris office reported that the purchase of American surplus was problematic: "Mission purchases in Paris have been moving at a very slow pace lately. The equipment they offer us often does not meet our needs; we encounter great difficulties regarding the quantity and type of goods, even though the equipment we buy is sometimes of secondary importance to our economy. … The mission in Paris will not be able to use up the American A-50 loan."[204]

The difficulty and slow pace of purchases of American surplus equipment were the result of the poor technical condition of the equipment offered to Poles and of its variety. In the case of vehicles, this fact gave rise to the problem

---

201 AAN, MS, sygn. 389, [List Thomasa MC Cabe'a do Oskara Langego], Waszyngton, 22 IV 1946 r., pp. 11–13.

202 AAN, MHZ, sygn. 2/2, Uzupełnienie do sprawozdania [Komisji do zbadania i przedstawienia wniosku o zatwierdzenie rozliczeń dotyczących kosztów akcji demobilu brytyjskiego i amerykańskiego], [1950], unnumbered pages.

203 AAN, CUP, sygn. 1938, [Zakup sprzętu motoryzacyjnego z demobilu amerykańskiego], Paryż, 28 II 1947 r., pp. 61–63.

204 AAN, MS, sygn. 1612, Notatka w sprawie przedłużenia czasu trwania umowy o demobilu, [23 XII 1947 r.], p. 74; ibid., Notatka dla Podsekretarza Stanu do spraw Handlu Zagranicznego ob. Ludwika Grosfelda w sprawie przedłużenia kredytu pożyczki A-50 na rok 1948, Warszawa, 30 VIII 1947 r., p. 231.

of costs associated with providing technical support and securing the necessary spare parts, and given the diversity of vehicle makes and models, the problem was becoming serious. No wonder, then, that the Subcommittee on Foreign Purchases under the CUP "basically took a negative [stance] toward making further purchases from American surplus."[205] Ultimately, however, the Polish-American agreement was extended to February 1, 1948. The Poles continued to purchase American equipment until the end of January, but from around the second quarter of 1947, they also bought American equipment outside of France—in the case of vehicles, in Belgium, Germany, and Norway, but also in England.[206]

Purchases of British military surplus were managed by the mission in London. In June 1947, the Polish government concluded a financial agreement with the British government under which the Poles were granted a loan of £6 million, of which 3.9 million would be spent on surplus equipment.[207] Initially, representatives of the Polish mission submitted a request to the British Ministry of Supply for the purchase of 7,000 trucks with a load capacity of 1.5 to 4 tons. However, these plans were soon revised, and as a result, instead of buying a larger number of vehicles at once, purchases were made through auctions of single vehicles.[208] In this case, as well, it proved impossible to spend the entire amount of the loan. In the end, the total expense on British surplus equipment was £4.4 million, for which over a thousand trucks were purchased, as well as a "certain" number of passenger cars for a total amount of over £250,000.[209] It seems (at least in light of available sources) that vehicles acquired through the "B-6" programme were in a slightly better technical condition, although—it was emphasised—they were

205 AAN, CUP, sygn. 1939, Do ministra przemysłu i handlu, 2 XII 1947 r., p. 208.
206 AAN, MPiH, sygn. 3833, Sprawozdanie no. 20 z działalności Wydziału Demobilu w ciągu roku 1947, Warszawa, 10 II 1948 r., pp. 1–2.
207 Ibid., pp. 3–4.
208 AAN, MPiH, sygn. 294, Dotyczy: samochodów, 19 I 1948 r., pp. 8–11.
209 Ibid., Dostawy z Demobilu Angielskiego B-6 od początku akcji do 28 II 1949 r., p. 62; ibid., sygn. 3870, Zestawienie samochodów, [no date], p. 44; ibid., Sumaryczne zestawienie wycenionych i przecenionych pojazdów mechanicznych z Demobilu B-6, A-50 i UNRRA, Gdańsk-Oliwa, 10 I 1949 r., p. 61; ibid., sygn. 3833, Wykaz sprzętu zakupionego za pożyczkę z demobilu angielskiego B-6 w czasie od 1 VII do 30 VII 1948 r., p. 193.

not new: " … legally speaking, these are nearly unused vehicles, having travelled 200 to 500 miles, but they have no spare wheels, no batteries, no tools, and due to lack of maintenance, they will require an inspection in Poland—especially the electrical systems."[210]

At one point, the possibility of purchasing Allied surplus equipment located in the Middle East was also investigated. Poles were offered loans on terms resembling those in the "A-50" and "B-6" programmes. The equipment tied to this offer was in much better condition than the European alternative; the problem was the high cost of transport.[211] Ultimately, the choice between buying "a good car with expensive transport from the Middle East, or a bad car in need of major repairs with relatively cheap transport from the American zone" was made in favour of lower transport cost.

A small number of vehicles—both trucks and passenger cars—were also purchased from the Red Army in late April and early May 1948. The transaction, worth 25 million zlotys, included more than 400 vehicles. Some of the purchased vehicles must have been in quite good technical condition because a few of them had sealed hoods before transport, a safeguard against theft not so much of the vehicles themselves, but of spare parts. In addition, the purchased cars were protected by a specially appointed guard. However, a subsequent report stated that this did not prevent armed groups from attempting to loot the cars.[212]

From the moment it became clear that buying a car, even one in a middling technical condition, was very difficult, purchases of surplus equipment were treated in a very ad hoc manner. At the meeting of the Subcommittee on Foreign Purchases of the Automotive Commission, Jan Śmigielski protested that "[w]e should avoid buying second-hand equipment … willy-nilly," and demanded that purchases be carried out in a planned manner: "We must have such a plan. The buyer must have in his hand a detailed list of what we need and he should be guided by that list when choosing surplus units."[213]

---

210 Ibid., sygn. 3870, Biuro UNRRA, Demobilu i Reliefu, Londyn, 29 IV 1948 r., pp. 18–19.

211 AAN, KERM, sygn. 214, Komisja Motoryzacyjna. Podkomisja Zakupów Zagranicznych Sprzętu Motoryzacyjnego. Protokół 2-go posiedzenia, 24 IX 1947 r., p. 22.

212 AAN, KRN, sygn. 27, Protokół 25 posiedzenia Komisji Komunikacyjnej Krajowej Rady Narodowej w dniach 24 i 25 X 1946, pp. 184–191.

213 AAN, KERM, sygn. 214, Komisja Motoryzacyjna. Podkomisja Zakupów Zagranicznych Sprzętu Motoryzacyjnego. Protokół 2-go posiedzenia, 24 IX 1947 r., p. 17.

Meanwhile, in practice, Polish experts responsible for the selection and purchase of vehicles were guided by completely different priorities. Often acting under the pressure of time (e.g. with a loan agreement coming to an end), they opted for a purchase despite the "poor" condition of the vehicle—the English word "poor" being used in the Polish-language special purchase catalogues—for a very mundane reason: these vehicles would be used later as a reservoir of spare parts for domestic cars.[214] Such was the case in late October 1947, when Polish experts were offered a number of jeeps whose technical condition left much to be desired. A bid was made on the assumption that "these cars will be useful for parts for [vehicles] previously purchased and delivered to the country."[215] Further purchases of equipment from this source were deemed undesirable by specialists from the Subcommittee on Foreign Purchases of the Automotive Commission at CUP, who wrote to the MPiH on this matter.[216]

As can be seen, the Polish representatives did their best to use the funds granted for the purchase of surplus equipment. In the meantime, it transpired that buying wrecks for spare parts was not really useful. The processing capacity of the State Workshops and Automobile Works, estimated at one hundred major car repairs per month, was quickly exhausted and garages were unable to accept another batch of vehicles. In September 1947, it was estimated that ongoing equipment repairs would last until April of the following year, which meant that the next batch of purchased vehicles could not be put into operation until 1949 or 1950.[217] According to the daily press, the mechanics working there often performed miracles. In 1948, in the building of the Experimental Station of the Department of Automotive Services of MON,

---

214 AAN, CUP, sygn. 1938, [Sprawozdanie Polskiej Misji dla Zakupu Demobilu Amerykańskiego], Paryż, 26 II 1947 r., p. 61; ibid., sygn. 1939, Sprawozdanie, Paryż, 20 X 1947 r., p. 149.

215 For example, in September 1947, the Poles purchased 2,300 trucks and semi-trucks, of which 25–30% already qualified for the scrapyard "due to the inability to purchase spare parts"; ibid., Telefon z Paryża—misja Zakupu—p. Marczak, [wrzesień 1947 r.], p. 133; ibid., [Sprawozdanie Polskiej Misji dla Zakupu Demobilu Amerykańskiego], Paryż, 28 X 1947 r., p. 66.

216 Ibid., Do Ministra Przemysłu i Handlu, 2 XII 1947 r., p. 208.

217 AAN, KERM, sygn. 214, Komisja Motoryzacyjna. Podkomisja Zakupów Zagranicznych Sprzętu Motoryzacyjnego. Protokół 2-go posiedzenia, 24 IX 1947 r., p. 20.

an automotive exhibition was opened showcasing the work of repair plants, with restored cars on display: "We can see how new parts are created from worn-out parts, seemingly suitable only for scrap, how they are regenerated and reshaped by extrusion, how precise tools are made out of necessity, etc. To the side and in the courtyard there are completely renovated cars, tractors, tanks, among them jeeps constructed from scrapped car parts … ."[218]

Persons wishing to purchase a car had to apply to state administrative bodies for a vehicle allocation. On this basis, car distribution lists were prepared, and sales were handled by the newly established Motozbyt Automotive Industry Trade Center.[219] Distributors, however, constantly experienced long delays because as soon as the buyers realised the technical condition of the vehicles available to them, they very often abandoned the purchase.

A certain number of vehicles ("several thousand," by Tomasz Szczerbicki's estimate) went to Poland as part of the recovery of property plundered from Polish territories. In the years 1945–1952, this was the purview of several commissions, which imported cars from Germany.[220] As part of the recovery effort, several vehicles belonging to the government-in-exile in London were also imported as part of the "L-49" programme, involving two passenger cars: a Ford, which was brought into Poland, and a Škoda, which was sold in London.[221]

---

218 Z. K., "Ze szmelcu eleganckie pojazdy. Wojskowe Zakłady Remontowe mają się czym pochwalić," *Głos Ludu* 1948, no. 117, p. 4.

219 The Motozbyt Automotive Industry Trade Center was established on April 10, 1948, in place of the Motozbyt Automotive Industry Sales Office. Its responsibilities included the domestic and foreign purchase and sale of cars, tractors, motorcycles, and other items manufactured by automotive industry enterprises. Matters of foreign purchases included in the order were previously within the competence of the Varimex State Society for Foreign Trade, but on November 1, 1948, they were assigned to Motozbyt; AAN, MHZ, sygn. 7/42, Zarządzenie Ministra Przemysłu i Handlu z 10 IV 1948 r. wydane w porozumieniu z Ministerstwem Skarbu i Prezesem Centralnego Urzędu Planowania o utworzeniu przedsiębiorstwa państwowego pod nazwą "Centrala Handlowa Przemysłu Motoryzacyjnego Motozbyt", pp. 54–54 v; ibid., Protokół zdawczo-odbiorczy przekazania agend, dotyczących importu samochodów oraz sprzętu motoryzacyjnego, Warszawa, 2 XI 1948 r., pp. 251–256; ibid., Komunikat no. 8, Warszawa, 16 IV 1948 r., p. 293.

220 T. Szczerbicki, *Samochody w PRL*, p. 17.

221 AAN, MS, sygn. 1537, Sprawozdanie z działalności Biura Rewindykacji, UNRRA, Demobilu i Reliefu za IV kwartał 1949 r., p. 9.

Some of the vehicles that ended up in Polish hands as a result of the activities of the Central Liquidation Office were former German property. In 1949 alone, the District Liquidation Office in Warsaw seized items listed in Group III (which covered, among other things, means of transport) to a value of 360 million zlotys at 1939 prices. Unfortunately, it has not been possible to determine what percentage of this amount involved vehicles.[222]

Vehicle wrecks abandoned by retreating German troops were also used, especially as a source of spare parts. However, as the front moved westward, it also left behind vehicles that were not fit only to be scrapped. Teams of "searchers" combed the countryside looking for vehicles that could still be started and used by state agencies and institutions. Marian Sękowski, a member of one such team operating in Western Pomerania, described a rivalry for the cars between the searchers, peasants, and Soviet soldiers.[223] Searchers from Central Poland, mainly from Warsaw, also came to these areas in search of usable cars and spare parts.[224] As Sękowski recalled years later: "We never passed by vehicle wrecks at the side of the road. One could always wring something useful out of them."[225]

Vehicles with a wartime past formed the basis of the Polish automobile fleet for the next few years. It is worth noting that in this regard, Poland was not unique among Eastern Bloc countries. For example, the foundation for the Soviet fleet were American cars received under the Lend-Lease programme (mainly Studebakers, Dodges, GMCs, Jeeps, and Fords) and captured vehicles, usually abandoned by retreating Wehrmacht troops, along with vehicles generally regarded as the Red Army's spoils of war.[226]

2.3.2 "A Low Price and an Elegant Appearance"—Automobile Imports

According to official data prepared by the Ministry of Transportation, in the first half of 1948, there were over 93,000 motor vehicles on Polish roads, of

---

222 AAN, GUL, sygn. 77, Wykaz wartościowy ujętego ewidencyjnie i rozprowadzonego majątku ruchomego, Warszawa, [24 I 1950 r.], pp. 65–76.

223 M. Sękowski, Pamiętnik warszawskiego taksówkarza, Warszawa 1985, p. 405.

224 Ibid., p. 406.

225 Ibid., p. 438.

226 For more, see L. H. Siegelbaum, *Cars for Comrades*, pp. 215–217.

which just over 26,000 were passenger cars and less than 30,000 were trucks. The vast majority of them were used vehicles from the aforementioned sources: UNRRA deliveries, military surplus, as well as reparations and reclamations. New, imported cars accounted for a small percentage of the total. Furthermore, the mostly disastrous technical condition of the vehicles meant that Poland could only maintain the size of its fleet at a stable level through foreign purchases. For example, in February 1949, there were 32,650 passenger cars in Poland, but almost 4,000 had been withdrawn from use due to poor technical condition. This loss could not be replaced by imports, which amounted to only 1,500 vehicles.[227]

One source of foreign supplies were French companies. Pursuant to a Polish-French agreement concluded on August 1, 1946, passenger cars worth over 125 million francs were to be sent to Poland, paid for in Polish coal.[228] Interestingly, Polish purchases were preceded by a quite thorough research of foreign automotive markets; in October 1946, a specialist from CZM was in France for this purpose. Within three weeks, he had visited all the most important French factories. His observations on the state of automobilism in France are interesting: "France (Paris) uses only old prewar machines of all brands. In freight traffic, one sees only American surplus machines, secured by France due to their presence in high numbers in its territory. One finds the same brands as seen in UNRRA deliveries to Poland."[229] The quality and state of production of the most important French companies also raised doubts: "Due to war damage to French automobile production, one finds technical solutions [from] 1939 being used … . While visiting showrooms, one finds a general lack of new construction ideas and technical applications, along with a complete lack of wartime lessons and achievements."[230] It turned out, however, that—having only began production—French companies were unable to provide a satisfactory number of cars to the Polish market because

227 AAN, PKPG, sygn 5175, Planowany stan pojazdów mechanicznych w roku 1950, tajne, p. 3.
228 AAN, MF, sygn. 21/384, pp. 27–35.
229 AAN, CUP, sygn. 1937, Sprawozdanie z podróży do Francji 3–21 październik 1946 r., p. 57.
230 Ibid., p. 56.

it exceeded their production capacity.[231] Neither Citroën, nor Simca was able to meet that demand. In 1946, neither of these companies could offer cars to Poland because of previous obligations towards other contractors and low production levels (Citroën produced only 100 units per day of models 11 and 15). Only Peugeot and Renault pledged to deliver small numbers of cars in that year: twenty-five Peugeot 202 s and seventy-five four-cylinder Renaults. Larger deliveries would take place in 1947—140 and 1,000 cars, respectively. Moreover, both companies were ready to grant Poland licences to build passenger cars. Some import contributions were also offered by the Delage company, which mainly produced sports cars and limousines. However, due to its poor financial condition (and a shortage of sheet metal), Delage could only deliver passenger car chassis to Poland.[232] The French companies were clearly unable to meet Polish automotive needs, but Poland was eager to conclude contracts. The CZM representative wrote:

> The French government should be persuaded to agree to supply automotive machines to Poland from the nearest factory stockpiles. It should be emphasised that this machinery be sold at prices in line with the concluded Polish-French agreement. … The decision-makers, both in Poland and in France, should be impressed upon to speed up the signing of a Polish-French railway agreement. The absence of this agreement and the absence of a Ministry of Transportation representative results in an effective ban on transports through the American zone and prevents any deliveries to Poland. It should be noted that sea transport prices are v[ery] high.[233]

Once the "Contract concerning compensation by Poland for French businesses affected by the Polish Act on Nationalisation of January 3, 1946" was signed, it was planned that a five-year credit and investment agreement would be signed with France, foreseeing a compensation of 4.5 million tons of coal for French investment products. Half of the products were to be automotive items.[234]

---

231 AAN, CUP, sygn. 1937, [List L. Gross-Gronomskiego] w sprawie zakupu samochodów w ramach polsko-francuskiej umowy handlowej, Paryż, 15 X 1946 r., p. 59.

232 Ibid., Sprawozdanie z podróży do Francji 3–21 październik 1946 r., pp. 54–55.

233 Ibid., p. 56.

234 AAN, MPiH, sygn. 3493, Protokół dotyczący dostaw węgla polskiego do Francji od roku 1948 do 1952, pp. 46–47; AAN, MF, sygn. 373, pp. 63–64.

However, problems with French automobile imports continued over the next few years, caused both by the French, who—confronted by coal supply issues—did not fulfil the promised shipments, and by the Poles. Leon Gross-Gronomski, a Varimex representative in Paris, warned that due to incorrect instructions from the Ministry of Shipping and Foreign Trade, there were problems with the issuance of a letter of credit at Bank Polski intended for payment for cars. As a result, the French factories not only did not want to hand vehicles over to the Poles, but also refused to warehouse them until financing for their purchase was secured. There was therefore a risk that vehicles initially intended for Poland could be sold to other interested parties. Only an intervention at the ministerial level sufficed to solve this problem.[235]

In his report, Gross-Gronomski repeatedly complained about the relations with both officials at the Foreign Ministry of Shipping and Foreign Trade and the commercial attaché at the embassy in Paris. The former showed no interest in purchasing the automotive equipment provided for in the Polish-French agreement.[236] In response to pressure from Varimex to go to France as soon as possible and explore the local market, the Department of Import and Export at the MŻiHZ reportedly stated that "French merchants and industrialists will come to us on their own." In addition, the ministry representative who was sent to Paris lacked the necessary powers to complete the transaction, while the attaché at the embassy took no interest in the ongoing trade negotiations and did not send his representatives to the talks.[237]

Many imported vehicles came from Czechoslovakia, where Poland purchased 2,000 vehicles immediately after the war.[238] Meanwhile, under an agreement from July 4, 1947, Poland received more than 1,500 passenger cars.[239] In addition, a complete service station for Czech-made cars was

---

235 AAN, CUP, sygn. 1938, Sprawozdanie z pobytu we Francji od 3 do 30 I 1947 r., p. 37.

236 Leon Gross-Gronomski argued that the point in the contract concerning automotive products was constructed too vaguely and did not contain information on the makes and quantities of vehicles to be purchased, nor their prices and delivery dates; ibid., p. 36.

237 Ibid., p. 36.

238 AAN, MHZ, sygn. 18/45, Import [Czechosłowacja], unnumbered pages.

239 Ibid., Dostawy z Czechosłowacji do Polski w ramach list importowych clearingowych na lata 1947–1948, unnumbered pages.

purchased, and it was decided that a parts depot would be organised.[240] A year later, another batch of passenger cars was imported. While this transaction was concluded, it was noted at a meeting of the Subcommittee for the Purchase of Automotive Equipment of the Automotive Commission that Poland could afford to buy twice as many cars.[241] In the following years, imported Škodas were an important part of purchasing plans: in 1950, approximately 3,000 vehicles of this make were brought into Poland.[242]

Chevrolets, manufactured by the American giant GMC, were a popular sight on Polish roads; they were imported through a company office in Copenhagen. In 1948, almost 700 Chevrolets reached Poland in this way, mainly of the Fleetmaster model.[243] American cars were expected to play the role of state vehicles because, as the Budget and Economic Office of the Praesidium of the Council of Ministers believed, they had "a relatively low price and an elegant appearance."

Representatives of ministry found another important partner in the matter of importation of cars and automotive equipment in Italy. Cooperation with Italy will be discussed later; in this context, one would mention a trade agreement signed on December 27, 1947, under which Poland was to receive automobiles, accessories, service equipment, and tyres, among other stock, to a value totalling US $1.7 million in exchange for coal.[244]

Some automotive imports also came from the USSR.[245] The five-year trade agreement signed on January 26, 1948 provided for the purchase by Poland of

---

240 AAN, MHZ, sygn. 7/42, Czechosłowackie Zakłady metalowe i maszynowe (KOVOSTROJ) Dotyczy: umowy w sprawie urządzenia w Polsce stacyj obsługi dla pojazdów mechanicznych czechosłowackiego pochodzenia, Warszawa, 15 IX 1948 r., pp. 278–283.

241 AAN, KERM, sygn. 215, Protokół z posiedzenia Podkomisji Zakupów Zagranicznych Sprzętu motoryz.[acyjnego] odbytej 21 IV 1948 r., pp. 1–2.

242 AAN, PKPG, sygn. 5175, Import sprzętu motoryzacyjnego w roku 1950 wg rodzaju i wartości, projekt planu—tajne, p. 2.

243 AAN, MHZ, sygn. 18/45, Obroty towarowe Polski z Danią w latach 1945–1952. Import, unnumbered pages.

244 AAN, KERM, sygn. 217, [Informacja Departamentu Importu Ministerstwa Przemysłu i Handlu o umowach handlowych zawartych z zagranicą dot. sprzętu motoryzacyjnego] wyłącznie do użytku służbowego, Warszawa, 14 X 1948 r., pp. 18–19.

245 AAN, Polskie Towarzystwo Handlu Zagranicznego "Varimex" (hereafter: Varimex), sygn. 4/1, Spis przedmiotów importowanych w 1947 r. wg alfabetu, p. 82.

multiple "automotive goods": tractors, GAZ trucks, and ZIS limousines (two units of the state car model 110), as well as airplanes.[246] The agreement also provided for the import of an assembly plant for GAZ-20 Pobeda automobiles. The plant would produce 12,000 units per year. At the same time, the Soviets were to grant Poland a licence for the production of these vehicles, with the delivery date set for 1950.[247] This is significant because Polish representatives were engaged in advanced negotiations with Italian Fiat at the same time regarding the purchase of a production licence for the medium-engine model 1100. We will return to this matter later in this chapter.

Poland also imported automotive products from England and the USA.[248] From the former came mainly car parts and tyres, but also motorcycles and agricultural tractors. From the United States came engines for Jeeps, spare parts, and tyres.[249]

2.3.3 "Czech, Italian and Anglo-Saxon Opportunities"— In Search of Licences for the Automotive Industry

The import of automobiles, as emphasised several times already, was only meant to supplement Poland's existing automotive fleet; the main source of new vehicles was to be domestic production. Of course, officials realised that the development of a native passenger car would be much more difficult than, for example, of a truck, as preparations for the launching of the production of Stars were slowly being completed. In this context, the search for foreign licences began. Conducting it was the Central Board of the Metal Industry (CZPM), which was tasked with "exploring current trends in the automotive markets."[250] There was also a plan to purchase several vehicles selected

---

246 Ibid., p. 17.

247 AAN, KERM, sygn. 218, Wytyczne do użytku służbowego, Warszawa, 14 X 1948 r., p. 32.

248 AAN, MPiH, sygn. 2356, Statystyka handlu zagranicznego za okres od 1 I do 31 IX 1948 r., pp. 2–12.

249 AAN, KERM, sygn. 217, [Informacja Departamentu Importu Ministerstwa Przemysłu i Handlu o umowach handlowych zawartych z zagranicą dot. sprzętu motoryzacyjnego] wyłącznie do użytku służbowego, Warszawa, 14 X 1948 r., pp. 21–22.

250 Ibid., sygn. 215, Pismo Centralnego Zarządu Przemysłu Metalowego do Centralnego Urzędu Planowania Departament Komunikacji i Łączności. W sprawie zakupu samochodu wzorcowego, 23 III 1948 r., p. 14.

from among "leading brands" and carry out technical tests to determine their usefulness in Poland.[251] The aim of the search was very specific: to find a medium-engine vehicle with a chassis universal enough that it could be transformed from a passenger car into an ambulance or a small truck without major technical problems.

The initial reconnaissance carried out by experts from the CZPM showed that these requirements could be met by the English Jowett Javelin. According to Polish engineers, it had excellent features, both under the hood and in the chassis, thanks to which, unlike Opels, it could be easily converted into a delivery vehicle.[252] The application for the purchase of a single vehicle, which would be subjected to further technical tests, was approved very quickly, and the vehicle soon arrived to Poland. Test results confirmed the positive opinions about Jowett Javelin, though in the end, the idea of buying a British licence or importing more units was rejected. Interestingly, these were not the only contacts between the Polish authorities and the British automotive industry. In addition to the aforementioned imports, the commercial attaché of the Polish Embassy in London received an offer from the British company Vauxhall Motors Ltd. concerning, among other items, passenger car models 14 series J1B/JIB and HIX. The attaché suggested to the CZM, to whom the application was addressed, that maintaining contacts with the Luton-based company "which is well-disposed toward us would be very desirable."[253]

Due to intense Polish-French contacts regarding the importation of passenger cars into Poland, plans were obviously being made to explore the possibility of purchasing licences in France. I have already mentioned that two French companies were interested in this type of transaction: Peugeot and Citroën. Stefan Askanas, Director of the Department of Transportation and Communications at CUP, was tasked with choosing which of the proposed vehicles (with an engine capacity of up to 1600 cm^3) would be the best option. The possibility of acquiring a licence in France was to be discussed further during a meeting of the expert Polish-French Commission. Preparing for the talks, Polish representatives were advised to obtain "perfect" understanding of the topic and to keep in mind the existence of other sources of licences.

---

[251] Ibid.
[252] Ibid.
[253] AAN, CUP, sygn. 1937, [Vauxhalle dla Polski—oferta z Luton], p. 86.

In case they "stuck with a French passenger car, [they were to] demand all technical, organisational, and financial assistance in order to launch full production in Poland within 2 years, on the framework of Andre Citroën's offer from 1934 and Ford's offer from 1937."[254] After a more thorough analysis, however, the French was not considered satisfactory; the licenses offered did not represent a sufficiently high technical level. This opinion did not change even when a third company added its proposal to the other two. Prepared by Renault, this offer referred to "the license for a vehicle which it will no longer produce."[255] Finally, it was decided that the demand for passenger cars of the type offered by French companies could be met with imports from other countries, especially Pobeda cars from the USSR.[256]

The document quoted above, addressed to Director Askanas, contained information about other talks conducted at the same time regarding the purchase of licences for the production of passenger cars. This document described those talks as representing "Czech, Italian and Anglo-Saxon opportunities." The "Anglo-Saxon opportunity" was an offer made to the Polish government by GMC, an important partner because of the contacts and business connections the American company had had with Poland before World War II, which were still a vivid memory. Talks began very soon after the war's end. GMC presented a proposal to Poland concerning spare parts for Chevrolets, but also including the possibility of building a Chevrolet car factory in Poland.[257] The Americans offered comprehensive assistance both in the detailed planning of the plant and in the sharing of information on vehicle assembly. They also promised to provide support from American specialists.

Less than two months later, in September 1946, CZM received an anonymous "Statement." The author of this short document proposed two means of establishing relations between Poland and GMC. The first called for a representative office of the American company to be set up inside Poland, which would sell "all kinds of passenger cars, trucks, tractors, buses … at

254 AAN, KERM, sygn. 210, Notatka dla Pana Dyr. Askanasa, Warszawa, 21 VII 1947 r., p. 71.

255 Ibid., Komisja Motoryzacyjna. Protokół 9-go posiedzenia, 12 V 1947 r., p. 104.

256 AAN, CUP, sygn. 1940, [Pismo] Do Centralnego Urzędu Planowania, Warszawa, 24 III 1948 r., p. 64.

257 Ibid., sygn. 1937, Pan M. Skotnicki, Dyrektor Departamentu Zcentralizowanej Motoryzacji Ministerstwa Komunikacji, [lipiec 1946], pp. 38–41.

prices and on conditions to be determined." The second concerned plans to build an assembly plant for cars of the American brand in Gdańsk. This plant was to be the only GMC facility of this type in Central and Eastern Europe. The neighbouring Czechoslovakia was to be Poland's competitor for the second proposal.[258]

At the time this document was created (September 1946), Polish authorities had likely already decided to purchase several dozen Chevrolet cars for official use. The American company's office in Copenhagen was thus asked to prepare an appropriate offer. Soon thereafter, the Kraków-based Technical and Trade Company (Spółka Techniczno-Handlowa), the probable source of the "Statement," claiming to be the sole GMC representative in Poland, questioned the planned transaction in a letter to the Prime Minister, demanding to be included in the project and to be paid a commission.[259] The company's letter was answered by the Department of Import and Export of the MŻiHZ, which rejected the claims of the company, citing the general director of General Motors International in Copenhagen, A. Madsen, who stated that during his stay in Poland, "he concluded no agreement with anyone regarding the general office of the company." Incidentally, as he rightly pointed out, such an office had "no reason to exist, due to the centralisation of purchases in institutions run by the State."[260] The "Statement" also provoked a strong reaction from CUP. The aforementioned Stefan Askanas confirmed the licensing talks with "GM[C], Ford, Fiat, etc. ... concerning the production of cars in Poland" and emphasised the overriding role played by CZM, which was responsible for matters of sale and purchase of motor vehicles.[261] Contacts with the GMC representative office in Copenhagen were maintained for some time, although, as Askanas emphasised, the reasons were mainly courtesy and "the need to procure spare parts" since there was "no prospect of maintaining closer relations with General Motors in the future."[262]

---

258 AAN, URM, sygn. 5/471, Memoriał, pp. 3–6.

259 Ibid., Do obywatela Prezesa Rady Ministrów w Warszawie, Kraków, 2 XI 1946 r., p. 10.

260 Ibid., Notatka w sprawie listu firmy "Auto", Kraków, ul. Zwierzyniecka 25, z dnia 2 XI 1946 r. do ob. Prezesa Rady Ministrów, Warszawa, 16 XII 1946 r., p. 13.

261 Ibid., Do ob. Dyrektora mgr. Z. Kłopotowskiego Prezydium Rady Ministrów, Warszawa, 12 II 1947 r., p. 14.

262 AAN, CUP, sygn. 1940, Ministerstwo Przemysłu i handlu [w sprawie] przyjazdu przedstawiciele General Motors, Kopenhaga, 21 IV 1948, p. 84.

Talks with Czechoslovakia reached quite an advanced stage. Initially, the proposal put forward by Poland's southern neighbour was considered "strong, with favorable prospects."[263] The Polish government showed interest in the offer prepared by Škoda and Tatra. Škoda offered to sell the 1101 model to the Poles, but doubts were raised concerning its dated design, with a body made of wood and sheet metal, its high price, and its outdated appearance. Ultimately, Škoda's offer was rejected. In turn, Tatra wanted to sell models 57B and 107 to Poland, but the former was a rather antiquated construction which the Czechs themselves planned to stop producing soon. The latter model, on the other hand, had not yet entered mass production. However, the Polish government showed the most interested in the offer put forward by the Jawa factory in Prague and its Aero Minor II model. This small car, based on the German DKW design, attracted attention both because of its size and because of the resulting lessening of the cost in operation. However, the high price demanded by the Czechs resulted in the rejection of this offer, as well.[264] Two years later, a few units of this car were purchased in order to carry out technical tests.[265]

Talks with Czechoslovak enterprises were resumed briefly in the first half of 1948, but again without results. It was at this time that the possibility of cooperation between the machine industries of the two countries arose, involving the production of automobiles, among others. The Polish government, already engaged in advanced talks over a licence with Fiat, tried to use this fact to its advantage. The problem was that the Czechoslovaks were reluctant to agree to share production, which would require making technologies and patents available to Poland. During talks held in May 1948 in Prague, Eugeniusz Szyr stated: "We will not agree to a technical cooperation so long as it is easier for us to reach an understanding with Fiat than with comrade [František] Fabinger [general director of the Union of Metal and Engineering Industry, Reditelstvi Kovodélného a Strojirenského Prumyslu,

263 AAN, KERM, sygn. 210, Komisja Motoryzacyjna. Protokół 9-go posiedzenia, 12 V 1947 r., p. 104.

264 AAN, CUP, sygn. 1938, Sprawozdanie z konferencji w dniu 30 V 1947 r. w Kovostroju, pp. 196–197.

265 AAN, KERM, sygn. 220, Protokół z VI posiedzenia Komisji Importu Motoryzacyjnego, Warszawa, 26 I 1949 r., p. 33.

KOVO]. ... Therefore, it is not surprising that we prefer to talk to Fiat ... . This illustrates why we have concluded an agreement with Fiat."[266]

It was with the Italian Fiat that the talks reached the most advanced stage, having began already in 1946 and ended in April 1948.[267] The licence agreement signed at that time called for the production of a modified Fiat 508 in Poland, which was then to be replaced by the modern model 1100; production of the latter in Italy would only begin in 1950. The licence covered the construction of a factory which would produce 10,000 vehicles per year (with a one-shift operation). At the end of July 1948, Eugeniusz Szyr approved the creation of the enterprise: the aforementioned FSO in the Warsaw suburb of Żerań. A year later, two production halls were ready, built with the help of Italian experts.[268]

Throughout the duration of the Polish-Italian talks, the Soviets expressed strong reservations. During the Polish industry representatives' visit to Moscow in January 1948, during which the terms and conditions of the trade agreement between the two countries were established, Joseph Stalin himself urged the Poles to abandon negotiations with Fiat. He was concerned that Fiats on Polish roads would make it difficult to unify the vehicle fleet of Central and Eastern Europe, "which must be treated not only as transportation equipment, but also as combat equipment." In the same conversation, Stalin proposed to give Poland a free licence to produce Soviet GAZ passenger cars and trucks.[269] The Soviets continued to criticise the Polish-Italian agreement even almost a year after it was signed. During a meeting of the Polish-Soviet section of the Scientific-Technical Commission, one Soviet delegate presented the USSR's position on this issue: "Knowing the case of 'Fiat', [the Soviet Union] considers it wrong for people's democracies to build automobile factories for different types of cars (Poland—'Fiat', Hungary—'Steyer', etc.)."[270]

---

266 AAN, KC PPR, sygn. 295/XI-393 (mf 2354/5), Stenogram z drugiego dnia konferencji gospodarczej, odbytej 20 III 1948 r. w Pradze, pp. 91–92.

267 D. Jarosz and M. Pasztor, *Skazani na podległość. Z dziejów stosunków polsko-włoskich w latach 1945–1958*, Warszawa 2013, pp. 196–202.

268 Z. Konieczniak, *FSO. Fabryka Samochodów Osobowych 1951–1986*, Warszawa 1986, pp. 13–14.

269 H. Różański, *Śladem wspomnień i dokumentów (1943–1948)*, Warszawa 1987, p. 510.

270 AAN, PKPG, sygn. 2977, Notatka z konferencji w Ministerstwie Handlu Zagranicznego ZSRR w dniu 28 IV 1949 r., p. 50.

In light of the fact that the meeting in the Kremlin took place on January 14, 1948, and the licence agreement with Fiat, which the USSR strongly criticised, was signed on April 14, 1948, it is worth highlighting Poland's persistence in the decision to conclude the agreement with Italy. When they finally reneged on the contract, it was only as a result of strictly political factors.[271] The establishment of the Council for Mutual Economic Assistance (Comecon) at the beginning of 1949 and its two sessions that took place in August and September of that year also likely played a part. At these sessions, binding decisions were made regarding joint automotive production. The Czechoslovak concept that it should be based on Czechoslovak industry, which was the most technologically advanced and had the longest traditions, conflicted with Polish attempts to start production of cars under a Fiat licence.[272]

Probably in late September or early October 1949, a letter addressed to the Commercial Counsellor's Office of the Polish Embassy in Moscow, written by Julian Gren—then acting MPiH plenipotentiary for the implementation of the Polish-Soviet investment agreement—informed the embassy about Poland's resignation from the Italian licence and engagement in efforts to obtain Soviet assistance. Plans were to use the investment in Żerań, which had already started.[273] In the end, it was decided that the agreement of January 26, 1948 between Poland and the USSR would be updated to include the construction of a complete factory producing Pobeda passenger cars and the granting of a licence for the production of these cars.[274] At the same time, the Poles were negotiating with Fiat on dissolving the contract signed in April 1948. It was finally agreed in a protocol dated April 27, 1951, that Poland would grant appropriate compensation to the Italians.[275]

---

271 See D. Jarosz and M. Pasztor, *Skazani na podległość*, pp. 200–201. In 1959, M. Piłacki and L. Mikołajków wrote that one of the reasons for the withdrawal from the Polish-Italian cooperation was the embargo imposed on machine tools that were to be delivered to FSO from England, Italy, and West Germany; M. Piłacki and L. Mikołajków, "Samochód—narzędzie pracy czy luksus?" *Wiedza i Życie* 1959, no. 10, p. 614.

272 V. Fava, *The Socialist People's Car*, pp. 82–84.

273 AAN, PKPG, sygn. 2977, [Julian Gren] Do Biura Radcy Handlowego, no date, pp. 126–127.

274 Ibid., Protokół do Umowy między Rządem Rzeczpospolitej Polskiej a Rządem Związku Socjalistycznych Republik Radzieckich o dostawach do Polski sprzętu przemysłowego na kredyt z 26 I 1948 r., pp. 128–129.

275 D. Jarosz and M. Pasztor, *Skazani na podległość*, p. 202.

The GAZ passenger car, which Joseph Stalin called *Pobeda*, meaning Victory, was a construction developed at the turn of 1944. The generalissimo supposedly ordered that the car be equipped with an economical, four-cylinder engine. The car resembled the prewar Opel Kapitän.[276] However, it is worth noting that several postwar cars, such as the Czechoslovak Tatra 600, the German Kaiser, or the British Standard Vanguard, also had a similar shape. The Pobeda was the first car available in the USSR on general sale, although its price (16,000 roubles) made it practically inaccessible to the broader masses. This GAZ passenger car would go on to be produced for over 12 years. In total, almost 260,000 units of this model left the factory in Gorky. Poland was the only foreign country where this vehicle was produced.[277]

The issue of Poland using a Soviet licence instead of an Italian one to initiate production of passenger cars requires additional commentary. In light of available sources, the decision to begin production might well have been made earlier, as indicated by two events. During the aforementioned Polish-Czechoslovak talks held in Prague on cooperation between the machine industries of both countries, Eugeniusz Szyr mentioned the Soviet offer regarding motorisation.[278] In April 1948, a conference was held at the Technoeksport Union, Soviet foreign trade central office, during which Polish automotive specialists suggested purchasing several copies of the Soviet cars for technical inspection. This was supposedly related to the planned construction of an assembly plant for these vehicles, as stipulated in the contract of January of the same year.[279] A similar piece of information is dated

---

[276] Andrei Miniuk believes that Soviet solutions were copied from German originals. In any case, the same supposedly happened with the Moskvitch, the construction of which relied on appropriated plans for the Opel Kadett; A. I. Miniuk, "The Use of German Industrial and Scientific Technical Potential in the Development of the Soviet Motor Industry," in: *Towards Mobility: Varieties of Automobilism in East and West*, ed. D. Schlinkert, M. Grieger, and U. Gutzmann, Wolfsburg 2009, pp. 79–80.

[277] L. H. Siegelbaum, *Cars for Comrades*, pp. 62–64.

[278] E. Szyr said at the time: "The Soviet Union wants to enable us to produce cars. Likewise, it is building a new steel mill for us in accordance with the latest achievements of steelworks in the Soviet Union"; AAN, KC PPR, sygn. 295/XI-393 (mf 2354/5), Stenogram z drugiego dnia konferencji gospodarczej, odbytej 20 V 1948 r. w Pradze, p. 80.

[279] AAN, MPiH, sygn. 3532, Protokół z konferencji w Zjednoczeniu "Technoeksport," odbytej 16 IV 1948 r., pp. 36–37.

October 1948, and refers to the planned importation of an assembly plant for cars of this make.[280] However, all of this happened after the contract with the Italian Fiat had been signed. It can therefore be assumed that the Soviet cars were meant only to supplement the passenger vehicle fleet. Both Fiat 508 and its planned successor, model 1100, had completely different characteristics than the Soviet GAZ M-20. Most importantly, they were smaller, with a lower engine capacity and a chassis that was not as versatile. The Pobeda, in turn, was closer to the English Jowett Javelin, which had been successfully tested in Polish conditions and offered many more possibilities in terms of body versions. Only by the second half of 1949 was the plan to build a fleet of passenger cars based on Fiats produced in Poland abandoned, and the concept of homogeneous vehicles throughout the entire Soviet bloc that the USSR promoted retained.

2.3.4 "Żerań Is Running"—FSO Warsaw

In the end, the first vehicles left the assembly lines on November 6, 1951. They were Warszawas completely assembled from parts delivered to Poland by the Soviets. The date was not accidental; it marked the thirty-fourth anniversary of the outbreak of the October Revolution, and the workers of Żerań took an active part in the so-called October action. "The car industry in Poland is born. … Żerań is running," Polish officials announced triumphantly, and the factory was visited by all of the most important people in the country at that time, including Bolesław Bierut.[281] A month later, writer Jan Józef Szczepański paid a visit, making sure to note in his diary under the date "December 6, 1951," the broad propaganda campaign that accompanied the start of production: "Yesterday, I visited the factory in Żerań. All the press hype was a typical, staged show. Apart from five cars assembled for the opening ceremony, the factory released nothing. Only now are they finishing work on all the equipment that was listed as completed ahead of schedule in the newsreel."[282] However, Szczepański was not entirely accurate. The newsreel in

280 AAN, KERM, sygn. 218, Wytyczne do użytku służbowego, Warszawa, 14 X 1948 r., p. 32.

281 M-20 Warszawa, PKF 47/51; Archiwum Polskiego Radia (hereafter: APR), sygn. 466/2, Reportaż z Żerania—wóz no. 000004.

282 J. J. Szczepański, *Dziennik*, vol. 1: *1945–1956*, Kraków 2009, p. 300.

question, which included a report from the November ceremony, there were no mention of the entire factory having started, only of how assembly hall no. 1 was in operation fifty-four days ahead of schedule. Of course, this does nothing to change the fact that the pace of construction and of the launch of the largest factory in Warsaw at that time did not meet the expectations, for reasons that were not only the Poles' fault.[283]

Figure 1. FSO Warszawa on the assembly line at the Passenger Car Factory, 1957, National Digital Archives, Zbyszko Siemaszko, 3/51/0/6.2/57

Almost three years after the October celebrations, individual FSO departments were still unable to produce all components. The engine facility was experiencing what sources describe as an "uncontrollable" production of piston rings, bearings, and cylinder block castings. The chassis department was struggling with the production of suspension components, including the rear axle. At the same time, the press and fittings shops still lacked

283 Opowieść o FSO. Historia tej warszawskiej fabryki, ed. Z. Boniecki, R. Gajewskiego, and E. Pietrzak, Warszawa 2010, p. 38.

crucial equipment.[284] About 150 machine tools were missing, including 29 of Soviet production. As of September 1, 1954, of the almost 3,000 machines planned for the factory, only around 70% were delivered. Furthermore, the missing machines were so important for production that their absence often blocked the entire process. Cooperation with Polish suppliers was disastrous, especially when it involved plants subordinated to the Ministries of Small Industry and Crafts, Chemical Industry, and Machine Industry.[285] All this contributed to very poor production results not only for vehicles, but also for individual components. According to the adopted plan, in 1954, 2,500 engines were to be produced, along with 1,400 drive shafts and 1,400 front suspensions. Meanwhile, after three quarters, production volumes were at a dramatically low level. By September 1, 1954, the FSO crew managed to produce only 680 engines, 450 drive shafts, and 10 front suspensions. Not a single steering wheel was assembled, and only twenty shock absorbers were made, although the plan called for 1,400 of each.[286] A special memo for PKPG observed: "The start of automobile production at the Żerań Passenger Car Factory raises concerns with serious delays and a lack of certainty regarding potential improvement to development in the future."[287] The situation at FSO was said to be critical and only an intervention by the highest authorities, both state and ministerial, would ensure that the intended vehicle production could be achieved.[288] It was not until 1956 that work on the Warszawa production assemblies was completed, and from that moment forward, fully domestic vehicles began to leave the FSO assembly lines.[289] That said, the production time for this car in Polish conditions significantly exceeded Soviet standards, which stipulated that the production of a single Warszawa would require 240 hours. Meanwhile, at FSO in 1957, when Żerań released about 20,000 of these cars, it was calculated that 364 hours of labour were required

284 AAN, PKPG, sygn. 379, Uwagi głównego inżyniera projektu tow. inż. Aleksijewa o FSO, [1954], pp. 4–8.
285 Ibid., Uwagi o niedociągnięciach w kooperacji z FSO, [1954], pp. 41–49.
286 Ibid., Uwagi o stanie rozruchu produkcji w Fabryce Samochodów osobowych na Żeraniu, Warszawa, [1 X 1954 r.], p. 2ff
287 Ibid., Notatka w sprawie rozruchu produkcji samochodów na FSO, [październik 1954 r.], pp. 8–10.
288 Ibid.
289 K. J. Mórawski, *Syrena*, p. 19.

to make each of them. It was not until 1961 that results were achieved that came close to Soviet standards.[290]

Figure 2. FSO Warszawa on the assembly line at the Passenger Car Factory, 1957, National Digital Archives, Zbyszko Siemaszko,sygn. 3/51/57/4

Years later, in an interview for the *Motor* weekly, Tadeusz Wrzaszczyk offered a rational assessment of the purchase of the licence for the production of GAZ cars. He emphasised their significant disadvantages (outdated technology, high labour costs and material consumption), but also their advantages, the most important of which included the construction of the factory itself, the training of its staff, and the sharing of the technology involved in the production of some car elements. In other words, this licence laid the foundations for the Polish automotive industry's future development.[291]

290 S. Szostkiewicz, *Przemiany w strukturze załogi Fabryki Samochodów Osobowych w latach 1956–1961*, Wrocław–Warszawa–Kraków 1965, p. 137.

291 "Igranie z ogniem," *Motor* 1995, no. 51/52, p. 4.

2.4 Stalinism on wheels

2.4.1 Drivers

In the Polish realities of the 1940s and the first half of the 1950s, owning an automobile was a luxury available only to a chosen few. As noted by officials in one of the CUP departments, the change taking place in Poland relative to the interwar period—i.e. a several-fold increase in the number of trucks with a concurrent significant decrease in the number of passenger cars—was something "completely normal and even useful, given the difficulties in transport and the new face of Poland." Therefore, the immediate future for people who wanted to own an automobile was not bright: "A passenger car will be an unattainable dream for the common man for a long time, but this is completely understandable if one takes into account that social income must primarily be directed toward reconstructing the country's economic life."[292] Unfortunately, this opinion, expressed probably in 1946, quite accurately described the postwar reality. Destroyed by warfare, Poland was too poor to be able to entertain the development of private motorisation on a larger scale. As Aleksander Rostocki recalled, when a batch of 1,000 East German IFA cars (model F8) was imported to Poland in 1951 and their price was set at 13,000 zlotys—more than twenty-one average monthly wages, it turned out that there were no buyers. In the end, it was decided to allocate half of them to various institutions as company cars, and distribute the rest among representatives of those professions that required their own means of transport.[293] Nonetheless, many Poles dreamed of having their own automobile and some of them tried, at all costs, to turn these dreams into reality.

In 1955, according to official statistics, there were about 20,500 personal cars in Poland (see Table 4). We are thus talking about an increase of several thousand over the course of a decade. Some of the ways in which Poles could buy an automobile (mainly when it was necessary to run a business or carry out a profession) have already been mentioned. Certain opportunities for private individuals to obtain a vehicle were provided by the exchange of state-owned

292 AAN, MK, sygn. 219, Zakres prac dokonywanych w komunikacji [przygotowany przez Departament Komunikacji i Łączności Centralnego Urzędu Planowania], no date [prawdopodobnie 1. połowa 1946 r.], unnumbered pages.

293 *Rynek motoryzacyjny*, ed. Z. Krasiński, Warszawa 1980, p. 55, table 1.

cars. From time to time, the daily press published information about the importation of automobiles from abroad, some of which were intended for open sale, alongside classified ads announcing the sale of used vehicles.[294]

Table 4. Number of motor vehicles and two-wheelers in Poland in 1945–1956 (in thousands)

Year	Passenger Cars		Two-Wheel Vehicles	
	Total	Private	Total	Private
1945	8.8	–	3.0	–
1950	40.1	–	58.9	–
1954	36.1	–	135.9	–
1955	40.3	20.5	169.7	163.0
1956	44.7	24.7	236.4	229.8

Source: A. M. Restecki, Zrealizowane oczekiwania. Miliony samochodów osobowych w r. 1975, "Motor" 1966, no. 30, p. 3; "Rocznik Statystyczny" 1957, p. 211; "Rocznik Statystyczny" 1959, p. 230; "Rocznik Statystyczny" 1960, p. 264.

At that time, all of "automotive life" was focused around an organisation whose origins date back to the partitions, and which brought together enthusiasts of automobilism and motoring in the prewar period: the Polish Automobile Club (AP). Most of its members who were deeply involved in "automotive life" survived the war. The association was thus quickly reactivated. In September 1945, an AP General Assembly was held, convened by prewar board members. Provisional authorities were then elected, headed by Janusz Regulski, who before the war had been the AP vice-president.[295] In June of the same year, at the initiative of CZM director Mieczysław Skotnicki, the first postwar AP General Assembly was held, attended by delegates of branches operating in fourteen provincial cities practically since the end of World War II.[296] A month later, the AP Board of Directors was put together, with Minister of Transportation Jan Rabanowski as president and vice-presidents

294 For example: "Nowe samochody rozprowadzi 'Motozbyt'," *Głos Ludu* 1948, no. 131, p. 5; ibid., no. 134, p. 7.

295 J. Regulski, *Blaski i cienie długiego życia*, Warszawa 1980, p. 402.

296 It is worth noting that around the same time, 105 motorcycle clubs and sections were affiliated with the Polish Motorcycle Association; "Automobilklub Polski rozpoczął znowu pracę," *Motoryzacja* 1946, no. 1, p. 24.

Piotr Jaroszewicz, Wiktor Grosz (both representing the military), Mieczysław Skotnicki, and Janusz Regulski. In August of that year, the first issue of the club's official press organ *Motoryzacja* was published.[297]

A group of people involved in motorisation quickly gathered around the AP, and the club itself began its usual work promoting motorsport and advancing issues related to transport and road safety; for example, its representatives were included in a committee set up to organise examinations for future drivers.[298] Teams were created whose task it was to provide professional advice on the operation and maintenance of motor vehicles. Expertise was at the heart of the AP's work, and the great diversity of Poland's vehicle fleet meant that this expertise was often worth its weight in gold.[299]

AP members devoted a great deal of energy to reactivating traditional car rallies organised under the club's auspices. The first Car Rally of the Polish Automobile Club took place in September 1946, and the following year the AP organised a car and motorcycle street race in Warsaw along with the Thirteenth International AP Car Rally. The use of the word "international" in this context was an exaggeration because the only foreign competitor was an employee of the Czechoslovak embassy. More important, however, was the fact that the AP subscribed to the tradition of prewar events, as indicated also by the continuous numbering of those events (the "Thirteenth" AP car rally) since the period of the Second Republic. The event found itself within the orbit of interest of the most important people in the country; members of the Politburo of the PZPR Central Committee viewed the rally as "damaging." They feared that state drivers would take part in subsequent events using official cars. For this reason, they worked to tighten control over particular cars

297 Automobilklub Polski 1909–2009. Monografia, ed. B. Mierkowski, Warszawa 2009, pp. 33–35.

298 The commissions operating at that time at the automotive departments of voivodeship offices also included representatives of voivodeship offices and of the Transport Workers Trade Union; AAN, MK, sygn. 1136, Zarządzenie Ministra Komunikacji z 23 V 1947 r. o opłatach za egzaminowanie osób, ubiegających się o pozwolenia na prowadzenie pojazdów mechanicznych, unnumbered pages.

299 *Automobilklub Polski*, pp. 36–37.

and their "purposes of travel."[300] The fourteenth race took place in 1948, and this time, alongside Polish drivers, over twenty drivers from Czechoslovakia took part. The event was held under the honorary patronage of President Bolesław Bierut, who received the participants at Belvedere Palace after the rally ended.[301]

However, this was the beginning of the end for the AP community. The darkening political atmosphere of Polish Stalinism affected people involved in motorisation. In 1948, Janusz Regulski was accused of "anti-popular" activity; he was arrested and sentenced to 14 years in prison, from which he was released on the wave of the political thaw of 1956.[302] Józef Docha, president of the Polish Motorcycle Association, was also imprisoned. As a result of brutal interrogation, he died in 1951. AP members were considered "an element hostile or indifferent to the working class" and "barely sympathetic." This was hardly a surprise because—as a report for the Transportation Department of the Central Committee of the PZPR proclaimed—"in pre-September [1939] Poland, automobile owners or users were alien to us in terms of class." A looming problem for Poland's rulers was a kind of elitism among the AP membership. The organisation, which numbered about 3,500 members after merging with the Polish Motor Association (PZM), would expand its ranks to 17,000, mostly comprised of "a considerable number of workers …, and of a mentally sound and politically sophisticated element." At the same time, officials realised that the AP played an invaluable role, including from the authorities' point of view, as a promoter of automotive technology.[303] The intention was thus to put the several decades of experience of AP members in the field of motorisation to some use. The plan for the gradual takeover of AP was as follows:

---

300 AAN, KC PPR, sygn. 295/V/5 (mf 2090/1), Protokół no. 14 posiedzenia BP [KC PPR] z 14 VI [19[47], p. 92.

301 *Automobilklub Polski*, pp. 88–90.

302 H. Korczyk, "Janusz Regulski," in: PSB, vol. 30, 1987, p. 744.

303 AAN, KC PZPR, sygn. 237/XIII-143, Protokół z posiedzenia Sekcji Samochodowej przy Wydziale Komunikacyjnym KC PZPR odbytej 26 X 1949 r., unnumbered pages.

> The ideological foundation of each training reading, diligent work in the training of car drivers and motorcyclists, organising competitions in connection with the country's political life, and finally social events, are the links that, skilfully combined in a rationally thought-out plan, will allow the rise of a new man, and this will make it possible to move away from the harmful influence of the elements mentioned at the outset, which undoubtedly still exist today and must disappear as soon as possible.[304]

Despite this, the AP continued to operate as before, including organising automobile races. This was the case with the International Technical and Experimental Truck Rally in 1950, in which six Stars took part along with vehicles from Czechoslovakia and Hungary.[305] It is hard not to see this as an attempt by AP members to fit into the current climate conducive to motor vehicle transport so as to pursue automotive passions under ideological camouflage.

The club's formal liquidation began on January 29, 1950, when an AP General Assembly of Delegates was held and passed a resolution on its dissolution. An identical motion was passed by members of the PZM General Assembly of Delegates, which was held at the same time. The next day, at a joint meeting, delegates established a single joint organisation to replace existing structures, called the Polish Automobile Association.[306] The official reasoning for the merger cited "organisational and economic calculations," though it is difficult not to see it as a part of the broader policy of consolidation of various communities (e.g. architects, artists, and writers) in a Stalinist reality.

The dismembering of the AP was a carefully prepared process. The idea to combine the two organisations—of car and motorcycle enthusiasts—emerged in the second half of the 1940s, but faced a quite mundane hurdle. AP and PZM were included in the structures of international automotive organisations, the Fédération Internationale de l'Automobile (FIA) and the

---

304 Ibid.

305 W. Rychter, *Dzieje samochodu*, Warszawa 1979, p. 416.

306 *Automobilklub Polski*, p. 38. In Czechoslovakia, the Automobile Club was liquidated in 1951; V. Fava, "The Elusive People's Car. Imagined Automobility and Productive Practices along the 'Czechoslovak Road to Socialism' (1945–1968)," in: *The Socialist Car*, p. 21.

Fédération Internationale de Motocyclisme, respectively, and FIA statutes prohibited such a merger; if the Polish associations moved forward with the merger, they faced expulsion from the international groups. This, in turn, would result in considerable financial losses, meaning, among other things, that they would no longer enjoy the right to issue international driver's licences. Therefore, the new organisation created from the merger of AP and PZM needed a well-conceived statute, one accepted ahead of time by the FIA. At the end of 1949, talks began at the international level to define the shape of the future body, which concluded successfully in December 1949. At that point, nothing stood in the way of the AP's liquidation, which took place in early 1950.

The aforementioned CUP document also addressed the issue of vehicles owned by private companies. On the one hand, as the document's authors noted, possession of such vehicles was conditioned by real professional needs, and on the other, it constituted a serious burden for the already overstrained fuel reserves. Restricting the supply of fuel to private vehicles (described as "vegetative" in the document) was intended to significantly limit their movement. The savings would go to the state-owned fleet, and those who wanted to buy fuel above the specified norm would have to pay commercial prices.[307] In the long term, the savings campaign was to also cover automobiles belonging to administrative bodies and state-owned enterprises. This issue will be discussed below.

Other restrictions aimed at private automobile users involved the range of vehicle travel. The ordinance issued in early January 1951 by the Council of Ministers allowed vehicles belonging to private persons and non-socialised enterprises to travel only within the administrative borders of the cities where the vehicle was registered. In the case of people living in smaller towns (up to 100,000 inhabitants), the movement area was defined as a radius of 20 km "calculated along the exit roads to the administrative borders of these towns." In the case of people living in Warsaw and Łódź who were engaged in commercial transport, it was possible to increase the vehicle range. Doctors, dentists, veterinarians, and labour competition winners living in these two cities could also obtain such permits. The January regulation limited the total

307 Ibid.

monthly mileage of automobiles owned by individuals and private companies to 200 km. A private user could only drive a passenger car with a functioning odometer and an engine with a displacement no larger than 2 litres.[308]

Although Polish authorities eventually abandoned the idea of a complete ban on registering automobiles belonging to private persons—a rather realistic move—this did not mean an automatic consent to the liberalisation of regulations regarding the purchase of vehicles. In the early postwar years, people who wanted to buy any car had to meet several conditions. Private entrepreneurs and craftsmen had by far the fastest, though not necessarily the easiest, path to purchasing a vehicle. Both had to present a certificate issued by the Chamber of Commerce and Industry (in the case of people working in industry or trade) or the Chamber of Crafts (in the case of craftsmen) about the need to own a vehicle. The object of such a transaction could be only so-called redundant vehicles—i.e. excess vehicles sold by the state administration. Here, the chances to obtain a new vehicle were slim. Furthermore, redundant vehicles were usually of the post-German or surplus variety, the maintenance of which was unprofitable for the state due to their poor technical condition.[309]

After receiving an allotment, and in addition to paying the price set by the institution selling the vehicle, the buyer was obliged to subscribe to the Premium Bond for National Reconstruction (PPOK).[310] A CUP ordinance required the vehicle buyer to purchase PPOK bonds in the amount of the full value of the vehicle. This requirement caused a great deal of opposition, since it was calculated that "taking into account the price of the car, the bond amount, and the costs of bringing the cars—all of which showed deficiencies of one kind or another—back into running order, the final cost was beyond

308 Dz. U. 1951, no. 4, poz. 29. This ordinance prohibited the use of passenger cars with an engine displacement larger than 2.5 litres and the following makes and models of cars in commercial transport: Audi "Front," Ford "V8 22," Ford "GPW," Jeeps, Wanderer "W45," "W50" and "W250."

309 AAN, Izba Przemysłowo-Handlowa (hereafter: IPH), sygn. 1195, [Pismo informacyjne IPH dotyczące] sprzedaży samochodów poniemieckich do Centralnego Zarządu Motoryzacji, Warszawa, 19 III 1947 r., unnumbered pages.

310 Dz. U. 1946, no. 2, pos. 11.

the means of the companies applying for the allocation."[311] For this reason, in the second quarter of 1946, only 167 automobiles were distributed among entrepreneurs associated with the IPH and the Head Council of Merchant Associations of the Republic of Poland, which was a negligible percentage of the quota assigned to these institutions.[312]

The bond obligation was explained as a means of payment for the privilege of using the prices and privileges available to ministries and state institutions.[313] The amount that had to be paid by some vehicle buyers was reduced very quickly. This was the case with co-op members, who received a 50% discount.[314] Another way to reduce the additional costs incurred for the PPOK was to convert the vehicle so it could drive on liquefied petroleum gas.[315] When the PPOK action was suspended, many car buyers had not yet paid the required amounts. Finally, after discussions within the Ministry of Treasury, it was decided that from that moment forward, the payments (10% of the value of the vehicle) would be directed to the fund for the reconstruction of Warsaw.[316]

The applications submitted in the early postwar years to state institutions dealing with the distribution of automobiles among private entrepreneurs are a highly interesting historical source. Almost all of them contain indications that the company applying for a vehicle was cooperating with state industries. For example, when applying for a Citroën passenger car, Stanisław Jeromiński's Commercial and Industrial House (Dom Handlowo-Przemysłowy) in Warsaw's Praga district argued that, due to high turnover,

---

311 AAN, IPH, sygn. 1195, [Pismo informacyjne IPH] do Centralnego Urzędu Planowania dotyczy: szacunku pojazdów mechanicznych, Warszawa, 29 VII 1946 r., unnumbered pages.

312 Ibid., sygn. 1196, [Pismo IPH] do Centralnego Urzędu Planowania dotyczy subskrypcji PPOK od nabywców samochodów z demobilu kanadyjskiego, 20 V 1946 r., unnumbered pages.

313 Ibid., sygn. 1195, Protokół z konferencji w dniu 4 II 1946 r. w sprawie przydziału samochodów przedsiębiorstwom prywatnym zgrupowanych w Izbie Przemysłowo-Handlowej i Naczelnej Radzie Zrzeszeń Kupieckich RP, unnumbered pages.

314 Ibid., sygn. 1196, [Pismo IPH] do Centralnego Urzędu Planowania dotyczy subskrypcji PPOK…, unnumbered pages.

315 Ibid., Protokół z konferencji w dniu 4 II 1946 r.

316 Ibid., sygn. 1156, PPOK "Akcja motoryzacji", 7 XI 1947 r., unnumbered pages.

his company paid "significant taxes and tributes to the state treasury."[317] On the other hand, the company Składy drewna i materiałów budowlanych (Timber and Building Materials Depot) belonging to Józef Maciejewski was, in the owner's view, "a key contributor to the reconstruction of the Capital and to the supply of industry and crafts."[318] Private entrepreneurs often mentioned the location of their companies' headquarters, usually outside city centres, a fact which caused considerable difficulties in cases where public transport opportunities were limited. As a representative of one packaging company in Warsaw wrote in its application: "Given the constant contact that we need to maintain with the Central Directorates, as our clients, and the fact that it is impossible to secure a telephone line extension due to the lack of cable in this district, no other mean will suffice than automobile transport."[319] In turn, the Polish Foreign Trade Society Elektrim ("Elektrim" (Polskie Towarzystwo Handlu Zagranicznego Elektrim), one of the largest enterprises for the export and import of electrical engineering and power industry, which had two cars—a jeep ("damaged and incomplete") and a Steyer ("also damaged")—began its efforts to purchase a new vehicle at the beginning of 1947. Until January 1948, they were unsuccessful.[320] Much rarer were applications which simply stated, for example: "We are interested in one new passenger car, American."[321]

Equally interesting is the application, or more precisely the comments to it in an official's hand, addressed to the Chamber of Commerce and Industry by the Paint and Varnish Factory (Fabryka Farb i Lakierów). This company, based in Helenówek near Pruszków, just outside of Warsaw, had applied for a Škoda or Citroën passenger car. Of course, the application's author did not

---

317 Ibid., sygn. 1155, [Dom handlowo-przemysłowy Stanisław Jarominski, Warszawa-Praga] w sprawie przydziału samochodu osobowego marki Citroen, Warszawa, 30 VI 1947 r., unnumbered pages.

318 Ibid., Dotyczy przydziału nowego samochodu osobowego, Warszawa, 28 VII 1948 r., unnumbered pages.

319 Ibid., [Fabryka opakowań blaszanych PEM, Warszawa, ul. Burakowska no. 5/7], 22 V 1948 r., unnumbered pages.

320 Ibid., [Polskie Towarzystwo Handlu Zagranicznego dla elektrotechniki "Elektrim"] dotyczy przydziału samochodu, Warszawa, 4 I 1948 r., unnumbered pages.

321 Ibid., [Laboratorium dr Stanisław Klawe, Warszawa], Warszawa, 19 I 1948 r., unnumbered pages.

fail to mention extensive contacts and business conducted with state-owned enterprises. At the end of the application, the company representative wrote: "please give all possible consideration." To which the IPH official added: "but this will be unlikely because, to the best of my knowledge, private companies do not receive allocations."[322]

2.4.2 Roads

I have already mentioned what the war damage to road infrastructure looked like. Moving the country's borders to the west made it necessary to integrate the merged areas. These new territorial acquisitions had a relatively dense road network compared to pre-1939 Poland. For every 100 km^2 of land annexed to Poland, there were approximately 45 km of paved roads. On the other hand, in the former territories it was almost half as much (24 km per 100 km^2).[323]

In the first postwar years, the priority was to rebuild and standardise the road network. Eugeniusz Buszma, later the director of the Central Public Roads Authority, estimated that integration of the road systems of the old and new territories would require the construction of over 25,000 km of roads within the pre-1939 borders (excluding areas annexed to the USSR). Buszma went so far as to claim that it was "an issue that is, one might say, burning."[324] However, this process turned out to be extremely costly. Two years after the end of the war, the Central Planning Office prepared a list of equipment and materials necessary for the reconstruction of roads, waterways and railways, and which of them had to be imported. The total value exceeded US $365 million, of which over US $27 million was allocated to roads, including for the purchase of, among others, machines necessary to repair road foundations and pavement. At the same time, it was estimated that from May 1945 to January 1947, the value of the rebuilt objects reached 10%

---

322 Ibid., [Fabryka Farb i Lakierów, podanie o przydział samochodu osobowego] do Izby Przemysłowo-Handlowej w Warszawie, 3 VI 1948 r., unnumbered pages.

323 A. Zawistowski, "Wzrost podporządkowany doktrynie politycznej," pp. 185–186.

324 E. Buszma, "Problem dróg samochodowych w Polsce," *Drogownictwo* 1946, no. ½, http://www.nowedrogi.pl/index.php?option=content&task=view&id=32&Itemid=93 (accessed: January 21, 2011).

of the estimated damage costs.[325] Only 13 km of new roads had been built and 1,500 destroyed roads had been renovated.[326] This was a very slow pace.

In addition to reconstruction, it was also necessary to maintain already existing transportation routes in a condition that would allow them to be used. In the last quarter of 1945, the Roads Department of the Ministry of Road and Air Transport planned for the maintenance of bridges on state and provincial public roads alone to an amount of over 32 million zlotys. However, plans were quickly revised and only 20 million was allocated for this purpose.[327] At the start of the Three-Year Plan, Poland had a total of over 95,000 km of hard-surface roads and 157,000 km of dirt roads, which meant that there were 30.7 km of roads per 100 km^2 of territory. Regarding road infrastructure, the first postwar economic plan, prepared by Czesław Bobrowski's team, called specifically for the construction of 4,500 km of new roads and almost 39,000 running metres of bridge.[328] In the end, success was only partial. While new construction, modernisation, and reconstruction produced over 97,000 km of hard-surface roads, increasing the ratio to 31.2 km per 100 km^2, there were still huge disparities between individual regions of the country. Furthermore, in terms of the density of hard-surface roads, other European countries had definitely surpassed Poland. Among the examples is Germany, which at the end of the 1940s had over 40 km of hard roads per 100 km^2, or Czechoslovakia, which boasted 54 km of roads per 100 km^2. In Poland, only the Śląsko-Dąbrowskie voivodeship, which had 55 km of hard road per 100 km^2, reached the European average. Meanwhile, the Rzeszów voivodeship was in last place, with a mere 12 km per 100 km^2.[329]

---

325 AAN, CUP, sygn. 1466, Zestawienie potrzeb dla odbudowy komunikacji w urządzeniach i materiałach, które nie są wcale produkowane w kraju lub też produkcja krajowa jest niewystarczająca, Warszawa, 3 VII 1947 r., unnumbered pages.

326 J. Kaliński, *Plan odbudowy gospodarczej 1947–1949*, Warszawa 1977, p. 177.

327 AAN, CUP, sygn. 2927, Wniosek Departamentu Dróg Kołowych [Ministerstwa Komunikacji] w sprawie kredytów dodatkowych na utrzymanie mostów drogowych w okresie 1 X—31 XII 1945 r., Warszawa, 6 XI 1945 r., p. 261.

328 Dz. U. 1947, no. 53, pos. 285.

329 AAN, KC PZPR, sygn. 237/XIII/140, Protokół z posiedzenia Sekcji Drogowej przy Wydziale Komunikacyjnym KC PZPR z 19 III 1949 r., unnumbered pages; ibid., Gospodarka drogowa w Polsce Ludowej, unnumbered pages.

The Six-Year Plan was more ambitious. It planned for the construction of 6,000 km of new roads, the reconstruction of 9,000 km of old roads, and the redevelopment of 4,000 km of existing roads, providing them with modern, hard surfaces. The plan was to also rebuild 34,000 metres of bridges, previously mostly wooden, now to be made of steel and reinforced concrete. It was generally assumed that thanks to these measures, the vast majority of war damage would be repaired, and that the network of the most important traffic arteries would be modernised. The differences in the density of roads between the country's central, eastern, western, and northern regions were also to be reduced. Ultimately, during the Six-Year Plan, the length of hard-surface roads increased by 6,500 km, reaching 267,600 km, though the increase in improved surface roads was definitely lower, amounting to just over 1,200 km, a number that was smaller than in the years 1946–1949.[330] In 1952 alone, the cost of building and rebuilding roads and bridges reached 463.4 million zlotys, which meant that 88% of the financial plan had been implemented. By 1953, 90% of the plan had been implemented, and although the planned length of new and reconstructed roads was exceeded by several kilometres, the fact was that the goals regarding construction, widening, redevelopment, and reinforcement of bridges were not achieved.[331] In the end, in 1955, there were over 98,000 km of hard-surface roads in Poland, which meant a road density of 31.7 km per 100 km^2. However, only slightly more than 25,000 km of that length had an improved hard surface, and large regional disparities remained. In terms of the density of hard-surface roads, the Wrocław (55.4 km/100 km^2), Opole (48.8 km/100 km^2), Stalinogród (41.5 km/100 km^2), and Gdańsk (40 km/100 km^2) voivodeships led the way. The road network was the worst in the Lublin (14.4 km/100 km^2), Białystok (18.5 km/100 km^2), and Rzeszów (22.2 km/100 km^2) voivodeships.[332]

---

330 "Rocznik Statystyczny Transportu" 1967, pp. 6–7; A. Rostocki, W. Wieniawski, *Motoryzacja w liczbach 1969*, Warszawa 1970, p. 229; cf. AAN, PKPG, sygn. 2951, Memoriał w sprawie stanu dróg państwowych i powiatowych oraz w sprawie potrzeby wznowienia robót przy ich utrzymaniu, [1953 r.], pp. 11–18.

331 AAN, Urząd Rady Ministrów, Kancelaria Tajna (hereafter: URM KT), sygn. 6/322, Ocena wykonania planu robót drogowo-mostowych o znaczeniu ogólnopaństwowym w ramach P[lanu] I[nwestycyjnego] Ministerstwa Transportu Drogowego i Lotniczego na 1953 r., pp. 31–37.

332 "Rocznik Statystyczny 1956", 1956, p. 210.

2.4.3 The Law

After the end of World War II, the binding legal acts with regard to road traffic on the lands that were within the borders established at the Yalta and Tehran conferences were the Act of October 7, 1921, regulating public roads[333] and the Ordinance of October 27, 1937, on the movement of motor vehicles on public roads.[334] Despite several changes, the latter remained in force for over twenty-five years, until it was replaced by a completely new code, which became law of the land on October 1, 1962.[335]

Meanwhile, the regulations on vehicle registration were changed many times. The first legal regulations concerning this issue, as well as the marking of motor vehicles, were issued at the end of 1944.[336] In October, the head of the Department of Transportation, Posts, and Telegraphs issued a circular in response to repeated appropriation of automobiles owned by PKWN, despite the fact that their drivers possessed all required documents: a travel order, a driving record book, and a certificate confirming the vehicle's ownership. The circular reminded readers about the requirement of registration of each car and motorcycle with the Transportation-Construction Department at the relevant voivodeship offices, where vehicles were provided with a plate and registration document, a so-called passport.[337] At the end of August 1945, KRN deputies in the Transportation Committee of the Sejm called on Osóbka-Morawski's government to decentralise vehicle registration and transfer responsibility for it to voivodeship automotive offices. As mentioned above, this duty was vested in the centralised PUS.

The first registrations of vehicles on liberated Polish territories took place in April 1945. Theoretically, the regulations of October 1937 were to apply, but PUS relied on its own regulations and introduced a centralised registration system for civilian cars. This process, which was highly burdensome because it lasted for months, met with a great deal of criticism and provoked the

---

333 Dz. U. 1921, no. 89, pos. 656.

334 Dz. U. 1937, no. 85, pos. 616.

335 Dz. U. 1962, no. 61, pos. 295.

336 In September 1944, the head of the Department of Transportation, Posts, and Telegraphs issued an ordinance on the marking of motor vehicles and the method of issuing registration plates; "Dziennik Urzędowy Ministerstwa Komunikacji" (hereafter: Dz. Urz. MK) 1945, no. 2, pos. 18.

337 Ibid., no. 3, pos. 26.

aforementioned reaction from the Transportation Commission. However, PUS refused to introduce changes. Some modifications aimed at tightening the vehicle registration process were implemented in November 1945. Based on rules established during the inter-ministerial conference held on November 12 and 14, PUS issued the rules of vehicle registration. Circular no. 41 of November 20, 1945, established that on December 15, all so-called trial (*próbne*) plates would be invalidated, and would henceforth be used only for the purpose of transporting the vehicles to a technical examination. Vehicles which had not obtained a permanent registration and still used plates marked with the abbreviation "*PR*," were to be confiscated.[338] The issuance of trial plates prior to the circular was regarded as inconsistent with paragraph 30 of the regulation on the movement of motor vehicles of October 27, 1937.

Regulating the issue of vehicle registration also represented an attempt to limit many disruptive phenomena. As a PUS circular noted, it was a common practice to buy automobiles, motorcycles, and spare parts without checking the legality of their origin. The high demand for vehicles meant that the transactions often involved stolen cars: "Due to the temporary demand for cars of this origin, robberies and thefts of automobiles are multiplying for the purpose of disposing of them in an uncontrolled and illegal way. … some honest people, honest workers, or, as was the case in a few instances, demobilised soldiers, lose their savings by unknowingly purchasing motor vehicles from fences or even directly from a thief, the ownership of the vehicle not being recognised by the state." PUS simultaneously asserted that thorough checks were carried out during the registration process to verify a vehicle's origin. At the same time, the circular reminded readers that formerly German automobiles and motorcycles, along with those imported and distributed by KERM, could be legally purchased only through PUS.[339]

338 AAN, URM, sygn. 5/466, Obwieszczenie, pp. 11–11 v; ibid., Okólnik no. 41, Warszawa, 20 XI 1945 r., pp. 21–22. Trial plates were issued for a period of 3 to 7 days, depending on the distance between the parking place of the motor vehicle and the seat of the office where the technical inspection (on which registration was conditioned) was carried out. It was impossible to extend this period. Individual voivodeships and districts, including Warsaw, received four-digit numbers in the so-called "PR" series; ibid., MAP, sygn. 488 (mf B-1473), Zasady korzystania z numerów próbnych dla pojazdów mechanicznych, p. 13; ibid., Okólnik no. 41, Warszawa, 20 XI 1945 r.

339 Ibid., Ostrzeżenie, 5 XII 1945 r., p. 12.

This decision by PUS caused an almost immediate reaction from vehicle users, especially those tied to local administration, who were deprived of their means of transport literally overnight. The Chancellery of the Prime Minister received requests from all over Poland to extend the validity of trial plates, cancel the circular, and streamline the process of obtaining permanent registration certificates, which "so far has been taking many months."[340] Perhaps due to this decisive reaction PUS announced a slight softening of the rules for issuing trial registration plates and extension of the validity of trial plates in the next circular (no. 46), but only for vehicles from foreign deliveries; trial plates for such automobiles could be "renewed in justified cases until a permanent record card is issued."[341] Decisions were also made that extended the validity of trial plates used by certain social and political organisations. Such a situation developed in early March 1946, when the PUS Office of Operations assented to the issuing of test plate certificates, allowing unrestricted operation of vehicles from UNRRA deliveries used by the Voivodeship Coordinating Commission of Political Parties for the West Pomerania District.[342] Obviously, it was politically necessary to keep these vehicles moving.

Returning to PUS, its activities in this area was the subject of devastating criticism. In the first issue of *Motoryzacja*, an author identifying himself as "E.O." wrote that "it must be said that any restrictions on registration—both regarding who may register a vehicle in their name and regarding the method of registration—are not *based on any legal provision* [italics in original]." However, the author admitted that these restrictions had been necessary in the first months of the postwar state administration, but the regulations issued by PUS were inconsistent with the code of 1937. "This regulation," E.O. wrote, "... did not, and could not, provide for any narrowing of the circle of

---

340 See e.g.: ibid., Telegram, 18 XII 1945 r., p. 7; ibid., Telegram, 18 XII 1945 r., p. 8; ibid., Telegram, 14 XII 1945 r., p. 16.

341 Ibid., Okólnik no. 46, [grudzień 1945 r.], p. 28. Furthermore, wherever it could be justified by "economic necessity and the interest of the state," trucks of German origin presented for registration by state economic organisations and the Społem Economic Association could receive certificates for trial licence plates valid until permanent cards were issued.

342 Ibid., [Pismo informacyjne] Do Biura Prezydialnego Rady Ministrów, Warszawa, 6 III 1946 r., p. 33.

persons who could be owners or users of motor vehicles. ...[T]he limitation of the right of ownership would have to be mandated by legislation, and such an act did not exist before the war and does not exist still."[343] Elsewhere, the legal provisions created at PUS regarding vehicle registration were called "vague," the office itself "omnipotent," and its actions "dictatorial."[344]

It was not until July 28, 1946, that the deputy minister of transportation issued an order regulating vehicle registration and allowing, for the first time, the registration of vehicles by private persons, who had previously been deprived of this right. The order repealed all previously binding circulars and orders issued by both PUS (no longer in existence) and CZM, with the exception of two documents: circulars no. 59 of March 27, 1946, and no. 62 of April 9, 1946. The order of July 28 included an instruction regulating vehicle registration in accordance with the provisions of the 1937 code, supplemented by the CZM regulations of June 28, 1946.[345]

According to binding regulations, motor vehicles were registered by second-level offices from the area where the vehicle was garaged based at the owner's request. The submitted documents were to be accompanied by the original proof of ownership of the vehicle, though notarised or officially certified copies were admissible. Any documents which stated "without doubt that the vehicle as a whole (not in part, or as a wreck, etc.) is identical to the one submitted for registration" could be submitted as proof. Those wishing to register a vehicle had to present documents issued by the Polish authorities or relevant institutions, authorised companies who sold vehicles (depots and outlets belonging to the Central Automobile Works, Centralne Zakłady Samochodowe), court judgements, proofs of purchase from a public auction, etc. If the vehicle came from abroad, foreign documents were honoured, though the registrant had to attach proof that duty had been paid. The registration office could also restrict the movement of motor vehicles to specific areas (e.g. *powiat* or voivodeship). The instruction also regulated

---

343 E. O., "Unormowanie sprawy rejestracji," *Motoryzacja* 1946, no. 1, p. 31.

344 Old., "Ponowna rejestracja pojazdów mechanicznych," *Motoryzacja* 1947, no. 8, p. 452.

345 "Wiadomości urzędowe Centralnego Zarządu Motoryzacji," *Motoryzacja* 1946, no. 1, p. 37.

matters of re-registration in the event of a change of vehicle owner.[346] All vehicles not re-registered by September 30, 1946 became the property of the State Treasury.[347]

In terms of the number of registrations, the results of the order of June 28 were worse than expected. Within a month after the regulations came into force, 941 private motor vehicles were registered, and 28 vehicles that had previously belonged to various state offices and institutions were re-registered as private vehicles. In August, the results were much better: 2,738 and 101 vehicles, respectively.[348] However, if we note that the registration deadline was September 30, this increase is not surprising. No doubt, delays in registration of vehicles also resulted from the fees that vehicle owners were obligated to pay. At stake here was the required payment for the District Liquidation Offices, which distributed former German vehicles. As noted at a meeting of the Transportation Commission, the situation was further complicated by rumours of possible price cuts in July and August. This had an impact because many circles expressed the opinion that the fees were too high, which the IPH agreed with, proclaiming that "private enterprises should play a part in the re-privatisation of motor vehicles, [and] only carry minimal burdens, in a fair proportion to the actual value of the automobile." As was noted, "too high an estimation [of fees] will painfully affect private enterprises, for which the privately owned car is not a luxury item but a means of running a business."[349] Only with the publication of the circular of August 9, 1946, by the Central Liquidation Office, concerning the estimation of vehicle values, was the matter resolved.[350] The fees charged for the technical inspection were also too high. In 1949, by order of the Minister of Transportation, those fees

346 AAN, KRN, sygn. 27, Protokół z 35. posiedzenia Komisji Komunikacyjnej, Warszawa, 1 X 1946 r., pp. 522–534.

347 Ibid., IPH, sygn. 1196, W sprawie przerejestrowania samochodów prywatnych, Warszawa, 2 VIII 1946 r., unnumbered pages.

348 Ibid., KRN, sygn. 27, Protokół z 35. posiedzenia Komisji Komunikacyjnej, pp. 522–523.

349 Ibid., IPH, sygn. 1195, [Pismo informacyjne IPH] do Centralnego Urzędu Planowania dotyczące szacunku pojazdów mechanicznych, Warszawa, 29 VII 1946 r., unnumbered pages.

350 Ibid., KRN, sygn. 27, Protokół z 35. posiedzenia Komisji Komunikacyjnej, p. 523.

were set at 250 zlotys for a motorcycle, 400 zlotys for a new truck or passenger car, and 700 zlotys for a used vehicle.[351]

Another difficulty pointed out by officials was the fact that the instructions from the Ministry of Transportation instructions did not spell out which documents could confirm the ownership status of a vehicle in practice, and which could do so at least in theory. The list included, among others, all registration cards issued by German occupation authorities in place of pre-war registration cards, as well as German registration cards issued in Polish territories incorporated into the Third Reich.[352] The significance of this problem is evidenced by the fact that, in early October 1946, the Transportation Committee of the Sejm saw fit to address the Central Liquidation Office in reference to two issues. The first concerned the prolongation of the agreement with the Ministry of Transportation regarding the extension of the deadline for paying fees for vehicles and their legal registration in recognition of the mass influx of applications after the deadline specified in the instruction of June 1946. The second issue involved the recognition of the right of Poles to possess automobiles whose ownership documents were issued by German authorities during the war in both the *Generalgouvernement* and Polish territories incorporated into the Third Reich.[353]

2.4.4 Official Vehicles

No doubt, the shiny limousines belonging to Polish dignitaries that Maria Dąbrowska described in her diaries, parked in front of the theatre in Nowy Świat Street in Warsaw on a July evening in 1948, made a great impression on society.[354] However, the creation of a fleet of automobiles intended for state officials was a very difficult process from the outset because postwar shortages in almost all areas of life also affected access to official and state cars.

The lack of cars for top government officials was especially painful. Henryk Różański recalled how, in early August 1944, he managed to find and start

---

351 Ibid., MK, sygn. 1144, Zarządzenie Ministra Komunikacji z 5 X 1949 r. w sprawie opłat za badanie techniczne pojazdów mechanicznych, unnumbered pages.
352 Ibid., KRN, sygn. 27, p. 524.
353 Ibid., sygn. 30, [Pismo informacyjne] do Prezesa Głównego Urzędu Likwidacyjnego ob. Siwińskiego Ignacego, 10 X 1946 r., p. 132.
354 M. Dąbrowska, *Dzienniki powojenne 1945–1949*, Warszawa 1997, pp. 251–252.

"a Mercedes holed up in some garage," which would then serve Hilary Minc, head of PKPG, responsible for the country's economic policy, for some time.[355] In September of the same year, PKWN received a hundred new Jeeps from the USSR, which Prime Minister Osóbka-Morawski distributed among government employees.[356] However, this was a drop in the bucket in terms of the actual needs. Furthermore, these cars were soon almost completely dismantled for spare parts while parked.[357] In late November, the Prime Minister issued a circular ordering the "most economical use" of vehicles belonging to individual ministries. This amounted to an acceptance of the fact that all vehicles not in use at a given time could be transferred to other ministries after prior arrangement.[358] Attempts to create a fleet of state vehicles for members of the government, the KRN, and the diplomatic corps undertaken in July 1945 led General Karol Świerczewski, Deputy Minister of MON, to request a donation of a dozen or so vehicles used by the Second Polish Army for this purpose.[359] Only later was it decided to import American Chevrolets, Buicks, and Cadillacs.[360]

Vehicles produced by GMC came to Poland via Scandinavia. One such delivery from November 1946, consisting of a Cadillac, six Buicks, and thirty-five Chevrolets, turned out to contain damaged vehicles ("the fenders are bent, the paint is chipped, there are dents on some of the bodies. Almost all of the tools have been stolen"). In spite of this, the Polish authorities did not file a complaint because the damage could be repaired on site quite cheaply, and the need for cars was urgent. However, in the relevant telephone message, Stefan Askanas makes an interesting note, suggesting that the distribution of vehicles should be done by drawing lots.[361] This may indicate that the

---

355 H. Różański, *Śladem wspomnień i dokumentów (1943–1948)*, Warszawa 1987, p. 150.

356 Ibid., pp. 154–155.

357 AAN, Polski Komitet Wyzwolenia Narodowego (hereafter: PKWN), sygn. I/102, Raport, 14 XI 1944 r., p. 96.

358 Ibid., Okólnik, 29 XI 1944 r., p. 1a.

359 AAN, URM, sygn. 5/39, Do Dowódcy II-ej Armii Wojsk Polskich generała Świerczewskiego, Warszawa, 12 VII 1945 r., pp. 20–20 v.

360 AAN, CUP, sygn. 1939, Telefonogram, 30 XI 1946 r., p. 205. The Buicks were intended for Prime Minister Józef Cyrankiewicz and Marshal Michał Rola-Żymierski; ibid., sygn. 1937, [List attache wojskowego Ambasady Polskiej w Waszyngtownie gen. Izydora Modelskiego], 14 IX 1946 r., p. 84.

361 Ibid., sygn. 1939, Telefonogram, 30 XI 1946 r., p. 205.

hunger for official cars within the public administration was enormous. For many years, Artur Starewicz would drive a Fiat 500 that had been confiscated during the agrarian reform.[362]

However, the most important state dignitaries simply had to ride exceptional cars, and President of the KRN and (as of 1947) President of the Republic of Poland Bolesław Bierut was to receive a truly special vehicle. In early April 1948, the Paris office of Polish Foreign Trade Company Varimex (Polska Centrala Handlu Zagranicznego Varimex) received an order to purchase a convertible for the Polish head of state. The guidelines that reached Paris—a four-door vehicle with a black or dark blue body and red leather interior—excluded any mass-produced vehicle. After investigating the French automobile market, the Varimex employee entrusted with the task informed the Warsaw headquarters: "You can't buy a ready-made four-door convertible here. You have to make arrangements. Therefore, I talked to various body factories and came to the conclusion that the best is Chapron, who produces some very nice stuff."[363] This was a reference to Henri Chapron, an engineer and builder of car bodies, author of designs that earned a permanent place in the history of the world automotive industry. He specialised primarily in modifying the bodies of luxury brands, mainly French limousines, transforming them into real works of designer art. His most famous works include modifications of the famous Citroën DS which Roland Barthes said "has fallen from the sky."[364] One of Chapron's works, a Mylord—a converted Citroën SM convertible, was sold at auction in 2014 for over half a million euros.

The cable from Varimex employee went on: "[T]he chassis must be long enough for a 4-door convertible. And currently only one, Delahaye, has a chassis that is long enough." Once again, the choice was the best possible: the company founded by Émile Delahaye in 1895 was famous for its luxurious limousines. The body in question came from the 180 model. Originally, the car was powered by a six-cylinder engine with a displacement of 4.5 litres and an output of 120 HP. Chapron's would take until the end of the year

---

362 Artur Starewicz's account, Hoover Institution Archives, Jane L. Curry Collection, Box 9. I would like to thank Michał Przeperski for sharing this source.

363 AAN, CUP, sygn. 1940, Sprawozdanie za okres od 2 do 8 IV 1948 r., Paryż, 9 IV 1948 r., p. 69.

364 R. Barthes, "The New Citroën," p. 88.

to complete the car at the cost of 3.5 million francs. The Varimex employee suggested in closing: "However, it seems to me that if the color combination in the order is not ritually observed, green upholstery will look better in a black convertible than a red one."[365] In the end, the transaction was never completed, though this does not change the fact that in the realities of that time, such a car would have been an exceptional item within the socialist bloc.

The story of the purchase of a convertible for Bolesław Bierut was only an isolated episode. The majority of the automobile fleet used by state officials and the administrative apparatus in general during the early postwar years consisted mainly of used cars, motorcycles, and bicycles, complemented by a few imported cars. Moreover, in the early 1950s, official cars were mostly outdated; they had exceeded mileage limits and could not guarantee safe driving.[366] The Transportation Department of the Central Committee of the PPR complained that the Polish automobile fleet was characterised by "an incredible variety of types of machines and a catastrophic lack of spare parts."[367] Both difficulties (the technical condition and the multitude of makes and models) presented state car repair shops with an immense challenge. The problem of spare parts was handled in various ways: former German warehouses that had survived the war were put to use, while some parts were produced at own expense or in private plants or purchased on the open market.[368]

In the latter case, keeping the vehicles running often required paying a price that was considered speculative. As Franciszek Wichrzycki, head of the Autotransport Department at the Government Praesidium, wrote to Prime Minister Osóbka-Morawski, the common explanation ran as follows:

> Since spare parts could not be obtained at official prices for the simple reason that they were not available, we have been forced, and will often be forced in the future, to buy [what we need] at so-called free market prices. There are few vehicles, and

365 AAN, CUP, sygn. 1940, Sprawozdanie za okres od 2 do 8 IV 1948 r., Paryż, 9 IV 1948 r., p. 69.

366 Ibid., PKPG, sygn. 378, Notatka w sprawie ilości i stanu samochodów osobowych, Warszawa, [lipiec 1952 r.], p. 25.

367 AAN, KC PPR, sygn. 295/XI-81 (mf 2315/15), Sprawozdanie z działalności Wydziału Komunikacji KC PPR za miesiące wrzesień–listopad 1946 r., [4 XII 1946 r.], p. 11.

368 AAN, KERM, sygn. 219, Protokół no. 1 oględzin warsztatów remontowych Pocztowego Urzędu Przewozowego Kraków, przy ul. Cystersów 21, [maj 1949 r.], p. 156.

> putting one in running order without spending even a few hundred or even thousands of zlotys on spare parts given the limited pool of cars amounts to sabotage. Buying a Jeep clutch disc on the open market when two of them are in stock is not a crime nor an oversight when you consider how important this spare part is. Since there are currently several hundred Jeeps in Poland, I declare that we are ready to purchase any amount of these discs, if we have the opportunity.[369]

The cost of spare parts was an extra burden on an already fragile state budget. In 1949 alone, 5 million francs were earmarked for the purchase of Jeep components.[370] Unfortunately, the availability of the desired parts slowly became a problem (including for political reasons). Many car models were no longer produced and it became impossible to obtain components necessary for repairs and servicing. In 1948, the planned import of spare parts for former UNRRA vehicles would amount to 1.6 billion zlotys. Ultimately, Poland managed to purchase the needed equipment for less than 30% of the sum.[371] One of the most sought-after elements were ball bearings, the lack of which resulted in the withdrawal of a large number of vehicles from use.[372]

Not only old cars but also new ones suffered from breakdowns. Grzegorz Halak, technical director of the State Workshops and Automobile Works, noted that after only two years of operation, Renault and Chevrolet passenger cars required a major overhaul. In a letter to the Ministry of Labor and Social Policy, he observed:

> It is certain that until the end of 1948 and during 1949, 90% of cars of the aforementioned brands will need to pass through repair workshops. Currently, an increasing number of cars imported in the period 1946–1947 are no longer on the road. Our garages in Warsaw, whose programme includes the repair of these vehicles, cannot perform the task assigned to them due to the acute shortage of spare parts for the aforementioned vehicles. It should be emphasised that, for unknown reasons,

---

369 AAN, URM, sygn. 5/39, Do Prezesa Rady Ministrów, 27 II 1945 r., p. 12.

370 AAN, KERM, sygn. 222, [Dot. wniosków importowych], Warszawa, [5 III 1949 r.], p. 18.

371 Ibid., Sprawozdanie z działalności w roku 1948 Dyrekcji Naczelnej [Centrali Handlowej Przemysłu Motoryzacyjnego Motozbyt], Warszawa, marzec 1949 r., p. 248.

372 AAN, MPiH, sygn. 2430, [Memoriał inż. Grzegorza Halaka Dyrektora Technicznego Dyrekcji Państwowych Zakładów i Warsztatów Samochodowych do Departamentu Planowania Ministerstwa Przemysłu i Handlu], Warszawa, 28 IX 1948 r., pp. 3–4.

> the imported vehicles were not provided with the necessary spare parts, which is already exposing the economy to great losses.[373]

Perhaps, in order to partially avoid this problem, CUP officials used the quality and condition of roads in particular regions of the country as one of the criteria for allocating new cars; theoretically, more durable cars were directed to eastern areas, and those of weaker construction to other areas.[374] The same was done with trucks.[375]

The problem of the great variety of makes and models of vehicles on Polish roads was closely related to the issue of availability of spare parts. Polish officials mentioned this problem already in early 1947,[376] but it took another two years for them to make binding decisions. By 1948, in an issue of *Życie Gospodarcze*, Aleksander Rostocki was citing some quite alarming statistics. He calculated that there were 380 different kinds of vehicles on Polish roads.[377] Data on vehicles used by officials at the Ministry of Transportation showed that the ministerial fleet of passenger cars consisted of over fifty different makes and models. Therefore, the clause in the government resolution of February 23, 1948, which described the state automobile fleet as "unified and rationally distributed in terms of brands and types," cannot be seen as anything other than wishful thinking.[378]

In practice, for repair shops, the variety of types and brands of vehicles meant that many of them could not be provided with technical support. In order to control this automotive chaos (described elsewhere as a "terrifying" or "gaudy mosaic"[379]), KERM determined in a resolution dated February 12,

---

373 Ibid.

374 AAN, MPiH, sygn. 2429, [Dot. przydziału samochodów osobowych i furgonetek], Warszawa, 30 VI 1948 r., p. 119.

375 Ibid., Sprawozdanie z lustracji gospodarki samochodowej w Centralnym Zarządzie Przemysłu Naftowego, Warszawa, 26 III 1948 r., p. 20.

376 It was then that the first proposals were made for dividing vehicles on Polish roads according to makes and models and providing technical support only to those that were specifically selected, see A. Wiślicki. "O bliskie perspektywy samochodów osobowych," *Motoryzacja* 1947, no. 2, pp. 250–251.

377 A. Rostocki, "Sprawa taboru samochodowego," *Życie Gospodarcze* 1948, no. 7, pp. 298–300.

378 Dz. Urz. MK 1948, no. 6, pos. 75.

379 AAN, CUP, sygn. 2921, Motoryzacja w Trzyletnim Planie Odbudowy, p. 11.

1949, which makes could be described as typical (and thus assured of the supply of parts and subjected to capital renovations) and which as non-typical (without technical support). Passenger cars classified as typical included the following models: Chevrolet Fleetmaster, Citroën III, Fiat 110, Škoda Tudor, and Willys. The fleet of vehicles used by the MON and the MBP was excluded from these regulations.[380]

As mentioned above, in the first half of 1948, among a total of over 93,000 cars, 26,000 were passenger cars. According to a report prepared by the Ministry of Labor and Social Policy, there were nearly 12,000 cars in the "purely state sector," excluding vehicles belonging to cooperatives, of which just over 41% were "typical." The remaining "non-typical" vehicles were in very poor technical condition. Furthermore, it was assumed that over the course of 1949, half of them would have to be withdrawn from service due to wear and tear and to their "complete unprofitability of operation." Statistics prepared by CUP a year later served only to confirm the terrible condition and degradation of the automobile fleet. Just before the KERM resolution came into force in February 1949, out of 32,662 passenger cars, only 7,538 were classified as typical, that is, only 23%.[381]

Clearly, the "typicality" of a particular make or model was determined not by popularity reflected in the number of vehicles but by the availability of spare parts. This meant that the state administration was suddenly put in a very difficult situation. Taking into consideration the previous instruction to state offices to abandon "redundant and surplus cars,"[382] the already very small number of cars shrank even more, and each vehicle became worth its weight in gold. Before that, however, the movement of cars belonging to state offices was limited for cost-saving reasons, first by circular no. 19 of the Council of Ministers dated May 22, 1948, on the use of passenger motor vehicles, and then by a resolution of the same body, dated February 23, 1949.[383] These regulations divided vehicles into three categories: the letter "R" in the

---

380 "Monitor Polski" (hereafter: M.P.) 1949, no. 59, pos. 797.

381 AAN, CUP, sygn. 2994, Stan samochodów osobowych na 1 II 1949 r., p. 211.

382 AAN, KERM, sygn. 218, Protokół posiedzenia ścisłego Prezydium Komitetu Ekonomicznego Rady Ministrów, 27 VIII 1948 r., pp. 11–12.

383 AAN, MAP, sygn. 488 (mf B-1473), Okólnik no. 19 w sprawie używania osobowych pojazdów mechanicznych, Warszawa, 22 V 1948 r., p. 70; ibid., Zarządzenie ministra administracji publicznej w sprawie zasad używania samochodów osobowych,

registration marked official cars to which the most important state representatives (including voivodes) were entitled; a "D" was used for company cars intended for the transportation needs of specific organisational units in order to facilitate their work. The last category were "F" ("function") vehicles, which were used in the performance of official duties by an employee and were therefore a work tool. Additionally, strict limitations were imposed on travel distances. Provincial administrators could travel by car within a radius of 20 to 50 km, depending on the density of the public transport network. At the *powiat* level, the distance limit for official cars was restricted to the administrative boundaries of the territorial unit. Only state cars were not subject to such restrictions.

These were not the first regulations implemented to reduce unnecessary travel. Restrictions on the use of cars belonging to the state administration related closely to quite common abuses committed by officials at various levels. Such attempts to control these abuses were made, for instance, in 1946. In that instance, the Department of Transportation and Communications of the CUP cited a proposed regulation from the Ministry of Transportation regarding vehicle registration, which was to be published in the middle of the year, intended to remove state privileges from private cars from the fleet of machines owned by institutions and nationalised enterprises—privileges such as easier access to parts or fuel.[384] Another example of measures taken to regulate the use of official vehicles is found in the regulations set forth by the Ministry of Industry. As part of a savings campaign, regulations in 1947 were introduced that completely prohibited the use of official cars for purposes other than official activities, and the use of a car for a business trip required the consent of a superior each and every time. It was also prohibited to use the vehicles within a radius of 150 km "from the parking place to a destination to which access is possible by train or bus."[385]

będących w posiadaniu władz i urzędów administracji ogólnej oraz samochodu terytorialnego, Warszawa, 22 III 1949 r.

384 AAN, MK, sygn. 219, Zakres prac dokonywanych w komunikacji [przygotowany przez Departament Komunikacji i Łączności Centralnego Urzędu Planowania], no date, unnumbered pages.

385 AAN, IPH, sygn. 1196, Instrukcja korzystania ze służbowych środków lokomocji, Warszawa, 6 III 1947 r., unnumbered pages.

The regulations introduced by the resolution of the Council of Ministers in 1948 sparked immediate protest. In particular, vehicle range limits were questioned as "unrealistic." Among the critics was the mayor of Katowice, Aleksander Willner, who believed that maintaining the recommended radius of movement was simply impossible in the Upper Silesian metropolitan area. One reason he cited were the frequent visits by foreign delegations, which were toured around both Upper Silesia and Lesser Poland (Oświęcim-Auschwitz, Kraków, Zakopane); another was the fact that many holiday homes were located in towns several dozen (Jastrzębie Zdrój, Gorzyce), or even one hundred (Wisła) kilometres away from Katowice.[386] Various ministries, including the Ministry of Transportation, Reconstruction, Agriculture, and Agrarian Reform, sent several dozen requests to Premier Józef Cyrankiewicz for exemption from restrictions for their subordinate offices. They were lifted only for the director of the Roads Department, because—as noted in the justification—"each journey, whatever it is, gives him the opportunity to collect professional material for all directorial activities. Supervising roads is so closely related to car travel that all such trips should be considered advisable and purposeful."[387] The Prime Minister did not approve the requests of the President of the Central Office of National Measurements, the Vice-President of the Central Spatial Planning Office, the Director of the State Veterinary Institute in Puławy, or the Director of the Central Board of the State Repatriation Office or his deputy. In these cases, rather than creating a troublesome precedent, it was deemed sufficient to grant permission for further travel with a delegation allowance on a case-by-case basis. Administrators could also use public transport (often being provided with free travel privileges or discounts for tickets in sleeping cars or on airplanes). During one meeting of the Motorisation Subcommittee, officials concluded that "the resolution [of February 1949] in its current form is facing very great challenges and in many cases, it is becoming unrealistic."[388]

---

386 AAN, MAP, Dot. promienia wyjazdów dla samochodu prezydenta miasta Katowic, Katowice, 16 VIII 1948 r., pp. 130–132.

387 AAN, URM, sygn. 16/147, Notatka dla Obywatela Premiera dotyczy wniosków o zwolnienie z ograniczeń samochodowych, Warszawa, 30 VII 1948, pp. 1–3.

388 AAN, KERM, sygn. 219, Protokół z 12. posiedzenia Podkomitetu Motoryzacyjnego, Warszawa, 31 III 1949 r., p. 29.

As stated, the division of vehicles into typical and non-typical was not guided by the number of individual makes and models, but by the availability of spare parts. Decisions over which types of vehicles were to be deprived of technical support were based on the assumption that those selected would naturally go out of use and be replaced first by imported cars, and then by vehicles of domestic production. The assumptions of the six-year plan predicted an annual loss of non-typical vehicles between 4,000 and 6,000 units: while 39,000 vehicles out of a total of 73,200 were non-typical in early 1950, it was assumed that, when the number of cars increased to 112,500 in 1955, only 500 non-typical ones would remain.[389] As it later turned out, these calculations were unrealistic because even legal regulations distinguishing typical and non-typical makes and models did not prevent, for example, PKPG from trying to impose on Motozbyt the need to supply non-typical vehicles with spare parts.[390]

Even after the KERM resolution came into force, most state automobile repair shops still repaired both types of vehicles. The Postal Transport Office in Kraków used twenty-two vehicles, most of which were typical (eight trucks and five passenger cars), with parts being supplied by Motozbyt and other trading centres. However, the repair shops still serviced non-typical cars, although spare parts for them came from formerly German warehouses and private sources or were made in-house. A similar situation was found in repair shops of the Wrocław PUP.[391] A commission that investigated the issue of such repairs in the entire country proposed to "secure and improve" the supply of spare parts for both typical and non-typical vehicles. This was necessary to keep the cars moving.[392]

---

389 AAN, CUP, sygn. 2994, Protokół z 2. posiedzenia Komisji do opracowania wytycznych do planu 6-cio letniego motoryzacyjnego. Wielkość taboru samochodowego, Warszawa, 6 XI 1948 r., p. 83.

390 AAN, KC PZPR, sygn. 237/XIII-143, Protokół z posiedzenia Sekcji Samochodowej odbytej w dniu 30 VIII 1949 r. w Wydziale Komunikacyjnym KC PZPR, unnumbered pages.

391 AAN, KERM, sygn. 219, Protokół no. 1 z oględzin warsztatów remontowych Pocztowego Urzędu Przewozowego Kraków, przy ul. Cystersów 21, [maj 1949 r.], p. 156; ibid., Protokół no. 2 z oględzin warsztatów remontowych Pocztowego Urzędu Przewozowego, Wrocław, ul. Kolejowa, pp. 159–160.

392 The proposal also included a highly interesting and revealing description of the condition of non-typical vehicles: "Looking at the [non-typical] cars mentioned above,

The Central Cooperative Union (CZS), which was not a part of the official car distribution system, also protested against these regulations. The units subordinated to that organisation had a fleet of cars based mainly on non-typical vehicles; although still running, those vehicles were largely worn out and supplemented only by a small number of typical vehicles. Therefore, when the resolution came into force, CZS officials had to seriously limit operations.[393]

It is impossible to clearly assess whether the division into typical and non-typical vehicles brought the expected results. Certainly, as sources show, this problem persisted to a significant degree in the mid-1950s. One example is the fleet belonging to the Ministry of Light Industry. In February 1956, of the almost 1,500 vehicles used by ministry employees, the majority (927) were old, surplus, or formerly German vehicles, "so, non-typical ones, withdrawn from use on the road *en masse* every year."[394] It is highly probable that this was not an exceptional situation.

The typical/non-typical division had another, quite unexpected result. Once the vehicles of the state had been somewhat organised, a new problem arose. Analysing the classifieds and advertisements published in the *Motor* weekly, one may reach the conclusion that the warehouses of various institutions and enterprises were inundated with parts for makes and models of cars specified in the resolution of February 1949. Both in the late 1950s and over the next decade, classified ads about the sale of components for these cars abounded. Ads for Chevrolet Fleetmasters and Skoda 1101s appeared

---

we can see that they have undergone various renovations in different conditions. The engine and chassis type are so mismatched that parts are not interchangeable. They are usually stitched together from several cars of one make, but also from elements of different makes. The original parts that are obtained often require significant modifications and adaptations. Inspecting these cars after renovation is also problematic because the materials work several times longer than originally intended and are now worn out. Without appropriate, very expensive devices, it is impossible to determine this. Further, it is impossible to predict eventualities that may occur any moment now. We anticipate that the life of these vehicles can only be extended through individual renovations"; ibid., Wnioski Komisji powołanej do zbadania gospodarki technicznej w warsztatach i zajezdniach Min. Poczt i Telegrafów, pp. 182–184.

393 Ibid., [Pismo Centralnego Związku Spółdzielczego do KERM] dotyczy: rozciągnięcia na spółdzielnie uchwały KERM w sprawie pojazdów mechanicznych, Warszawa, 28 III 1949 r., p. 21.

394 AAN, URM KT, sygn. 6/249, Uwagi do załącznika no. 2, 29 II 1956 r., p. 43.

particularly frequently, with individual companies intent on "liquidating [the parts] at low prices."[395] Following the resolution that specified the typical and non-typical vehicles, state repair shops were likely forced to secure as many spare parts as possible, which remained unused when the old stock fell into disuse.

* * *

In the PRL, state anniversaries were usually an opportunity for the proud presentation of current achievements. Such was the case on the ninth anniversary of the PKWN manifesto. An anniversary article was published in *Technika Motoryzacyjna*, stating: "In the automotive industry that is of utmost interest to us, we have made achievements that we would not dare dream of in a capitalist system." These "achievements" included the launch of the production of agricultural tractors at the Ursus Mechanical Works (Zakłady Mechaniczne "Ursus"), the 20,000th unit having rolled out in 1953, and the production of entirely Polish Star trucks in Starachowice, 10,000 of which were assembled by that date. Last but not least, the Bolesław Bierut Factory at Żerań, "based on partial supplies from the Soviet Union ... produces powerful and 'beautiful' Warszawas."[396]

Reflecting the standard propaganda of that time, Leon Minc argued in *Motoryzacja* that the Polish automobile fleet, "after all the postwar and accidental 'acquisitions' fall away," would promptly reflect the socialist character of the domestic economy. The goal was therefore to reduce the number of models in the fleet as much as possible and emphasise the predominance of trucks, primarily of domestic production (Star and Lublin), supplemented only by passenger cars and "rational imports." As the author noted, in a capitalist system, competition between individual car manufacturers leads to the production of a vast number of models, which is justified neither by technical reasons nor by the needs of users, and frequent design changes are only for external effect, "as a means of advertising to attract customers."[397]

---

395 See e.g. *Motor* 1961, no. 22, p. 15.

396 "W rocznicę Manifestu PKWN," *Technika Motoryzacyjna* 1953, no. 7, p. 1.

397 L. Minc, "Wpływ ustroju społecznego na rozwój samochodu, cz. 1," *Motoryzacja* 1953, no. 12, pp. 331–332. Interestingly, the opinions expressed by Minc in the series

The analysis of the ease of driving and maintenance of the vehicles, as well as the availability of spare parts, led Minc to stress the significant advantage of vehicles produced under the socialist system: "Soviet designers directed their efforts to ease the labour of truck drivers as much as possible. … [T]he work of the operating staff is significantly simplified and the operating conditions of the vehicle are improved." These concerns were of no interest to capitalist producers, who focused more on making it easier to drive passenger cars, which "are much easier to operate" than trucks and buses, "because the resulting increase in ownership costs is not advantageous and brings no … profits."[398] Another objection was tied to the completely irrational—in Minc's view—development of certain features of capitalist cars, "which are in fact only useful for advertising." These included vehicle speed, which often exceeded 160 km/h, entering "the range of racing speeds, which … are completely useless [for everyday operation]." The final conclusion regarding capitalist manufacturers was bleak: "[T]he internal contradictions of a capitalist society constantly distort and inhibit the technical development of automobile design." On the other hand, socialist automobile industries had a bright future: "The development of automotive technology in [socialist] countries is subject only to the real and significant interests of the national economy, where there can be no limitation to rational technological progress."[399]

That having been said, it was impossible not to notice the enormous need for a new passenger car on Polish roads, one which would fill the gap that the Warszawa could not fill. Even determined propaganda efforts did not suffice ("The constantly growing prosperity of the working masses has created a demand for a small-displacement car for personal use," but "a lot

---

of articles that followed from this one are consistent with the statements of Henry Ford, who sought at all costs to prevent any design changes to his legendary Model T: "Ford believed [his competitors'] yearly stylistic changes were perversions of the consumer society he had helped create. 'We have lost our buying sense and fallen entirely under the spell of salesmanship. … [N]owadays the American people seem to listen and be sold; that is, they do not buy. They are sold things; things are pushed on them'."; Greg Grandin, *Fordlandia: The Rise and Fall of Henry Ford's Forgotten Jungle City*, New York 2009, p. 92.

398 L. Minc, "Wpływ ustroju społecznego na rozwój samochodu, cz. 2," *Motoryzacja* 1954, no. 1, p. 7.

399 L. Minc, "Wpływ ustroju społecznego na rozwój samochodu, cz. 3," *Motoryzacja* 1954, no. 2, pp. 37–39.

of effort and time will still be needed before small-displacement cars appear on the streets of our cities next to the famous and beloved 'Warszawa'").[400] The number of permits for the use of passenger cars, which was growing month to month, provides evidence of this fact.

As is clear, the Stalinist reality of the first postwar decade in Poland left little room for individual motorisation. Even if officials briefly considered the creation of a passenger car factory in the country with production at an average European level, as the economic plans suggest, this ideal was ultimately abandoned due to external political conditions. Nevertheless, the idea of individual motorisation was very much alive, especially among automotive experts. At the same time, the dynamic situation west of the Iron Curtain showed that without a strong automotive industry and private motorisation, it was difficult to keep up with Western societies in virtually every aspect.

2.4.5 Automotive Europe at a Crossroads—From a People's Car to a Popular Car

Western European societies slowly recovered from the trauma of war and entered an era of prosperity.[401] One of its symbols was individual motorisation, whose development had been interrupted by World War II, but which soon regained its prewar pace.

For a closer look at this phenomenon, we need to go back to 1908, when Henry Ford introduced his legendary Model T into production, giving rise to the development of mass individual motorisation. He and his successors (literally but also figuratively) showed that it was possible to build cheap, relatively reliable cars, available to everyone. European manufacturers, however, continued to produce models whose prices exceeded the financial capabilities of the average citizen. This situation was worsened by the economic crisis, among whose effects was a low demand for cars, which did not match the supply.[402] Many manufacturers correctly predicted that after overcoming the economic difficulties, Western societies will want access to a cheap, relatively reliable car in the style of the Ford T. The greatest impetus for the construction of affordable and popular cars came from Ferdinand Porsche, who was

---

400 J. Burgin, "Niektóre aktualne problemy motoryzacji," *Motoryzacja* 1954, no. 1, pp. 1–2.
401 See T. Judt, *Postwar: A History of Europe since 1945*, Random House 2010.
402 J. J. Flink, *The Automobile Age*, Cambridge–London 1988, p. 189ff.

responsible for the technical side of the Nazi drive to popularise individual motorisation—initially in the form of a car called the KdF-Wagen, known after the war as the Volkswagen Käfer: the popular Beetle.[403]

For Adolf Hitler, the development of the automotive industry was a means to overcome the economic crisis, but not only that.[404] In addition to the highway construction programme,[405] the "people's car" was intended to be a catalyst for the modernisation of German society. Only a motorised nation could be a modern nation.[406] To use and develop Henry Ford's concept was the logical consequence of this belief. In his first speech after becoming Chancellor of Germany, Hitler announced that his government would facilitate the development of mass individual motorisation—the purchase of a new car was to be exempt from taxes; obtaining a driver's licence would be easier; the highway code would be amended; and the production of a small people's car was to begin, along with the construction of a network of modern roads. Work was carried out by the aforementioned Porsche, who, after talks with Hitler, established the basic design requirements for the car. It was to be small but spacious enough to accommodate four people; its maximum speed would reach 100 km/h; fuel consumption was set at 6 litres per 100 km; and the engine was to be air-cooled, which would prevent problems during frosty winters. The car was supposed to be cheap (Porsche suggested a valuation of 1,500 marks, though Hitler demanded a price 500 marks lower),[407] reliable,

---

403 The abbreviation "KdF" came from the name of the organisation "Kraft durch Freude" (German: Strength through Joy), which organised tourist events and recreation in the Third Reich.

404 See e.g. W. König, *Volkswagen, Volksempfänger, Volksgemeinschaft. "Volksprodukte" im Dritten Reich: Vom Scheitern einer nationalsozialistischen Konsumgesellschaft*, Paderborn 2004.

405 An interesting view of Hitler's highway construction programme is presented by Michael Burleigh in *The Third Reich: A New History* (New York 2001). Burleigh emphasises primarily the programme's propaganda value, arguing that its actual importance, especially economic, was much smaller than is usually believed; ibid., pp. 256–258.

406 R. Koshar, "Cars and Nations. Anglo-German Perspectives on Automobility between the World Wars," *Theory, Culture & Society* 21, 2004, no. 4/5, p. 122.

407 W. Sachs, *For the Love of the Automobile: Looking back into the history of our desires*, Oxford 1992, pp. 60–61.

and technically advanced enough not to lose much value over years of use.[408] Many of these requirements were addressed in an earlier design by engineer Hans Ledwinka, who was responsible for the Czechoslovak car brand Tatra. This model, the prototype V570, never entered mass production, but it had a significant influence on Porsche's final design.[409] In 1938, a special savings programme was introduced for future KdF-Wagen owners, consisting of monthly deposits of 5 marks into special accounts. Over 330,000 Germans accumulated 280 million marks in this manner.[410] In 1939, a factory with an expected production capacity of 1.5 million KdF-Wagen cars a year was ready. Mass production of the people's car was halted by the outbreak of World War II. Located in Lower Saxony, in the Stadt des KdF-Wagens, the plant could not produce passenger cars, but it did assemble military vehicles (including the so-called Kübelwagen and Schwimmwagen, based on Volkswagen) and parts for V-1 missiles.[411]

After hostilities ended—indeed, while they were still going on—the idea of a popular car was revived, and the pursuit and production of a car that met the condition of "popularity" began again. One example is the Czech company Avro, which secretly continued work on a prototype of a small car powered by a two-stroke engine. French engineers and designers (Pierre Bézier and Fernand Pickard) also worked on prototype cars, intended to be

---

408 A. Zieliński, *Rozwój koncepcji samochodu osobowego w XX wieku*, Warszawa 2005, pp. 146–147.

409 The issue of the similarity between the two models became the subject of legal action initiated by the Czechoslovak manufacturer, but this was interrupted by the events of 1938. A judgement was only handed down after the trial was resumed, in 1961, ordering Volkswagen to pay 3 million marks in compensation; P. Keiller, "Sexual Ambiguity and Automotive Engineering" in: *Autopia*, ed. P. Wollen and J. Kerr, London 2002, pp. 346–348.

410 This savings programme did not provide savers with any cars. After the war ended, funds accumulated by German citizens in savings accounts were confiscated by the USSR. In 1954, the Federal Court of Justice of West Germany released Volkswagen from liability for the money collected for "KdF-Wagen" cars, and the whole matter was resolved only by a settlement in 1961, which stipulated that any person who had accumulated a sufficient amount in his savings account had a right to a credit of 600 marks for a "Volkswagen" or to 100 marks in cash; J. J. Flink, *The Automobile Age*, p. 265.

411 R. Volti, *Cars and Culture: The Life Story of a Technology*, Baltimore 2006, p. 78.

completely different from prewar cars: cheap to produce and inexpensive to purchase and operate.[412]

In Western Europe, the 1940s and 1950s were a period of emergence for individual motorisation, which—despite better statistics than in Poland—still could not be called universal. In the early 1950s in Spain, there was one passenger car for every 314,000 people; in France, one car per twelve households; the same was true in Germany. Condition were superior in Great Britain, where 14% of households had a car, although there, was great geographical diversity: approximately 25% of the 2.2 million passenger cars were registered in London.[413]

In reference to the British case, one should note the quite pronounced social stratification, which will later be important from the Polish point of view. Wherever factories and plants representing modern industries were located, and wherever employee salaries were therefore higher than elsewhere, a relatively high level of motorisation was observed. For example, in Luton near London in the early 1960s, 45% of workers had their own cars, while in Workington in Cumbria on the north-west coast of England, only one in ten workers employed in the local steel mill owned a car. Similar values were recorded in Glasgow and Middlesbrough, which were considered old industrial areas. Overall, most private cars were registered in the south and in the Midlands, in such cities as Coventry and Birmingham. An equally telling indicator was the type of house occupied by private car owners. While in the suburbs, inhabited by the worker "middle class," 80% of households possessed a driver's licence, for those living in so-called council (public) housing, this figure was 25%. Most people in the British Isles undeniably aspired to own a car, but many of them found that purchasing one represented a significant financial burden until the development of the used car market at the turn of the 1970s.[414] Reliance on used cars was typical for Western Europe in general:

---

412 J. P. Bardou, J. J. Chanaron, P. Fridenson, and J. M. Laux, *The Automobile Revolution: The Impact of an Industry*, Chapel Hill 1982, p. 166.

413 T. Judt, *Postwar*, p. 401; M. Akhtar and S. Humphries, *The Fifties and Sixties: A Lifestyle Revolution*, Basingstoke—Oxford 2001, p. 154.

414 In 1968, more than half of all British households did not have a car. In Leicester, only 39% of households had one. Even in Birmingham, Britain's major car city, 60% of households remained without a vehicle until 1971. At the same time, while in 1950 the number of all motor vehicles on the islands was 4.4 million, of which passenger

in the 1960s, for every new car purchased four used ones were sold.[415] In turn, in France, a study on the degree of "being used to cars" conducted in 1967 and published in 1971, showed that passenger cars typically belonged to members of particular professions, particularly freelance workers, almost all of which (99.2%) owned a vehicle. Subsequent places were occupied by industrialists and large merchants (93.3%), senior staff (90.8%), middle staff (79.5%), small entrepreneurs (74.3%), farmers (64.7%), foremen and skilled workers (60.5%), and clerks (56.2%). At the bottom of the list were unskilled workers (47.9%) and agricultural workers (46.1%).[416]

The automotive industry in the United States (the undisputed world leader in 1950 with 85% of world automobile production) and the United Kingdom (the largest exporter of vehicles in the world) faced a great task: to meet the automotive needs of vast masses of people. Compared to the 1930s, the situation had reversed; while one of the causes of the economic difficulties in the prewar period was low demand for cars, the postwar West seemed to face an almost unlimited demand. This was due not only to increasing purchasing power of the people, but also to the fact that, because war put a stop to new production, most cars dated back at least to the 1930s, which meant that their technical capacity was slowly coming to an end.[417]

It was therefore necessary to provide a society recovering from the stagnation of war with cheap cars that could, at least to some extent, satisfy the growing demand for cars and rejuvenate the ageing automobile fleet. Cheap often meant small, which translated into lower fuel consumption and lower fees, which in most European countries had risen to exorbitant levels, placing cars in the category of luxury goods. The high price of gasoline, in part due to taxes, also increased the already high cost of a vehicle.[418] The automotive

---

cars accounted for just over half, by 1965 this number increased to 13 million, and in the early 1970s it reached 15 million, with the share of passenger cars increasing to 77%; S. Gunn, "People and the car," pp. 224, 228–229.

415 J. P. Bardou, J. J. Chanaron, P. Fridenson, and J. M. Laux, *The Automobile Revolution*, p. 213.

416 M. Roche, "Samochód," in: *Psychologia życia codziennego*, ed. M. Reuchlin, trans. Z. Zakrzewska, Warszawa 1983, p. 384.

417 R. Volti, *Cars and Culture*, pp. 88–89.

418 It was probably fuel prices and fuel availability (rationing in the postwar period) that played a decisive role in the "small car revolution." This became evident later, during

industry of Western Europe met the expectations of potential buyers for a cheap car, and the impulse came from a rather unexpected direction.

At this point, let us return to Germany, specifically to the car factory—or rather military vehicle factory—in the city of Fallersleben, which was destroyed by Allied air raids and occupied, first by Americans and then by the British (who changed the city's name to Wolfsburg). Initially, the factory was turned into repair workshops for the British army, but over the following months, German workers began production of a Volkswagen car, the first mass-produced model in postwar Europe.[419] Heinz Nordhoff, previously long-time director of the BMW plant and the Opel truck factory in Brandenburg, was appointed general director.[420] One of the first units of the newly manufactured automobile was sent to England, with the suggestion that the factory in Wolfsburg be treated as part of British war reparations. However, this idea was considered unprofitable; one commentator supposedly reflected that "a type of car like this will remain popular for two or three years, if that. To build the car commercially would be a completely uneconomic enterprise." American advisers to Henry Ford II expressed similar doubts. Rejected by the Allies, the factory was finally handed over to the German federal government, which ceded control of the *Volkswagenwerk* to the state of Lower Saxony. From that point on, production volume increased continuously, and in 1954, Volkswagen GmbH became the fourth largest car manufacturer in the world, just behind the American "Big Three" (Chrysler, Ford and GMC).[421] The company's success was due to the best-selling vehicle of all time: the VW Beetle.

The years 1947 and 1948 saw the appearance of other models that set trends in the development of individual motoring: Renault 4CV, Citroën 2CV, Morris Minor, and Fiat 500. These were small cars with a quite simple structure, economical in use.[422] There would be no return to the times

---

the Suez crisis in 1956, when gasoline prices went up in France and manufacturers almost immediately began to reduce the size of engines installed in their cars; ibid., p. 92; J. J. Flink, *The Automobile Age*, p. 294; J. P. Bardou, J. J. Chanaron, P. Fridenson, and J. M. Laux, *The Automobile Revolution*, p. 214.

419 A. Zieliński, *Rozwój koncepcji samochodu osobowego*, p. 173.

420 W. Rychter, *Dzieje samochodu*, p. 377.

421 J. J. Flink, *The Automobile Age*, pp. 320–326.

422 A. Zieliński, *Rozwój koncepcji samochodu osobowego*, pp. 175–183.

of prewar, when passenger cars were luxury items. Postwar Europe could not afford expensive, fuel-hungry cars; in 1946, Renault chairman Pierre Lefaucheux noted that the idea of the passenger car as a product intended only for the select few was outdated and, as such, destined to die.[423] By 1958, there were already 39 million vehicles on Western European roads, many of them two-wheelers, whose number was estimated at approximately 18 million. Since the war, 4.5 million new passenger cars rolled off factory floors. Already, a symbolic changing of the guard was taking place: among car producing countries of Europe, West Germany came in first place, with an output of 1.5 million cars annually. Second place went to Great Britain, the previous leader and a top producer since the 1930s. The British produced about 100,000 fewer cars than the Germans, but remained ahead of the French (1.1 million) and the Italians (400,000).[424]

For most inhabitants of the Eastern Bloc, the second half of the 1950s also brought hope for at least partial involvement in the automotive boom. In Czechoslovakia in 1955, there were 139,000 registered passenger cars. A year later, the number rose to 141,900, and in 1957, to almost 160,000. By the end of the decade, 216,300 automobiles were riding the Czechoslovak roads. Growth in the number of passenger cars was only one of the symptoms of change; the general climate around individual motoring was improving. One example of this development is the language used to speak and write about this topic. The press devoted increasing attention to motoring, noticing the growing aspirations for a higher standard of living among the Czechoslovak population and the resulting growth in the demand for cars.[425]

The situation was slightly different in the Soviet Union, where a private car was a strictly rationed commodity. Lewis H. Siegelbaum estimated that in the first half of the 1950s, roughly half of the passenger cars produced were intended for sale to individual buyers—between 16,000 and 64,000 units per year. In 1960 and 1965, sales stalled at around 60,000 units, in spite of a significant increase in production. Nevertheless, high prices (a GAZ M-20 cost 16,000 roubles; a Moskvitch, 9,000 roubles) meant that only

423 J. P. Bardou, J. J. Chanaron, P. Fridenson, and J. M. Laux, *The Automobile Revolution*, p. 173.
424 P. Duignan and L. H. Gann, *The Rebirth of the West*, pp. 506–508.
425 V. Fava, *The Socialist People's Car*, p. 129.

a select few—those favoured by the ruling elite—could actually afford to buy them: "leading workers" and state-owned farm workers, academics and writers.[426] Additionally, major figures promoted collective public transport in place of private ownership. However, limited access to vehicles did not mean that the society that the society had a significantly different outlook to that of Western European countries. Watching *The Grapes of Wrath*,[427] set in the United States during the Great Depression, Soviet viewers seemed not to notice the misery of the depicted workers; instead, after the screening, many of them asked how it was possible that in a capitalist America in decline, the poor characters in the film could afford their own cars and fuel. Perhaps they subconsciously registered something that John Urry articulated decades later, when he wrote that the car had become so democratised in the United States that even the losers of the Great Depression had one.[428] Viktor Sukhodrev, a personal translator of many of the most important people in the Kremlin who was dubbed "the English voice of Soviet leaders," recalled a moment from Nikita Khrushchev's his visit to America in 1959. The First Secretary of the Communist Party of the Soviet Union stated in a tone that brooked no objection that Soviet citizens have no interest in owning either an apartment or a car. While translating Khrushchev's words into English, Sukhodrev thought to himself: "But I want a car! I want an apartment!" His was certainly not an isolated case. In Moscow, crowds of onlookers habitually gathered in places where the cars of Western diplomats were parked, admiring the limousines of the West. American correspondent of the United Press International agency Aline Mosby claimed that her British MGA sports car, which she drove around the Soviet capital, was the city's greatest attraction after Lenin's mummy.[429] Only with the government shake-up of 1964 did a significant change occur.

2.4.6 The Automotive Thaw

The first signs of change in the Polish authorities' approach to private motorisation appeared, not unexpectedly, in the spring of 1952. On the pages of

---

426 L. H. Siegelbaum, *Cars for Comrades*, pp. 217–218, 224.
427 *The Grapes of Wrath*, dir. John Ford (1940
428 J. Urry, "Życie za kółkiem", p. 423.
429 Ibid., pp. 224–226.

Przekrój (*The Cross*-Section the iconic Polish weekly socio-cultural magazine), Wiktor Lenczewski began a twenty-four part series entitled "Easy driving course."[430] In the first part, he wrote: "Our country is motorising at a dizzying pace. In Lublin and Starachowice, we build trucks; in Żerań, the beautiful and modern 'Warszawa'."[431] The second part included a rather suggestive description of the crowded streets of Moscow, populated by thousands of small and commonplace Moskvitches.[432] As Justyna Jaworska rightly observes, this section was likely intended to forestall "charges from the censor that [the article] promoted a consumerist and petty-bourgeois lifestyle."[433] In subsequent parts, readers of the *Przekrój* learned about the technicalities of brakes, engines, etc. Of course, the entire series and its successor ("How to Drive") were written with the weekly's typical absurd sense of humour.[434] However, this does not change the fact that *Przekrój* started promoting the development of private motorisation, and would continue to do so for more than a decade.

Another signal came from Witold Rychter,[435] a prewar promoter of motor sports and a pioneer of motorisation, then an appraiser and court expert in car accident cases, and later co-creator of the Highway Code of 1961. In the spring of 1954, Rychter published an article entitled "Problemy samochodu ludowego" (The Problem of the Popular Car) in *Horyzonty Techniki*. His starting point was the fact that leading miners were being rewarded with passenger cars and motorcycles. He continued: "Isn't it possible for more citizens in our country to own a car? As the theses proclaim, the national wealth is increasing … . [T]he possibility of purchasing a car is becoming

430 The series began in no. 371 (1952).

431 W. Lenczewski, "Łatwy kurs kierowania samochodem. Lekcja 1," *Przekrój* 1952, no. 371, p. 13.

432 W. Lenczewski, "Łatwy kurs kierowania samochodem. Lekcja 2," *Przekrój* 1952, no. 372, p. 13.

433 J. Jaworska, *Cywilizacja* Przekroju. *Misja obyczajowa w magazynie ilustrowanym*, Warszawa 2008, p. 212.

434 The first part of the new series by Władysław Podżega was published in November 1952. (*Przekrój* 1952, no. 396).

435 Witold Rychter wrote many books on automotive topics, as well as memoirs (*Moje dwa i cztery kółka*, Warszawa 1983), in which he describes the beginnings of motorisation in the Second Polish Republic and the postwar period, along with his activities in the promotion of motorisation and motorsports.

more and more realistic. However, we are only interested in cars that are accessible for us in terms of both price and operational usefulness. The time is approaching when each of us workers in the socialist industry will be able to purchase a car without much effort."[436] It was impossible to avoid the slogans of the period, but the author managed to smuggle a few facts into the text (apart from quite obvious criticism of the car currently in production, i.e. the Warszawa) that did not fully fit into the communist value system. According to him:

> When we talk about a car, we think not only about the pleasure of a relaxing Sunday ride or a vacation spent roaming around in a car among the most beautiful surroundings. A car is also a convenient means of transportation …; it is a vehicle that takes us from the suburb to the workplace; a vehicle that will allow a doctor to quickly reach a patient in the countryside and wherever there is no convenient transport, but there is a road; a vehicle—that will allow you to complete tasks, perform the work of a travelling instructor, a veterinarian, an agrobiologist…[437]

So not only pleasure, but above all, work. Then, Rychter listed the most important features of the people's car (identical to those identified by Ferdinand Porsche): affordability, economical operation, sufficient interior capacity, durability. Of note is the issue of price; Rychter assumed that such a vehicle should be available to working people—"a higher-earning worker or a working member of the intelligentsia."[438] Moreover, even before, when individual passenger car owners were mentioned (rarely though that happened), they were leading workers, the working intelligentsia, writers, artists, and academics.[439] In August 1955, Rychter further developed his views on the trends in individual motorisation. This time, however, his text contained a large dose of

---

436 W. Rychter, "Problemy samochodu ludowego," *Horyzonty Techniki* 1954, no. 2, p. 50.

437 Ibid.

438 Ibid., p. 51.

439 S. Askans, "Fabryka Samochodów Osobowych—widomy symbol pomocy ZSRR," *Technika Motoryzacyjna* 1953, no. 7, p. 318. In early 1956, A. Marczewski and R. Lange wrote in *Motoryzacja*: "There is an automotive hunger among members of the creative associations: artists, writers, architects, actors, and journalists, as well as among the professional intelligentsia: engineers, doctors, and veterinarians, and finally, among a large crowd of economic activists"; A. Marczewski and R. Lange, "Głos w sprawie motoryzacji," *Motoryzacja* 1956, no. 1, p. 24.

information about the so-called toy cars—vehicles ranging in size between a motorcycle and a small car, often three-wheelers, which were relatively cheap to operate due to their dimensions and performance.[440] Rychter suggested that the construction and production of such a "micro-car," modelled on the German Goggomobil or the Italian Isetta (or built under licence), should represent the initial stage of the motorisation of the Polish society.[441]

The question of a car for the masses was subsequently raised by other authors. There were, for instance, overviews of makes and models of the small cars that were taking Western European markets by storm at the time. Kazimierz Studziński reported that in 1953, the West German automotive industry produced over 500,000 cars per year, 75% of which were popular cars, and 25% medium-sized vehicles. In France, popular cars accounted for almost half of the total production, the leaders being the Renault 4CV (68,000) and Citroën 2CV (almost 25,000).[442] An important contribution came from engineer Fryderyk Bluemke, a designer of combustion engines. His two articles addressed basically the same issue—the creation of a popular car for the working world. Bluemke recommended the commencement of work on the construction of a four-wheeled vehicle with a load capacity of 200 kg and a weight of 400 kg (for comparison, the popular Polish "Maluch" weighed around 600 kg) such as the Renault 2CV or the IFA P40 models. The article also included a comparison of several dozen models of small cars with technical data.[443] Bluemke's articles prompted a lively reaction, but the political events that completely changed the reality in the country had already taken place by then.

---

440 W. Rychter, "Samochodziki," *Horyzonty Techniki* 1955, no. 8, pp. 353–359; see also: "Jeszcze o samochodzikach," *Horyzonty Techniki*" 1955, no. 12, pp. 536–537.

441 W. Rychter also mentioned local amateur designers, whose vehicles, which tended to bear cute names such as Hortek (after the title of *Horyzonty Techniki*) or SAM ("Samochód amatorski tygodnika Motor," Amateur Car of *Motor* weekly), were frequent examples of coping with car hunger on one's own; W. Rychter, "Samochodziki," p. 358.

442 K. Studziński, "Samochody popularne państw zachodnich i NRD," *Technika Motoryzacyjna* 1954, no. 10, p. 310.

443 F. Bluemke, "Rozważania nad polskim samochodzikiem," *Horyzonty Techniki* 1956, no. 9, pp. 394–398; F. Bluemke and M. Łukawski, "Samochodzik popularny dla świata pracy," *Technika Motoryzacyjna* 1956, no. 9, pp. 298–301.

Clearly, the development of motorisation behind the Iron Curtain was slowly coming into view in Poland in the mid-1950s. Some circles associated with the automotive industry tried to put pressure on those in power, using the written word to persuade them to take the matter into closer consideration. However, these activities were very limited in scope. Change only became possible after the government shake-up in 1956.

In Second Gear under Gomułka

3.1 Course change—the year 1956

The year 1956 was a watershed—not only in political terms. The 20th Congress of the Communist Party of the Soviet Union, the death of Bolesław Bierut, the June events in Poznań, the uprising in Hungary and the return of Władysław Gomułka—all these events demonstrated that the previous formula of exercising power had exhausted itself, and taken together, they represented a new opening for the society. As one reader, nicknamed "Kibic," wrote in *Życie Warszawy*: "October 1956 is here. Maybe you never thought about it, but this date means different things to different groups of people. … For some, October means the chance to meet family in the East or West. For others, a return to an abandoned workshop. And for others still, getting rid of a 'hump' in their biography."[444] People began to talk much more boldly about consumer needs that had been ignored by the authorities. As one writer put it in *Motor* in 1956, "[i]n the life of the Polish nation, 1956 was a watershed. We changed some of our assumptions, straightened-out concepts—in other words, restored proper meaning."[445] There was hope that the "straightened-out concepts" would also include "individual motorisation." This sentiment was echoed by "Kibic": "Right, but what about motorisation?"[446] Stefan Kisielewski, a prominent composer, writer, and journalist, came up with an "automotive" joke: "Poland is like a broken car, and in October, when they

444 Kibic, "No i co z tą motoryzacją?" *Życie Warszawy*, December 15–16, 1957 r., p. 3.
445 K. Wilczyński, "Rok 'Nijaki'. Ostatnie kartki kalendarza," *Motor* 1956, no. 52, p. 4.
446 Kibic, "No i co z tą motoryzacją?"

started repairs on it, they only fixed the horn."[447] "Former car assembler" Stanisław Lem wrote in *Przekrój* in 1957:

> The days when a private car had to hide beneath a rusty body are behind us. No more mimicry of chipped paint or bent sides. Wartburgs no longer attract the attention of dumbstruck natives; Warszawas, tiddler Fiats (600 s), Multiplas, occasionally Standards, Spartaks, and Moskvitches, and from time to time a ZIM or some whale of a beast from across the seas now grace the streets of Kraków and Warsaw, lying modestly in wait outside city houses. The only thing that can maybe still make passers-by kneel and peek at the "bottom" is the latest, glassed-out "American." Thus, we are cautiously entering a new stage in the motorisation of the country.[448]

The signal for criticism arrived with the 8th Plenum of the Central Committee of the PZPR. Alongside the reckoning with Poland's Stalinist past came criticism of its failed economic investments. At the plenum, the topic of the FSO factory at Żerań was raised several times. On the second day, Władysław Gomułka criticised both the size of the Żerań factory and the Warszawa automobile that it produced, emphasising the high costs and the small number of manufactured cars of a kind that "probably no one in the world produces today."[449] Hilary Minc tried to defend the achievements in motorisation, linking problems with the Żerań factory with lagging investments in industrial infrastructure. Defending the Warszawa, he pointed out that it was "currently the best car available in the [socialist] camp."[450] This did nothing, however, to change the common opinion about the quality of products of the Żerań factory. Gomułka's words marked a turning point, signalling that open criticism of decision-makers and their policy towards private car owners became permissible.

The post-October wave of criticism affected not only the decision-making centre; calls for a settling of accounts were addressed at almost all levels of power.[451] The Politburo of the Central Committee of the PZPR decided that,

---

[447] J. Zawieyski, *Dzienniki*, vol. 1, Warszawa 2011, p. 384.

[448] S. Lem, "O polskiej drodze do motoryzacji," *Przekrój* 1957, no. 645, p. 20.

[449] "VIII Plenum KC PZPR," *Nowe Drogi. Organ teoretyczny i polityczny Komitetu Centralnego Polskiej Zjednoczonej Partii Robotniczej* 1956, no. 10, p. 22.

[450] Ibid., p. 126.

[451] Cf. A. Leszczyński, *Sprawy do załatwienia. Listy do* Po prostu *1955–1957*, Warszawa 2000, p. 26.

given the general public belief that the expenses on the highest administrators of the state were unjustified, some privileges had to be limited. It was noted that certain comrades and their families showed no moderation or modesty in the exploitation of these privileges. Limitations were thus imposed on the number of cars designated for personal use, now reduced from two to one, although the possibility of purchasing vehicles in instalments was retained.[452] Merely a year earlier, Wiktor Eugeniusz Nowakowski wrote in his diary: "Now that workers are the dictatorial class, they look with concern, if not hatred, at the lines of beautiful, luxury cars of foreign brands standing in front of a special shop for the chosen few, opposite our cooperative on Puławska Street. A shop stocked with everything."[453] When Indian Prime Minister Jawaharlal Nehru visited Warsaw in June 1955, Nowakowski observed: "Foreign and domestic dignitaries parading by in cars brings to mind the reaction of all those who were envious of car owners before the war. ... In the past, capitalists were envied by communists, today former capitalists envy communists, or rather those calling themselves communists."[454] A similar observation was recorded by poet and essayist Mieczysław Jastrun in his diary at the beginning of April 1955.[455] Leopold Tyrmand, writer, publicist, and intellectual, in turn, wrote: "I reckon that an armed uprising against the regime, if it ever comes, will begin at bus stops in just such [unmercifully cold] weather. I have not seen such a savage hatred in the eyes of the unemployed in the West seeing millionaires drive past in their cars as I found in the gaze of Varsovians who saw pass the limousines of communist dignitaries after waiting for hours for their bur to come."[456]

Yet, it was not the dignitaries' limousines that caused the greatest resentment. People noticed that, while the authorities spent almost the entire post-war period trying to prove that the private automobile was an ideologically foreign concept, entire swathes of the society, usually those in positions of power, enjoyed easier access to this forbidden fruit without it being perceived

452 AAN, Władysław Dworakowski—spuścizna, sygn. 471/11, Notatka dla Biura Politycznego KC PZPR w sprawie ograniczenia przywilejów materialnych dla działaczy państwowych, partyjnych, związkowych i wojskowych, [15 X 1956 r.], pp. 268–270.

453 W. E. Nowakowski, "Okruchy systemu," *Karta* 2014, no. 76, p. 91.

454 Ibid., p. 94.

455 M. Jastrun, *Dziennik 1955–1981*, Kraków 2002, p. 14.

456 L. Tyrmand, *Diary 1954*, Evanston, 2014, p. 159.

as a sin against the communist way of life. Meetings of the Central Unit against Fraud and Corruption are a perfect showcase for the extent of this phenomenon. At its meetings, the words "automobile" or "motorcycles" came up all the time. As a participant in a meeting in late November 1957 put it: "I understand that the director has an automobile, I have nothing against it, but I don't agree with the fact that he has three, because that's out of order." Nevertheless, three cars were not the highest number on record. One of the directors of the Katowice fish central, already serving a sentence for abuse of power, reportedly owned six cars and a motorboat. From this perspective, the two cars owned by "the guy from Motozbyt on a [salary of] 1,500 zlotys" hardly made an impression.[457]

The demand for "socialist justice" was also expressed in letters addressed to central authorities. One anonymous letter addressed to Polskie Radio (*Polish Radio*) and Trybuna Ludu (*People's Tribune*, the official press organ of the Central Committee of the Polish United Workers' Party) states: "We ask whether the handsome fee of a few thousand zlotys earned through car speculation is less of a swindle than when a driver smuggles a passenger and gets fired for it?" The letter was inspired by a case involving a member of the directorial staff of the Ministry of Construction who sold passenger cars, including a Citroën, purchased as surplus from the Security Service. He then reportedly sold the cars at a significant profit. The Ministry of Control became interested in the matter, but—as the letter stated—the audit revealed no irregularities. Nevertheless, the author concluded: "We will not go far this way, because when the head rots and stinks, the stench and putrefaction will spread to the entire country, until everything collapses and we'll have another Poznań…"[458]

Similar sentiments were expressed in an article published in the December 1956 issue of *Motoryzacja*, which reads, for instance:

> Over the last eight years, we have built a powerful automotive industry, which is not far behind that of Czechoslovakia in terms of production space, and boasts

---

[457] AAN, Komitet Centralny Polskiej Zjednoczonej Partii Robotniczej (hereafter: KC PZPR), sygn. 237/XXXII-7, Materiały z narady z 27 XI 1957 r., pp. 9, 16, 19; cf. ibid., sygn. 237/XXXII-9, Informacja z pracy zespołów do walki z nadużyciami i korupcją, Warszawa, 7 XII 1957 r., p. 22.

[458] Ibid., sygn. 237/XXVII-23, Biuletyn no. 41/209, Warszawa, 12 VIII 1957 r., pp. 4–5.

> modern machines, presses, and equipment that make it undoubtedly the best among all the people's democracies, including the USSR. We are millionaires, Polish Fords, and yet we go about by foot and without shoes; if this situation in the industry persists, we may end up going without pants. … If Eisenach, with three heavy presses, churns out 16,000 "Wartburgs" this year, and 22,000 the next, and Żerań, with more than 25 presses, makes 6,000 "Warszawas," and that while roof and floor moldings are shipped from Gorky, this fact speaks for itself.[459]

The author of the article also criticised the idea of purchasing a licence for and initiating production of a micro-car in Poland (an idea of Fryderyk Bluemke). Although he agreed that micro-cars were an important means of motorisation, filling the gap between a motorcycle and a larger car, he used technical and operational data to prove that they brought limited savings, and when it came to driving comfort, especially considering Poland's poor road conditions, a micro-car was not a good solution.[460] This opinion was echoed by Tadeusz Szujski, who saw micro-cars as an important addition to the vehicle fleet, next to scooters, motorcycles, and small- and medium-displacement cars. Potential buyers consisted of "many thousands of active workers, thus far relatively low-paid, with various specialties, often of an advanced age."[461] Even the writer, poet, and publicist Jerzy Putrament, who was not perceived as an advocate for motorisation, wrote in a column in *Życie Warszawy*:

> If our authorities treat passenger cars as a luxury both today and tomorrow, and even in the rather distant future, when socialism is established in Poland—one

459 Z. Mróz, "Nasze kłopoty motoryzacyjne," *Motoryzacja* 1956, no. 12, p. 309.

460 *Idem*, "Jeszcze o mikrosamochodach," *Motoryzacja* 1957, no. 5, pp. 138–139. This opinion corresponds to the situation of micro-cars on Western markets at the time. By then, they had been operating in quite limited numbers, and the boom was largely caused by the international situation (Suez crisis), which resulted in fuel problems—a return to gasoline rationing in Great Britain. However, it quickly turned out that this was actually the beginning of the end for "toy cars." Fuel problems prompted car companies to devise cars with greater driving comfort than micro-cars but with similar economics of use; L. J. K. Setright, *Drive On! A Social History of the Motor Car*, London 2002, p. 174ff. The "twilight of micro-cars" was correctly predicted in Poland by Kazimierz Loesch ("Rozwój samochodzików w Europie," *Technika Motoryzacyjna* 1957, no. 12, p. 417). See also S. Brzosko, "Niektóre zagadnienia związane z małym samochodem popularnym," *Technika Motoryzacyjna* 1958, no. 8, pp. 289–294.

461 T. Szujski, "Samochodzik ma rację bytu w Polsce," *Technika Motoryzacyjna* 1956, no. 11, p. 367.

> has little hope for even a small, but rapid improvement in today's disastrous state of affairs. ... The car has already become an indispensable everyday household item in leading capitalist countries, not only for the bourgeoisie. The car greatly increases the productivity of its user. [...] To hell with these red signs that push Polish motorisation into dead ends.[462]

The editorial office of *Po Prostu* received a particularly interesting letter containing a proposed solution to the "automobile problem." Its sender believed that instead of expensive limousines for dignitaries, a greater number of cheaper cars should be purchased, and some of the money saved in the process could be used to buy motorcycles for "ordinary" people: "While this is a fantastical image, I see no reason why it can't be implemented in the near future."[463] A survey published by *Motoryzacja* (the question was: "What should be done so that Poland is motorised as quickly as possible and at the lowest possible cost?") received responses from various circles, both technical experts and ordinary citizens. The tenor of the emotions sensed by Poles waiting for their own four wheels is illustrated by a note from the editors, informing readers that many of the answers could not be published because "they contain unprintable statements addressed to those responsible for the current condition of our motorisation." However, balanced voices generally prevailed, though not without a pinch of malice: "Today, we are building our own road to socialism, let us finally see proper cars on it and in appropriate numbers. Let owning a car not be, not the attribute of a well-connected dignitary, but the privilege of the working man. Let the problem of acquiring spare parts not become an international issue, and the purchase of a tyre or inner tube not lead down the shady paths of smugglers from Czechoslovakia."[464]

Lesław Łowczyński demonstrated a very sober view of the problem, analysing the purchasing power of the Poles, the likely price of a small-displacement vehicle (most respondents were of the opinion that the price should not exceed 30,000 zlotys), and the annual operating costs, to find that it was impossible for people earning 5,500 zlotys to obtain the 150,000 zlotys that was presumed necessary for the purchase

---

462 J. Putrament, "Rozmyślania kierowcy (Sprawa rozwoju polskiej motoryzacji)," *Życie Warszawy*, October 6, 1956, p. 3.

463 Quoted in: A. Leszczyński, *Sprawy do załatwienia*, p. 27.

464 "Nasi czytelnicy mówią," *Motoryzacja* 1957, no. 5, p. 121.

and maintenance of a car. Thus, Poland would need to turn to microcars, which—in Łowczyński's opinion—could be produced by "small workshops around the country."[465] A more comprehensive solution to the problem was proposed by Adam Popiel, who focused primarily on the development of automobile production in Poland broadly defined, that is, on the possibility of purchasing a licence for a small car, such as the German Goggomobil or the Italian Fiat 600, a reduction in the number of medium-displacement Warszawas being produced, and the development of the small-displacement Syrena, a long anticipated car that was still not available for sale.[466]

3.2 The "parliament of polish motorisation"

On January 7 and 8, 1957, a meeting was held in Warsaw, attended by representatives of ministries and several institutions involved in transport and motorisation. Among the initiators of the meeting were: the Automotive Circle of the Scientific and Technical Association of Polish Mechanical Engineers and Technicians, the Automotive Section of the Scientific and Technical Association of Transportation Engineers and Technicians, and the Transport Economics Section of the Polish Economic Society. Over the course of two days, six papers were delivered on automotive issues and their importance for state policy. During discussions, several harsh words were uttered against decision-makers responsible for the state of motorisation. For those taking part in the meeting, there was no doubt that it could only take place because of the events of 1956.[467] Mieczysław Madeyski drew attention both to the fact that Poland lagged behind other European countries (Poland was 17th, out of 22, in terms of the number of cars, ahead

465 L. Łowczyński, "Samochodzik czy samochód popularny dla świata pracy," *Technika Motoryzacyjna* 1957, no. 2, pp. 70–71

466 A. Popiel, "W sprawie samochodu popularnego," p. 72.

467 "The 20th Congress of the Communist Party of the Soviet Union, and more recently the 8th Plenum of our Party, have created an ideal opportunity for correcting the mistakes of the past and embarking on a path that corresponds to the role that we should play among the family of nations building socialism"; "Krajowa Narada Motoryzacyjna w dniach 7 i 8 stycznia 1957 roku w Warszawie," *Technika Motoryzacyjna* 1957, no. 3, p. 77.

only of Yugoslavia, Hungary, Romania, and Bulgaria) and to state policies that prevented the development of individual motorisation.[468] Referring to Madeyski's speech, one participant, Wiktor Sudra from the Warsaw University of Technology—who had been involved in assessing the Fiat factory project in the late 1940s[469]—compared the situation of car owners during the Second Polish Republic and in the twelve postwar years, reaching a bleak conclusion. According to him, "[t]he thesis must be clearly put forward that no car means economic illiteracy, economic backwardness; it represents the main obstacle to economic development of the country." He also spoke of a "lack of understanding [regarding the development of individual motorisation] throughout the past 30 years."[470]

During the meeting, participants once again directed criticism at misguided investments of the Six-Year Plan. They agreed that the country should focus its attention on producing a small-displacement car and pointed to Western European countries as paradigmatic examples for the development of the automotive industry; the clear implication was that they would serve as a potential source of licences. Kazimierz Loesch from the Design Office of the Automotive Industry said: "The Soviet automotive industry, on which we have relied so far, represent a high level of technology and technological experimentation, but in terms of design, the automotive industry of other countries is at a higher level. Such is the case with industries of England, France, and the German Federal Republic."[471] However, the most lasting effect of the meeting was the proposal for an Automotive Council (Rada Motoryzacyjna, RM) as an advisory body to the government. The decision to establish such a council was announced in September 1957,[472] and its first meeting took place on January 3, 1958.[473] According to the resolution that constituted the council, the responsibilities of the 27-member body included, among others: developing prospective projects for the advancement of the automotive industry; offering opinions on prototypes of motor vehicles and

---

468 "Sejm polskiej motoryzacji," *Motor* 1957, no. 3, pp. 8–9.

469 *Słownik Biograficzny Techników Polskich*, no. 6, Warszawa 1995, p. 142.

470 "Sejm polskiej motoryzacji," p. 10.

471 "Krajowa Narada Motoryzacyjna w dniach 7 i 8 stycznia 1957 r. w Warszawie," *Technika Motoryzacyjna* 1957, no. 4, pp. 154–155, 158–159, 162.

472 "Monitor Polski" (hereafter: M.P.) 1957, no. 81, pos. 487.

473 M. Madeyski, "Rada Motoryzacyjna 1958," *Motoryzacja* 1958, no. 1, pp. 1–4.

in the matter of prices for vehicles and consumables; as well as proposing motions and offering opinions on urban solutions and adapting them to the requirements of motorisation. The council's first chairman was Ryszard Strzelecki, then-Minister of Transportation.[474] It should be emphasised that the council had no executive power; its role was purely advisory. It was a forum for exchanging views and shaping opinions, one significant for the official state policy on motorisation was unclear. Simply put, it was a safety valve.[475]

---

474 Ibid. The full composition of the Automotive Council was as follows: chairman Ryszard Strzelecki (Minister of Transportation); deputies Kiejstut Żemajtis (Minister of Heavy Industry), Lieutenant General Jerzy Bordziowski (Chief of the General Staff of the Polish Army), Professor Adam Minchejmer (Warsaw University of Technology); secretary: Jan Rustecki (Ministry of Transportation); members of the praesidium: Wiktor Sudra (Warsaw University of Technology), Marian Madeyski (Szczecin University of Technology); members: Kazimierz Olszewski (Ministry of Chemical Industry), Henryk Mania (Ministry of Small Industry and Crafts), Piotr Stolarek (Ministry of Municipal Economy), Gen. Cezary Nowak, Stanisław Mroczek, Antoni Tymaniecki, Jan Kon, Stefan Halicki, Jerzy Koszyk, Edward Laskus, Jan Dąbrowski, Aleksander Rostocki, Roman Pijanowski, Leonard Tomaszewski, Mieczysław Dembicki, Jerzy Werner, Zygmunt Filipowicz, Zbigniew Makarczyk, Jerzy Grodecki, Mieczysław Wantoła.

475 However, this does not change the fact that many automotive plans and hypotheses developed by the RM working teams turned out in retrospect to have accurately predicted the direction in which the Polish automotive industry was heading. One of the most important documents presented by the Automotive Council were guidelines adopted in 1964, entitled "The automotive economy in the future perspective, 1961–1980," which consisted of a two-part study on "Automotive economy 1961–1980—a comprehensive summary of sectional plans in the prospective plan for the development of motorisation in Poland." These were supposed to be directional guidelines for further action within the framework of the subsequent five-year plans. Two years earlier, the council adopted resolution no. 4/18/62 concerning passenger car needs in Poland in the years 1962–1980. It included the following paragraph: "The development of individual motorisation is closely related to the development of economic life and the technical and organisational progress of the society. The desirability of the development of individual motorisation and the appropriateness of popularising the use of passenger vehicles as individual means of transportation results from the significant saving in social time, increasing overall efficiency and enabling rest and recreation. In addition, the development of domestic production and an increase in the number of vehicles contribute to an increase in the share of services in relation to production, which is beneficial for the national economy." One of the most important tasks facing decision-makers was to achieve such a level of motorisation in society that the development of motorisation would primarily

Half a year after the meeting, the need for changes in the matter of motorisation and the direction that they should take were discussed during a joint meeting of parliamentary committees on Heavy Industry, Chemical Industry and Mining, and Transportation and Communications. In addition to parliamentarians, the discussion was attended by representatives of the Ministry of Transportation, the Ministry of Heavy Industry, universities, and members of the Planning Commission of the Council of Ministers, a body that replaced the liquidated PKPG. The introductory speech was delivered by a representative of the Ministry of Heavy Industry, who painted a rather dark picture of the Polish automotive industry. In terms of the number of inhabitants per car (670), Poland occupied a very low position in Europe, far behind Western countries (the ratio for Italy was 64:1), as well as some of the Eastern Bloc countries (for example, Czechoslovakia, where the ratio was 94:1). Moreover, the structure of the fleet was completely different than in Western countries, because in Poland, the number of trucks was twice as high as that of passenger cars. The conclusion was obvious: "We have too few passenger cars." Moreover, the report highlighted problems that plagued the Polish automotive industry, which—due to insufficient materials but also high financial outlays—was unable to produce a larger number of better-quality products. At one point, the Żerań FSO even had to stop the production of Warszawa cars because of a shortage of … cotton wool and thread. The prospective plan prepared at the Ministry anticipated that by 1970, the Polish automotive industry would be able to produce over 120,000 passenger cars per year. Aside from production volume, the range of available cars would also increase: the Warszawa, already in production, would be joined by the Syrena, slowly entering production, as well as a popular car and a micro-car. The report announced that the Warszawa would be replaced over time by a more modern construction. In the discussion that concluded the meeting, the ministry representative presented an interesting—indeed, bold—vision for the direction the Polish automotive industry was to follow: motorcycles, trucks, and medium-displacement passenger `cars were to be produced based on domestic designs, and popular small-displacement cars would be licenced from the West, but only if a large enough scale of production was agreed

depend on the supply of vehicles; *Prace Rady Motoryzacyjnej 1958–1964*, Warszawa 1965, pp. 45, 72.

upon. The Warszawa would be modernised and remain in production until the early 1960s, but Polish engineers would concurrently work on the design of a car intended to eventually replace the vehicle assembled at FSO since 1951. Additionally, the Żerań factory, which had been so far reportedly running at about 40% capacity, would achieve full production, i.e. 25,000 cars per year, thanks to—among other changes—being provided with missing machinery needed for the purpose. Poland's automobile industry would also devote more attention to the aesthetics of the manufactured vehicles. For this purpose, a plan was conceived to establish cooperation with specialists, including from Italy.[476]

3.3 Finding our own way: cooperation, licensing, or…

Another recurring theme in the debate on motorisation was the issue of a possible cooperation among socialist bloc countries in the production of their own cars. It was obvious to Polish authors that the requirements for the production of their own car were too high, and practically speaking, the only path forward involved partnerships within the bloc. In this regard, there were two candidates—Czechoslovakia and the German Democratic Republic. Although nothing came of these plans, it is worth noting that a new element had appeared in official statements: the socioeconomic importance of the development of motorisation was recognised to a far greater extent than before. For a growing number of experts, a car meant an increase in the technological advancement of the society and an improvement in the everyday life. There were even some "pleasures" that could be derived from owning a car.[477] In *Przegląd Techniczny*, Jan Dąbrowski drew attention to the

---

[476] AAN, Kancelaria Sejmu, sygn. 150, Protokół ze wspólnego 9. posiedzenia Komisji Przemysłu Ciężkiego, Chemicznego i Górnictwa oraz Komisji Komunikacji i Łączności, 5 VI 1957 r., pp. 212–227.

[477] J. Piastowski, "…nam jeździć zakazano," *Rada Robotnicza* 1960, no. 6, p. 4. On the cooperation between socialist countries in the production of vehicles, see e.g. D. Fikus, "Samochód—marzenie i rzeczywistość," *Polityka* 1965, no. 19, p. 8; E. Waszczuk, "Znaki zapytania motoryzacji," *Życie Warszawy*, December 7, 1961, p. 3; L. Ciamaga, "Tani samochód," *Życie Gospodarcze* 1959, no. 50, p. 5; J. Bujniewicz, "W sprawie taniego samochodu," *Życie Gospodarcze* 1960, no. 8, p. 8; A. Rostocki, "Rozszerzmy

simple "desire to have one's own vehicle," a desire that was becoming a true "social phenomenon."[478]

Interestingly, opinions disputing the need to develop individual motorisation were very rare. One example is an opinion piece published in *Prasa Polska*, whose author, Tadeusz Sznurkowski, commented on the discussion taking place in the press, questioning whether the alarmist tones were justified. He argued:

> Judging by the amount of materials our press publishes on automotive topics … one would assume that these are everyday items that most of the society cannot do without. The numbers indicate that [only] several tens of thousands of people in Poland have their own passenger cars. … Due to their price and maintenance costs, cars are available only to a relatively small group of people with high earnings. Buying a car is within their means. Most importantly, they feel the need to have one. … However, the press is full of descriptions of cars and their production. They contain photos and descriptions of prototypes, both domestic and foreign, of various types. … It puts forward countless proposals that, if implemented, would put Poland among the world leaders in terms of motorisation.[479]

While the argument is not entirely valid (the author did not even see the possibility of technical advancement offered by the development of motorisation), he raised a rather important issue—the purchasing power of the Polish society. In 1961, Aleksander Rostocki soberly assessed the situation in *Życie Warszawy*: "We are not currently in economic conditions that would enable a dynamic development of individual motorisation (passenger cars). However, efforts should be made to enable those who want to possess a car to fulfill their desire."[480]

However, the most important contribution to the discussion on the direction of development of Polish motorisation came with an article published in

---

motoryzacyjną współpracę KDL," *Życie Gospodarcze* 1960, no. 11, p. 4; I. Gawryluk, "Mariaż samochodowy NRD–Polska," *Życie Warszawy*, March 27, 1963, p. 3.

478 J. Dąbrowski, "Prywatne samochody osobowe warunkiem szybkiego rozwoju naszej motoryzacji," *Przegląd Techniczny* 1959, no. 21, pp. 16–18.

479 T. Sznurkowski, "Pod dyskusję: słuszna polityka czy przysłowiowa 'kropla wody'?" *Prasa Polska* 1958, no. 8, pp. 10–11.

480 A. M. Rostocki, "Nie jestem przeciwnikiem motoryzacji," *Życie Warszawy*, December 27, 1961 r., pp. 3–4.

Polityka in 1969, entitled "For a socio-cultural concept of motorisation."[481] At the time, its author—Józef Pajestka—was deputy chairman of the Planning Commission. The text was very balanced and emphasised the still-limited purchasing power of the Poles. Above all, Pajestka tried to dispel the belief that a car was a luxury good. According to him, this was an idea "imported" together with Western cars, alien to the realities of socialism, but common in large Polish cities. For the car to play a specific socio-cultural role, strengthening social bonds, facilitating communication, and accelerating overall progress, it needed to have a presence not so much in large cities, as in small-town Poland. Pajestka argued: "I think that no other product of material civilisation could change life in the 'province' as profoundly as the car." In conclusion, he stated: "The car is a wonderful product of human material civilisation. Used properly, it can serve as an extremely important lever of socialism's socio-cultural and economic progress."[482]

After the article was published, the editorial office of *Polityka* received many letters of support for the ideas expressed by its author. Wróblewski, who had published a piece on a similar topic in the same weekly a year before,[483] decided to follow the author's trail to Radomsko, the city Pajestka had described in his article. Once there, he found that the need for a car was indeed great: "First of all, no one had any ideological objections against such a vehicle, and no one was afraid that poorer folks would envy the rich, that motorists would drive wherever they wanted, etc. It was estimated that if such vehicles could be bought without any restrictions, soon there would be

481 J. Pajestka, "O społeczno-kulturową koncepcję motoryzacji," *Polityka* 1969, no. 3, p. 3.

482 For more on the circumstances of the publication of J. Pajestka's article, see M. Rakowski, *Dzienniki polityczne 1969–1971*, Warszawa 2001, pp. 10–11; see also M. Jastrząb, "The idea of developed socialist society and a private car" (I would like to thank the author for sharing this text).

483 In 1968, A. K. Wróblewski published an article in the weekly entitled "Gdyby utopia miała kółka" (If utopia had wheels), in which he tried to answer the question whether Polish society was able to afford a cheap car. Censors reacted to the article, concerned that writing about the automotive industry could trigger a "consumptionist mood" among Poles; they were also put off by the journalist's pessimistic tone. Officials reviewing Wróblewski's text even suggested that it be transferred to another, less widely read magazine; A. Kozieł, "Prasa w latach 1944–1989," in: *Prasa, radio i telewizja w Polsce. Zarys dziejów*, ed. D. Grzelewska et al., Warszawa 1999, pp. 152–153.

six thousand of them in the county, compared to only six hundred now."[484] The article was seized by a censor. However, other voices came through, only strengthened Pajestka's arguments. Bolesław Adamczewski laid even more stress on the role of motorisation in the lives of young people ("young people prefer to snobs in a car, rather than workers on foot") and the fact that, even as the society was becoming richer, a car—specifically, a Fiat 125p—was an unattainable product for the majority: "In all or almost all important areas of material life, the distance between Poland and rich countries ... is being reduced. ... However, in the field of motorisation, we are far behind. We won't catch up with them in a Fiat 125p."[485]

However, it was not expert opinions that changed the official policy towards private motoring. Only with the shake-up in state leadership and the replacement of Władysław Gomułka by Edward Gierek in 1970 did far-reaching changes occur in this field. Comrade Wiesław's reign since 1956 had raised hopes, but as for their fulfilment, however partial, it would only arrive under his successor.

3.4 Praise the positives, discreetly ignore the negatives

The political thaw of 1956 also affected the heavy industry, which until then had been focused primarily on military needs. Part of the released processing capacity could now be directed to civilian production. The resolution of June 21, 1956 of the Praesidium of the Government of the PRL required that plants subordinate to the Ministry of the Automotive Industry which were not "sufficiently burdened with special production in the 5-Year Plan" produce consumer goods.[486]

---

[484] A. K. Wróblewski, *Polska na kółkach*, Warszawa 1989, p. 29.

[485] B. Adamczewski, "Bez uprzedzeń," *Polityka* 1969, no. 5, p. 5.

[486] AAN, Urząd Rady Ministrów, Kancelaria Tajna (hereafter: URM KT), sygn. 218/3, Uchwała Prezydium Rządu Polskiej Rzeczypospolitej Ludowej no. 391/56 z 21 VI 1956 r., pp. 66–68. Among factories covered by the resolution that furnished the automotive industry were: the Kraśnik Factory of Metal Articles (Kraśnicka Fabryka Wyrobów Metalowych), the Dębno Metalworks (Zakłady Metalowe), the Bydgoszcz Railroad Signalling Factory (Bydgoska Fabryka Sygnałów Kolejowych), the Precision Tool Factory (Wytwórnia Wyrobów Precyzyjnych) in Czarna Wieś, the Kielce Metalworks), the Installing Equipment Factory (Zakłady Wytwórcze Sprzętu Instalacyjnego) in

The development of motorisation on the other side of the Iron Curtain proved that, by serving as a catalyst for dramatic advances (mainly technological) throughout the entire economy, the automotive industry could also generate very real profit. Meanwhile, experts from PKPG and MHZ kept abreast of on events in Western Europe.[487] In the mid-1950s, an interesting phenomenon took place there: for the first time, the American car industry, still the world leader in automotive production, saw increasingly serious competition from British and West German exports. Moreover, in both Great Britain and the Federal Republic of Germany, foreign sales mostly involved the highly popular small-displacement cars, many of which also found their way to the American market. In 1953, Great Britain exported passenger cars worth US $270 million; a year later, that value increased to US $306 million. In the same years, Germany's foreign car sales amounted to US $135 million and US $233 million, respectively. West German cars also began to conquer markets where British brands had previously dominated. The values cited above must have made clear to Polish decision-makers how much capital was at stake. Clearly, if the leading automotive industries of Western Europe were to serve as a model, automotive production in socialist economies had to rely on the export potential of passenger cars, primarily small-displacement, with engine size not exceeding 1,200 cm^3. However, equally important for potential Western European buyers were high technical efficiency, economical fuel consumption, and responsiveness to changing fashions. A well-supplied

---

Poniatowa, the Skarżysko-Kamienna Metalworks, and the Radom Metalworks; ibid., Załącznik do uchwały Rządu, pp. 69–70.

487 In June 1956, the Economic Cooperation Department of the Ministry of Foreign Trade conducted introductory talks on establishing cooperation with Swiss companies and institutes in the area of automotive industry. The search for contacts became the responsibility of the Commercial Counsellor's Office in Brno, among others. The Polish government could offer "experience in the field of production technology: passenger cars, trucks, tractors, and tool production …. We imagine a cooperation in the form of an exchange of documentation, bulletins, prospectuses, and factory practices at the cost of the delegating entity." In addition, a sales adviser was tasked with assessing whether the Swiss were interested in passenger cars, trucks, and motorcycles produced in Poland; AAN, Ministerstwo Handlu Zagranicznego (hereafter: MHZ), sygn. 17/3, Wydział Współpracy Gospodarczej [MHZ]—Nawiązanie kontaktów z firmami i instytutami w Szwajcarii, Warszawa, 8 VI 1956 r., unnumbered pages.

service network offering access to spare parts was also important.[488] In short, this list of requirements seemed comprised exclusively of insurmountable obstacles for the automotive industries of Central and Eastern Europe.

Passenger cars produced in Poland, and specifically the only one intended for export—the Warszawa—were far from desirable in the eyes of foreign buyers, especially in the financially attractive Western markets.[489] FSO director Grzegorz Halak, who showed *Horyzonty Techniki* editors around the plant right after production began in November 1951, told them: "Look at everything you want. Praise what is good and criticise what is bad," which was an invitation they eagerly accepted.[490] In early 1958, *Motor* described the first automobile produced in Poland as one that had "the structure and the technical and operational performance at the level of the years 1942–1945, and if we take into account specific indicators and design solutions, even the period before World War II."[491] In spite of this, the Warszawa remained an important component of Polish export. In the years 1954–1956 alone, almost half of all FSO cars were sent abroad, mainly to members of the Communist Bloc, and less often to Asia and Africa.[492] While this direction of exports (to socialist countries) could be justified ideologically ("Under the plan, exports to the USSR and the People's Democracies constitute our contribution to the development of these countries and serve to further expand cooperation with them"[493]), it was clear to everyone that sales within the bloc were forced by the fact that the products of the Żerań factory did not meet global requirements, especially those of Western European markets.

To improve the Warszawa's reputation, advertising campaigns were launched in the mid-1950s, aimed at potential buyers of the cars manufactured

488 AAN, Państwowa Komisja Planowania Gospodarczego (hereafter: PKPG), sygn. 62, Kapitalistyczny rynek maszyn i urządzeń transportowych, Ściśle tajne, 10 I 1955 r., pp. 7–16.

489 Z. M., "M-20 'Warszawa' unowocześniona," *Motoryzacja* 1956, no. 3, pp. 70–72.

490 "M-20 Warszawa schodzi z taśmy," *Horyzonty Techniki* 1951, no. 12, p. 513.

491 *Motor* 1958, no. 3.

492 *Opowieść o FSO*, pp. 158–159.

493 AAN, PKPG, sygn. 482, Omówienie planu handlu zagranicznego na 1951 rok, Warszawa, 1950, p. 16.

at FSO. There were even television commercials. After seeing one of them, Aleksander Rostocki wrote in *Motor* that

> the [advertising] film about the "Warszawa" begins by showing the Żerań plant at work, then one of the engineers goes on holiday in a "Warszawa." On the way, he picks up a "hiker"—a handsome blonde—and while driving with her, he explains the advantages of the "Warszawa." At the same time, the film shows how easily the "Warszawa" handles bad roads (the best part of the film), how well the brakes work, etc. In the end, the driver marries the "hiker" and the "Warszawa" makes their everyday life easier.[494]

Positive reviews of the Warszawa appeared in the press, such as the one published in *Kurier Polski*, which cites Motoimport representatives as saying: "Not a single 'Warszawa' export was returned to us due to alleged poor quality." As they went on to claim: "contrary to the opinion of many domestic 'experts', the 'Warszawa' is regarded on foreign markets as a car with a successful design, especially the chassis and engine, and at the same time as one of the most durable and strongest cars that can deal with bad roads. … Does this mean that foreign buyers have no objections? No. In fact, they have three: the bodywork could be nicer, the 'cosmetics' could be better, and… they would like more of them."[495] It was at this time that the first advertising brochures intended for the export market also saw print. Of course, it was clear that the quality of the brochures put out by Western companies was beyond the reach of Poles. On the brochures advertising the Warszawa, it was opined: "It is true that they are far from, for example, the Mercedes or Fiat advertising brochures. … Naturally, they cannot compare to the rich colours of American brochures." Nonetheless, the overall effect was thought to be positive, and the Warszawa advertising brochure itself highlighted the car's "positives … while discreetly ignoring its negatives."[496] Of the latter, there were a lot.

While planning the work in the automotive industry, the Design Office of the Automotive Industry characterised the Warszawa as having an excessively heavy structure, an insufficiently powerful engine, and an unappealing body.

---

494 A. Rostocki, "Dobra reklama pilnie poszukiwana," *Motor* 1959, no. 3, p. 3; cf. T. Szczerbicki, *Samochody w PRL*, p. 49.
495 A. Zap., "Cudze chwalicie," *Kurier Polski*, March 1, 1958.
496 T. Szczerbicki, *Samochody w PRL*, p. 49.

The situation would improve only slightly with the planned modernisation and the creation of the M21 model, intended to be "more adapted for export."[497] These plans were undeniably promising. FSO contacted Carozzeria Ghia SpA, an Italian car design company. Just the names of makes Ghia cooperated with (including Volkswagen, Ferrari, and Alfa Romeo) were impressive. The cost of a new body for the Warszawa designed by Ghia was US $60,000. However, nothing came from this cooperation.[498] The modernisation of the Warszawa was merely cosmetic. Today, we would simply call it face-lift: the radiator grille and the front turn signal lamps were given a slightly more modern look, and side mouldings were added. The engine power and torque were also increased by raising the engine's compression ratio.[499] It is therefore not surprising that the next expert opinion on this car did not differ significantly from the previous one. A document prepared by specialists from the Automotive Industry Association (ZPM) states that the Warszawa still deviated significantly from global standards, which were characterised by "outstanding driving comfort and handling, and an excellent

---

497 AAN, Biuro Konstrukcyjne Przemysłu Motoryzacyjnego (hereafter: BKPM), sygn. 14, Plan 5-letni koncepcyjny w zakresie konstrukcji przemysłu motoryzacyjnego, [1955?] p. 12.

498 It is not entirely clear whether the Polish government bought the Italian project. Szczerbicki claims that due to considerable opposition both from Polish designers (including Stanisław Panczakiewicz) and public opinion (mainly regarding the fee), "the whole fuss with Ghia achieved nothing in particular," but he does not provide any specifics (*idem*, *Samochody PRL*, p. 122). Elsewhere, FSO is said to have bought the project, though the cost of the machines that would produce the Italian-designed body would reach $2.5 million. This meant at least a 30% increase in the price of a Warszawa, which was already considered high; J. M., "Dorobek i plany przemysłu motoryzacyjnego," *Życie Gospodarcze* 1959, no. 35, p. 8. The fact that, despite criticism from various quarters, Poland may have purchased the Ghia body design is indicated by the reaction to the black car model in 1:10 scale, representing the prototype of the Warszawa 210, shown during the Exhibition of Technical Progress of the Automotive Industry in 1961. The car resembled the Ford Falcon and—as the professional press described it—"It is not the 'Ghia' kept secret by FSO. … The body design bought from the Italian 'Ghia' cost $60,000; today, there are no plans for the future that would involve it"; (sj), "Wystawa motoryzacyjna. Technika w kraju i na świecie," *Życie Gospodarcze* 1961, p. 3; see "Igranie z ogniem—wywiad z Tadeuszem Wrzaszczykiem," *Motor* 1995, no. 51/52, pp. 4–5, 8.

499 T. Szczerbicki, *Samochody w PRL*, p. 379.

finish." Meanwhile, the car, which had been in production since 1951, had a number of disqualifying defects: "uncomfortable driver's seat, uncomfortable passenger seats, a lack of hydraulic transmission, a brake pedal that requires great pressure, the car also has a tendency to skid, ... [and] an outdated gear system, unsuited to modern driving requirements."[500] In spite of this, the car was still being exported.[501] However, the target markets for foreign sales—Africa, Asia, and Latin America—were characterised by a hot or tropical climate and usually difficult road conditions, necessitating that the vehicles be adapted to operate in such conditions.[502]

Research on the profitability of exporting the Warszawa, carried out in late 1960 and early 1961 by the Motoimport Central Foreign Trade Office (CHZ) on behalf of the Ministry of Heavy Industry (MPC) and MHZ, showed that the model had been generating losses since 1958. The calculations indicated that in 1959 alone, each dollar obtained from the sale of a Warszawa cost 160 zlotys, which was primarily a consequence of the poor quality of the car and a low demand for cars of its class on world markets. Nonetheless, the decision

500 AAN, Ministerstwo Przemysłu Ciężkiego (hereafter: MPC), sygn. 37/167, Monografia i wstępne kierunki programu rekonstrukcji branży, Warszawa, listopad 1965 r., p. 25.

501 In October 1959, the 50,000th Warszawa left the Żerań FSO assembly lines. By the end of that year, a total of 54,134 units had been produced. Of this number, 13,453 were sold abroad; J. Dehnel, "'Rodzinna uroczystość'. 50 000 samochodów FSO-Warszawa," *Motor* 1959, no. 42, p. 3.

502 Further modernisations of the Warszawa were carried out in 1960, when the model 201 was put into production, and in 1962, when production of the model 202 began, which was equipped with an overhead valve engine began. In 1964, production of models 203 and 204 was launched, both with a sedan body, without the characteristic hunchback silhouette. Stanisław Lem described it as follows: "It looks funny, a result of compromises, but maybe your eyes will get used to it. The rear lights are the size of a large book (a plastic square), probably the largest in the world, the white front flashers look like saucers. And the face is funny, like an old-face mask, when the back is rounded like an ass"; S. Lem and S. Mrożek, *Listy 1956–1978*, trans. T. Lem and R. Niziołek, Kraków 2011, p. 364, see also p. 372. Interestingly, the markings used by FSO were previously patented by Peugeot, which even filed an official protest in this matter. Because of this, the designations of individual Warszawa models were changed (to 223 and 224), and they remained so until the end of production, i.e. February 28, 1973, when the last car, number 255119, rolled off the production line; T. Szczerbicki, *Samochody w PRL*, pp. 380–388; M. Górski, *Historia konstrukcji samochodów FSO. 1951–2011*, Warszawa 2013, pp. 11–12.

was made to continue exporting the car in order to maintain production at the Żerań factory and foreign exchange earnings, the result being that Polish products became less and less popular, especially on Western markets.[503] In 1963, Polish officials noticed that, due to the obsolete design of automotive products, "we fell out of the [capitalist] foreign markets" and the only regular importer outside of the Communist Bloc was Turkey—and even Turkey was planning to reduce its purchases.[504]

It is worth noting that the quality of the products of the Polish automotive industry was not the only significant obstacle for importers. The Polish government was also unable to fulfil its obligation to deliver appropriate quantities of spare parts for the vehicles it sold abroad. Foreign contractors protested at various levels, describing huge delays in deliveries. Such was the case, for example, with exports to the Hungarian People's Republic. Due to mutual agreements, in 1966, Poland was obliged to sell Hungary spare

---

503 AAN, MHZ, sygn. 4/511, [Pismo informacyjne] dotyczy: kontroli przeprowadzonej w Biurze Motoryzacyjnym CHZ "Motoimport" w zakresie eksportu samochodów, Warszawa, 17 IV 1961 r., pp. 7–9. In 1960, the main recipients of automotive equipment were Bulgaria, Hungary, Czechoslovakia, China and Turkey. Smaller quantities were sold to Mongolia, Romania, Vietnam, the USSR, East Germany, Greece, Saudi Arabia, Guinea, Iraq, and Chile. The last four were new markets, "conquered" in 1960.; ibid., sygn. 4/512, Sprawozdanie z kontroli przeprowadzonej w CHZ "Motoimport" w okresie od 28 II do 17 V 1961 r., unnumbered pages.

504 AAN, Urząd Rady Ministrów (hereafter: URM), sygn. 72/35, Notatka w sprawie przewidywanego eksportu maszyn i urządzeń w 1963 r., p. 28. Trade contacts with Turkey were established, in part, through Poland's participation in the International Fair organised in Izmir. In 1954, a Warszawa and a truck produced in Starachowice, along with other vehicles, were presented there. Interestingly, other exhibitors presented a much greater variety. The USSR brought to Izmir models from ZIM, Moskvitch, ZIS, and GAZ; England presented products of the Vauxhall factory and various models of Hilman, Humber, and Austin brands. The Italians showed the Fiat 1200 along with Vespa and Lambretta scooters. Why did Polish products enjoy so much interest and popularity (all of the exhibited items were sold during the fair)? Perhaps it had something to do with the habits of Turkish drivers and the condition of the local roads. As the report from the event in Izmir states: "All [Turkish] automotive equipment is used very intensively, which, combined with very poor condition and improper maintenance, has caused the rapid destruction of the vehicles. Both passenger cars and trucks are systematically overloaded"; AAN, MHZ, sygn. 60/45, Sprawozdanie z delegacji służbowej na Międzynarodowe Targi w Izmirze 1954 r., Warszawa, 14 X 1954, pp. 179–181.

parts for Polish cars for a total of 2.5 million roubles. However, by the end of November, completed deliveries only accounted for 1.5 million. When the protests failed, Hungary threatened to "suspend the importation of Polish cars."[505] A Motoimport representative summoned to the ministry confirmed the situation: "Complaints issued by the Hungarian authorities about the lack of consistency in deliveries, failure to provide the requested full range of items, failure to fulfill obligations and arrangements are unfortunately consistent with our records in most cases." However, the problem concerned not only the manufacturer of a specific product range. Long delays were primarily the result of late deliveries between various partners cooperating in the production of parts.[506]

3.4.1 Unwanted and Temporary—The FSO Syrena

In the eyes of individual vehicle users and those aspiring to own a car, the first sign of the arrival of the Polish government's new automotive policy might well have been the joint resolution of the PZPR Central Committee and the Government Praesidium adopted in May 1953, which contained one paragraph that would have brought a smile to the faces of all those dreaming of universal motorisation: "A popular, time-saving means of transport should be built for use in business and leisure activities, intended for workplace innovators (*racjonalizatorzy*), leading workers, activists, academics, leading representatives of the intelligentsia."[507] Though this passage contains several ambiguities (how are we to understand the mysterious "means of transport"?) and foresees limitations in access, it represented a real light at the end of the Stalinist tunnel.

The fate of the Syrena, which became this light, was influenced by the planned temporary nature of the car, which ended up in production for almost thirty years. The entirely Polish car, built from scratch by Polish designers, faced limitations from the very beginning of its existence, even while still on the drawing board, burdened as it was by the stigma of a "transitory" and "temporary" product. In June 1953, on the basis of instructions

505 Ibid., sygn. 2/4, [Informacja], Warszawa, 15 XII 1966 r., unnumbered pages.
506 Ibid., dot.: współpracy pomiędzy CHZ Motoimport a CHZ Mogurt, Warszawa, 11 V 1966 r., unnumbered pages.
507 Quoted in K. J. Mórawski, *Syrena*, p. 17.

issued by the deputy chairman of the PKPG, a special unit was established at the Office of the Chief Designer at FSO, whose task was to prepare and select a concept for a small-displacement car, and then to develop its design and manufacture prototypes. The car was to be designed for the average, individual user, and was not intended for export.[508] While working on the vehicle, its designers, headed by engineer Karol Pionnier, had to take into account the low technological level of the domestic industry and the lack of service facilities. The Central Automotive Industry Authority also required designers to make maximum use of domestically produced components from the Warszawa in the newly designed car, to quickly start production and to reduce costs. Additionally, the target number of units produced was set at only 4,000 per year, which was presumed sufficient for the transition period, until a modern small car factory could be built in Poland, plans for which began to be discussed in the mid-1950s.[509]

Ultimately, Pionnier's team prepared two concepts for the new car. The first one called for the use of a four-stroke, air-cooled engine and a fully loaded, possibly a semi-loaded body on a floorpan. This design was inspired by Volkswagen. The second concept was defined as transitional from the very beginning. It was based on cheaper solutions used, for instance, in DKW cars—that is, a two-stroke liquid-cooled engine and a non-load-carrying body based on a load-bearing frame. The choice of the simpler concept was due to economic reasons; to limit the cost of producing the new car, especially considering the small number of units intended to be produced, technologically advanced solutions were abandoned for the sake of profit.[510]

The first three pre-prototype units of the new car, which the FSO workers called "Syrena," came out at the end of 1953. In other words, between the beginning of construction work and the presentation of the car in front of the Ministry of Mechanical Industry on December 31, 1953, only 7 months had passed! The units differed in certain details, the most important of which concerned the body. Two had a body based on a wooden structure, a concept developed by engineer Stanisław Panczakiewicz. The third, whose body was made of steel, came from engineer Stanisław Łukasiewicz. Panczakiewicz,

---

508 J. R. Dehnel, Syrena faktem, "Motor" 1958, no. 38, p. 10.
509 K. J. Mórawski, *Syrena*, pp. 20–21.
510 Ibid., p. 25.

who was a determined proponent of the use of wood, was guided by the "temporary nature" of the entire project. In turn, Łukasiewicz's concept was defined by the fact that many of the elements used in the pre-prototype came from the Warszawa. Once again, the final choice of the concept for the new FSO car was determined by economic considerations. In 1956, the implementation of the production of elements for the Warszawa at the Żerań factory finally ended, which meant that from that moment on, cars leaving the assembly lines would be almost completely "Polish." This also gave a green light for the Syrena. Moreover, earlier production limitations (maximum 4,000 units per year) were no longer valid; it was estimated that the current capacity would allow for a volume two and a half times greater. In this situation, a wooden roof was out of the question.[511]

While the preparation of the concept, pre-prototypes and prototype units of the Syrena occurred at a truly Stakhanovite pace, the implementation of mass production was slow. Initially, sales were planned for the second half of 1956. At the end of July, it was announced that FSO was "only a few months away" from producing the first 100 units of the car. At the end of 1956, one writer opined: "For several years, it [the Syrena] has been on everyone's lips in all kinds of publications. It has been also appeared to be stuck on the production line."[512] Finally, on March 20, 1957, the first Syrena left the FSO gates. By the end of the year, 200 units were produced, and in the following year, another 660. This relatively small number was the result of the primitive methods of manufacture; the bodies of the first 500 Syrenas to leave the Żerań factory were made by hand from start to finish. Data on the required production time is interesting. In 1957, it took 550 hours to produce a Syrena (we might recall that the labour required for a Warszawa was 364 hours). After four years, that number was reduced to 241, which was still a very long time (for the Warszawa, after the same time, it was 220 hours).[513] It is therefore not surprising that the planned level of 10,000 units was achieved only in 1965, although—as noted above—it was still only half as much as what

511 Ibid., pp. 26–27.
512 K. Wilczyński, "Rok 'Nijaki'," p. 4.
513 S. Szostkiewicz, *Przemiany w strukturze załogi Fabryki Samochodów Osobowych w latach 1956–1961*, Wrocław–Warszawa–Kraków 1965, p. 137.

was necessary to meet the growing needs of the Polish society.[514] The first batch of Syrenas was delivered to users who were experts in the design and operation of cars. They were required to submit regular reports describing how these cars handled during normal use.[515]

In June 1958, the first officially sold Syrena was purchased by a physician, Zofia Manicka. She was assisted in the purchase by FSO's director, whom she met by chance in the factory's office building, while looking for information about when the vehicle's long-awaited production would start. The second unit from the first pool of two cars was bought by Janusz Rozum from the weekly *Zwierciadło*. As it later transpired, the order was decided by the FSO director, who said: "Ladies first, and whatever's left goes to you."[516]

Reviews of the new car began to appear immediately after regular sales began in 1958 and Syrenas hit the Polish roads. One of the first units went to Jerzy Łukasik, who covered 130,000 kilometres in the car in less than two years. In a statement published by *Motor*, he said: "Initially, there were only problems. Bad shock absorbers, failing condensers, leaking windows, defective gearbox." Of particular interest is a passage listing the spare parts every Syrena user should have with them "just in case": a fan belt, generator brushes, spare rubber hoses for the radiator, and a spare cable and a set of sliders for the transmission system.[517] Interestingly, drivers praised some of the vehicle's features (good handling in corners; excellent visibility while driving thanks to panoramic windows front and rear; passenger comfort, both in the back and in the front, although not for the driver, with the gear lever sticking out from the steering wheel). Nevertheless, they were quick to point out the low quality of the finish. After testing the Syrena on the experimental track at the Żerań factory, *Motor* journalist Andrzej Zieliński summed up his impressions in a statement for Polish Radio: "The car itself is very good, the engine is indestructible, but the accessories are faulty."[518]

---

514 AAN, KC PZPR, sygn. 1730 (mf 2894), Kierunki rozwoju przemysłu motoryzacyjnego. Ministerstwo Przemysłu Ciężkiego, [1964 r.], p. 510.

515 AAN, Komitet Ekonomiczny Rady Ministrów, sygn. 6/249, Rozdzielnik samochodów osobowych przeznaczonych dla osób prywatnych. Załącznik no. 3, [1956 r.], p. 67.

516 T. Szczerbicki, *Syrena*, Poznań 2016, pp. 364–367.

517 *Motor* 1960, no. 27.

518 Archiwum Polskiego Radia (hereafter: APR), sygn. 3934/11, Siedem dni w Polsce i na świecie, 1959.

In Stefan Sękowski unit, the water temperature indicator and speedometer were found to be damaged upon receipt of the car. While the former was replaced immediately under warranty, he had to pay for the latter. Moreover, after a closer inspection of the car, it turned out that not a single screw or nut was properly tightened in the chassis or in the engine. All these faults were discovered within 24 hours of receiving the Syrena. More problems came to surface under continued use: faulty workmanship on the engine pistons, imperfect construction of the radiator mounting bracket and of the connection between the exhaust pipe and the muffler, and poor design of the engine mounts, which stopped functioning after some time. These and other problems, such as, for example, the engine flap not closing properly, did not prevent reviewers of the car from describing it as "really good and pleasant." In *Horyzonty Techniki*, Pionnier commented on Sękowski's text: "Unfortunately, it must be said that the 'Syrena' still does not fully meet European 'standards' in terms of workmanship and assembly accuracy. … Finally, I would like to remind you once again: the 'Syrena' was constructed in difficult conditions. It is a compromise resulting from the need to use many parts from the parent 'Warszawa', and is therefore a by-product that could never have existed in any other way."[519] When Aleksander Rostocki, chairman of the Automotive Council in the 1960s, was asked during an interview with *Życie Warszawy* what car he drives, he replied: "Of course, the best car in the world!" To the journalist's follow-up question ("Would it be the only Rolls-Royce in Poland?"), Rostocki responded: "God forbid. It's the Syrena!" The persistent journalist pursued further: "Will you let us in on a secret: is it true that this car has the proverbial fountain, but it only works when it rains and is directed at the driver's lap?"[520] Rostocki defended himself: "Foul insinuations. … The one I own, for example, is so tight that only daily exercise keeps me physically fit enough to open the door."[521]

Criticism directed at FSO led to the development of further models of the Syrena. Its modernisation was announced at the highest level of

---

519 S. Sękowski and K. Pionnier, "Cienie i blaski samochodu Syrena," *Horyzonty Techniki* 1959, no. 12, pp. 535–539.

520 The word "fountain" (wodowtrysk, lit. waterspout) was commonly used in the mid-twentieth century as a "proverbial," ironic reference to extravagant luxury."

521 "W perspektywie 300 tysięcy wozów rocznie," *Życie Warszawy*, 23 July 1964, p. 3.

government.[522] The first in a series of successors to the 100 model was a car marked 101, which was produced in 1960, even though production of the 104 model had already been announced and would eventually begin in 1966.[523] Subsequent models appeared cyclically: the 102 in March 1962 and the 103 in the fourth quarter of the following year. Unfortunately, the changes did not improve the car's overall quality, outside of the use of the engine from the East German Wartburg in several hundred units from a few models.[524] The Syrena's operating instructions included a request from the FSO crew to inform them "about any problems noticed … so we can quickly fix them."[525] Users eagerly took advantage of this option, though some of the modifications requested by them and by *Motor* readers—such as a redesign of the dashboard to optimise the positioning of indicators, an increase in the number of storage compartments, and the inclusion of reclining seats—were introduced either after a few years (for example, reclining seats in 1975) or not at all.[526] One cannot lay the blame for all of the car's problems solely on poor workmanship at FSO. As the director of the Żerań factory explained in *Życie Warszawy*: "Thirty-seven percent of 'Syrena's' parts are supplied by cooperators, including rubber, glass, upholstery, electrical engineering, water and fuel pumps, etc. But these 37% of the car's parts account for as much as 60% of all complaints."[527] However, this does nothing to change the fact that all the loudly proclaimed modernisations were, in fact, just cosmetic, and the Syrena increasingly became an object of crude jokes and anecdotes. One such joke, popular in the 1960s, compared the Polish car to a Rolls-Royce.

---

522 "'Wytyczne rozwoju gospodarki narodowej w latach 1959–1965', referat członka Biura Politycznego, tow. Stefana Jędrychowskiego (12 III 1959 r.)," in: *III Zjazd Polskiej Zjednoczonej Partii Robotniczej. Stenogram. Warszawa, 10 III—19 III 1959 r.*, Warszawa 1959, pp. 360–361.

523 The basic novelty of the Syrena 104 was its new, three-cylinder engine. The exhaust and ignition systems were also changed; the carburetor and cooling system were modernised. However, compared to other cars of this class, it was still structurally outdated, employing solutions that other manufacturers had stopped using at least a decade earlier; K. J. Mórawski, *Syrena*, pp. 60–65.

524 Ibid., pp. 46–47, 50–51.

525 *FSO Syrena. Instrukcja obsługi*, Warszawa 1960, p. 5.

526 K. J. Mórawski, *Syrena*, pp. 44, 58–59.

527 Quot. from: ibid., p. 59.

What was the difference between them? The Syrena had a decorative strip running down the side; the "American"[528] limousine did not.[529]

It is difficult not to draw a comparison here with the Trabant produced in Zwickau. This popular car was a contemporary of the Syrena: both cars officially went on sale in 1958. The Trabant, named in reference to the Soviet Sputnik, was made of Duroplast, a material that was the pride of the East German chemical industry, and equipped with a two-cylinder, two-stroke, 23 horsepower engine driving the front axle. Six years later, a minor modernisation of the drive unit allowed the horsepower to increase to 26. This was the last major change to the car's design. Another 25 years had to pass before it received a new engine, borrowed from its West German rival, Volkswagen. Its overall appearance remained the same. However, it is worth emphasising that East German decision-makers did not really care about improving the car, which generated substantial profits for the state in its current shape. Between 1970 and 1987, 730 million East German marks were invested in production; profits from sales were estimated at 5.5 billion marks.[530] At the end of the 1980s, the Trabant was the most popular passenger car in East Germany, with almost two million of them in use. One had to wait many years for a new Trabant; the shortest waiting time was 12.5 years and the longest was 15 years, depending on the model. It was still the most easily available car, despite its price, which amounted to several times the average monthly salary. By comparison: a Wartburg cost 2.5 times as much, requiring three years of savings, and one had to wait from 14 to 16.5 years to buy one. The waiting period for imported cars ranged from 13.5 to 17 years.[531]

With regards to Poland, it is of note that despite all of its obvious shortcomings and defects, the Syrena became increasingly popular in the Polish society. Its price was definitely a factor. In 1961, over 10,000 Syrenas rode

528 It was common at the time to refer to anything from the West, including the British Rolls-Royce, as "American."

529 *Humor z Polski. Dowcipy z lat 1948–2008*, ed. E. Rychlewska, Poznań 2008, p. 139.

530 J. R. Zatlin, *The Currency of Socialism: Money and Political Culture in East Germany*, New York 2007, p. 220.

531 The Trabant was produced until April 1991. Over the years, more than 3 million units of this car were produced; ibid., p. 225; S. Wolle, *Wspaniały świat dyktatury. Codzienność i władza w NRD 1971–1989*, Warszawa 2003, pp. 313–314; I. Merkel, "Der Trabant," in: *Erinnerungsorte der DDR*, ed. M. Sabrow, München 2009, pp. 363–373.

on the Polish roads, accounting for approximately 10% of all passenger cars then in private hands. Syrena enthusiasts established numerous clubs. In a short time, as Mórawski notes, fans of the Syrena outnumbered the much older groups of Warszawa, Wartburg, and Škoda fans.[532] In the early 1960s, it was announced that production of the Syrena would reach 15,000 units per year over the next five years. However, this promise proved very difficult—if not impossible—to keep. In 1961, 4,900 Syrenas left the Żerań factory. A year later, the number increased to 5,600, and in 1965, it reached 11,800. The magic threshold of 10,000 units was thus exceeded, though those numbers remained well below the planned amounts. The level of 15,000 units per year was only passed in 1968.[533] Once again, one is obliged to cite the findings of Mórawski, who wrote that several factors contributed to these results. On the one hand, for FSO, the production of the Syrena "was still an unprecedented and, in its own way, pioneering undertaking," and problems related to the implementation of the production cycle simply did not allow for the achievement of expected production volumes. On the other hand, the cooperative nature of the entire project meant that a great deal of the blame lay with companies cooperating with Żerań. This was the case, for example, with the Mechanical Equipment Factory in Bielsko-Biała, which failed to deliver drive units for Syrena on time.[534]

The document prepared by BKPM, mentioned earlier in this chapter, had another interesting feature. Among all of the automotive industry products intended to meet growing market needs—next to the "medium passenger car," that is, the Warszawa—there was supposed to be a "cheap car for general use." This was not the Syrena, whose production was still in its infancy. Moreover, plans foresaw a short production run ending concurrently with the discontinuation of the current version of the Warszawa, the M20. The Syrena was to be replaced by a new and cheap car designed to drive on Polish roads, intended for "use by the masses of private users." Its price would be low because of large production volume, expected to reach 25,000 units a year, using the facilities of the FSO Żerań. The car would weigh 750–850 kg, and

532 K. J. Mórawski, *Syrena*, p. 43.
533 *Opowieść o FSO*, p. 156.
534 K. J. Mórawski, *Syrena*, p. 44.

its top speed would be 100–120 km/h.[535] The idea to build a new factory for small-displacement passenger cars was entertained several times throughout the 1960s, accompanied by calls to the end the production of the Syrena.[536] However, since the final decision was always that such a factory would not be built, the production of the Syrena would continue, with another modernisation announced.[537]

Clearly, then, dark clouds constantly gathered over the Syrena and the spectre of halted production loomed. It is, therefore, not surprising that the stigma of its temporariness, mentioned earlier in this chapter, was difficult for the Syrena to shed. The fact that the Syrena was not intended for export certainly also played an important role in this stigmatisation. It was simply not worth too much investment. Even when, in the early 1960s, the Ministry of Foreign Trade proposed to include the Syrena in the Polish export plan, the idea was ultimately dropped in light of the poor workmanship quality and obsolete construction.[538] Similar proposals were made as late as 1963, at which point the MPC even appointed a special commission to explore the possibility of promoting the Syrena as an export product. Ultimately, however, it was decided that the car could not meet the requirements of foreign contractors. The negative assessments stemmed from design errors that prohibited both a major modernisation of the car and changes in manufacturing technology. The Syrena clearly lagged behind cars of a similar class produced in other countries.[539] In other words: only wholesale changes to its structure, including the construction of the body and chassis, would allow for the introduction of multi-series production, and only that production model could be profitable.

---

535 AAN, BKPM, sygn. 14, Plan 5-letni koncepcyjny w zakresie konstrukcji przemysłu motoryzacyjnego, pp. 12–16.

536 AAN, Ministerstwo Komunikacji (hereafter: MK), sygn. II/2, Protokół no. 2/60 z posiedzenia prezydium Rady Motoryzacyjnej odbytego 26 IV 1960 r., p. 522.

537 APR, sygn. 3951/1, Z Kraju i ze Świata, 1961.

538 AAN, MHZ, sygn. 4/511, Dotyczy: kontroli przeprowadzonej w Biurze Motoryzacyjnym CHZ "Motoimport" w zakresie eksportu samochodów, Warszawa, 17 IV 1961 r., p. 8.

539 "The technical parameters of this car, such as its weight, the weight to acceleration ratio, etc., are impossible to compare with any cars of this class in the world. The use of a two-stroke engine in a car is already an anachronism, if we take into account the design trends around the world"; AAN, MPC, sygn. 37/167, Monografia i wstępne kierunki programu rekonstrukcji branży, Warszawa, listopad 1965 r., p. 26.

In July 1962, the Politburo of the Central Committee of the PZPR, the highest executive body of the Communist party, commissioned Piotr Jaroszewicz to prepare "definitive" conclusions regarding the production of the Syrena, but no archival evidence of the deputy prime minister's activities has been found.[540] Three years later, when the decision was made to purchase a licence for the production of the Fiat 125, the fate of the Syrena seemed to have been sealed. While approving the decision to begin the production of a new car in Żerań, the Politburo decided at the same time to discontinue the Syrena, only ensuring the supply of spare parts for the car. Until production ceased, the Syrena would be produced in numbers requiring no additional investment outlays.[541] Ultimately, however, it turned out that, due to the fact that a significant number of the Big Fiat (*duży fiat*, an affectionate nickname for Fiat 125's produced in Poland) were exported and to its relatively high price, the discontinuation of the Syrena would create a wide gap in the passenger car market in Poland—a gap that would be difficult to fill with imported cars.[542] Therefore, it was decided in 1967 that the production of the Syrena would continue. As *Motor* reported, "the decision was driven by the needs of the citizen, the technical capabilities of the industry, and the economic conditions calculated on the scale of the national economy."[543] It became obvious that it was impossible to produce Big Fiats, Warszawas, and Syrenas at the same time in the same factory. The fate of the Syrena was thus finally sealed. Its production would be taken over by the Mechanical Equipment Factory in Bielsko-Biała, which had previously manufactured engines for the Syrena. The relocation took two years and production at the new location began in August 1972, after another government reshuffle. Initially, the factory at Bielsko-Biała produced the 104 model, using components inherited from FSO, eventually replacing it with probably the most successful Syrena in history, the 105. Once again, the stigma of the car's temporary status was felt, because the "Bielsko period" of the Syrena coincided with the anticipated

---

540 AAN, KC PZPR, sygn. XIA/176, Protokół no. 75 posiedzenia Biura Politycznego 11 VII 1962 r., p. 213.

541 Ibid., sygn. 1733 (mf 2895), Protokół no. 11 posiedzenia Biura Politycznego 16 II 1965 r., p. 80.

542 AAN, MK, sygn. II/2, Protokół no. 1/69 z posiedzenia Rady Motoryzacyjnej przy Radzie Ministrów, odbytego 26 VI 1969 r., p. 378.

543 *Motor* 1967, no. 34.

start of production of a small-displacement car licenced by Fiat. Thus, the 105 model, although the most successful, underwent no revolutionary changes, since the above-mentioned reclining seats or the change in the orientation of the doors cannot be considered as such. However, the Syrena took on many elements from the Big Fiat: door locks and a window lowering mechanism, but also side windows with a larger surface, which significantly improved driving comfort.[544]

Initially, it was planned that the production of the 105 would continue until the production of the Fiat 126p was fully underway, and that it would end no later than in the mid-1970s.[545] However, once again, plans had to give way to reality and economic factors. It was not until June 30, 1983, that the last Syrena rolled off the production lines at the factory in Bielsko-Biała, which had combined with several other plants and the newly built factory in Tychy to create the Fabryka Samochodów Małolitrażowych (Small-Displacement Car Factory). Thus ended the almost thirty-year history of the first, and so far only, completely Polish passenger car.[546] In total, the two Polish automobile factories produced over half a million units of Syrenas of various models.[547]

---

544 K. J. Mórawski, *Syrena*, pp. 86–87.

545 AAN, KC PZPR, sygn. XI/664, Podstawowe problemy rozwoju przemysłu maszynowego w latach 1971–1975, Warszawa, marzec 1971, p. 14.

546 In February 1981, the rules for the sale of passenger cars changed once again and prepayments were introduced. The huge demand for passenger cars meant that within a month, Poles completely exhausted the stock of cars for sale. Waiting times for processing the prepayments were extended, in the worst case to ten years. Interestingly, prepayments for Syrenas, which were also covered by the new sales system, were accepted even when it was known that the model was no longer going to be produced; see H. Wilk, "Zmotoryzowane lata osiemdziesiąte," in: *Społeczeństwo polskie w latach 1980–1989*, ed. N. Jarska, J. Olaszek, Warszawa 2015, pp. 174–177; *idem*, "'Ciągle ścigam cenę samochodu'—oficjalna dystrybucja samochodów w Polsce w latach 1980–1989," *Polska 1944/45–1989. Studia i Materiały* 2015, no. 13, p. 148ff.

547 It is worth mentioning that Syrenas slowly disappeared from the Polish landscape. The end of production in June 1983 did not cause, as Mórawski called it, "a mass 'escape' of Syrena owners towards other vehicles, and the vast majority of cars were still in operation." Significantly, in the early 1990s, Polmozbyt warehouses had large stocks of spare parts for this car, and the high interchangeability of components with the Warszawa, and therefore with Żuk and Nysa (which were still being produced), meant that users had no major problems repairing their vehicles; K. J. Mórawski, *Syrena*, pp. 112–113.

On the threshold of its seventh decade, *Motor* once again asked its readers what future they foresaw for individual motoring in Poland. Not surprisingly, many opinions concerned the Syrena. Readers talked about the first Polish passenger car and recalled with nostalgia the mid-1950s, when the first cars of this brand left the Żerań factory. Critics were effectively drowned out by memories about what was, after all, the not-so-distant past: "'I learned to drive in a Syrena', 'a reliable companion on holidays and Sunday trips', 'I drive all the time, all year round, in winter it [the Syrena] starts perfectly!'"[548] Wacław O. wrote to the weekly that "the motor-pump they call the Syrena has been riding all over our country for 15 years. Those with more courage go far beyond Poland, traverse the mountains and the wildernesses. Even abroad, no one points a finger at them and they rarely need to be towed home." However, he also admitted "that the Syrena really is a reliable, modern car that fulfills the hopes and expectations of every buyer."[549] The Syrena's main advantages, it seems, were its relative availability and low price, while its quality remained at a dramatically low level.[550] An engineer from Warsaw who also decided to share his thoughts on the future of the Syrena with the readers of *Motor* suggested that the constantly growing population of the domestic technical intelligentsia and highly qualified workers will not be able to afford the much more expensive Big Fiat and "will forever miss the opportunity to buy a car."[551] It is also notable that the Syrena's simple design—given widespread shortages of spare parts and problems with car maintenance—led many users to acquire technical skills needed to repair their cars on their own.

---

548 *Motor* 1970, no. 17.

549 L. Rejewski, "Co z syreną?" *Motor* 1970, no. 21, p. 1.

550 As T. S., a resident of Stężyca in Kashubia, wrote in a letter to *Motor*: "During the two years of driving my Syrena [purchased new], I changed the speedometer four times, the gear stick three times, the front wheel bearings (total crap after 2,000 km), joints, etc. etc. … On July 28 [19]70, however, I noticed that the paint was peeling off the rear fenders. It exposed the sheet metal, oh, but if only it were actually sheet metal! It's really just a chunk of rust that is barely holding together. You can easily poke your finger right through 'it'"; "'Myśliciel' o syrenie," *Motor* 1970, no. 36, p. 2; cf. "Jakość syren," *Motor* 1970, no. 39, p. 3.

551 (Rej.), "Co dalej z Syreną?" *Motor* 1970, no. 34, p. 2.

The more than half a million Syrenas produced over the course of almost thirty years, played an invaluable role in the development of individual motorisation in Poland. Somewhat in spite of popular opinion (which was quite right about the car's poor quality), the Syrena contributed significantly to the motorisation of the Polish society. It was often viewed as a symbol of progress in everyday life. This was the case for Szczepan and Leokadia Głuszak, who wrote in their diary: "In 1967, we bought a new car, a 'Syrena 104,' and then we introduced modernity into the apartment itself: we installed central heating, running water, and a bathroom."[552]

As various surveys show, Poles usually started their personal motoring adventure with a Syrena. With only a small margin of error, we can claim that these half a million Syrenas were the basic vehicle for large swathes of the Polish society in the PRL, a fact determined primarily by price. Outside of the Mikrus, the Syrena was the cheapest new car until Fiat 126p came along. It is also of note that this car was intended only for private users.[553] Perhaps the popularity of the Syrena was also due to patriotic considerations, compared to the Warszawa, which was often called "an unpleasant stray from the East."[554] Such "local patriotism" was typical of virtually all societies in the Communist bloc: Germans, Czechs and Slovaks, Romanians, and residents of the USSR were most likely to use the products of their own automotive industries. Usually, the reason was that Trabants, Škodas, and Dacias were the cheapest and most easily available four-wheelers on the market, though pride in the fruits of the labour of the domestic factories certainly also played a part (especially in East Germany and Czechoslovakia, where locally made vehicles were entirely of domestic origin). This remained true even when the quality of the cars was inferior to that of their counterparts in the Western world.[555]

552 "Dwa pokolenia," in: *Ludowa i socjalistyczna. Pamiętniki Polaków 1918–1978. Antologia pamiętnikarstwa polskiego*, eds. B. Gołębiowski, M. Grad, and F. Jakubczak, Warszawa 1983, p. 215.

553 A small number of units were delivered to companies and state institutions, where they served as service vehicles. These Syrenas were used by, among others, the Citizens' Militia, the Polish Post Office, the army, and the forest service; T. Szczerbicki, *Syrena*, p. 193.

554 R. Sulima, *Antropologia codzienności*, Kraków 2000, p. 38.

555 L. Gatejel, "The Common Heritage of the Socialist Car Culture," p. 148.

3.4.2 From Kitchen Utensils to a Micro-car: The Short life of WSK Mikrus MR-300

In late November 1958, a particularly interesting announcement appeared in the weekly *Motor*, informing readers about the appearance of a new car on the market. Produced jointly by Communication Equipment Factory (Wytwórnią Sprzętu Komunikacyjnego, WSK) plants in Mielec (chassis and body) and Rzeszów (engine), this micro-car, aptly named the Mikrus[556], would "gradually start selling in the second half of November", according to the weekly. Aside from detailed technical specifications of the vehicle, the article contained a list of voivodeship offices of Motozbyt that were to distribute it.[557] Although attentive readers could have noticed that the date of the "gradual start of sale" and the moment of publication of the announcement were alarmingly close, it was yet another harbinger of a coming automotive spring.

The first prototypes of the Polish micro-car were built in early 1957. The fact that they were built in plants that had previously produced equipment for the army was due to the release of production capacity during the thaw. Thus, the WSK Rzeszów plant—which had been producing, for instance, Lis-2 engines that powered MiG-15 aircraft manufactured in Mielec—suddenly had to switch to completely new production: from motorcycle and car parts, through milk centrifuges, to cutlery and tableware.[558] On the wave of the Western fascination with micro-cars, several prototype vehicles were created in different parts of the country using various, often cottage-industry methods. The first vehicle of this type was built at the turn of 1953 at the Automotive Industry Experimental Center (ODPM), and was named the Pionier. The car was designed as a cross between the Czech Aero, the East German DKW, and the Gada—a car whose designer was one of the Polish engineers employed at the ODPM. However, the Pionier was not well

---

[556] The vehicle's full name was WSK Mikrus MR 300. "WSK" was the name of the plants producing the car (Wytwórnia Sprzętu Komunikacyjnego), while the initials "MR" referred to the cities where its components were produced: Mielec and Rzeszów. The number "300" referred to the engine displacement; A. Garbacz, *Mikrus. Auto, któremu nie pozwolono dorosnąć*, Stalowa Wola 2011, p. 4.

[557] *Motor* 1958, no. 47, p. 15.

[558] M. Płocica and B. Winiarski, *Mikrus MR-300. 3 lata produkcji, 50 lat historii*, Kraków 2011, pp. 16–17.

received by PKPG decision-makers.[559] Another proposed micro-car was the Smyk, prepared by the Design Office of the Automotive Industry in Warsaw, a vehicle that could not enter production because the factory at Żerań was busy making Syrenas.[560] A similar fate befell the Silesian Brzdąc.[561] Only the Mikrus, developed in the Subcarpathian region, received more attention and favour from decision-makers.

Almost from the very beginning, observers noticed a strong external similarity between the Polish car and the West German Goggomobil. It is known that while working on the Mikrus prototype, talks took place regarding the purchase of a licence from Hans Glas. Conditions were even agreed for the production of the Goggomobil at WSK Rzeszów. Ultimately, due to the excessive demands of the West German company, the idea was abandoned, a fact which did nothing to prevent the Poles from using the automobile produced by Hans Glas as an "extensive" inspiration or even—as the WSK Rzeszów technical director Bogdan Mędrzecki recalled—a model.[562] One of the creators of the Mikrus, Hieronim Kubiak, admitted years later that the degree to which the West German micro-car inspired the Polish design was very significant. After the Goggomobil was first observed during one of the Tatra Motorcycle Rallies in the mid-1950s, planting the seed for the idea of constructing a similar car in Poland, it was decided to purchase three Goggomobils and use them as a model for a Polish micro-car.[563]

After various adventures,[564] the first prototypes came together in mid-1957, and were officially presented in Mielec on July 22 of that year. Alongside the Mikrus, the Meduza was also presented—a different body concept based on the Mikrus chassis, which, however, did not enter production. Both cars then

---

559 A. M., "Marzenia na kółkach," *Świat* 1957, no. 41, p. 12.

560 Ibid., pp. 12–13, 18; (Pojm.), "Pierwsze spotkanie ze 'Smykiem'," *Życie Warszawy*, October 22–23, 1957, p. 1; R. Sosiński, "Jedziemy Smykiem," *Horyzonty Techniki* 1957, no. 12, pp. 542–546; A. M., "Marzenia na kółkach."

561 J. Kochanowski, *Rewolucja międzypaździernikowa Polska 1956–1957*, Kraków 2017, pp. 264–265.

562 M. Płocica and B. Winiarski, *Mikrus MR 300*, pp. 23–25.

563 A. Garbacz, *Mikrus*, pp. 5–6.

564 Among others: the choice of 10-inch wheels for the car was determined by the fact that it was the most popular size of tyres produced at that time, because its supplier, the Rubber Industry Plant (Zakłady Przemysłu Gumowego) in Dębica, had just started producing tyres of this size for agricultural machines; A. Garbacz, *Mikrus*, p. 22.

travelled to Warsaw for presentation at the Ministry of Mechanical Industry. According to some sources, two Mikrus cars were taken to the capital by truck, and only started moving on their own wheels after reaching the outskirts of the city. A sarcastic comment noted: "you teach a child to go for walks by carrying it in a pushchair."[565] The prototype presented in Warsaw met with great interest from Józef Cyrankiewicz and Piotr Jaroszewicz themselves, both of whom reportedly took the car for an hour-long ride on the streets of the capital. A positive decision regarding further production was apparently made then and there.[566]

In the end, the Mikrus went on sale on December 12, 1958, at a price of 50,000 zlotys per unit, more than thirty-seven average monthly salaries, despite previous statements naming a value 20,000 zlotys lower. Some commentators at the time even described the Mikrus as a car "for micro-people with macro-pockets."[567] The first three units went to the Kraków office of the Union of Fighters for Freedom and Democracy, to Józef Jacheć from Zdzieszowice, and to Father Saturnin Sikorski from the parish of Czersk, near Warsaw.[568] The remaining units from the first hundred produced were handed over to private users, on the condition that they would relay information about the car's handling in various road conditions.[569]

It is difficult to clearly assess how successful the Mikrus was as a design concept, but the car definitely had a very limited potential. As the user manual proclaims: "Two front seats for adults and a rear seat for children ensure full driving comfort. Due to limited space, carrying three or four adults is only possible for short distances … . The advanced technical parameters and typical equipment of the Mikrus fully qualify it as a 'family' means of transport, and the operating costs put it almost on par with the costs of operating a motorcycle with a sidecar, while ensuring the driving comfort of an average small car."[570] However, these advantages could not outweigh its numerous disadvantages. Among them was the trunk, which, though it

565 A. M., "Marzenia na kółkach," p. 13.
566 M. Płocica and B. Winiarski, *Mikrus*, pp. 61–65; A. Garbacz, *Mikrus*, p. 8.
567 A. M., "Marzenia na kółkach," p. 18.
568 T. Szczerbicki, *Samochody w PRL*, p. 181.
569 J. Tarczyński, "Mikrus MR 300," *Motor* 1984, no. 27, p. 15.
570 *WSK Mikrus MR-300. Instrukcja obsługi*, Warszawa 1960, p. 4.

boasted a 200-litre capacity, was located under the front hood and accessible only from inside the car—a fact that opened the car to derisive ridicule. Similar derision was expressed in an article about the Smyk, comparing it to the Mikrus as a competitor for primacy among Polish micro-cars.[571] At the same time, the Mikrus had many technical shortcomings.[572] Subjected to a road test by experts from the Motor Transport Institute in Warsaw, it received very low marks, for both for design and performance. Nonetheless, great hopes were placed on the Mikrus. In *Odgłosy*, Leon Janowski wrote: "In the domestic automobile fleet, the 'Mikrus' plays the role of a Cinderella that will never catch a prince .... Well, it turns out that if you drive the Mikrus skilfully, it handles various kinds of terrain no worse than such vehicles as the Fiat 600, the Multipla, the DKW, or the famous Citroën 2CV."[573]

However, most users did not have a very high opinion of the car; they commonly referred to the Mikrus ironically as a vehicle on a "European scale" or as a "crippled car."[574] In a letter to television, one Mikrus owner wrote that, due to frequent breakdowns and defects, despite "the best care in operation, the car is parked more often than it is driven."[575] After driving a brand new Mikrus a mere 800 kilometres, a doctor from the Wrocław Voivodeship, reported serious failures of the engine, suspension, and electrical system, which, in practice, made it impossible for him to do his job. Moreover, the need to bear the cost of repairs (they were not covered by the warranty) meant that he could not afford to pay the monthly instalments.[576] He ended his letter to *Fala* in a very emotional tone: "Today, my car stands as an exhibit covered in a thick layer of dust, unusable .... For five years, I saved, sometimes denying myself the most desired entertainment, only to be exploited

---

571 "During the test drive of the 'Mikrus' and 'Meduza', a pair of horses easily overtook the fourteen mechanical horsepower. The engine was hotter than the nag"; elsewhere, it was reported: "The 'Mikrus' prototypes can barely manage the hills on their usual Rzeszów–Mielec route; A. M., "Marzenia na kółkach," p. 18.

572 Ibid., pp. 153–154.

573 L. Janowski, "Koń a sprawa polska czyli rzecz o motoryzacji," *Odgłosy* 1959, no. 27, p. 6.

574 Archiwum Dokumentacji i Zbiorów Programowych Polskiego Radia i Telewizji (hereafter: ADiZPRiT), sygn. 1050/29, Biuletyn nr 85 w sprawie samochodów Mikrus produkcji WSK-Mielec, 1 XII 1959 r., unnumbered pages.

575 Ibid.

576 Ibid., 20 XI 1959 r., unnumbered pages.

and wronged in this way. Let the factory in Mielec take responsibility for its defective product, I will hand it back to them with no compensation."[577]

In spite of all these critical views about its design and operation, the Mikrus raised hopes that the status of Polish motorisation would improve. It was even included in the exhibition summarising the achievements of 15 years of the PRL, which took place at the 28th Poznań International Fair in 1959.[578] Displayed on an striking, polished rotating platform, the vehicle made a very good impression. It was received well not only by Poles, but also by Western guests visiting the exhibition halls in Poznań. Inquiries about the possibility of exporting the Mikrus were submitted, for instance, by Swedes.[579] The car's success in Poznań led to its inclusion in the exhibition of the achievements of the PRL on its fifteenth anniversary, which was to be held in Moscow; even before the exhibition opened to the public, journalists spoke favourably about the Mikrus. However, the positive press came to nothing because the Mikrus did not live to see the exhibition's opening and was replaced by the Junak motorcycle. At the same time, on September 20, 1959, the plants in Mielec and Rzeszów received a letter from the MPC ordering the immediate suspension of the assembly and production of the Mikrus.[580]

There are various theories about the reasons for this order. according to Mieczysław Płocica and Bartosz Winiarski, it was undoubtedly Polish authorities who decided to discontinue the production of the car, but this raises questions about the causes of this decision. One theory is that the Soviets were indirectly responsible for the demise of the Mikrus, since they were pursuing advanced work on the construction of their own micro-car, the ZAZ 965 (Zaporozhets). It is worth remembering that this was still a time when Polish engineers had to be careful not to prove themselves more efficient than their Soviet counterparts.[581]

---

577 Ibid.

578 S. Askanas, "XXVIII Międzynarodowe Targi Poznańskie. Ekspozycje motoryzacyjne," *Motoryzacja* 1959, no. 5, p. 118.

579 M. Płocica and B. Winiarski, *Mikrus*, pp. 155–157.

580 A. Garbacz, *Mikrus*, pp. 10–11.

581 Incidentally, it is worth noting that the public formulated a similar opinion to explain the central authorities' decision in 1965 to discontinue work on prototype models of the Warszawa 210, the Syrena 110, and the Syrena Sport. However, after Karol Mórawski, we can assume that the discontinuation of any and all activities stemmed

Płocica and Winiarski provide at least three other possible causes: a demand from Hans Glas GmbH concerning licensing rights; "jealousy within the domestic automotive industry"; and a "pure economic calculation," which later became the official justification for the cessation of production.[582] In the first case, the only source is the recollection of automotive journalist Stanisław Szelichowski, who claimed that the Germans did, in fact, note an excessive similarity between the Mikrus and the Goggomobil, and were therefore preparing to file a lawsuit against Poland. No trial ever took place because the Poles ended production of the disputed car on their own.[583] In the case of internal animosities supposedly sealing the fate of the Mikrus, Stanisław Szelichowski blamed FSO representatives, who viewed the micro-car as a threat to the Syrena, just as the latter was entering mass production, due to the supposedly inferior quality of the car from Żerań to the product of the plants in Mielec and Rzeszów.[584] The third possible reason—economics—seems most plausible. Almost from the very beginning, when it turned out that production costs of the Mikrus were very high, government representatives seriously doubted the project's profitability. Already in early 1959, at the plenary meeting of the Automotive Council, Minister of Heavy Industry Kiejstut Żemajtis, described the decision to produce the micro-car as "questionable." The external conditions that enabled unprofitable ventures were disappearing. Żemajtis proclaimed: "The 'Mikrus' is being produced in an aviation plant at a time when it had a fallow period. Currently, the plant has been loaded with its proper production." He also considered it highly probable that, in the face of new production tasks, it would not be possible to reach the number of units that would make Mikrus profitable.[585] The car's relatively high price was the result of high production costs, which were estimated at 54,000 zlotys in 1959. A loss of several thousand zlotys after a full implementation of production and an increase in the number of

---

more likely from economic reasons, including especially the high costs associated with starting production of new vehicles, which, in turn, was an important argument for the decision to begin looking for foreign know-how; K. J. Mórawski, *Syrena*, pp. 54–55.

582 M. Płocica and B. Winiarski, *Mikrus*, p. 161.

583 Ibid., p. 160.

584 Ibid., pp. 160–166.

585 AAN, MK, sygn. II/2, Protokół no. 1 z plenarnego zebrania Rady Motoryzacyjnej, 9 I 1959 r., pp. 74–76; cf. A. M. Rostocki, *Kochajmy stare gruchoty*, Warszawa 1977, p. 160.

units released would turn into a profit of 5,000 zlotys on each Mikrus sold by 1962. It was calculated that, by 1963, the profit would increase to 10,000 zlotys, while production costs would drop to 37,000.[586] Rather short-term plans, reaching only as far as the year 1959, anticipated that 5,000 Mikrus vehicles would roll out of the WSK Mielec factory. In the end, 1,700 units were produced over the course of three years.

Poles reacted to the cessation of production with great surprise and regret. In an emotional letter to the Polish Radio, a resident of Zawiercie wrote: "On November 10 of this year, it was announced to the world in the press that the youngest child of our four-wheeled transport, the Mikrus, has died. It died a natural death, unable to withstand the competition of her adult siblings ..., the Syrena and the Warszawa, or pass the test of time. ... But it wasn't the Mikrus who didn't pass the test, it was the people."[587] Years later, Alexander Rostocki reflected on the Mikrus in nostalgic tones: "In our times, the car has ceased to be ... the fruit of enthusiasm, of joyful creativity, of the zeal of a single person, or even a group of people. It is a machine built with cold calculation by nameless design offices and produced by many plants in cooperation with each other, based on precisely defined technologies developed by specialised design and research units. The Mikrus was an exception."[588]

3.4.3 "The pace of technical progress is imposed on us by life, by the situation, by the world in which we live": The Fiat 125p

In July 1957, Józef Cyrankiewicz issued an order appointing a special commission to explore the matter of the production of a popular car. The commission was headed by Eugeniusz Szyr.[589] The result of its work was a report entitled "Conclusions concerning the launch of production of a popular car," whose

---

586 M. Płocica and B. Winiarski, *Mikrus*, pp. 111–115.

587 ADiZPRiT, sygn. 1050/29, Biuletyn nr 85 w sprawie samochodów Mikrus produkcji WSK—Mielec, 23 XI 1959 r., unnumbered pages.

588 A. M. Rostocki, *Kochajmy stare gruchoty*, p. 161.

589 In addition to E. Szyr, the committee also included representatives of MPC, MK, MON, URM, BKPM, the Institute of Machine Industry Organisation, the Planning Commission of the Council of Ministers, the Central Automotive Production Board, and Motoimport; Archiwum Dokumentacji Historycznej PRL (hereafter: ADH PRL), Kolekcja Eugeniusza Szyra, sygn. III/17, unnumbered pages; cf. J. Kochanowski, *Rewolucja międzypaździernikowa*, p. 265ff

arguments coincided almost entirely with what experts had been proposing: the popular car should be a four-seater and relatively economical (consuming no more than 8 litres of fuel per 100 km). The report called for a production target of 120,000 units per year, which would meet both domestic and export needs. Initially, the new vehicle was to be manufactured in Żerań, but the planned production volume meant that a new factory would have to be built. Potential locations were even suggested: Warsaw, Lublin, Poznań, and Łódź. The commission also recommended that production be based on a purchased licence, and to this end, it had even initiated investigation of foreign markets. Among companies that expressed initial interest in cooperating with the Polish government were the French companies Renault and Simca, contacts with which were established during the Poznań fair.[590] Italian Fiat and British Triumph also expressed interest in cooperation with Poland.[591] Ultimately, the talks did not amount to anything concrete, and the study prepared by the commission—as Eugeniusz Szyr noted years later—was rejected due to resistance from the highest authorities (primarily Władysław Gomułka).[592]

The argumentation presented in the report did not appeal to industry circles. In early 1958, during the first plenary meeting of the Automotive Council, Minister of Transportation Ryszard Strzelecki described the development of individual motorisation in the following terms: "It seems that we can solve the problem of individual motorisation only by launching and expanding production of our own passenger cars, corresponding in design features and price to the particular nature of our country."[593] The diplomatic tone of the minister's statement was probably dictated largely by a desire to maintain a positive atmosphere around the government. Yet, the rhetoric, in both tone and content, quickly reverted to the previous norm. During the following meeting of the Automotive Council in late 1958, Strzelecki said: "[W]ithout denying the need for a popular car, our country's economic

---

590 ADH PRL, [Pismo Kazimierza Secomskiego do Eugeniusza Szyra], Warszawa, 2 IX 1957 r., unnumbered pages.

591 AAN, MK, sygn. II/2, Protokół no. 7/P z posiedzenia Prezydium Rady Motoryzacyjnej, 28 IV [19]58 r., p. 417.

592 ADH PRL, Kolekcja Eugeniusza Szyra, [Pismo Kazimierza Secomskiego], unnumbered pages.

593 AAN, MK, Przemówienie Ministra Komunikacji Ryszarda Strzeleckiego na I Plenarnym Zebraniu Rady Motoryzacyjnej, [3 I 1958 r.], p. 18.

situation does not allow for the production of such a car to be given priority over a number of other needs of the society and the development of other industries that have a significant impact on the harmonious development of the national economy."[594] This statement was echoed by Minister Żemajtis, who left no doubt as to the shape of private motorisation in the coming years, even announcing that no changes in state policy towards individual motorisation would be possible until 1965. Nevertheless, he allowed for some light at the end of the tunnel. MPC representatives were conducting talks with Czechoslovakia at the time on possible cooperation in the production of passenger cars. If negotiations broke down with Poland's southern neighbour, the ministry would initiate discussion about the purchase of a licence, so long as it did not take on a "colonial character."[595] The main concern here was that until Polish industry was able to produce entire cars from parts manufactured in Poland, it would have to rely on the costly import of components from a licensor.[596]

It should be noted that members of the Automotive Council were among the greatest critics of the state's automotive development policy. Again and again at council meetings, clashes took place with government leaders, who were consistently invited to attend. This was the case at the end of April 1960, when a sharp exchange of opinions took place between Deputy Minister Antoni Czechowicz and Wiktor Sudra from the Warsaw University of Technology, representing the Automotive Council. The former was of the opinion that the production of a popular passenger car was not a priority for the economy, and potential production should be based on a cooperation with Czechoslovakia, an idea that was being seriously considered at that time. Czechowicz also noted that if talks with the southern neighbour failed, the Syrena would have to be thoroughly modernised, which would not require the construction of a new, large plant. Sudra took the opportunity to criticise Czechowicz, claiming that the opinion of the council was not being taken into account when decisions were made on matters concerning the automotive

---

594 Ibid., Protokół no. 5 z zebrania plenarnego Rady Motoryzacyjnej, 12 XII 1958 r., p. 66.

595 Ibid., Protokół no. 1/P z posiedzenia Prezydium Rady Motoryzacyjnej, 2 I 1959 r., p. 451.

596 Ibid., Protokół no. 7/P z posiedzenia Prezydium Rady Motoryzacyjnej, 28 IV [19]58 r., p. 416.

industry. What this referred to were the questions of a popular car (the council was in favour of the production of such a car), the modernisation of the Warszawa (the council considered it to be pointless), and the suspension of production of the Mikrus (the council wanted it to be maintained).[597]

The idea of a cooperative arrangement with Czechoslovakia, mentioned several times above, began to take shape in 1959. The Kremlin had been pressuring other communist bloc countries through Comecon to make joint plans for the development of particular forms of production and to implement investments between at least two member countries.[598] Guidelines for the development of the Polish national economy in the years 1959–1965 presented in the closing resolution of the Third Congress of the PZPR even included a section requiring the foregrounding of specialisation and cooperation within the socialist camp when planning industrial production.[599] The Czechoslovak delegation that arrived in Warsaw in 1959 consisted of representatives of the Ministry of General Machine Construction. At a meeting with MPC representatives, it was deemed advisable to consider the necessary conditions for the initiation of joint, mass production of a passenger car with an engine displacement of up to 1000 cm^3. It was assumed that within a decade, a vehicle assembly plant would be established in each country, and that production of components would be divided between them to ensure low unit costs and a reduction in investment outlays. It was also decided that relevant ministries in East Germany would be informed about the possibility of joining the cooperation.[600] In subsequent years, talks on joint production continued with

---

597 Ibid., Protokół no. 2/60 z posiedzenia Prezydium Rady Motoryzacyjnej, 26 IV 1960 r., p. 522.

598 R. Skrzypek, *Polityka PRL wobec państw socjalistycznych w latach 1956–1970. Współpraca napięcia konflikty*, Poznań 2010, p. 211; see also Piotr Jaroszewicz's speech during the 3rd Congress of the PZPR: *III Zjazd Polskiej Zjednoczonej Partii Robotniczej. Stenogram. Warszawa 10 III—19 III 1959 r.*, Warszawa 1959, pp. 430–433.

599 *III Zjazd Polskiej Zjednoczonej Partii Robotniczej*, p. 1092.

600 AAN, Komitet Współpracy Gospodarczej z Zagranicą (hereafter: KWGzZ), sygn. 20/54, Protokół z rozmów między delegacjami Ministerstwa Przemysłu Ciężkiego Polskiej Rzeczypospolitej Ludowej i Ministerstwa Ogólnego Budownictwa Maszynowego Republiki Czechosłowackiej, Warszawa, [15–18 IV 1959 r.], unnumbered pages. The Czechoslovaks announced that they would soon start producing their own passenger car with an engine of up to 1000 cm^3 and any cooperation would be possible only after its completion, planned for the early 1970s; ibid., MPC, sygn. 13/5, Notatka z

the participation of representatives of East Germany, and though these talks produced no binding decisions, the idea of a small, popular car remained. The three countries were to jointly produce half a million units of the vehicle per year, because only at such a production volume would it be possible to implement modern, automated production and broad cooperation between the countries involved. This approach would also make it possible to reduce investment expenditures by 30–40%.[601] It cannot be denied that Poland would be the greatest beneficiary of a possible cooperation between these automotive industries, because it would gain access to its neighbours' technology.[602] This was not the first attempt by the Polish government to enter into cooperation with another people's democracy.[603] Just like in the 1940s, the Czechoslovaks were rather cautious about the Polish proposals. During Gomułka's meeting with Antonín Novotný in the High Tatras in March 1963, the First Secretary of the Communist Party of Czechoslovakia politely announced that "in many areas there are the most favourable conditions for mutual, beneficial cooperation," while also indicating that Czechoslovakia would first have to reach an agreement with Moscow, because the USSR provided Czechoslovakia with almost 60% of its raw materials and was the recipient of 30% of Czechoslovak export production. In conclusion, Novotný even suggested that the fate of the Polish proposals be made dependent on a tripartite agreement between Poland, the USSR, and Czechoslovakia. A memo from the talks between the first secretaries relates: "Concerning some of the Polish proposals with regard to the so-called 'Agreement of Producers', the First Secretary of the Communist Party of Czechoslovakia failed to

rozmów grupy specjalistów PRL i CSRS w sprawach związanych z pogłębieniem współpracy w dziedzinie przemysłu samochodowego w generalnej perspektywie do 1980 roku, [9 VI 1961], unnumbered pages.

601 AAN, KC PZPR, sygn. 237/XXXI-253, Notatka w sprawie rozszerzenie współpracy polsko-czechosłowackiej w zakresie wspólnej produkcji samochodów ciężarowych, autobusów i samochodów osobowych. Załącznik no. 3, [po 8 III 1963 r.], pp. 30–31.

602 R. Skrzypek, *Polityka PRL*, pp. 223–227.

603 See AAN, Komitet Centralny Polskiej Partii Robotniczej (hereafter: KC PPR), sygn. 295/XI-393 (mf 2354/5), Stenogram z polskich przemówień w czasie partyjnej konferencji gospodarczej polsko-czechosłowackiej, odbytej 19 III 1948 r. w Pradze, pp. 62–123.

provide a specific answer. This involved those areas of the machine industry that were related to Czechoslovak supplies to the Soviet Union."[604]

Arrangements regarding the specialisation of industrial production within Comecon were made during the sixteenth session of the organisation in 1962. In the machine industry, 590 items were covered, and Poland was assigned 162 types of products, of which 19 it was to produce on its own, 63 in cooperation with one other country, 56 with two, 18 with three, and 6 with four. The largest beneficiaries were the USSR (387 products, including 132 independently) and East Germany (214 and 49, respectively). Poland was ahead of Czechoslovakia (158 and 21). At the same time, however, determining the product list turned out to be a difficult task. Individual countries tried to qualify for as many as possible, with the most highly developed countries working to prevent others from using their technologies; this concerned primarily East Germany and Czechoslovakia. The Germans were particularly aggressive, launching production that was not provided for in the specialisation arrangements, as happened with excavators, which were supposed to be manufactured in Poland and the USSR. Additionally, both Czechoslovakia and East Germany strove to claim the most profitable products.[605]

The fact that the Polish government was seriously interested in the joint production of cars within Comecon is also evidenced by a confidential report prepared in April 1963 by the Planning Commission of the Council of Ministers for the Office of the Comecon Executive Committee.[606] One major

---

604 AAN, KC PZPR, sygn. 237/XXXI-253, Notatka informacyjna o wynikach rozmów Pierwszego Sekretarza KC PZPR Towarzysza W. Gomułki z Pierwszym Sekretarzem KC KPCz Towarzyszem A. Novotným, które odbyły się w Wysokich Tatrach w dniach 14–15 III 1963 r., pp. 1–5.

605 AAN, KC PZPR, sygn. 237/XXXI-342, Notatka dla Sekretarza KC tow. B. Jaszczuka w sprawie realizacji ustaleń specjalizacyjnych podjętych przez organa RWPG na lata 1962–1965, 12 II 1964 r., pp. 2–8.

606 The passenger car assembly plant project, prepared a year earlier by the Automotive Industry Design Office, called for the production of a small, 700 kg passenger car with an engine of up to 1,000 cm3, capable of accommodating four people, with a maximum speed of 120–140 km/h and a fuel consumption of 6–7 litres per 100 km. The cost of starting an assembly plant that would be able to produce 30,000 vehicles per year was estimated at 200 million zlotys. The project anticipated that some components would be imported from Hungary; AAN, MPC, sygn. 43/16, Projekt wstępny montowni samochodów małolitrażowych, kwiecień 1962, unnumbered pages.

focus for economic development in the PRL in the following twenty years was the automotive industry, which would produce two types of passenger vehicles: medium- and small-displacement. A popular passenger car with a displacement of approximately 1000 cm^3 would be manufactured initially at Żerań and, starting in the 1970s, in a new, specially built factory. The development of this branch of the machine industry was supposed to then result in cooperation in the production of parts and assemblies for jointly manufactured passenger cars and trucks. Each country participating in this joint venture was to have its own assembly plant.[607]

One potential direction of cooperation in the production of passenger cars was East Germany, but Poland's western neighbour focused its attention on the USSR, though the Kremlin was not interested in any joint activities because it was following its own programme of development of motorisation. Moreover, East Germany was a key market for Soviet automotive exports: in 1956, imported cars accounted for 7% of all vehicles in the country. In subsequent years, this figure continued to grow, reaching 32% by the end of the 1960s. Most of these imports were cars manufactured in Togliatti, Gorky, or Moscow. There were also attempts to establish cooperation between East Germany and Hungary. In this case, failure was due to the attitude of the Hungarians, who wanted to produce only certain spare parts and deliver them to East German factories. Talks about joint automobile production between Czechoslovakia and East Germany definitely reached the most advanced stage, but the Prague Spring brought the entire process to a halt.[608]

As is evident, attempts to engage in cooperation within the Comecon were made, but they yielded no significant results due to various factors, including political ones. In the Polish case, mutual hostility was probably the key factor. The domestic automotive industry was facing new challenges, but satisfactory results could not be reached only by modernising own production, which

---

607 Ibid., KC PZPR, sygn. 1724 (mf 2892), Podstawowe kierunki rozwoju gospodarczego PRL w okresie 1961–1980, pp. 267–268.

608 B. Ciesla, "Difficult Relations. German Automobile Construction and the Economic Alliance in Eastern Europe, 1945–1990," in: *Towards Mobility: Varieties of Automobilism in East and West*, ed. D. Schlinkert, M. Grieger, and U. Gutzmann, Wolfsburg 2009, pp. 96–97; L. Gatejel, *Warten, hoffen und endlich fahren*, pp. 111–115.

remained unable to support export plans even after modernisation. What remained was cooperation, but for that, Poland had to turn westward.[609]

One of the main topics of the Fourth Congress of the PZPR in mid-June 1964 was "setting a course for change in the structure of the Polish industry." In his introductory speech, Władysław Gomułka drew attention to the structure of domestic industrial production, which—compared to economically developed countries (he used East Germany as an example from the Eastern Bloc and England as one from Western European)—was characterised by a very low dynamic of industrial development, especially in machine building. An increase in production within this branch of industry would give a positive impulse to the export structure, since the sale of machinery and equipment was seen as "the key to a path to the expansion of our economy." A technical reconstruction would take place, especially in the machine and chemical industries.[610] In terms of the production of machines and equipment, in 1950, Poland had an output 7.5 times lower than the Federal Republic of Germany, 18–19 times lower than England, 6.5 times lower than France, and 4 times lower than Italy. Over the course of ten years, these indicators improved slightly: Poland managed to catch up with Italy, but still lagged behind France (reaching only half the output) or England (a quarter of the output).[611] How much there was to be done in this regard is illustrated in the tables showing the value of machinery and equipment imports and exports in 1956–1963. Each year, the value of sales abroad was lower than the value of purchases.[612]

609 Romania also chose the western direction. Offers were submitted by Volkswagen, Ford, and BMC, among others. Ultimately, the choice fell to Renault, a contract with which was signed in 1966. Under the contract, a new factory was established near the city of Pitești, producing Dacias which were modified versions of the French giant's models 8 and 12; L. Gatejel, "The Common Heritage of the Socialist Car Culture," p. 146; eadem, *Warten, hoffen und endlich fahren*, pp. 148–154.

610 *IV Zjazd Polskiej Zjednoczonej Partii Robotniczej, 15–20 czerwca 1964 r.*, Warszawa 1964, pp. 63–64, 110, 264.

611 T. Pałaszewska-Reindl, *Konsumpcja dóbr trwałego użytku w Polsce*, Warszawa 1966, p. 88.

612 In 1963 alone, Polish exports of machine industry goods were worth 2.3 billion zlotys, while imports amounted to 2.7 billion zlotys. In both cases, the value of these groups of goods constituted approximately one-third of the value of all foreign trade; *Rocznik Statystyczny*, 1965, pp. 335–336; cf. AAN, MHZ, sygn. 19/3, Eksport z

The direction of changes reflected in the final resolution of the Fourth Congress only confirmed actions initiated earlier. Already during the 10th Plenum of the Central Committee of the PZPR, officials identified the machine industry as foundational for the future "modernisation and technical reconstruction of the national economy."[613] In February 1964, at a meeting of the Politburo of the Central Committee, its members ordered the development of a programme for the reconstruction of the machine industry, orienting it towards production for export. It was anticipated that by 1970 this industry would account for half of all exports.[614] The reconstruction was supposed to follow the guidelines presented in the "Assumptions for the development of the machine industry in the years 1966–1970," adopted at the same meeting, the very first sentence of which indicated a significant change in approach: "Assessments of the achievements and progress of the machine industry can no longer rely on comparisons with the prewar period and the first postwar years." From then on, the reference point would be "development trends in the machine industry in countries with a developed industry." Shortcomings were also noticed in the area of passenger cars, where "needs ... are greater than the possibilities of production."[615] The MPC calculated that in 1964 alone, the planned production of 9,500 Syrenas would satisfy only half of the demand for these vehicles. With a fleet of 175,000 cars in in 1963, Poland had one passenger car per every 175 people, which placed the country nearly last in Europe. In Czechoslovakia, the rate was

---

Polski maszyn, urządzeń i środków transportowych w latach 1949–1958 wg krajów sprzedaży, p. 23; ibid., Import do Polski maszyn, urządzeń i środków transportowych w latach 1949–1958 wg krajów sprzedaży, p. 24. Poland was also one of the largest importers of machine industry products within the Comecon. In 1964, as many as 42.7% of the value of all Polish imports from other countries in the bloc stemmed from machinery and equipment; ibid., sygn. 2/5, Zmiany w strukturze towarowej obrotów we wzajemnej wymianie handlowej krajów członkowskich RWPG w okresie lat 1955–1964, unnumbered pages.

613 "Przemówienie tow. Franciszka Waniołki wygłoszone na X Plenum KC PZPR 16 kwietnia 1962 r." in: *X Plenum Komietu Centralnego Polskiej Zjednoczonej Partii Robotniczej, 16–18 IV 1962 r.*, Warszawa 1952, p. 5.

614 AAN, KC PZPR, sygn. XIA-178, Protokół no. 96 posiedzenia Biura Politycznego, 26 II 1964 r., pp. 140–141.

615 Ibid., sygn. 1730 (mf 2894), Założenia rozwoju przemysłu maszynowego w latach 1966–1970, Warszawa, 19 II 1964, pp. 384, 390.

one car per 78; in East Germany—1:109; but in Italy and France—1:20 and 1:8, respectively. The ministry's ambitious plan anticipated that in 1970, the ratio would drop to one passenger car per ninety-four people. To achieve this goal, automobile production had to double. When formulating the "directions of development until 1970," ministry representatives assumed financial outlays of 5.3 billion zlotys for the development of the automotive industry in the years 1966–1970. Most of this amount would cover the expansion of plants producing trucks and tractors. Approximately 600 million zlotys were allocated for the development of passenger car production. A part of that sum was to be used to purchase licences for the production of certain vehicle components.[616]

In early October 1964, at its next meeting, the Politburo of the Central Committee gave the green light to talks with potential licensors. The starting point for the meeting was the weakness of the national economic plan for 1965, especially in terms of exports of machinery and equipment to capitalist countries. In the unanimous opinion of the participants, the plan was "stretched in many respects and does not correspond to the developmental directions … outlined by the Fourth Party Congress." It was therefore necessary to focus especially on exports. The Politburo indicated the basic lines of action: expanding opportunities for cooperation with capitalist countries in the development of export industries; securing funds for the importation of elements whose absence hindered the export production of the machine industry; transferring the best technical staff to industries producing for export; and taking decisions "on the purchase of necessary foreign licences."[617] The archives of the MHZ retained a memo confirming the establishment of contacts with the French automotive industry and the Renault company,[618] but it was with the Italian Fiat that the talks reached the most advanced stage.

After an unsuccessful attempt to initiate cooperation at the turn of the 1950s, contacts probably would not have been re-established in the 1960s if it was not for the Zavodi Crvena Zastava factory in Kragujevac, Serbia,

616 Ibid., Kierunki rozwoju przemysłu motoryzacyjnego. Ministerstwo Przemysłu Ciężkiego, pp. 509, 512, 514.
617 Ibid., sygn. XIA-178, Protokół no. 4 posiedzenia Biura Politycznego, 2 X 1964 r., p. 90.
618 AAN, MHZ, sygn. 35/26, Departament traktatów II, Warszawa, 28 VIII 1965 r., pp. 137–138.

which had produced the Zastava 600, a licenced version of the popular Fiat 600, since 1954.[619] Italy was an important trading partner for Yugoslavia even in the 1920s and 1930s. The outbreak of World War II severed ties between the two countries only temporarily, and the split between Belgrade and Moscow made the renewal of economic exchange with Western countries an extremely crucial matter. Suffice it to say that almost immediately after Yugoslavia and Italy resolved the issue of Trieste, an economic cooperation agreement between the two was signed.[620] A contract with Fiat was concluded on April 12, 1954, because the Italian company outbid not only other Italian companies, but also French, English, and American competitors.[621] It is worth emphasising that the first half of the 1950s was a period of global expansion for Fiat: new factories opened in Latin and South America (Argentina, Brazil, and Venezuela), in Mexico, and in Europe (Spain, Austria, the Federal Republic of Germany, Poland, and the USSR).[622] Here, the crucial fact is that the production of model 1300/1500 began concurrently in the early 1960s in factories in Turin and Kragujevac. Polish experts rated this model of Fiat very highly; compared to its competitors, it stood out because of its modern design, low kerb weight, long repair intervals, and low fuel consumption. Polish officials also noted "the technological nature of the design, and therefore

---

619 M. Milijković, "Western Technology in Socialist Factory: the Formative Phase of the Yugoslav Automobile Industry, 1955–1962," Cold War History Research Center at Corvinas University of Budapest, 2013, p. 6, http://www.etd.ceu.hu/2013/miljkovic_marko.pdf (accessed: 18 May 2016). The first postwar attempts to launch automotive production in a former arms factory in Kragujevac took place in the early 1950s. It was then that Yugoslavia began producing jeeps under a contract with Willys-Overland from the USA. After a certain number of vehicles had been produced, the contract was terminated due to excessive financial demands on the part of the Americans; ibid., p. 65.

620 J. A. Gierowski, *Historia Włoch*, Wrocław—Warszawa—Kraków 1999, pp. 556–557, 568–569, M. Milijković, "Western Technology," p. 6; T. Wituch, "Spór o Triest—wczesny epizod 'zimnej wojny'," *Dzieje Najnowsze* 1997, no. 2, pp. 73–86.

621 D. Turnock, *The East European Economy in Context. Communism and Transition*, London—New York 1997, pp. 32–33.

622 M. Milijković, "Western Technology," p. 67; A. Władyka, *Wszystko o... Fiat*, Warszawa 1977, pp. 27–30.

the possibility of achieving low manufacturing costs," access to an organised service, and potentially high market interest in the car.[623]

The Crvena Zastava plant itself also made a good impression. When, at the end of December 1964, a delegation of the Polish MON visited the factory in Kragujevac, its representatives were amazed: "The Red Zastava plant is a modern plant, it has a modern machine tool park produced in capitalist countries. ... Internal transport is organised very well, especially in the case of assembly lines." The production volume was also impressive: in 1964, 34,000 Zastava 750 s rolled off the factory floor, and the plan was that by 1970, almost five times more cars of various models would be produced.[624]

Economic contacts between Poland and the Socialist Federal Republic of Yugoslavia were re-established in the second half of the 1950s. It was then that the Polish-Yugoslav and Yugoslav-Polish Chambers of Commerce were established, followed by the Polish-Yugoslav Committee for Economic Cooperation.[625] In 1958, trade between the two countries amounted to approximately US $46 million (Poland exported goods worth US $22.3 million and acquired imports worth US $24 million), those numbers increased systematically in the following years, almost reaching US $100 million in 1964, with the export-import ratio of 50.2 to 48.8. Undoubtedly, the fact that the value of trade between the two countries doubled was the result of a long-term agreement on the supply of goods signed in December 1960. Initially, it was assumed that total trade would reach US $100 million within five years, but the projected value was subsequently increased several times. Polish exports to Yugoslavia included complete facilities, ship engines, mining and metallurgical equipment, machine tools, textile machinery, coke, hard coal, chemical and pharmaceutical raw materials, tobacco, eggs, and resins. The goods that flowed in the other direction included marine engines, ships, food

---

623 AAN, KC PZPR, sygn. 1733 (mf 2895), Informacja o prowadzonych rozmowach w sprawie możliwości produkcji samochodów osobowych przy współpracy z Jugosławią, [10 XII 1964 r.], p. 102.

624 Ibid., Zjednoczenie Przemysłu Motoryzacyjnego (hereafter: ZPM), sygn. 77/TK/1965, Wyciąg ze sprawozdania z pobytu polskiej delegacji wojskowej w Jugosławii po linii Zarządu Technicznego Wojsk Pancernych Zjednoczenia Przemysłu Ciągnikowego i Służby Samochodowej MON, [styczeń 1965 r.], unnumbered pages; D. Turnock, *The East European Economy in Context*, p. 33.

625 A. Wieczorkiewicz, *Polska Jugosławia. Gospodarka współpraca*, Warszawa 1972, p. 97.

industry equipment, mercury, agricultural machinery, aluminium oxide, zinc concentrates, magnesites, lead, cable industry products and non-ferrous metals, tobacco, wine, and prunes.[626] An additional impulse to bring economic relations even closer came with the agreement on industrial cooperation signed in June 1964.[627]

At the end of December 1963, during talks at a meeting of the Polish-Yugoslav Joint Commission on Industrial Cooperation held in Belgrade, Yugoslav delegates mentioned for the first time the possibility of cooperation in the automotive industry; they proposed that "Poland should consider accepting the documentation for the production licence for Fiat 1800 and 2300 cars along with derivatives," and establishing cooperation in the production of small-displacement cars assembled in Kragujevac. The Polish delegation had not yet considered this possibility, but decided to initiate talks on the importation of larger numbers of Zastavas (5,000–6,000 units per year) in exchange for power equipment manufactured in Poland. The contract was to be worth US $30 million.[628] Further talks on Polish-Yugoslav cooperation in the automotive industry took place in September 1964. A Polish delegation comprised of representatives of the MHZ and the Committee for Foreign Economic Cooperation (KWGzZ), led by Stefan Jędrychowski, met their Yugoslav counterparts in Belgrade and expressed the willingness to continue the existing cooperation, while proposing an expansion into new areas, including the production of equipment for energy facilities, railways, tractors, construction machines, and passenger cars. Polish delegates encouraged the Yugoslavs to submit an official proposal and specify the conditions of cooperation in the field of motorisation.[629] The Yugoslavs initially

626 Ibid.; AAN, MHZ, sygn. 31/70, Materiały informacyjne i propozycje dla delegacji polskiej na spotkanie delegacji partyjno-rządowych Polski i Jugosławii, Warszawa, 20 VI 1964 r., unnumbered pages.

627 Ibid., Wspólne oświadczenie delegacji partyjno-rządowych Polskiej Rzeczypospolitej Ludowej i Socjalistycznej Federacyjnej Republiki Jugosławii (część gospodarcza), Warszawa, październik 1965 r., unnumbered pages.

628 Ibid., URM, sygn. 72/37, Sprawozdanie delegacji polskiej Polsko-Jugosłowiańskiej Komisji Mieszanej ds. współpracy przemysłowej z rozmów przeprowadzonych na I spotkaniu w Belgradzie, 2–8 XII 1963 r., pp. 238–239.

629 AAN, MHZ, sygn. 31/70, Notatka o konsultacji i rozmowach organów planowania PRL i SFRJ, odbytych w dniach 11–16 września 1964 roku w Belgradzie. Poufne, unnumbered pages.

announced the transfer of a partial licence for the production of the Fiat 1300/1500 model to Poland (to which they were authorised in their contract with the Italian company) and responded positively to the Polish proposal to share production of the components of the new car. At the turn of the 1970s, the Polish government wanted to supply the Kragujevac plant with engines and clutches, and to receive in return suspension components and rear axles from Yugoslavia. The Yugoslavs, on the other hand, were interested in various body parts and castings produced in Poland.

Meanwhile, in October 1964, representatives of the Automotive Industry Association began preliminary talks with Fiat, which expressed its willingness to cede the licence to Poland. Further negotiations took place at the end of December, when a Polish delegation met with the management of the Italian company. From the beginning, the Polish side conditioned further talks on the inclusion of Yugoslavia in a shared cooperation. The Italians had only one requirement: a three-sided cooperation would be accepted if the production of specific components was divided between the parties at established volumes. In addition, Fiat guaranteed all technical, material, and training assistance. It also assured the Polish government that it would not interfere if Yugoslavia provided it with the licence for the new car free of charge. In that case, Fiat's role would be limited mainly to technical support, especially in the initial production period.

The situation changed after another round of talks with the Yugoslavian side. A disagreement emerged concerning the list of components that were to be manufactured in factories in both countries. There was also the issue of foreign sales, which were highly important for Polish exports. Yugoslavia demanded that Poland not sell new cars to countries with extant or future Yugoslav assembly plants.[630] This would significantly reduce the sales market for Polish cars, even as broadening that market was a key condition for the Polish government. Fiat, on the other hand, created no such obstacles (apart from exports to Italy). Moreover, it offered assistance in the distribution of new cars manufactured in Żerań through the network of its representative offices around the world.[631]

---

630 AAN, KC PZPR, sygn. 1733 (mf 2895), Notatka w sprawie uruchomienia w Polsce samochodu 1300/1500, warszawa, [10 II 1965 r.], pp. 117–118.

631 *Fiat w Polsce (sprzedaż licencji)*, Warszawa 1980, pp. 8–9.

The issue of licensing was considered again by the Politburo, which accepted a concept for the development of the automotive industry presented at its meeting on February 16, 1965, and agreed to start talks with Fiat, while negotiations continued on the possibility of cooperation with the Kragujevac plant. An order went out for the preparation of accurate cost calculations for two eventualities: a trilateral Polish-Yugoslav-Italian cooperation or one without Yugoslavia. Additionally, decisions were made about the future of models currently manufactured at FSO: the production of the Syrena was to be maintained "at a level that requires no additional expenditure"—that is, limited to spare parts—and would end with the appearance of the Fiats. Meanwhile, the assembly of various types of Warszawas was to be continued.[632]

Negotiations with Fiat began in May 1965. The Italian delegation arrived in Warsaw and handed representatives of the Automotive Industry Association with a questionnaire necessary to develop a preliminary draft of the licensing agreement. The document was filled out and sent to Turin in June 1965.[633] During negotiations with Fiat, the Yugoslav plan was slowly abandoned. In addition to the reasons mentioned above (restrictions on exports, problems in agreement on the production of the components of the new car), Fiat also boasted experience in providing the kind of training and technological resources necessary for the efficient expansion of the Żerań plant. The fact that Fiat had an array of patents, which were much more likely to be transferred to Poland after a licence agreement was concluded, was also important.[634]

Fiat's offer was thus the most advantageous. To some extent, the choice of the Turin company was also influenced by historical contacts, both from the interwar period and from the late 1940s. Andrzej Władyka, one of Pol-Mot's directors, summed up the decision: "There were several reasons. Fiat produced

---

632 AAN, KC PZPR, sygn. 1733 (mf 2895), Protokół no. 11 posiedzenia Biura Politycznego w dniu 16 II 1965 r., p. 80. Ultimately, however, the Syrena was produced for almost twenty years, until 1983, while the last Warszawa rolled off the Żerań assembly line in March 1973.

633 AAN, MHZ, sygn. 59/3, Dotyczy: Współpracy z Fiatem, Warszawa, 29 VI 1965 r., unnumbered pages.

634 AAN, KC PZPR, sygn. 1733 (mf 2895), Informacja o prowadzonych rozmowach w sprawie możliwości produkcji samochodów osobowych przy współpracy z Jugosławią, [10 XII 1964 r.], p. 106.

modern and popular small- and medium-displacement cars. It had extensive experience in transferring know-how and launching production under licence, not only in capitalist countries."[635] Władyka's opinion was confirmed by Tadeusz Wrzaszczyk, then-director of ZPM: "The purchase of the licence resulted primarily from the need to quickly overcome the distance separating our automotive industry from its world-leading counterparts. A thorough analysis has shown that a licence is fully justified economically and solves the problem relatively quickly with the highest degree of certainty of good results. … In addition, this car suits us, it is economical to produce … ."[636]

The agreement between Fiat and Motoimport was signed on December 22, 1965, and approved by the Economic Committee of the Council of Ministers on January 21, 1966.[637] It is worth noting that the negotiations were conducted in secret and any information about them was restricted by censorship. Wróblewski recalls that the only official mention had been published in *Kurier Polski* and stated that FSO employees were taking intense Italian language courses. This information apparently sparked a wave of rumours.[638] The fact that a contract had been signed was officially announced almost a year after the fact.[639] The licence cost US $2.5 million, payable after seven years. This amount could be reduced depending on the volume of automotive equipment purchased from Fiat within six years: if Poland spent US $25 million in this way, the licence fee would be waived. Andrzej Górecki, later director of Pol-Mot, played an important role in producing the agreement. The Italians were represented by, among others, Armando Fiorelli, who was involved in organising the production of Fiats in interwar Poland.[640] The agreement included many smaller contracts. The basic licence allowed for

---

635 A. Dłutek, *Kooperacja polsko-włoska Fiat 126p: zakup licencji: opis przypadku*, Warszawa 1979, p. 6.

636 "Polski 'Fiat'—kiedy i jaki?" *Motor* 1966, no. 47, p. 3.

637 AAN, MHZ, sygn. 14/21, Uchwała no. 14/66 Komitetu Ekonomicznego Rady Ministrów z 21 stycznia 1966 r. w sprawie zatwierdzenia umowy licencyjnej oraz współpracy technicznej z firmą "Fiat," p. 6.

638 A. K. Wróblewski, *Polska na kółkach*, Warszawa 1988, p. 117.

639 Archiwum Państwowe w Gdańsku (hereafter: APG), Wojewódzki Urząd Kontroli Prasy, Publikacji i Widowisk w Gdańsku (hereafter: WUPPiW Gdańsk), sygn. 318, Aktualne zapisy i zalecenia, 1966, p. 14 (I would like to thank Michał Przeperski for pointing out this source to me); *Motoryzacja* 1966, no. 12, p. 1.

640 *Opowieść o FSO*, p. 73.

the production of a new model in Poland. Fiat was to provide the necessary documentation for the plants and specifications for individual elements. As mentioned above, the Italian company did not prevent Poland from exporting the new car to all countries, including those associated with Comecon, except Italy and Yugoslavia; it is worth noting that the USSR did not negotiate such an option for Lada. Along with the purchase of the licence, the two parties also reached an agreement on financing the purchase of equipment and accessories, which included the option of covering the cost of the licence through other purchases at Fiat, as mentioned above. Italian experts would also take part in modernising Żerań FSO. Factory equipment—machines, as well as welding and assembly tools—came largely from Fiat's partners in Great Britain, East Germany, the USA, and West Germany, but also from the USSR. Another advantage was that the new components and parts could be used in other vehicles manufactured in Poland. Likewise, from that moment on, Polish industry could also make use of several dozen patents owned by Fiat. The agreement came into force in February 1966, and in April of that year the Council of Ministers ratified the contract signed the previous December. FSO was thoroughly modernised, and the production of the Warszawa was moved to a hall taken over from the Warsaw Car Repair Works (Warszawskie Zakłady Naprawy Samochodów) at Stalingradzka Street. In the same month in Turin, a Motoimport opened an office tasked with coordinating technical and commercial cooperation between FSO and Fiat. In the second half of 1966, the training of Polish employees began in Italy, and work was underway to adapt Italian structures to Polish standards.[641]

Let us now return to Polish-Yugoslav cooperation. Despite abandoning the idea of purchasing a licence from Yugoslavia, both countries continued to support the idea of a cooperation in the production of car components. A framework contract for long-term technical cooperation, signed on April 24, 1966, called for the mutual supply of assemblies and parts for the production of 1300/1500 vehicles—the so-called standard assemblies. It was assumed that in the years 1967–1975 deliveries to both countries would create a turnover of approximately US $144 million and would be divided equally between

[641] AAN, MHZ, sygn. 14/21, Informacja o przebiegu uruchomienia produkcji samochodu "Polski Fiat 125p", pp. 213–214; *Opowieść o FSO*, p. 7; Z. Podbielski, *Polski Fiat 125p/ FSO 125p*, Warszawa 2009, p. 24; Fiat *w Polsce (sprzedaż licencji)*, pp. 8–9.

the partners.[642] The agreement was supposed to come into force by the end of November 1966, but due to misunderstandings regarding the pricing of parts subject to the cooperation, it was not ratified until May 23, 1967. In February 1970, an annex was signed bilaterally raising deliveries. Among the products Poland sent to Yugoslavia, were engines, complete car bodies, fuel tanks, disc brake calipers, suspension components, and steering tools, while deliveries in the opposite direction included rear axles, heaters and coolers, starters, pistons and pins, oil and air filters, wipers, and other elements.[643] Parts sold to Yugoslavia were used to assemble the Zastava 1100p in Kragujevac.[644] In the same year, Poland concluded an agreement with the USSR on the mutual supply of automobile parts.[645] Years later, Wróblewski wrote that Fiat gave socialist countries "a second Friendship Pipeline, because it bound with one cooperative chain various socialist countries that otherwise found it difficult to get along."[646]

The December agreement with Fiat concerned the production of the model 1300/1500, but on May 21, 1966, an annex to the agreement was signed, stipulating that the body of the new car assembled in Poland would be drawn from the 125 model, which was still being developed. The supposed reason were the objections expressed by FSO employees when they learned that Fiat planned to end (and did end) the production of model 1300/1500 in 1967, which meant that the factory at Żerań would be producing a car that had no equivalent anywhere else—hence the letter "p" added to the number "125."[647]

This begs the question: why did Poland decide to buy a licence for a car that the Italians considered already obsolete? Perhaps the deciding factor was the test drive that Premier Józef Cyrankiewicz took in the model 125 at the FSO factory track. Unfortunately, during the drive, the oil pan broke while

---

642 AAN, MHZ, sygn. 31/70, Projekt protokołu VIII Sesji Polsko-Jugosłowiańskiego Komitetu Współpracy Gospodarczej, unnumbered pages; ibid., Dotyczy: sprawozdania Ambasady PRL w Belgradzie z dnia 17 III 1966 r. o realizacji polsko-jugosłowiańskiej współpracy gospodarczej, 14 VI 1966, unnumbered pages.

643 Z. Podbielski, *Polski Fiat 125p*, p. 52; B. Ryś, *Rozwój polsko-jugosłowiańskich stosunków gospodarczych*, Łódź 1986, pp. 268–269.

644 W. Bukowski, *Samochody PRL-u*, Łódź 2010, p. 19.

645 *Opowieść o FSO*, p. 71.

646 A. K. Wróblewski, *Polska na kółkach*, p. 17.

647 Z. Podbielski, *Polski Fiat 125p*, p. 25.

going over a corrugated section of road surface, suggesting that the car could have problems on the bumpy Polish roads.[648] Other factors were probably more important. Apart from the operational advantages mentioned above, the Polish government favoured the older model 1300/1500 for technological reasons. A report on new designs and prototypes, prepared in April 1965 by the Department of Heavy Industry and Transportation of the Central Committee of the PZPR, which also discussed products of the automotive industry, was quite forthright about the limitations of this industry. It drew attention to the insufficient quality of the raw materials and steel used to build the cars or the electrical equipment installed in them. The authors of the report emphasised that only an improvement to the quality of materials and components would make it possible to obtain the maximum benefits from the future licence.[649] This gave rise to a fear that, given Polish limitations and the advanced design of the engine of the model 125, achieving the desired production quality would be problematic and expensive.[650] Secondly, together with the licence for the model 1300/1500, Poland purchased an old production line for engines for this vehicle, which the Italians had just withdrawn from the Turin factory. It was estimated that under Polish conditions, it could remain in use for a decade. In the end, it remained in use five years longer than that.[651]

The first Fiat 125p powered by a 1,300 cm^3 engine rolled off the Żerań assembly line on November 28, 1967, twenty-one months after the licence agreement had been signed. It was assembled exclusively from Italian parts. Half a year later, the 1000th unit left the factory, and by the end of 1968, annual production passed 7,000 units. The first cars with a larger engine (1,500 cm^3) came out in 1969.[652] According to various estimates, the final cost of starting the production of the popular Big Fiat was US $30–40 million.[653]

---

648 *Opowieść o FSO*, p. 74.

649 AAN, KC PZPR, sygn. 237/IX/105, Informacja o wynikach przeglądu nowych konstrukcji i prototypów, kwiecień 1965, p. 65.

650 Cf. St Szelichowski, "Jeździmy Polskim Fiatem 125p," *Motor* 1968, no. 15, p. 9.

651 Z. Podbielski, *Polski Fiat 125p*, pp. 26–27; A. Dłutek, *Kooperacja polsko-włoska*, p. 7.

652 Z. Podbielski, *Polski Fiat 125p*, p. 26.

653 Tadeusz Wrzaszczyk stated a higher amount in an interview for the weekly *Motor*; *Opowieść o FSO*, p. 83; A. Dłutek, *Kooperacja polsko-włoska*, p. 7.

The new product of the Żerań factory was eagerly awaited by everyone. *Motor* kept readers up to date on progress (but also delays) in preparations for the production of the Big Fiat, while also publishing information about the car itself.[654] The editorial team received one of the cars, marked with the number 6, for road tests, and first impressions were very positive: spacious, quiet, with a well finished interior ("The adjectives that come to mind are: quiet, warm—soft"), very good brakes ("We anticipate that after Fiat cars become more widespread, many a car will end up with a dented trunk because of the shorter ... braking distance"), and a sturdy suspension.[655] Incidentally, it is notable that the editors of *Motor* sent an official appeal to FSO to furnish the Big Fiat with a sign on the rear window warning other drivers about its powerful disc brakes. A few months later, however, the magazine relayed that the Żerań factory had ignored the appeal, even as "early observations have now been confirmed, when autumn rains lead dozens of Fiats to end up crashed."[656]

The Big Fiat went on sale in 1968. In conjunction, Bank Pekao informed those of its customers who had foreign currency accounts and savings of at least $1,000 about the possibility of purchasing "'Fiat 125p' passenger cars manufactured in Poland under an Italian licence" as part of internal export. The price was quite high and amounted to US $2,300. Wróblewski, with his typical irony, wrote in *Polityka* about the first "dollar" buyers of Polish Fiats: "The lucky ones! They bought a real car, thus far assembled from Italian parts. All that is left for us is tomato soup."[657] The price was later reduced to US $2,000.[658] The foreign currency obtained in this way was intended to cover the costs of cooperative imports from Italy.[659] It is worth noting that

654 S. Szelichowski, "Jaki będzie Polski Fiat," *Motor* 1967, no. 25, p. 5; "Polski Fiat z FSO już w montażu," *Motor* 1968, no. 7, p. 3.
655 S. Szelichowski, "Za kierownicą Polskiego Fiata," *Motor* 1968, no. 8, p. 5.
656 "Nasi dłużnicy," *Motor* 1968, no. 49, p. 11.
657 A. K. Wróblewski, "Fiat bez kompromisów," *Polityka* 1968, no. 13, p. 3.
658 T. Szczerbicki, *Samochody w PRL*, p. 341.
659 AAN, URM, sygn. 72/18, Notatka Zespołu Przemysłu Maszynowego z wykonania zaleceń grupy roboczej powołanej w maju 1966 r., ds. aktualizacji planu importu kooperacyjnego z KK w latach 1966–1970, pp. 175–176.

the "dollar" Fiats very quickly appeared at used car sales, where they were sold for between 270,000 and 280,000 zlotys.[660]

Sales in Polish zlotys began in September 1968, when Motozbyt began accepting prepayments for Big Fiats. Setting the right price was quite a challenge. The MPC believed that 140,000 zlotys was an appropriate value, and that it should only be reduced over time to 95,000 zlotys per car in case of vehicles with the 1300 cm^3 engine. The higher price was to remain in force until the market was adequately saturated with vehicles, though what that meant was not clear. At the same time, it was proposed that—whatever the final retail price might be—a 1,000 zloty special fee should be added for every car, which would be paid into a fund securing a network of sales agencies and service workshops responsible for carrying out repairs and warranty inspections. Big Fiats with a higher engine displacement were to cost 10,000 zlotys more.[661] In turn, the Ministry of Internal Trade (MHW) favoured a price of 155,000–160,000 zlotys. However, the State Price Commission (PKC) believed that the so-called equilibrium price should be no less than 220,000 zlotys. This amount was informed by the production volume planned for the first few years, which was not enough to meet the demand, as well as the low saturation of the automobile market and the very high car prices on the free market. In subsequent years, the price would decrease in proportion to the increase in production. It was planned that in 1970, when production reached the level of 50,000 units, the price would drop to 140,000 zlotys.[662] Finally, at the end of January, the PKC set the price for the Big Fiat with the 1,300 cm^3 engine at 160,000 zlotys.[663] However, by the time prepayments began to be accepted, the price had increased to 180,000 zlotys.[664] Therefore, if an average Pole, employed in socialised industry and earning just over

660 L. Rejewski, "Czy giełda daje obiektywny obraz?" *Motor* 1968, no. 14, p. 1.

661 AAN, Państwowa Komisja Cen (hereafter: PKC), sygn. 1/19, Notatka w sprawie ceny samochodu osobowego "Polski Fiat 125p" z silnikiem 1300 cm^3—produkcji FSO w Warszawie, p. 202.

662 Ibid., p. 203.

663 Ibid., sygn. 1/2131, Dotyczy: wniosku z dnia 17 XI 1967 r., p. 113.

664 "Jak i kiedy dokonywać przedpłat na zakup samochodów osobowych," *Motor* 1968, no. 35, p. 3. The market price for the Big Fiats that Motozbyt sold through the prepayment system was equal to the official price of the car; "Kupić, nie kupić…?" *Motor* 1969, no. 12, p. 1.

2,200 zlotys a month, wanted to buy a Big Fiat, they would have to save for almost seven years.[665] We can therefore assume that few could afford this car. The weekly *Przekrój* wrote about the price of the car with a wry tone: "Felczak is on his way to buying a Polish FIAT. He only needs 163,729 zlotys more."[666]

After only a year of use by Polish drivers, criticisms of the Big Fiat began to appear, dampening the enthusiasm with which the new car was initially greeted.[667] Some complained that cars manufactured in Żerań broke down more often and faster than "one would expect." It was difficult to find both the parts necessary for repairs and the specialists who could perform them. *Motor*, which received many letters criticising the quality of Polish Fiats, pointed out that delays of several months in the deliveries of components were caused by, for instance, strikes in Italy. However, the fact that parts for the Fiat were also suitable for Zastavas produced in cooperation with Poland meant that demand for those parts was much greater than the number of Fiats riding on domestic roads would suggest. However, journalists found no explanation for problems with finding an appropriate service centre for the cars from Żerań. This was directly related to the KERM resolution of 1967 which required that the Ministry of Transportation organise a service network. At the beginning of the fourth quarter of 1969, there were only 16 FSO-authorised TOS (Technical Automobile Service) stations. The creation of further stations was blocked by the Automotive Technical Support Association, which was unable to produce a sufficient number of specialised tools necessary to repair the Big Fiats, even though FSO had submitted the required documentation back in September 1967. The small, or at least insufficient, number of authorised repair stations meant great difficulties for users of the 125p. To maintain the warranty, they had to carry out repairs

---

665 Zdzisław Rurarz recalled years later that, after all, cars were cheaper than… bananas: "[I]f we bartered a Fiat 126P for bananas to one of the Central American countries, then the bananas we would import in this way could fetch four times more zlotys on the internal market than a single Fiat 126P. So, if both products were considered 'luxury items', then bananas were, relatively speaking, four times 'more luxurious' than the car, which is obvious nonsense"; Z. Rurarz, *Byłem doradcą Gierka*, Chicago—Toronto—Warszawa 1990, p. 112.

666 Quot. from: "Bez komentarzy," *Motor* 1968, no. 50, p. 4.

667 See, for example: R. Barnert, "10 000 km FIATem 125p (z doświadczeń użytkownika)," *Motor* 1968, no. 50, p. 9.

and inspections exclusively at the designated points. Therefore, they often had to travel very long distances.[668]

At the end of 1969, *Motor* editors decided to review the Big Fiat's almost two-year "presence" on Polish roads, interviewing several of its users, most of whom were famous Poles. Among the owners of vehicles produced by the FSO interviewed were Sobiesław Zasada, Jerzy Waldorff, Jan Kociniak, and Jan Kobuszewski. Deputy Minister of Light Industry Zdzisław Przygoda and Czesław Gosławski from the Central Command of the Citizens' Militia (MO) were also interviewed. It is unquestionably difficult to find any particular enthusiasm in the quoted statements. The interviewees trode carefully when talking about their Big Fiats. Gosławski described it as an "acceptable" car which has its faults, but "the advantages definitely outweigh the disadvantages." Bohdan Tomaszewski said that his Big Fiat "runs well, but I think I just got a good one. I often hear people complain about this car and I don't know if I was lucky or if the complainers were unlucky." Ernest Bryll, who had driven his Fiat over 39,000 kilometres, complained about the suspension, V-belts, and radiator. Andrzej Jedynak, technical director of the Polmo Automotive Industry Association, quite diplomatically "omitted to answer" the questions. The most "honest" opinion was that of actor Jan Kociniak, who said directly: "Well, for this price you have to be very happy…"[669] Another view, also published in *Motor*, drew attention to one more detail—namely, that buyers of new Fiats were practically prevented from choosing the colour of their car. In fact, the choice was limited to one or two colours, often very unattractive, used on the given batch of vehicles. For example, in Motozbyt in Katowice, customers could only buy yellow cars, which attracted little interest (As "J. S." wrote in a letter addressed to the weekly: "this color is nasty, no one wants to drive a 'cheese-like' car. … [W]here are the navy blue or mousey (gray) ones?"). The editors agreed with the buyers' complaints ("The high price [of the Big Fiat] also causes high expectations"), but advised them against being picky and to "take whatever is available."[670]

---

668 L. R. Wolski, "Wokół Polskiego Fiata," *Motor* 1969, no. 41, pp. 1, 3; T. Kucharski, "Kupiłem fiata," *Prawo i Życie* 1969, no. 12, p. 4.

669 "Dwa lata z Polskim Fiatem na ty," *Motor* 1969, no. 51/51, pp. 6–7.

670 "Fiat na szaro," *Motor* 1968, no. 47, p. 2.

Initially, the export of new Fiats was directed toward Poland's closest neighbours: Czechoslovakia, East Germany, and Hungary. Concurrently, the export of automotive industry products was reorganised. In March 1968, in place of Motoimport, the Polmo Foreign Trade Company of the Automotive Industry was established, which was not subordinated to the MHZ, but rather to the Ministry of Mechanical Industry, through ZPM.[671] A month later, the name of the newly established entity was changed to Pol-Mot.[672] In 1970, it was decided to expand the scope of exports, and Big Fiats began to reach Western Europe: the Netherlands, Austria, Greece, and Finland.[673] In the case of exports to the Netherlands, Poland signed an agreement with the oldest Dutch importer of cars manufactured by Fiat—the Lang company. In Finland, in turn, a special company called Autola OY, led by the famous Finnish rally driver Pauli Toivonen, was established to handle imports into Finland.[674] In subsequent years, Big Fiats also appeared in France, Germany, Belgium, Denmark, Sweden, Norway, and in Asia (Iraq, China, Thailand, Japan), Africa (Algeria, Ghana, Liberia), and the Americas (mainly Latin and South America, although a dozen or so copies were also sold to purchasers in the USA). During almost a quarter century of production, FSO cars were delivered to over 80 countries around the world, including places as exotic as Mali, Guinea, and Fiji. Among the socialist countries, Fiat 125p cars were sent primarily to Yugoslavia (115,000 units), Czechoslovakia (82,000 units), Hungary (67,000 units), Bulgaria (46,000 units) and East Germany (43,000 units). Interestingly, among the capitalist countries, the largest recipients were England (where almost 50,000 of the Polish vehicles were sold)

671 AAN, Ministerstwo Przemysłu Maszynowego (hereafter: MPM), sygn. 21/2, Zarządzenie no. 21/Org/68 Ministra Przemysłu Maszynowego z 18 III 1968 r. w sprawie utworzenia przedsiębiorstwa państwowego pod nazwą: Przedsiębiorstwo Handlu Zagranicznego Przemysłu Motoryzacyjnego "Polmo", pp. 1–2.

672 Ibid., Zarządzenie no. 30/Org/68 Ministra Przemysłu Maszynowego z 23 IV 1968 r. w sprawie zmiany nazwy przedsiębiorstwa państwowego: Przedsiębiorstwo Handlu Zagranicznego Przemysłu Motoryzacyjnego "Polmo" z siedzibą w Warszawie, p. 3.

673 As noted by Lewis H. Siegelbaum, until the end of the 1960s, the Finnish automobile industry was based primarily on cars produced in socialist countries. For example, between 1949 and 1961, the Scandinavian country was the main importer of Czechoslovak Škodas; L. H. Siegelbaum, "Introduction," in: *The Socialist Car*, p. 12; V. Fava, *The Socialist People's Car*, p. 144.

674 R. Przybylski, "Eksportowy hit PRL," *Rzeczpospolita*, November 27, 2007.

and France (27,000).[675] In total, over 586,000 Fiat 125p automobiles were delivered to Polish and foreign markets. However, if the previously mentioned standard assemblies exported to Yugoslavia and other countries are taken into account, this number increases to 874,000. The volume of export sales, which was quite large for the time, forced a rapid modernisation of the car's construction in response to the growing requirements of foreign customers, especially in the West.[676] For this reason, export models of the car were highly attractive to Polish buyers.[677]

Almost from the very beginning, the decision to licence the medium-displacement model was criticised by those in favour of a small-displacement passenger car that was supposed to energise the motorisation of Poland. Members of the Automotive Council, in particular, were at the forefront of this criticism, repeatedly clashing with government representatives regarding the development path that they had chosen. In May 1965, when Polish-Italian licence negotiations began, representatives of the council prepared a draft resolution assessing the development plans for the automotive industry for the years 1966–1970. They criticised the lack of any plan to produce small-engine cars and the repeated postponement of the production of a modernised Syrena

---

675 One of the Polish newsreel episodes from 1972 was devoted entirely to the Parisian sales office for the Fiat 125p, run by the Italian Autobianchi chain on Avenue Kléber and headed by a "Monsieur Chardonnet." There was also a service and maintenance station there; "Polski Fiat w Paryżu," Polska Kronika Filmowa, 72/39B, http://www.kronikarp.pl/szukaj,32512,strona-1 (accessed: 25 May 2016).

676 For example, in 1972, the decision was made to purchase a number of patents (at a total cost of over 900,000 zlotys) related to driving safety and comfort due to both the requirements set forth in the regulations of the United Nations Economic Commission for Europe (ECE) and concerns about competition. The ECE was a UN body established in 1947 to set standards applicable in member states, including road safety. The ten patents to be purchased included a heated rear window (so far such a window had been installed only in Fiat 125p models which were exported to Switzerland), an electric window washer pump, and a brake system failure signal (it was expected that both pieces of equipment would be required by most Western European countries as of 1973); AAN, ZPM, sygn. 0519/72, Wniosek ostateczny Fabryki Samochodów Osobowych o podjęcie decyzji w sprawie zakupu patentów dotyczących elementów wyposażenia samochodu licencyjnego FIAT 125p, związanych z jego modernizacją wg wymagań przepisów ECE w zakresie bezpieczeństwa i komfortu jazdy, Warszawa, 22 V 1972 r., unnumbered pages.

677 Z. Podbielski, *Polski Fiat 125p*, pp. 52–55; *Opowieść o FSO*, p. 159.

and Warszawa. Deputy Minister Józef Talma responded to this criticism by revealing the government's intentions to purchase a licence for the model 1300/1500, while suggesting that the inclusion of references to the need for small-engine cars in the resolution could harm the ongoing talks. This information did not appeal to the audience, who voiced quite strong criticism of the government's attitude through the lips of Aleksander Rostocki: "Based on my 20 years of observations, there has never been an appropriate statistical moment to adopt binding guidelines for the development of the automotive industry [regarding passenger cars]. This industry is still in the realm of projects and discussions. … Today's discussion has given us so many reasons to be pessimistic that we cannot expect such a statistical moment to come in the following years, either."[678]

It is worth noting that supporters of the development of passenger car production had gained quite an unexpected and powerful ally. A reshuffle in the Kremlin and the replacement of Nikita Khrushchev by Leonid Brezhnev helped bring about a 180-degree turn also in this area. Khrushchev, who opposed to the development of individual motorisation, focusing instead on the development of public transport, and was more likely to invest in a factory producing licenced bacon rather than passenger cars[679], was ousted as First Secretary and Prime Minister of the Soviet Union. Alexei Kosygin, who took over as Prime Minister, was a car enthusiast like Brezhnev. He had even said: "You know how stubbornly they pushed the idea that there was no need for broad development of passenger car production in our country. As if everyone should only be allowed to ride the bus."[680] The actions taken by the leadership at the Kremlin yielded such results as a contract with Fiat.[681]

---

678 AAN, MK, sygn. II/2, Protokół no. 3/65 z Posiedzenia Prezydium Rady Motoryzacyjnej odbytego 7 V 1965 r., pp. 628–630 v.

679 N. Nettleton, "Driving towards Communist Consumerism," p. 132.

680 "Radziecka motoryzacja w ofensywie," *Motoryzacja* 1965, no. 11, p. 236.

681 The Kremlin prepared carefully before signing the licensing contract. Initially, in addition to Fiat, German (Volkswagen) and French (Renault) companies were also taken into consideration. Ultimately, it was decided to choose the Italians and the 124 model, which took first place in the prestigious competition for the European Car of the Year 1967. The contract was signed on May 4, 1966, and was valued at US $900 million. According to one rumour, the first person to test the new car was Leonid Brezhnev, who made a test lap around the Kremlin in a specially imported Fiat 124. Production at the new AvtoVAZ factory in Togliatti on the Volga River began in 1969,

In the spring of 1966, it was announced that in the eighth five-year plan, for the first time in the history of the USSR, the production of passenger cars would increase from the previous 200,000 cars to 800,000. In Western Europe, these changes in Central and Eastern Europe were called "the rusting of the iron curtain, which could not handle the pressure of the wave of motorisation."[682]

However, in the Polish context, it is worth noting that the developments in the Soviet Union did nothing to change the attitude of the power elite in Warsaw. Criticism of that attitude also continued unchanged. Once again, Talma had to defend the decision to sign a licence for a medium-displacement car in front of members of the Automotive Council. This time, his statement came in a form that rather drastically cut off further discussion:

> Not all of the Automotive Council's opinions were taken into account in government decisions that clearly defined the directions of development of the automotive industry. Therefore, it would be pointless to return to debates about constructions that will not go into production, and it may even be harmful. ... The selection of models for production was agreed upon at the higher levels of all ministries, with acceptance of the correct principle that not all selections would be produced within the country. In the same manner, after extensive discussions, the decision was made to produce the 1300–1500 [c]m^3 passenger car.[683]

Decision-makers were nonetheless criticised from various angles. At a conference of the Provincial Committee of the PZPR in Katowice, which took place in early October 1968, Ryszard Dziopak, director of the Mechanical Equipment Factory in Bielsko-Biała and later director of the Small-Displacement Car Factory, said: "Among passenger cars, even the maximum production of the newly launched 'Fiat 125p' will not satisfy our needs and will not meet market demands. It seems to me that it is completely wrong for certain

---

and full production capacity of 600,000 cars per year was achieved in 1972. Initially, it was planned that the first Ladas—assembled exclusively from Russian parts—would celebrate the hundredth anniversary of the birth of Vladimir Lenin (April 22, 1870), but this deadline could not be met; L. H. Siegelbaum, *Cars for Comrades*, pp. 91–92; N. Nettleton, "Driving towards Communist Consumerism," pp. 132–134.

682 AAN, Telewizja Polska S. A. (hereafter: TVP), sygn. 2/1014, Biuletyn specjalny—kraje socjalistyczne no. 2900/12 12 1966, unnumbered pages.

683 AAN, MK, sygn. II/2, Protokół no. 1/66 z posiedzenia Prezydium Rady Motoryzacyjnej, odbytego 16 II 1966 r., p. 659.

managers of our economic life to run away from this problem, which I admit is a difficult problem."[684] It was an important moment because Dziopak, a man considered one of Edward Gierek's people, offered a kind of manifesto for the development of individual motorisation, which would be followed a few years later by the new government. In his speech, he emphasised the need for a new factory producing a small, popular car at a price of around 80,000 zlotys per unit to a foreign licence. His statement clearly shows that the comrades from Upper Silesia were not beating around the bush and, were developing their own plans for the motorisation of the Polish society regardless of the decisions taken in Warsaw. Władysław Gomułka, who was present at the conference, strongly vehemently quenched Dziopak's reformist tendencies. In his view, the Polish automotive industry, doomed to internal cooperation, could not achieve profitable production because the economic effects of the branches of industry that cooperated with it (such as metallurgy) were falling drastically short of satisfying: "I can't count how many of them there are, but the production of each car probably involves several dozen larger plants, linked together in cooperation. And this is not a simple problem, and most comrades are well aware of this fact." At the same time, he emphasised the extremely high costs associated with the purchase of licences, the initiation of production in general and, specifically, the production of the Big Fiat: "We will continue to incur costs for many years, not to mention the fact that we have had to allocate very significant funds to the purchase of various machines related to this production. So, in such conditions, can you afford a second [small-engine] car at the same time, while this is still going on? Here, too, I have very great doubts."[685]

684 AAN, KC PZPR, sygn. 237/VII-5418, Protokół z przedzjazdowej konferencji wojewódzkiej KW PZPR w Katowicach odbytej 7–8 X 1968 r., p. 74ff.

685 Ibid., p. 310–314. In his book about the Polish Fiat 126p, Przemysław Semczuk wrote that this conference saw a sharp exchange between Dziopak and Gomułka. The source of this information is not entirely clear. The minutes of the conference suggest nothing of the sort, and furthermore, Mieczysław Rakowski, who was present in Katowice, wrote in his diary: "The conference was calm and very businesslike, unlike the district conferences in Warsaw, where all the talk is about revisionism, Zionism, and other deadly sins, and the least attention is paid to specific matters"; M. F. Rakowski, *Dzienniki polityczne 1967–1968*, Warszawa 1999, p. 368.

Certainly, the Fiat 125p could not become the car that would motorise the Polish society, especially since it was never expected to be such a car. This fact was determined by the price, which, considering the income levels in the Polish society at that time, placed the Big Fiat de facto beyond the reach of the average family.[686] Research conducted by sociologists from Poznań in the early 1970s confirms this assumption. It uncovered that the Big Fiat was rarely the "first choice" for those starting their motoring adventure. Cheaper models and brands were much more popular (such as Syrena, Trabant, or Zastava). The Fiat 125p, in turn, was chosen much more often by people who had owned a car before.[687]

The choice of the model 125p for production was determined primarily by export considerations and the possibility that it could bring foreign currency into the country. As it later transpired, officials took advantage of this opportunity. The year 1968 was the moment when the exportation of Żerań-born Warszawas was at the highest levels in history, reaching 8,888 units (out of 17,780 produced). In the same year, 1,876 Fiat 125ps were exported (out of 7,101 produced). In subsequent years, the production and export of Big Fiats increased, while the Warszawa's numbers decreased—which was related to the fact that the latter reached the end of production in 1973. In the case of the Big Fiat, both values would reach their maximum level in the middle of the next decade: in 1975, production jumped to 114,327 units, of which 82,909 were exported; in 1976, 116,940 units left the factory floor, of which 83,413 were sold abroad.[688]

---

686 G. Pisarski, "Koncepcje wzrostu spożycia," *Życie Gospodarcze* 1968, no. 32, p. 4.

687 Z. Krasiński, *Czynniki ekonomiczno-społeczne rozwoju motoryzacji indywidualnej w Polsce w świetle badań ankietowych*, Poznań 1972, p. 98.

688 *Opowieść o FSO*, pp. 156–158; *Rynek motoryzacyjny w Polsce*, ed. Z. Krasiński, Warszawa 1980, pp. 48–49.

"...after the 1st, the 10th, the 20th, after the 1st, the 10th...": The Road of the Poles to an Automobile

In the early 1960s, 2.2 million Poles had a driver's licence, and this number was gradually growing. In 1964, it reached 2.9 million, and a year later, almost 3.3 million.[689] In the last year of Władysław Gomułka's leadership, it exceeded 5 million. Professional driver's licences accounted for less than 10% of this number,[690] which meant that over 27% of Poles of working age had a driver's licence—that is, almost every third adult Pole.

Until 1954, there were four categories of driver's licences in Poland, marked with Roman numerals. Category IV allowed one to drive a motorcycle, and category III was necessary for non-commercial use of a car weighing up to 1.5 tons; both were available to anyone over 16 years of age. Categories II and I were intended for professional drivers.[691] After 1954, the number of categories increased to seven, but only three were marked with numerals: I—for all vehicles; II—all vehicles except for buses; III—all cars excluding taxis. The other four were: non-professional licences for driving cars; licences for motorcycles; licences for tractors; and licences for trolleybuses.[692] Minor changes were instituted in 1962; the number of categories remained the same, but the numbering was restored wholesale, from I to VII. Those who wanted to have a driver's licence for non-commercial use had to apply for a

689 B. Sosień, "Smutny bilans jednego roku," *Motor* 1964, no. 7, p. 3.
690 J. Wojciechowski, "Motoryzacja w Polsce i problemy jej rozwoju," in: *Problemy bezpieczeństwa ruchu drogowego. Konferencja naukowo-techniczna*, Warszawa 1971, p. 508.
691 Dz. U. 1948, no. 27, pos. 186.
692 Dz. U. 1954, no. 3, pos. 6.

category III licence.[693] It was not until 1968 that officials decided to change the categories of permits once again, marking them with subsequent letters of the alphabet—from A to E and M and T.[694] These designations survived practically until the beginning of the twenty-first century.

Driving courses were offered by the Polish Automobile Association and the National Defense League (Liga Obrony Kraju, LOK). Since its inception in 1950, the Automobile Club's successor had trained over 1.2 million drivers. Initially, driving lessons were conducted using 46 cars at 10 centres, but by the mid-1960s, the number of cars increased to 700 and of training centres to 84. In turn, the LOK had trained nearly 1 million drivers since 1954. Its activities in this regard focused primarily on rural communities. By the mid-1960s, in addition to its eighty permanent training centres, the LOK had twelve mobile ones that travelled to different areas to provide driving lessons.[695]

A driver candidate took an exam before a committee, the composition of which changed over the years. In 1948, it consisted of representatives of the relevant voivodeship (examination boards operating by the automotive departments of voivodeship offices), the Transport Workers' Trade Union, and the Polish Automobile Club.[696] From 1952, it involved representatives of praesidia of the national council, the PZMot, and trade unions.[697] In 1968, the three-person committee had a place reserved for an MO representative.[698] The driver candidate had to demonstrate knowledge of road regulations, the operation of motorcycle and car components, and practical driving skills.

At the end of the 1950s, an investigation in Warsaw uncovered a gang that included members of the communication department of the local WRN. It came out that members of the gang involved in the driving licence examination boards, took money from the candidates in lieu of the exam. The applications for driving licences were then filled out with fictitious evaluations,

693 Dz. U. 1962, no. 61, pos. 295.
694 Dz. U. 1968, no. 27, pos. 183.
695 J. Wojciechowski, "Bezpieczeństwo ruchu drogowego w Polsce w okresie XX-lecia," *Motoryzacja* 1964, no. 7/8, p. 159.
696 AAN, MK, sign. 1136, Zarządzenie Ministra Komunikacji z 23 V 1947 r. o opłatach za egzaminowanie osób, ubiegających się o pozwolenia na prowadzenie pojazdów mechanicznych, unnumbered pages; Dz. U. 1948, no. 27, pos. 186.
697 Dz. U. 1952, no. 1, pos. 8.
698 Dz. U. 1968, no. 27, pos. 183.

and the documentation was supplemented with false certificates required for a driving licence to be issued. The cost of a driving licence without a test ranged from 500 zlotys to 1,500 zlotys. The scale of abuse was enormous. In 1957 alone, as many as 1,500 fake drivers licences were issued, and the collected bribes amounted to 1.5 million zlotys. During the investigation, it was also revealed that the gang-members were responsible for abuses in the distribution of cars withdrawn from the state administration fleet.[699]

Practically throughout the entire period of Władysław Gomułka's reign, the number of people with driving licences grew at a rapid pace. It can be assumed that the desire to own a private car was equally great. Unfortunately, possibilities in this area were very limited, for various reasons. Nonetheless, Poles tried to fulfil their dream. Between 1955 and 1970, the number of passenger cars in private hands increased from 20,500 to 453,400 units (see Table 5). The average annual increase therefore amounted to over 27,000 cars, and while it dropped to slightly over 14,500 per year in the second half of the 1950s, it grew back to more than twice as many during the 1960s. Despite this significant change, Poland was unable to compete with either East Germany or Czechoslovakia, where in the 1960s alone the annual increase in private passenger cars reached an average of 86,100 and 57,900, respectively. In Hungary, which did not have its own automotive industry, the number of passenger cars increased by over 20,000 on average in the same period, reaching a total of 240,000 in 1970, most of which (89%) belonged to private users.[700]

Table 5. Number of passenger cars and two-wheeled vehicles in Poland in 1955–1970

Year	Passenger cars (in thousands)		Two-wheeled vehicles (in thousands)	
	Total	Private	Total	Private
1955	40.3	20.5	169.7	163.0
1956	44.7	24.7	236.4	229.8
1957	61.9	40.8	331.1	325

(Continued)

699 AAN, KC PZPR, sign. XI-281, Notatka w sprawie nadużyć przy wydawaniu zezwoleń na prowadzenie pojazdów mechanicznych, Warszawa, March 4, 1958, pp. 86–89.

700 G. Peteri, "Alternative modernity? Everyday Practices of Elite Mobility in Communist Hungary, 1956–1980," in: *The Socialist Car. Automobility in the Eastern Bloc*, ed. L. H. Siegelbaum, New York 2011, p. 48; *Rocznik Statystyczny* 1972, p. 676.

Table 5. *(Continued)*

Year	Passenger cars (in thousands)		Two-wheeled vehicles (in thousands)	
	Total	Private	Total	Private
1958	83.9	58.5	461.3	454.1
1959	104.5	78.6	630.2	622.8
1960	117.4	90.8	771.4	763.5
1961	135.9	108.5	927.2	917.7
1962	162	131.7	1038.4	1027.3
1963	188.2	156.4	1181.4	1168.3
1964	211.2	187.7	1321.5	1308.6
1965	245.5	214.9	1464.8	1451.3
1966	289.4	257.6	1540.0	1526.4
1967	331.9	300.5	1597.9	1585.0
1968	374.6	345.2	1686.9	1674.3
1969	454.9	426.9	1800.2	1788.2
1970	479.4	453.4	1789.4	1778.4

Source: A. M. Restecki, "Zrealizowane oczekiwania. Miliony samochodów osobowych w r. 1975," Motor 1966, no. 30, p. 3; Rocznik Statystyczny 1957, p. 211; Rocznik Statystyczny 1959, p. 230; Rocznik Statystyczny 1960, p. 264.

After October 1956, Poles had several different options for purchasing a passenger car. The basic source, although not the most important one, was official sales through the state enterprise Motozbyt by way of the so-called allocations. Some of the cars were distributed through a programme. Poles could also buy new cars through so-called internal exports. In addition, a used or new car could be bought second-hand. It was definitely the easiest to buy a vehicle through this channel by way of a private transaction involving classified ads[701] or car exchanges, or from friends, and family.

701 In the first ten days of July 1962, in Warsaw alone, nearly half a thousand "Buy-Sell" ads were published about private cars; K. Wolicki, "Droga do raju," *Polityka* 1962, no. 32, p. 3.

4.1 Motozbyt

The distribution of vehicles was handled by individual ministries, which passed them on to the labour councils of particular workplaces. Leading workers and workplace *racjonalizatorzy* (innovators) had priority in this regard.[702] Private individuals who wanted to receive an allocation for a vehicle had to apply to the trade department of the WRN.[703]

The rules of distribution were not entirely clear to outside observers. As one journalist wrote in *Motor* in early July 1956: "In many ways, the current practice of selling cars to private persons looked like black magic. Nobody actually knew where to apply for an allocation, who makes the decision, and what the formalities are."[704] Even the appointment of a special commission, consisting of representatives of the trade unions, Motozbyt, the Federation of Engineering Associations (Naczelna Organizacja Techniczna NOT), the PKPG, the health service, and the creative unions, to decide on the method of allocating vehicles did not fix the problem because, as the article in *Motor* reported: "A representative of our Editorial Office tried to find out what number of cars would be distributed to private people in 1956. He received no answer. Top secret! We fear that commission members do not know, either. Even were it otherwise, it would still be fiction because some cars are still allocated directly, bypassing the commission. The first batch of ten Wartburgs was distributed by Prime Minister Jędrychowski. The commission had nothing to say about it."[705]

Sales were conducted by Motozbyt, which received applications for the purchase of a car for cash. In justified cases, instalment purchases were allowed. Established in April 1948, the company underwent major reorganisation in 1951: it was removed from the structures of the Ministry of Heavy Industry and incorporated into the Ministry of Road Transport and Aviation (MTDiL). The retail chain, then consisting of thirty-six offices (and one store being built in Warsaw), was taken over by the Ministry of Internal Trade.[706]

---

702 K. Radwan, "Dziś rębacz Szczepan Blaut kupił samochód," *Motor* 1952, no. 32, p. 8.

703 "Jeszcze raz o talonach na WFM-kę," *Motor* 1956, no. 19, p. 7; "Sprzedaż samochodów osobowych według nowych zasad," *Motor* 1961, no. 3, p. 3.

704 ZER, "Komisja i samochody," *Motor* 1956, no. 27, p. 3.

705 Ibid.

706 AAN, Ministerstwo Transportu Drogowego i Lotniczego (hereafter: MTDiL), sign. 198, Wytyczne Komisji M[inisterstwa] K[omunikacji] powołanej do przejęcia Centrali

Car service stations which previously operated as part of Motozbyt (there were nineteen of them in 1951) were transformed by order of the Minister of Road and Air Transport into an independent multi-purpose enterprise called the Technical Automobile Service (TOS) and subordinated to the Centre for Automotive Equipment Management.[707]

A car purchased from Motozbyt could not be used for commercial transport.[708] In addition, owners of new cars were only allowed to sell their vehicles to third parties through Motozbyt. Otherwise, the car would not be allowed on the road.[709] In November 1957, regionalisation of new car sales was introduced. From that point on, in accordance with an order issued by the Minister of Transportation, residents of particular voivodeships could buy new cars only in Motozbyt offices designated for a given voivodeship. The buyer had to make an advance payment in the amount of the full price of the car and only then was a date set for the collection of the vehicle. Moreover, the actual price was the one valid on the day of receipt. It could, therefore, happen that upon receipt of the vehicle, the buyer had to pay even more money.[710]

The purchase of a new car was only permitted if the interested party was able to document the need for a car "to perform official duties or professional, social, athletic, or other activities," or if they did not own a car in the three years preceding the purchase, which required a confirmation from the

---

Handlowej Przemysłu Motoryzacyjnego "Motozbyt," pp. 35–37; ibid., sign. 199, Tezy organizacyjnego ustawienia "Motozbytu" w ramach Ministerstwa Transportu Drogowego i Lotniczego, June 14, 1951, unnumbered pages.

707 Ibid., sign. 198, Zarządzenie nr 51 Ministra Transportu Drogowego i Lotniczego z 10 VII 1951 r., p. 73.

708 The restriction was removed in December 1956; MP 1956, no. 104, pos. 1201.

709 MP 1956, no. 43, pos. 527.

710 Sales were carried out by nine Motozbyt offices. Motozbyt sold cars in Warsaw (for the voivodeships of Warsaw and Białystok), Łódź (for the voivodeships of Łódź and Kielce), Poznań (for the voivodeships of Poznań, Bydgoszcz, Zielona Góra, and Szczecin), Wrocław (for the voivodeships of Wrocław and Opole). Gdańsk (for the voivodeships of Gdańsk and Koszalin), Kraków (for the Kraków voivodeship); in Katowice (for the Katowice voivodeship); in Lublin (for the voivodeships of Lublin and Rzeszów, but only until January 1959, when the office was moved to Rzeszów), and at a branch of the Gdańsk Motozbyt in Olsztyn (for the Olsztyn voivodeship). In 1965, only the voivodeships of Białystok, Bydgoszcz, and Zielona Góra had no new car sales office of their own; MP 1957, no. 98, pos. 572; Dz. U. 1959, no. 7, pos. 29; "Motozbyt odpowiada na pytania Motoru," *Motor* 1965, no. 33, p. 1.

praesidium of the national council at the potential buyer's place of residence. This did not apply to persons who resold their car through Motozbyt or had it de-registered as a destroyed or damaged vehicle.[711]

However, the regulations changed very often. Just a few months after the reorganisation of new car sales, in April 1958, "due to the sufficient supply of new cars being reached," the Minister of Transportation suspended the requirement for documenting the need to own a car because of official duties or activities (although doctors, veterinarians, those working in science, culture, and the arts, and other employees of state and cooperative institutions retained priority when purchasing new cars), as well as the obligation to resell cars through Motozbyt. Instalment sales were also introduced.[712] Another change took place in September 1961, when the authority to issue rules concerning matters such as trade in new cars was transferred to the Ministry of Internal Trade.[713] Pursuant to its regulation, the distribution of new cars between individual voivodeships was to be handled by national councils.[714] Imported cars could be purchased only for cash, and the entire amount had to be paid within 14 days of the date of issuance of the purchase permit.

At the end of the 1960s, another significant change of regulations governing the purchase of a new car was implemented. On July 6, 1968, by order of the MHW, prepayments for passenger cars were introduced. Buyers were obliged to pre-pay specific amounts corresponding to the retail price of the selected make and model. Prepayments could be made both for the current calendar year and for subsequent years. The deadlines for payments, their amounts, and the makes and models of cars were to be published in the press when announced. Both Polish and imported cars were sold in this way. For buyers, section 2 of the order was of particular importance. As in previous regulations, restraints were established for the purchase of new passenger cars. Doctors, veterinarians, and agricultural workers who used their own cars for work-related purposes could not buy new cars more often than once

711 MP 1957, no. 98, pos. 572.

712 MP 1958, no. 31, pos. 180; see also: (wb), "Za gotówkę i na raty można kupować samochody," *Motor* 1958, no. 20, p. 8.

713 MP 1961, no. 334, pos. 187. In April 1963, the orders of the Minister of Transportation of November 1957 and April 1958 were both suspended by the Minister of Internal Trade; MP 1963, no. 38, pos. 192.

714 "Sprzedaż samochodów osobowych według nowych zasad," p. 3.

every three years; taxi drivers, once every two years; and "ordinary" users, once every four years. A person whose vehicle was destroyed or damaged enough to make it unusable could seek ownership of a new car more quickly. In such cases, a confirmatory opinion issued by PZMot would be necessary. The restraints did not apply to persons who, after drawing a car in the PKO savings book lottery, did not collect it, but rather sold it immediately.[715] This system remained in force throughout the next decade, with minor changes.[716]

Constantly changing regulations meant that owning a car required—apart from the very significant financial outlay, which will be discussed later—the readiness to repeatedly battle bureaucracy and wait a long time for the desired allocation. It is therefore not surprising that the pages of *Motor* abounded with articles discussing people's "deep desire to sit behind their own wheel," the best example of which is the article "Why I won't buy a 'Warszawa'," signed by a "Disappointed" (*Zawiedziony*). Encouraged both by the "rising curve" of production and by data that "suggestively indicated a real chance for a purchase" of a car, the author had submitted an application to Motozbyt, recently tasked with processing car purchase applications. At the mercy (or lack thereof) of a commission consisting of representatives of Motozbyt, trade unions, and the health service, he harboured little hope for receiving the desired car: "[T]here are several hundred applications, and a dozen or so Warszawas, so there is no chance. I feel sorry for the commission. Even if Themis and all her sisters sat on it, it would not be able divide fairly."[717]

Some even tried to bribe those responsible for the distribution of purchase permits for cars or motorcycles. There were also cases in which permits were simply sold to the highest bidder. Many such cases were revealed in the post-October 1956 settling of accounts. Reports of irregularities in the distribution of vehicles came from different corners of Poland. Such was the case with the WRN in Kielce, whose activities in this area were discussed during a meeting of the Central Unit for Combatting Fraud and Corruption in November 1957: "[A] lot, a lot of abuses, and it is known today, although we have not reviewed the matter, that much will have to change in the

715 MP 1968, no. 31, pos. 212.

716 MP 1971, no. 36, pos. 234; MP 1974 no. 33, pos. 195; MP 1975, no. 36, pos. 234; MP 1977, no. 16, pos. 93.

717 zawiedziony, "Dlaczego nie kupię 'Warszawy'?" *Motor* 1956, no. 21, p. 4.

distribution system itself, because the current approach creates conditions favourable for abuse." Similar mismanagement occurred in Wrocław, where almost all employees of the transportation department of the WRN were allegedly involved "in various dirty affairs."[718] This was echoed by commenters from Poznań: "The central unit really should look into the office that issues vouchers for the purchase of cars and motorcycles. Specifically cars, because that is the very peak of insolence." It turned out that advertisements had been published in *Głos Wielkopolski*, offering the exchange of vouchers for motorcycles. It was soon revealed that one could obtain a car of any make in this way with no problems ("if a man wants a Fiat, a man gets a Fiat; if you want this, you will get this").[719]

One problem that remained was the small number of cars being sold to private users. It should be noted that the needs of the state administration always trumped the needs of the society. This was the case in early 1956, when the small pool intended for sale to private users was further diminished to meet the needs of central institutions. As a result, of the 400 Warszawas produced by FSO that were intended for sale to private owners, one-fourth were transferred to various ministries and the Citizens' Militia. At the same time, used cars from the fleet of MON were earmarked for sale on the private market. These were mainly Citroëns and Škodas.[720]

Small deliveries to the private market meant that one of the factors deciding who was allocated a new car was the order in which applications were submitted. On this basis, the central authorities in Warsaw created distribution plans for individual voivodeships that were then to be implemented by the local offices of Motozbyt. This arrangement had great potential for abuse. Toward the end of the 1950s, it was discovered that a group of Motozbyt employees in Poznań—including the office director, his deputy, and the manager of the retail department—manipulated the distribution list in exchange for

718 AAN, KC PZPR, sign. 237/XXXII-7, Materiały z narady z 7 XI 1957 r., pp. 39–40, 51.

719 Ibid., pp. 30–31, 39–40.

720 AAN, Urząd Rady Ministrów, Kancelaria Tajna (hereafter: URM KT), sign. 6/249, dot.: projektu uchwały Prezydium Rządu w sprawie bilansu pojazdów samochodowych na r. 1956, March 7, 1956, p. 11; Notatka protokólarna z konferencji odbytej 9 III 1956 r. u wiceprezesa Rady Ministrów Dr St Jędrychowskiego w sprawie uzgodnienia projektu uchwały Prezydium Rządu dotyczącego bilansu pojazdów samochodowych na r. 1956, p. 14.

bribes. At their trial, their clients joined them among the accused; one of them was the owner of the Autotechnika company, who skipped the queue to received an allocation for a Škoda at a cost of 3,000 zlotys, little more than two average monthly salaries. Aside from them, a doctor from Poznań and the director of the local PKS office were also accused of giving bribes in exchange for access to Fiat 600 cars. During the investigation, it turned out that the group had taken advantage of the fact that official prices for cars had changed several times between 1956 and 1959. The increase in prices often meant that even if someone was on the allocation list, they were not always able to buy the vehicle. Thus, people from further down the list, who could pay the required amount, would take their place. In Poznań, who moved up the list was determined by a bribe, while so-called touts were said to have run around the voivodeship looking for people for whom the new prices were too high and forcing them to abandon their allocation. The regulation prohibiting the acquisition of a new car more often than every three years was also skirted around: during the period in question, car owners concluded many fictitious loan agreements in amounts that usually corresponded to the value of a new car. It then quickly transpired that the "loaners" were unable to repay the money and would willingly give up their new car instead.[721]

In 1957, Motozbyt received only 2,000 Warszawas for sale to private individuals out of the 10,000 Warszawas produced that year. At the same time, the number of applications reached 5,000. The price was set at a fairly high level of 80,000 zlotys (by 1961, it grew to 120,000 zlotys), but the option of purchase in instalments was not available; it only became possible in 1958.[722] The long-awaited Syrenas, when they could finally be purchased directly (in 1957, 200 units were produced, and the following year, 3,000), were valued at 69,000 zlotys (for a hand-assembled unit), and then at 72,000 zlotys (an assembly line unit).[723]

Official car prices aroused great emotions. It is therefore not difficult to guess how the society reacted to the spectacular price increase at the turn of

721 W. Bryx, "Zmotoryzowana sitwa," *Motor* 1959, no. 47, p. 10.

722 Anyone who wanted to buy a car in instalments had to pay half the amount in cash and the rest in eleven monthly instalments of even value; "Bez załączników i poparcia można kupić samochód," *Motor* 1957, no. 11, p. 6.

723 "Aktualne ceny pojazdów mechanicznych," *Motor* 1962, no. 36, p. 15.

1957, by several dozen percent, the values ranging from 65,000 to 125,000 zlotys, depending on the model.[724] In mid-1957, an East German AWZ P70 cost 65,000 zlotys, a Fiat 600—72,000 zlotys, and a Wartburg—75,000 zlotys.[725] In the case of the Wartburg, the increase amounted to over 100% within a few months—from 36,000 zlotys.[726] It should be noted that the imported cars were also only available in small quantities: 450 P70s and 750 Wartburgs.[727] In 1961, prices increased again by several dozen percent: a new Warszawa now cost 120,000 zlotys; a Wartburg, depending on the model and equipment, between 86,000 and 95,000 zlotys; a Škoda Octavia, 95,000 zlotys; and a Moskvitch, 115,000 zlotys.[728]

Looking more closely at the price list of the most popular makes of car in Eastern Bloc countries, one finds that Poles paid the most for imported cars, in some cases almost double. For example, in Bulgaria, a new Moskvitch cost the equivalent of 64,000 zlotys, while in East Germany, a Trabant cost 37,500 zlotys. On average, the difference in prices was several dozen percent (see Table 6).

Table 6. Comparison of prices of selected cars in communist countries (in zlotys)

Country	Makes			
	Moskvitch	Škoda	Trabant	Wartburg
East Germany	72,500	67,500	37,500	77,500
Czechoslovakia	72,000	60,800	38,400	57,600
Hungary	76,800	76,800	58,800	75,600
Romania	98,000	92,000	64,000	90,000
Bulgaria	64,000	64,000	44,000	62,000
Poland	115,000	95,000	65,000	95,000

Source: A. K. Wróblewski, "Haszysz na czterech kółkach," Polityka 1965, no. 54, p. 8.

724 W. Kulik, "Polityka motoryzacyjna czy antymotoryzacyjna?" *Motor* 1957, no. 36, p. 3.

725 "Aktualne ceny," *Motor* 1957, no. 22, p. 5.

726 The new price list for passenger cars was published in the *Motor* weekly with the following note: "We already know the prices. It is not known when we will be able to obtain the vehicles for these prices, because the cars and motorcycles listed here are not available for sale; *Motor* 1956, no. 1, p. 3.

727 "Wiosenne rozważania," *Motor* 1957, no. 14, p. 4.

728 "Sprzedaż samochodów osobowych według nowych zasad," p. 3.

Table 7. Prices of passenger car models relative to average monthly earnings in socialist countries (in 1971)

Country	Fiat 125p	Moskvitch 412	Škoda S100	Wartburg
Poland	64	56	50	48
Bulgaria	68	53	33	38
Hungary	45	35	33	33
Czechoslovakia	36	32	31	29
East Germany	29	24	21	23

Source: Z. Krasiński, H. Mruk, and P. Rzepczyński, Handel i usługi na tle rozwoju motoryzacji indywidualnej, Warszawa 1977, Instytut Handlu Wewnętrznego i Usług, Biblioteka 153, p. 41.

The National Automotive Conference (*Krajowa Narada Motoryzacyjna*), held at the beginning of January 1957, also raised the problem of prices of new cars on the Polish market. One participant in the meeting even stated that "the prices of the passenger cars that we produce is absolutely unaffordable for working people," while foreign vehicles are imported in negligible quantities and "are sold at exorbitant prices."[729] These statements raised a highly important problem that the decision-makers would need to resolve. On the one hand, by offering Poles the chance to buy a new passenger car, they were meeting the growing demand for this means of transport; on the other, they obtained an excellent tool for draining the wallets of their citizen. The entire operation was seemingly aimed—at least in theory—at speculators and their supposedly large cash reserves. In reality, the cost was borne by those members of the society who dreamed of having their own car and had the money to make it happen.

During a meeting of the Economic Situation Review Commission, operating under the Economic Council, Czesław Bobrowski described the ongoing debate as "noise around the issue of cars." In his view, the aforementioned conference of early 1957 could be summed up as "some assembly resolving that this was the deathbed of motorisation and then explaining to the workers that it is also unfavourable for them."[730] At the meeting, Leopold Gluck stated: "[I]n the explanatory action, we must say that some goods are intended

[729] "Sejm Polskiej Motoryzacji," pp. 8–9.

[730] AAN, URM KT, sign. 22/11, Stenogram z posiedzenia Komisji Przeglądu Sytuacji Gospodarczej Rady Ekonomicznej z 1 VI 1957 r., p. 105.

to drain[!] the purchasing power of the speculators, as well as people with higher earnings, such as writers, intellectuals, architects, some doctors. … [T]his explanation will contribute to the idea that this is not an attack on the general level of real wages."[731] Cars, along with other luxury goods, such as furs, carpets, and glassware, were to effectively deprive some groups of carefully accumulated savings. At a meeting of the Council of Ministers, the idea was even proposed to include motorcycles and bicycles in this category of goods, but this proposal was criticised by the likes of Julian Kole, who stated openly at the said meeting:

> We must admit that we do not have a clear conscience when it comes to motorcycles and bicycles because we could be making more of them and use the resulting savings to achieve the same profit as with the price increase. … What does the society think of us? We should consider what is more important—the tens of millions of zlotys or public confidence in our policy. Which is why I am absolutely against any large-scale price changes in relation to items that are not of the same type as a car, or a carpet, or glassware.

Kole's statement was echoed by Jan Krupiński, who drew attention to the attitude of miners, who were said to have expressed strong dissatisfaction with the high prices of certain products. Michał Kalecki, a great supporter of this form of "drainage," closed the discussion by stating: "What this means is that miners are very rich. I don't understand how you can get rich so easily. It also turns out that they are also very far from class conscious. If that's how they treat this, calculating, for example, how many days of labour their Czech colleagues need to earn a car, they are depreciating their own labour."[732]

Taking into account the average wages of a worker in this period, the price of a new Warszawa was equivalent to almost six years' wages, and of a new Syrena—four years' wages (see Table 7).[733] An excellent illustration of this

---

731 Ibid., pp. 112–113.

732 Ibid., pp. 115–116, 127–128. It is of note that neither Michał Kalecki nor Czesław Bobrowski were supporters of the development of individual motorisation; they claimed that Poles and Poland simply could not afford it; Cz. Bobrowski, *Wspomnienia ze stulecia*, Lublin 1985, pp. 260–261.

733 In the USSR in the mid-1970s, the popular Zhiguli 2101 cost 5,500 roubles, which equated to three and a half years of average earnings of a worker. Additionally, the sales were conducted on the basis of a prepayment of 25% of the price of the car, the

is provided by a letter from a *Motor* reader, discussing how prices were too high and disproportionate to the quality of the products:

> Why do people prefer to buy imported cars instead of our domestic Syrenas? Is it really because they are snobs, or because Wartburgs, Trabants, Zastavas, Škodas, or Moskvitches are disproportionately cheap compared to the mistreated Syrenas? Is it only because the Syrena, produced in a Polish plant, is—often already on the day of purchase, just outside the Motozbyt gates—7,000 zlotys cheaper on the open market than the official price lists would indicate? Why was the imported Stadion television set so sought after? Why is it so easy to buy a Polish Nefryt or Koral [television sets]? We're not talking about 80,000 or 100,000 zlotys. ... The plastic Trabant outperformed the Syrena in this competition—not because it is better. I assure you that many people I talked to about this agree that none of us would buy an imported car if the technical level and quality of our small-engine car were at least similar. ... I share the opinion of many people who believe that if we cannot currently afford to produce better passenger cars, let's produce something else, more profitable, something that can be sold around the world, and let's buy good cars for that money. Not luxury cars, just good cars.[734]

The prices of cars, especially Polish makes, became a laughing matter in Poland. One joke told how, after a car accident in which an American and a Pole died, the former laments the fate of his wife, who from that moment on would have to struggle alone to pay the remaining instalments of the loan that they took out to buy the new car. "The installments are not too high, my wife will make do," he adds. The Pole is much more desperate; he crashed a Syrena, the car he had worked for all his life. Surprised, the American asks: "Why did you buy such an expensive car?"[735] In 1965, cartoonist Karol Ferster portrayed one lucky Zastava buyer who left Motozbyt with a new car, but without his pants.

---

remaining amount being paid upon receipt of the car. In the late 1970s and early 1980s, the average waiting time was eight years; L. H. Siegelbaum, *Cars for Comrades: The Life of the Soviet Automobile*, Ithaca 2008, pp. 239–240.

734 "Nie leczmy objawów," *Motor* 1965, no. 8, p. 5; emphasis in original.

735 *Humor z Polski. Dowcipy z lat 1948–2008*, ed. E. Rychlewska, Poznań 2008, p. 138.

Figure 3. Karol Ferster, „Zastaw się a postaw się"

In spite of this, Poles bought almost everything that Motozbyt had on offer. This was true of the French Simcas (the Aronde model), seventy of which sold out in just two days, at a price of 125,000 zlotys each. The demand for cars was so great that in early 1957, Motozbyt had to stop accepting applications for the purchase of small-displacement Western cars, and a month later also for domestic Warszawas.[736] In total, between 1956 and 1960, Motozbyt sold over 43,000 passenger cars to private individuals. In subsequent years, the sales were almost twice as high; in 1964, they reached 19,500. The highest-selling Polish-made vehicles were Syrenas (9,300) and Warszawas (4,500).

[736] J. Kochanowski, *Rewolucja międzypaździernikowa. Polska 1956–1957*, Kraków 2017, p. 260.

Imported cars (Trabants, Wartburgs, and Moskvitches) accounted for 5,500 of the units sold.[737]

At the end of 1964, *Motor* published an exposé of the automobile market in Poland. The first sentence spelled out the quite unfavourable conclusion: "The current year did not meet expectations in terms of deliveries of imported cars to private individuals." Further on, the article proclaimed that of the 12,000 cars imported, just over 10,000 were actually delivered—the blame was placed primarily on Poland's southern neighbours, who were unable to deliver all of the promised 3,000 Škodas. At the same time, the article went on to say, attempts were made to make up for the shortage of imports with Warszawas and Syrenas. However, at the end of 1964, the prospects for access to new, foreign cars were poor: "There will therefore be no possibility to obtain an allocation unless some existing candidates withdraw their names from the list of buyers."[738] A year later, the situation was much the same: "Likely the only car that will be available to buy without difficulty is the FSO Syrena. The industry will hand over 12,000 units of this car to Motozbyt. However, all those who decided to buy an FSO Warszawa will not have it easy. Only a small batch of 4,000 units has been allocated for individual sale."[739]

Delayed deliveries of new cars caused many complications, which the readers were eager to discuss, writing alarming letters to the editor. One of them (signed "Patient Reader") states, for instance, that receiving the allocation was only the beginning of a long road to "the desired moment when your hands ... will rest on the steering wheel and your back will sink into the backrest of your own 'wheels'," because the presented date of receipt of the vehicle was rather unreliable. Motozbyt informed buyers that the car allocation could be made "from deliveries of the 1st, 2nd, 3rd, or 4th quarter, and moreover, the supplier has the right to a delay of up to 3 months beyond the quarter mentioned in the notification."[740] Delays in car deliveries were caused by quite mundane problems; in the case of imported cars, foreign factories often had problems fulfilling orders.

---

737 "Chcę kupić samochód," *Motor* 1964, no. 31, p. 3.

738 Z. Przybyliński, "Czego możemy spodziewać się na rynku?" *Motor* 1964, no. 43, p. 1.

739 "Na krajowym rynku. Co będziemy kupować w roku 1966?" *Motor* 1965, no. 50, p. 1.

740 "List rozgoryczonego," *Motor* 1962, no. 11, p. 3.

One of the readers, who was allocated a Škoda 1,000 MB (price: 95,000 zlotys), to be delivered in the first quarter of 1966, waited over half a year for his car. He sent a letter to the editor at the beginning of July, and the holiday trip to Yugoslavia he had planned to take in his own car starting on August 1st ("paid for with the modest sum of 15,000 zlotys") was put in serious doubt. In his letter, he complained: "Since April, I've been hearing the same thing: 'cars will arrive after the 1st, the 10th, the 20th, after the 1st, the 10th….'"[741] Another reader had a similar problem; he had been waiting for his Warszawa for over half a year, since February 1965. Embittered, he wrote: "My queue is constantly going backwards. I will probably receive the car in November, but that's after the holiday season. Can this be called an easy, hassle-free purchase of a domestically produced car?"[742]

The aforementioned regionalisation of car sales, resulting from regulations introduced in 1957, led to situations described in early 1966. As winter came and the market was already partially saturated, Motozbyt warehouses in Warsaw were said to be "bursting at the seams," and cars could be "acquired in such a surprisingly normal manner that it seems strange in our conditions." The explanation was quite mundane: it soon transpired that foreign contractors who were behind on the delivery of new vehicles and wanted to avoid paying high fines for failure to comply with contracts flooded Motozbyt with cars at the end of the year. Thus, "desperate at the accumulation of supplies, Motozbyt management bought several hundred metres of fencing and blocked off several acres of land for the stored cars." However, while Motozbyt in Warsaw, which served the residents of the Warsaw and Białystok voivodeships, had too many cars to sell, other parts of the country faced continuous shortages.[743]

In August 1964, *Motor* published an interview with Motozbyt's economic director, Marian Szowa, discussing the situation on the market for new vehicles. Among the subjects addressed was the availability of new cars in particular voivodeships. It was revealed that most people who wanted to buy a car lived in the Warsaw, Katowice, Wrocław, Poznań, and Gdańsk voivodeships, which also meant that obtain a car allocation was the most

---

741 "Urlopowicze czekają na Skody 1000 MB," *Motor* 1966, no. 31, p. 2.

742 "Na Warszawy trzeba czekać," *Motor* 1965, no. 32, p. 2.

743 S. Kubiak, "Samochody na razie czekają na klientów," *Motor* 1966, no. 5, p. 3.

difficult in those voivodeships. Trabants, Warszawas, and Syrenas were more accessible, although in some regions of the country, all vehicles earmarked for the third quarter, and even many from the fourth quarter, had reportedly already been assigned. According to Szowa, the chances of purchasing other brands of imported cars "were almost non-existent"—delayed deliveries from foreign contractors were to blame. In the backdrop loomed the need to save foreign currencies.[744]

Even the rather unfavourable data from 1964 and forecasts for 1966 cannot obscure the fact that in the 1960s, the "sales curve" for cars in Poland was rising—in 1961, over 14,000 new cars were produced, and in each of the years 1962–1964, that number reached 20,000. The "geography of allocation" of those new cars is also interesting. In 1963, there were 15,800 new cars to be allocated, representing six makes: Warszawa, Syrena, Škoda, Moskvitch, Wartburg, and Trabant. The Warsaw voivodeship received the most vehicles—as many as 3,000—followed by the Katowice voivodeship (2,700), while the least cars went to the Białystok and Rzeszów voivodeships: 196 and 278, respectively. The city of Warsaw alone received almost 2,500 new cars (see Table 8). There is a clear division here between the rich centre, which could afford its own vehicles, and the poorer periphery.[745]

Table 8. Allocation of cars to individual voivodeships in 1963

Voivodeship/ city	Number of cars allocated	Make					
		Warszawa	Syrena	Škoda	Moskvitch	Wart-burg	Trabant
Warsaw	2.518	557	1.103	377	161	197	123
Warszawskie	527	117	231	78	34	41	26
Bydgoskie	498	106	218	76	33	40	25
Poznań	728	161	319	108	47	57	32
Poznańskie	661	149	289	98	42	51	32

744 "Chcę kupić samochód," p. 3.

745 This division was typical of the early stages of automotive development. Clay McShane noted a similar phenomenon in the USA at the beginning of the twentieth century. At that time, New York was second only to Paris in terms of the number of cars. Five years later, the *New York Times* estimated that more than 45% of all cars driving in the USA were registered in the city and state of New York; *idem*, *Down the Asphalt Path: The Automobile and the American City*, New York 1994, p. 175.

Voivodeship/ city	Number of cars allocated	Make					
		Warszawa	Syrena	Škoda	Moskvitch	Wart-burg	Trabant
Łódź	833	186	365	124	53	65	40
Łódzkie	383	86	168	58	24	28	19
Kieleckie	335	75	147	50	21	26	16
Lubelskie	354	76	155	54	23	28	18
Białostockie	196	42	86	30	13	15	10
Olsztyńskie	354	76	155	52	24	27	17
Gdańskie	890	196	390	134	57	70	43
Koszalińskie	282	62	124	42	18	22	14
Szczecińskie	412	90	180	62	27	33	20
Wrocław	900	201	394	134	57	70	44
Wrocławskie	914	204	401	138	58	71	44
Opolskie	507	114	222	76	32	39	24
Katowickie	2.711	603	1.188	407	171	211	131
Krakowskie	479	107	210	72	31	37	22
Rzeszowskie	278	65	121	40	18	21	13
Total	15.804	3.510	6.923	2.364	1.010	1.299	768

Source: Jak? Gdzie? Ile? Kupujemy samochody w 1963 r., "Motor" 1963, nr 3, s. 10.

A similar situation occurred in the USSR, East Germany, and Romania. Almost half of all car deliveries went to the Russian Soviet Federative Socialist Republic; in 1975 alone, this involved 350,000 out of a total of 715,000 vehicles. For comparison, 110,000 cars were sent to Ukraine, and only 20,000 to Belarus in the same year. Moreover, the two most important cities of the RSFSR, Moscow and Leningrad, received almost 20% of all vehicles. The same was true of East Germany and Romania, where most cars were sent to Berlin and Bucharest. According to Luminita Gatejel, one reason for this was a desire on the part of individual communist regimes demonstrate one's material success It was obvious that the Western world's attention would be focused on the capital cities of these countries, which therefore had to project to the outside world the image of a developed socialist society, in which mass motorisation played an important role. Another issue raised by Gatejel was the specificity of the local distribution systems, where particular articles were distributed vertically—i.e. from the most important cities and urban centres.[746]

4.2 Internal export

Another way to purchase a private car was through so-called internal exports organised by Polish Welfare Bank (Bank Polska Kasa Opieki PEKAO). The idea for this type of action appeared in the late 1940s. After the war, the assistance provided by the Polish diaspora to families inside Poland became increasingly extensive, taking the shape of parcels containing mainly clothing and food. Foreign companies preparing and shipping parcels to Poland started to appear in great numbers. Unfortunately, the high commissions that they cited did not correspond to a high quality of either services or goods.[747] In response, a group of deputies submitted an interpellation to the Sejm regarding the organisation of aid from the Polish-American community to families inside Poland. Specifically, they proposed that instead of goods, money orders should be sent, which could then be used to buy goods in Poland at favourable prices.[748] The aid system introduced in the order of March 30, 1948, by the Ministry of Industry and Trade and the Ministry of the Treasury enabled individuals living abroad to buy items in Poland for relatives and friends living inside the country using foreign currencies.[749] PEKAO was entrusted with the task of handling these transfers, which was due to the bank's special position as the only domestic financial institution with a network of offices abroad, including in the United States.[750]

The entire process went as follows: the client deposited a certain amount of money at a bank branch, with a dealer or at a cooperating company, and then placed an order for specific goods from a list, which would then be delivered to a specific person in Poland. Initially, the list contained only food, textiles, and fuel, but over time, the catalogue expanded. The bank also introduced

746 L. Gatejel, "Appealing for a Car: Consumption Policies and Entitlement in the USSR, the GDR, and Romania, 1950s–1980s," *Slavic Review* 2016, vol. 75, no. 1, pp. 133–134.

747 Z. Landau and J. Tomaszewski, *Bank Polska Kasa Opieki SA*, Warszawa 1990, pp. 62–63.

748 Ibid., p. 63.

749 "Dziennik Urzędowy Ministerstwa Skarbu" 1948, no. 42, pos. 149.

750 Z. Landau and J. Tomaszewski, *Bank Polska Kasa Opieki SA*, p. 63.

so-called PEKAO packages, which consisted of various products.[751] In the first year, turnover was low, amounting to only US $27,000, but it increased systematically in subsequent years. In 1952, the million dollar mark was crossed for the first time, and two years later, the total value of orders passed US $4 million. Initially, the most frequently purchased items were sewing machines, prams, and motorcycles, and in subsequent years, also cars.[752] Since 1953, at least 20% of turnover came from diplomatic internal exports. In other words, a significant part of the income derived from this action was achieved by Polish diplomatic officers, who used the system to acquire items that were unavailable or difficult to obtain inside the country.

The bank gradually expanded both the territorial scope of the campaign, initially addressed only to the Polish diaspora in the US, and the types of orders accepted. From our point of view, the year 1952 was a watershed, because it saw the introduction of "optional" orders When making such an order, the client sent whatever sum of money he wanted to Poland, without specifying a purpose. These amounts were then deposited in special PEKAO accounts for the recipients, who could freely dispose of the funds accumulated there—of course within the internal export offer presented by the bank. This form of assistance quickly gained popularity, and while in 1953, there were 5,600 PEKAO accounts of this type, by 1955 approximately 38,000 of them have been opened.[753] Another decision that expanded the scope of the campaign was the Ministry of Finance's consent to the use of further types of transfers in internal exports, as well as to the retaining of foreign currencies

---

751 Ibid., pp. 63–64.

752 For example, in 1952, the purchase of cars as part of internal exports yielded a total of US $4,600; AAN, Państwowa Komisja Planowania Gospodarczego (hereafter: PKPG), sign. 3425, Uwagi dotyczące akcji eksportu wewnętrznego, [1955], pp. 3–6; AAN, Ministerstwo Finansów (hereafter: MF), sign. 1/3, Sprawozdanie z akcji Eksportu Wewnętrznego za rok 1953, unnumbered pages; ibid., sign. 728, Konferencja prasowa w Banku Polska Kasa Opieki w Warszawie na temat Eksportu Wewnętrznego, [December 1948], unnumbered pages. Cleaning and personal hygiene products were very popular. In 1961, Swedish razor blades were so sought after that Bank PKO introduced rationing, limiting a single purchase to a maximum of 200 units; Archiwum Centralne Banku Polska Kasa Opieki (hereafter: AC PEKAO), sign. 163, Protokół nr 16 posiedzenia Komitetu Wykonawczego RB PKO SA odbytego 16 II 1961 r. o godz. 18.00 w lokalu Banku PKO, unnumbered pages.

753 Z. Landau and J. Tomaszewski, *Bank Polska Kasa Opieki SA*, p. 65.

and precious metals by Poles inside the country (see Table 9). Half a year later, in early 1957, PEKAO also decided to use internal exports to equip craft workshops with tools, machines, and materials.[754]

Table 9. The structure of sales within the framework of internal exports (in millions of zlotys)

Groups of goods and their origins	Years		
	1961	1967	1973
I. Group of goods			
food and tobacco products	23.3	10.5	12.8
textiles	15.8	8.0	17.8
clothing	25.8	27.0	14.5
medicine	0.1	4.5	-
vehicles	13.9	34.4	45.4
apartments	-	4.7	1.4
other	21.3	10.9	8.1
II. Origin of goods			
domestic items	75.8	31.0	57.3
imported items	24.2	69.0	42.7

Source: Z. Landau, J. Tomaszewski, Bank Polska Kasa Opieki S. A. 1929–1989, Warszawa 1991, p. 74.

These and other measures meant that the PEKAO action enjoyed considerable and—most importantly from the bank's point of view—constantly growing interest. While in 1958, goods for internal export were purchased in twelve countries using 240 sales offices, by 1969, 22 countries and 400 outlets had become involved. By the end of the 1960s, PEKAO was selling almost 5,000 products, the vast majority of which (3,800) came from capitalist countries, while only 400 were domestic. This arrangement was not accidental, since 45% of sales consisted of goods imported from the West and 15% of domestic goods, while only 6% of the items came from other socialist countries. The bank's representatives boasted that the range of goods available for internal

754 Ibid., p. 66.

export was constantly changing, both in terms of quality and quantity, "taking into account new technologies and fashions."[755]

During the entire period between 1948 and 1970, the total foreign exchange inflow reached US $386.4 million, over 84% of which was transferred in the 1960s; between 1948 and 1959, PEKAO received a total of only US $60 million.[756] Nonetheless, the bank was not prepared to handle such amounts. A report for 1960 even complained that "despite a significant increase in sales … the Bank has been unable to fully meet the customers' needs. This was due to the lack of a sufficient quantity of imported goods, given the high market demand for these goods, space, organisational and personnel deficiencies."[757]

As a side note, it is notable that in the case of car sales, the "space deficiencies" were particularly severe. The fact that PEKAO did not have its own covered parking lot for storing cars intended for sale had a negative impact on financial results. The bank was forced to use underground facilities in the National Bank of Poland (Narodowy Bank Polski NBP) building at Świętokrzyska Street in Warsaw, and those cars that did not fit there were directed to the courtyard in front of the building of the Ministry of Finance at Romuald Traugutt Street. In fact, none of these locations was suitable for storing cars. The NBP basements regularly flooded with water, and cars parked at the Ministry of Finance deteriorated in unfavourable weather conditions or were vandalised by unknown perpetrators. Both locations also lacked adequate facilities to carry out minor, but necessary, servicing activities.[758] Yet, PEKAO's biggest problem with not having its own parking lot was the absence of a sufficiently large space for storing cars that often arrived unannounced, even when the deliveries had been planned sufficiently in advance to avoid having to park cars outside during months with unfavourable weather conditions. This fact resulted in serious financial losses, because cars parked outdoors were harder to sell and PEKAO was often

---

755 AAN, URM, sign. 5.3/4, Podstawowe zadania Banku PKO w dziedzinie eksportu wewnętrznego, Warszawa, December 1969, pp. 489–492.

756 AC PEKAO, sign. 1171, Analiza działalności za rok 1973, unnumbered pages.

757 Ibid., sign. 163, Wstępne sprawozdanie z działalności Banku Polska Kasa Opieki SA w zakresie eksportu wewnętrznego, unnumbered pages.

758 Ibid., sign. 3617, Założenia inwestycji Banku PKO Oddział w Warszawie, Warszawa, September 1962, pp. 4–5.

forced to lower the price below the expected profit level.[759] The bank would even often not purchase the cars that it was offered because it had no place to keep them. This was the case with the offer to purchase a production series of Moskvitches in 1961.[760] Such was the source of the idea to build a covered parking lot at Lotników Boulevard and Obrzeźna Street. Initially, Bank PEKAO expected to begin and complete the investment in 1966, but financial constraints meant that complaints about the lack of suitable space to park car deliveries continued until 1970.[761]

Data on the sales conducted by the bank began to appear in the early 1960s. In 1961, Poles purchased a total of 711 cars as part of internal exports. The most popular model was the Warszawa, with 407 units sold. Fiats were also very popular, especially the 600 model (137 units). Of other Western brands, English Triumphs and one Mercedes car were also on offer. PEKAO also sold cars manufactured in the Eastern Bloc: 56 Moskvitches, 59 Škodas, and twenty-five Wartburgs. A Warszawa cost US $1,500; a Syrena, US $1,000. People interested in a Fiat 600 had to pay US $1,400. Other models of this make were more expensive: the Fiat 1100 and the Fiat 1300 cost US $2,000; the priciest Fiat 1800 cost as much as US $3,000. At that time the official dollar exchange rate was 4 złoty, However the black market rate—and de facto the only one available to the average citizen—was several times higher, amounting to about 100 złoty.

The data on the bank's profits is interesting: the average gain reached 77% of the purchase prices, and Western cars had the best purchase-to-sale price ratio. Those sales allowed PEKAO to make a 98% profit from each sale.[762] Władysław Gomułka himself pointed out at a conference of the Warsaw

---

759 Ibid., sign. 164, Protokół nr 42 z posiedzenia Komitetu Wykonawczego RB PKO odbytego 28 V 1962 r. w lokalu Banku, unnumbered pages; ibid., sign. 172, Protokół nr 78 z posiedzenia Komitetu Wykonawczego RB PKO 19 XI 1970 r., unnumbered pages.

760 Ibid., sign. 163, Protokół nr 72 z posiedzenia Komitetu Wykonawczego RB PKO odbytego 28 VII 1961 r. o godz. 17.00 w lokalu Banku PKO, unnumbered pages; See: ibid., sign. 164, Protokół nr 63 posiedzenia Komitetu Wykonawczego RB PKO odbytego 2 VII 1962 r. w lokalu Banku, unnumbered pages.

761 Ibid., sign. 3617, Prezydium Dzielnicowej Rady Narodowej Warszawa-Mokotów Wydział Budownictwa, Urbanistyki i Architektury, June 10, 1965, p. 40.

762 Ibid., sign. 164, Sprzedaż samochodów w 1961 r. oraz w okresie od 1 I 1962 r. do 12 IV 1962 r., unnumbered pages.

committee of the PZPR in early April 1962 that dollar sales as part of internal exports are an excellent source for the much sought-after foreign currency.[763]

The situation was similar in 1964. That year, PEKAO sold 723 cars, mostly Volgas and Warszawa 203 s—a total of 380 units. In addition to these two, the bank's offer also included various models of Fiat, Moskvitch, and Wartburg. The most expensive among them were Fiat models 1800 and 1300, which cost US $3,000 and US $2,600, respectively. The price of a Volga was set at US $2,100; a Moskvitch cost US $1,700.[764]

At the beginning of November 1966, a conference was hosted by Deputy Prime Minister Eugeniusz Szyr to discuss the matter of trade in goods of foreign origin. During the discussions, the argument was raised that speculative and criminal activities along with unaccounted-for imports created significant losses of foreign exchange for the Polish state. The scale of losses incurred by the State Treasury was evident in data from 1965. In that year, over 11,000 foreign currency and customs crimes were detected, totalling 78 million zlotys in value. Undetected crimes were probably several times higher. For this reason, Bank PEKAO, as well as the foreign trade company Baltona, were tasked with drawing from the market at least some of the foreign currencies that Poles, willingly or not, used to purchase goods derived from crime. It was assumed that coordinated and planned activities in this area could allow the Polish economy to recover approximately US $20–25 million that had been lost as a result of unaccounted-for imports and criminal activities.[765] This "new opening" for PEKAO is especially evident in car sales. While in 1966 PEKAO sold 1,500 cars, sales through the first seven months of the following year amounted to 2,200 cars. The expected introduction of Big Fiats to the internal export offer gave hope for even better results.[766]

---

763 AAN, KC PZPR, sign. 237/VII-4528, IX Konferencja KW [PZPR], April 3–5, 1962, p. 332.

764 T. Szczerbicki, *Syrena*, Czerwonak 2016, pp. 135–137.

765 AAN, URM, sign. 62/9, Protokół nr GS/59/66 z konferencji u Wiceprezesa Rady Ministrów Ob. E. Szyra 8 XI 1966 r. w sprawie "Omówienia całokształtu pozaplanowego obrotu towarami pochodzenia zagranicznego," pp. 2–3.

766 AC PEKAO, sign. 169, Protokół nr 42 z posiedzenia Komitetu Wykonawczego RB PKO odbytego 5 VI 1967 r. w lokalu Banku, unnumbered pages; Protokół nr 53 z posiedzenia Komitetu Wykonawczego RB PKO odbytego 14 VII 1967 r. w lokalu Banku, unnumbered pages.

These hopes were actually fulfilled. During the first nine months of 1968, PEKAO sold cars for a total of US $4.9 million (the end-of-year sales value reached US $5.8 million)[767], while the amount for all of 1967 was "only" US $4.2 million—still a record result in the bank's history up to that point.[768]

Ultimately, in the years 1967–1970, Poles purchased a total of 13,674 cars as part of internal exports conducted by PEKAO (see Table 10). This was a significant increase compared to the preceding period, when the average yearly sales were in the hundreds. Most of the cars purchased were manufactured in Poland—6,900 units over the course of four years, primarily Warszawas. When the Big Fiat was introduced for sale, the interest in the new licenced product from the FSO factory at Żerań was evident. Cars produced by capitalist countries easily found buyers; PEKAO sold 4,100 of them in the period in question. These were mainly French (Simca, Renault), German (NSU), and Italian (Fiat) cars. Of the Eastern Bloc makes, Poland's internal exports included mainly the East German Wartburgs, the Soviet Volgas and Moskvitches, and the Czechoslovak Škodas, although these only became available in the second half of the 1960s.[769] In total, 2,600 of them were sold.

Table 10. Passenger cars sold as internal exports by Bank PEKAO in 1967–1970

Make of car	Years			
	1967	1968	1969	1970
NSU	580	270	169	17
Renault	915	551	476	105
Simca	53	822	2	-
Hillman	25	16	1	-
Fiat (various types)	241	88	55	127
Others	-	14	72	266
Total—cars from capitalist countries	1.814	1.034	775	515
Škoda	100	97	166	87
Wartburg	148	200	200	146

767 AAN, URM, sign. 5.4/3, Podstawowe zadania Banku PKO w dziedzinie eksportu wewnętrznego, Warszawa, December 1969, p. 493.

768 Ibid., sign. 170, Protokół nr 73 z posiedzenia Komitetu Wykonawczego RB PKO odbytego 18 XI 1968 r. w siedzibie Banku, unnumbered pages.

769 Ibid., sign. 169, Zapotrzebowanie Banku na samochody osobowe na 1968 r. w ujęciu ilościowym i wartościowym, unnumbered pages.

Make of car	Years			
	1967	1968	1969	1970
Moskvitch	299	3	-	-
Volga	319	221	375	244
Total—cars from socialist countries	866	521	741	477
Warszawa	516	987	977	908
Fiat 125p		621	69	2.841
Total—domestic cars	520	1.604	1.050	3.757
Total	3.200	3.159	2.566	4.749

Source: AAN, GUC, sign. 25/140, Kompendium statystyczne administracji celnej 1946–1970, p. 34.

PEKAO sold cars at very high mark-ups. The average margin varied depending on the car's country of origin. Margins were clearly the highest for Western cars. At that time, they amounted to around 100%. For example, the price for a Fiat 1100, depending on the model, was between US $2,000 and US $2,200, while the unit cost was approximately US $1,000. Undisputed leadership belonged to the popular Fiat 600, which cost US $657 per unit and was sold with a markup of over 113%. A similar profit level was achieved with special orders, when a client selected a model not included in the internal export offer. This was the case with Fiat 2300, which the bank bought for US $1,700 and sold for US $3,600.[770] On the other hand, cars from socialist countries were sold with lower margins, ranging from 28% to 46%. Cars manufactured in the Żerań factory—Warszawas and Syrenas—found buyers at prices 64% and 33% higher than actual cost, respectively. As the minutes of the meetings of the Executive Committee of the Council of the Bank show, these margins were repeatedly questioned—for example in 1962, when Deputy Minister of Foreign Trade Józef Kutin criticised PEKAO's practices in this regard, suggesting that margins on cars be reduced to 40–50%, that is, by half.[771] It was only in July 1967 that the KERM decided on a specific

770 AC PEKAO, sign. 165, Protokół nr 18 posiedzenia Komitetu Wykonawczego RB PKO odbytego 4 III 1963 r. w lokalu Banku, unnumbered pages.

771 Ibid., sign. 164, Protokół nr 68 z posiedzenia Komitetu Wykonawczego RB PKO obytego 20 VII br. [1962] w lokalu Banku, unnumbered pages.

calculation for internal export prices: the average price of the given product on Western European retail markets plus 10–20%.[772] It should be noted, however, that new prices determined according to this principle were introduced very slowly, especially in the case of passenger cars, which will be discussed later on the example of the Big Fiat.

The bank often tried to respond dynamically to the situation on the market, raising or lowering prices depending on the demand for a specific make. This was the case with the Renault Dauphine. When it turned out in mid-1964 that 700 cars delivered by the French manufacturer could not find buyers and the bank's activities (including an intense advertising campaign) did not result in increased sales, the Executive Committee of the Council of the Bank decided to reduce the price from US $1,700 to US $1,500. This yielded immediate results, since by early 1964, only four units of the original number of 700 remained in PEKAO's hands. Almost immediately, therefore, it was decided to increase the price by US $50. Interestingly, a similar problem occurred concurrently with the sale of the Wartburg de Luxe, which PEKAO sold at US $1,650. In this case, even a reduction to US $1,450 did not significantly increase buyer interest in this East German car.[773]

Customers who wanted to buy a car as an internal export and paid in dollars were rather picky. That explains why PEKAO only offered Syrenas for a very short time. In spite of their poor reputation, these cars were sold for dollars starting in 1961.[774] The decision to include them in the internal export system was prompted by the interest that the bank's customers supposedly showed in buying them.[775] In the first year, customers purchased eighteen out

---

772 AAN, URM, sign. 5.4/3, Podstawowe zadania Banku PKO w dziedzinie eksportu wewnętrznego, Warszawa, December 1969, p. 494.

773 AC PEKAO, sign. 164, Protokół nr 67 z posiedzenia Komitetu Wykonawczego RB PKO odbytego 16 VII 1962 r. w lokalu Banku, unnumbered pages; ibid., Protokół nr 72 z posiedzenia Komitetu Wykonawczego RB PKO odbytego 10 IX 1962 r. w lokalu Banku, unnumbered pages; ibid., sign. 165, Protokół nr 17 posiedzenia Komitetu Wykonawczego RB PKO odbytego 28 II 1963 r. w lokalu Banku, unnumbered pages.

774 Ibid., sign. 163, Protokół nr 44 posiedzenia Komitetu Wykonawczego RB PKO SA, odbytego 15 V 1961 r. o godz. 18.00 w lokalu Banku PKO, unnumbered pages.

775 Ibid., Protokół nr 14 posiedzenia Komitetu Wykonawczego RB PKO odbytego 10 II 1961 r. o godz. 18.00 w lokalu Banku PKO, unnumbered pages. It was similar in the case of Polish-made two-wheelers. When the Bank received questions about the possibility of purchasing them for dollars, it was almost immediately decided to include them

of thirty units.[776] From the very beginning, the Syrena's inclusion in the system was problematic. Initially, the 102 model was offered, replaced in subsequent years by models 103 and 104. The starting price was US $1,000, of which the bank's profit amounted to about US $300. Units earmarked for internal export were offered with better equipment than those sold by Motozbyt.[777] However, due to lack of interest, the price had to be temporarily lowered to US $900. It was noted that, given the sufficient supply of Syrenas on the domestic market, PEKAO could not "win the moment of attraction." Besides, "richer" versions of the Syrena, until then available only through internal export, began to be directed to the domestic market. Moreover, uninterested in taking over the Syrenas PEKAO sought to hand over, Motozbyt lowered the price of its cars just before the premiere of the new model.[778] The price reduction did not change the Syrena's situation, nor did the introduction into the internal export market of a version of the car with a Wartburg engine.[779] In 1964, out of thirty units on offer, only twenty were sold, and the following year, only twelve. The reason was the high number of complaints received by PEKAO. Ultimately, in 1966, the Syrena disappeared from the bank's offer.[780] It is therefore clear that a customer who had an adequate supply of dollars and decided to take advantage of internal export would immediately rule out the purchase of a car that could prove undependable in operation.

---

in the offer. The Junak cost US $345, the Ryś moped, US $100, and the Osa scooter, US $245. These prices were higher than those on foreign markets, where they cost US $315, US $100, and US $200, respectively; ibid., Protokół nr 31 posiedzenia Komitetu Wykonawczego RB PKO odbytego 7 IV 1961 r. o godz. 18.00 w lokalu Banku PKO, unnumbered pages; ibid., Notatka w sprawie rozszerzenia asortymentu towarowego, Warszawa, March 29, 1961, unnumbered pages.

776 Ibid., sign. 164, Sprzedaż samochodów w 1961 r. oraz w okresie od 1 I 1962 do 12 IV 1962 r., unnumbered pages.

777 Ibid., Protokół nr 49 z posiedzenia Komitetu Wykonawczego RB PKO odbytego 11 VI 1962 r. w lokalu Banku, unnumbered pages.

778 Ibid., sign. 165, Wniosek Wydziału Handlowego w spr[awie] wprowadzenia posezonowej sprzedaży samochodów "Syrena" w okresie 1 XII 1963 do 29 II 1964 r., Warszawa, November 18, 1963, unnumbered pages.

779 Ibid., sign. 166, Protokół nr 11 z posiedzenia Komitetu Wykonawczego RB PKO SA odbytego 13 II 1964 r. w lokalu Banku, unnumbered pages.

780 Ibid., sign. 168, Protokół nr 17 z posiedzenia Komitetu Wykonawczego RB PKO odbytego 21 II 1966 r. w lokalu Banku, unnumbered pages.

Hence the limited interest in Syrenas, which were infamously unreliable, a fact that discouraged buyers.

It is worth emphasising that PEKAO selected the makes to be included in the price list for internal exports very carefully. The Syrena did not survive, and the Zastava 850, which was offered to the bank at the end of 1968, was not considered to be of interest to potential buyers. The Executive Committee of the Council of the Bank stated that the high price of the Yugoslav car, more expensive than the Fiat 600, along with predicted problems with the supply of spare parts, disqualified the car from Kragujevac as a candidate for internal export.[781] Meanwhile, other makes, usually Western ones, were bought up almost immediately. This was the case with Renault 10 Major cars, a batch of 100 of which sold out within a week.[782] Among the brands imported from

---

781 Ibid., sign. 170, Protokół nr 81 z posiedzenia Komitetu Wykonawczego RB PKO SA odbytego 23 XII 1968 r. w siedzibie Banku, unnumbered pages.

782 Ibid., sign. 167, Protokół nr 62 z posiedzenia Komitetu Wykonawczego RB PKO odbytego 30 VIII 1965 r. w lokalu Banku, unnumbered pages. Of note is a rather interesting matter related to the servicing of the Renault cars mentioned here. The contract concluded with the French company stipulated that Poland would be provided with technical documentation, special tools, and spare parts before the first delivery. When the French delayed the fulfillment of the contract, the problem of the technical service of these cars arose. The Automotive Technical Support Association did not agree to provide warranty services without appropriate documentation, parts, and tools. This caused a serious problem for PEKAO, which—unable to provide technical service—decided not to release cars it had already sold. The Office of the Commercial Counsel in Paris was called on to resolve the dispute. Renault representatives claimed that, in their opinion, Motoimport had the documentation for an earlier model (Renault 8), which could be used for the models sold by PEKAO. In addition, a representative of the French company would travel to Poland in late August and early September to conduct training in major technical service offices. Furthermore, the French company also pointed out that each Renault 10 sold by the Bank was equipped with two manuals (in French and German) and a set of service tools. Meanwhile, PEKAO noted that these manuals were intended for individual users, not repair shops, and the tools mentioned by the French side amounted to a jack, some spanners, a screwdriver, and a spark plug key, which were useless for warranty inspections or repairs. Ultimately, the French announced that the missing elements would be delivered by the end of October, and PEKAO decided to issue cars to customers, though no repairs would be made, only periodic inspections; ibid., sign. 167, Protokół nr 73 posiedzenia komitetu Wykonawczego RB PKO SA odbytego 18 X 1965 r. w lokalu Banku, unnumbered pages; ibid., Protokół nr 76 posiedzenia Komitetu Wykonawczego RB PKO SA odbytego 28 X 1865 r., unnumbered pages;

socialist countries, Volgas were also very popular, usually intended for use as taxis. PEKAO repeatedly had problems with fulfilling orders, which often exceeded the quantities supplied. Due to persistent interest of customers in these cars, the bank even decided to increase the price by US $150, to US $2,150, but even this did not discourage buyers.[783] At the end of the 1960s, the decision was even made to transfer several hundred Volgas previously intended for state officials into the internal export offer; in their place, the officials would receive Big Fiats.[784]

The popularity of internal exports among car buyers might well have also been due to the fact that Bank PEKAO usually tried to ensure access to original spare parts and technical service for the vehicles it sold. Internal export price lists often included entries for sets of small parts, the purchase of which was then offered directly to buyers of specific models. The same was true of car tyres.[785] In other words, Bank PEKAO tried to avoid repeating the mistakes made by Motozbyt, which was often unable to ensure an adequate supply of spare parts for the cars it sold. The bank documentation includes a highly interesting note in which PEKAO representatives respond to a proposal from the MHW that the sale of cars imported for internal export should be conducted by Motozbyt. The rather diplomatic response from the bank's representatives de facto demonstrates a fundamental difference between the two institutions in their approach to customers:

> Such cooperation would be possible if "Motozbyt" was willing to meet certain conditions, such as ensuring continuity of access to cars for customers of the bank, proper storage and maintenance of cars, appropriate organisation of the issuance of cars to ensures prompt and efficient customer service, provision of full warranty service, etc., conditions which are undoubtedly serious factors affecting

---

ibid., Protokół nr 78 posiedzenia Komitetu Wykonawczego RB PKO SA odbytego 8 XI 1965 r. w lokalu Banku, unnumbered pages.

783 Ibid., sign. 165, Wniosek na Komitet Wykonawczy Rady Banku w sprawie zmiany ceny sprzedaży samochodów osob[owych] "Wołga", Warszawa, December 5, 1963, unnumbered pages; ibid., Protokół nr 93 posiedzenia Komitetu Wykonawczego RB PKO SA odbytego 6 XII 1963 r. w lokalu Banku, unnumbered pages.

784 AAN, URM, sign. 5.4/3, Protokół nr 5/70 z posiedzenia Prezydium Rządu 10 III 1970 r., p. 437.

785 AC PEKAO, sign. 164, Protokół nr 42 z posiedzenia Komitetu Wykonawczego RB PKO odbytego 28 V 1962 r. w lokalu Banku, unnumbered pages.

> the circulation of foreign currencies in relation to car sales. Heretofore, despite the difficult conditions of storage and technical supply, the bank has maintained the practice of selling cars with only sporadic cases of customer complaints … .[786]

Next to the Volga, the biggest domestic export hit was the Fiat 125p, produced by FSO since the late 1960s. The licence purchased from the Italian company brought a real breakthrough to the Polish automotive industry. At the same time, however, it did not bring the expected change in the development of individual motorisation in the Polish society. The popular Big Fiat was not a car that could serve as the basis for an automotive boom: it was too large and, perhaps more importantly, too expensive to become the car of the ordinary citizen. Moreover, the authorities did not hide the fact that their main priority was gaining foreign currency, which they intended to obtain by directing most of the production of the Żerań FSO for export, including internal.

The Big Fiat appeared in PEKAO's offer in 1968 and immediately became highly sought after among the Bank's clients. Initially, the price was set at US $2,300, which was very steep. The first proposal made during a meeting of the Executive Committee of the Council of the Bank was US $200 lower, but officials ultimately decided in favour of the higher value. As the justification states, the price was determined by the high demand for cars imported from Western countries and by the prices of similar cars offered through internal exports. However, the primary concern was that the black market value of PEKAO bills would increase, reach the level of 90–100 zlotys to a dollar, which would bring them dangerously close to the values paid for the US currency on the black market.[787]

In early 1968, Big Fiats easily found buyers able to pay in dollars. A total of 611 units were sold over the course of ten months of that year, 77% of them by the end of the second quarter. On the free market, Big Fiats drew very high prices, even reaching 270,000 zlotys. However, beginning in mid-year, internal export sales began to decline, which led to a troublesome situation for PEKAO, which had previously reduced the offer of foreign cars, removing

---

786 Ibid., sign. 166, [Information from Bank PKO S.A. to the Ministry of Internal Trade regarding the sale of passenger cars and spare parts], February 25, 1964, unnumbered pages.

787 Ibid., sign. 169, Protokół nr 95 posiedzenia Komitetu Wykonawczego RB PKO SA odbytego 14 XII 1967 r. w lokalu Banku, unnumbered pages.

Volkswagen from the list of makes in order not to create excessive competition for Big Fiats. The purpose of the move was to ensure the best possible conditions for the sale of new cars from Żerań.[788] Time and again complaints were heard that the price of internal exports was too high, especially in comparison to other cars offered by the bank, such as the Renault 10 or the NSU, which were sold at prices that did not exceed US $2,000.[789] In this situation, to ensure a price preference "for cars produced domestically compared to vehicles produced abroad and the constant improvement in the market supply of the 'Fiat 125p' cars," it was decided to reduce their price to US $2,100.[790]

Another problem the Bank faced were the difficulties in fulfilling orders for Polish cars—the Warszawa and Fiat 125p—previously placed with Polmozbyt. An instruction prepared by the Planning Department of the MHZ in May 1968 prompted officials at Polmozbyt to suspend deliveries of its products because from that moment on, they would not count towards the production plan for export.[791] At one point, the situation became so dire that the bank was unable to fulfil orders for cars manufactured by FSO, and dissatisfied customers sent complaints against the bank to the central authorities. The conflict between PEKAO and Polmozbyt lasted until July 1969, when, as a result of mediation by the Ministry of Finance, the new car distribution list prepared by the Planning Committee of the Council of Ministers included a requirement for internal export.[792]

High prices and supply problems meant that between January and October 1969, PEKAO sold only 66 Big Fiats, and by the end of the year, a total of 100. Increasingly, buyers of these cars chose to purchase them using Polish zlotys because Motozbyt had 8,000 Big Fiats in stock in 1969, and the plan for the next year foresaw the delivery of a total of 10,000 units of the

788 Ibid., sign. 170, Protokół nr 39 z posiedzenia Komitetu Wykonawczego RB PKO odbytego 17 VI 1968 r. w siedzibie Banku, unnumbered pages.

789 Ibid., Wniosek na posiedzenia zarządu w sprawie zmiany ceny EW samochodów fiat 125p prod. krajowej, unnumbered pages.

790 Ibid., Protokół nr 74 z posiedzenia Komitetu Wykonawczego RB PKO odbytego 21 XI 1968 r. w siedzibie Banku, unnumbered pages.

791 Ibid., sign. 171, Protokół nr 1 z posiedzenia Komitetu Wykonawczego RB PKO odbytego 2 I 1969 r. w siedzibie Banku, unnumbered pages.

792 Ibid., Protokół nr 43 z posiedzenia Komitetu Wykonawczego RB PKO SA odbytego 24 VII 1969 r. w siedzibie Banku, unnumbered pages.

model to the market. In other words, the market was gradually becoming saturated, and even in open sale, the price of the Fiat 125p was barely higher than the nominal price (only 190,000 zlotys). At the same time, given that the value of the dollar at the black market reached as high as 130 zlotys at the turn of the year, the internal export offer became very unattractive.[793]

PEKAO also faced competition from foreign sales offices which began to sell new cars inside Poland. At the end of the 1960s, several companies offering such services were operating on the Polish market: Dom Agenturowy M. Czarnecki i S-ka sold Citroëns and NSUs; Timex SA sold Mercedes cars; Transactor SA supplied Volkswagens; and Transpol SA sold cars produced by the British Rootes Motors, primarily the then-popular Hillman. Polcomex SA and Mundial SA handled the importation of French brands (Renault, Simca, and Peugeot).[794] Prices offered by these sales offices were so attractive that even after adding delivery costs and customs duties, they were significantly lower than the bank prices.[795] Transactor SA, which dealt in Volkswagens, offered the cars at so-called factory export prices, which were 11% lower than the retail prices in West Germany. This discount applied only if the car was delivered directly to Poland. If the car was picked up in West Germany, a 4% export tax was added to the factory price. Polish diplomats who decided to purchase a car through this channel received an additional 10% discount.

---

793 Ibid., Protokół nr 61 z posiedzenia Komitetu Wykonawczego RB PKO SA odbytego 6 X 1969 r. w siedzibie Banku, unnumbered pages; ibid., sign. 172, Protokół nr 2 z posiedzenia Komitetu Wykonawczego RB PKO odbytego 12 I 1970 r., unnumbered pages.

794 AAN, Główny Urząd Ceł (hereafter: GUC), sign. 12/45, Notatka w sprawie sprzedaży samochodów przez firmy przedstawicielskie, działające w kraju w imieniu producentów z kierunków kapitalistycznych, Warszawa, February 7, 1970, unnumbered pages.

795 AC PEKAO, sign. 171, Protokół nr 64 z posiedzenia Komitetu Wykonawczego RB PKO SA odbytego 16 X 1969 r. w siedzibie Banku, unnumbered pages. In the years 1967–1969, Poles purchased over 2,800 cars in this way; AAN, GUC, sign. 12/45, Import samochodów osobowych w latach 1967–1969. Zestawienie zbiorcze, unnumbered pages; ibid., Import samochodów osobowych w latach 1967–1969 realizowany przez Państwowe Przedsiębiorstwa Przedstawicielskie, unnumbered pages.

The only problem was that the payment had to be deposited directly into a West German account.[796]

Given the circumstances mentioned here and the visible decline in interest in the offer of the bank shown by dollar-paying customers, the decision was made in March 1970 to reduce prices for the Big Fiat as a result of the "minor revolution" in the development of prices for products sold as internal exports and of the sales market of new passenger cars imported from abroad in general. The bank took a long time to implement the aforementioned KERM regulation on prices from July 1967, probably out of a desire to maintain a high markup on specific goods, which ensured high foreign currency inflows. Only the significant drop in sales forced the bank to revise prices in accordance with the regulation of 1967. This was the case with cars, which provided comparatively the highest foreign currency earnings out of the entire internal export offer. When it turned out that the value of cars sold in 1969 dropped by US $1.2 million compared to the previous year, it became clear that maintaining a markup of 80–85% would be impossible in the long run. Moreover, as official data showed, Poles bought over 6,100 unaccounted-for imported cars in the same year, to a total value of $6.9 million. This amounted to 30% of all cars imported into the country.[797] Such large and diverse array of imports made it even more difficult to provide access to both technical service and spare parts.

Therefore, the idea was formulated to direct demand for Western passenger cars at least partially toward the Żerań factory's latest product. For this purpose, the Central Customs Office developed a plan for a new customs and pricing policy for the Big Fiat. First of all, preferential sales conditions and price levels would be proposed to everyone who wanted to buy the car. Customers would be able to buy a Fiat 125p, as before, for dollars as an internal export and (this was a new idea) at Pol-Mot for convertible currency. In both cases, prices would be lower than had been the case so far. At the same time,

796 Ibid., Notatka w sprawie sprzedaży samochodów przez firmy przedstawicielskie działające w kraju w imieniu producentów z kierunków kapitalistycznych, Warszawa, February 7, 1970, unnumbered pages.

797 AAN, GUC, sign. 12/45, Założenia protekcyjnej polityki celnej i cenowej w stosunku do eksportu i sprzedaży na rynku wewnętrznym samochodów marki "Polski Fiat," unnumbered pages.

cars imported into the country through the so-called unaccounted-for (that is, private) trade would be subject to high customs duties and taxation.[798] In practice, these regulations were to apply primarily to Western cars, because they constituted the overwhelming majority of vehicles imported outside of the official channels.

During a debate over the price for the Big Fiat in internal exports, it was agreed that customers would likely be brought back to PEKAO only if the price was closer to the level found on the domestic market, assuming the black market dollar exchange rate ($1 for 100 zlotys). Hence, the price recommended by the Bank was US $1,600 for a car with the 1300 cm^3 engine and US $1,800 for a car with the 1500 cm^3 engine.[799] The Government Praesidium agreed to the proposal and accepted the new prices for the Big Fiat at its meeting on March 10, 1970. At the same time, the price of the car on the domestic market was also set in dollars. Those who wanted to buy a Fiat outside of internal exports had to pay US $1,300–$1,400 dollars.[800] The new sales conditions were to be implemented almost immediately after the decision was announced, that is, on March 17. It is of note here that this was the first time that the price of a car was decided by one of the highest political bodies in the country.[801]

It did not take long for the decision to yield results. Within about three weeks (from March 17 to April 8), the bank sold 100 vehicles, and midway through 1970, it had sold as many as 1,290 Big Fiats. Ultimately, a total of 2,841 of these cars were sold by the end of the year as part of internal exports,

---

798 Ibid., Notatka syntetyczna założeń protekcyjnej polityki celnej i cenowej w stosunku do eksportu i sprzedaży na rynku wewnętrznym samochodów osobowych marki "Polski Fiat," [February 1970], unnumbered pages.

799 AC PEKAO, sign. 172, Protokół nr 2 z posiedzenia Komitetu Wykonawczego RB PKO odbytego 12 I 1970 r., unnumbered pages; ibid., Notatka w sprawie cen samochodów Polski Fiat 125p, Poufne, unnumbered pages.

800 When purchasing a Big Fiat on the domestic market, buyers agreed not to sell the vehicle for three years. Otherwise, they had to pay a 25% duty.

801 AAN, URM, sign. 5.4/3, Decyzja nr 26/70 Prezydium Rządu z 10 III 1970 r. w sprawie zmiany polityki celnej w stosunku do samochodów importowanych w obrocie pozaplanowym oraz zwiększenia wewnętrznego eksportu wewnętrznego samochodu licencyjnego Fiat 125p, p. 628.

generating US $4.7 million.[802] However, it was not all smooth sailing. When PEKAO's customers had bought up all of its Big Fiats within a month, the bank asked Pol-Mot for another 2,680 units. Lack of foresight meant that the waiting time before PEKAO customers could pick up their cars doubled to between 3 and 4 weeks. Only after an intervention by the central authorities did Pol-Mot restart deliveries.[803] The dollar sales of Big Fiats on the domestic market also increased significantly—almost ten times more units of this model were sold than in 1969, when sales totalled 110 units.[804]

However, while the price manoeuvre had a positive effect in the case of the Big Fiat, the same cannot be said about the internal export of Western cars. At the meeting of the Executive Committee of the Council of the Bank on March 26, 1970, it was decided to temporarily suspend the sale of cars imported from capitalist countries. The reason cited was clause 1.1a in the Government Praesidium's decision of March 10, which ordered that the price of cars from capitalist countries offered for internal export be set at the level of retail prices in Western European countries plus a markup of 10–20%. At the same time, the bank was to apply the principle of optimal profit, raising or lowering prices depending on demand. Due to the competitiveness of the aforementioned sales offices of foreign car companies, prices for internal exports would be almost identical between the bank and the offices, not including customs duties and transport costs. At the same time, the expectation was that the internal export sales would secure at least a 60% foreign currency profit. However, there was a contradiction here, because, in order to ensure the specified foreign currency profit, the bank had to keep prices at the current level and even raise some of them by several percentage points. Indeed, the new prices for Western cars in internal export, introduced in May 9 of that year, were higher. The Renault that previously cost $1,850, now had a price tag of $2,530. Various models of Fiat offered by PEKAO increased in price by $400 or more per unit. A Soviet Volga equipped with an engine

802 AAN, GUC, sign. 12/45, Informacja obrazująca zagadnienie przywozu w obrocie pozaplanowym samochodów osobowych i dostawczych, [1971], unnumbered pages.

803 AC PEKAO, sign. 172, Protokół nr 41 z posiedzenia Komitetu Wykonawczego Rady Banku 4 VI 1970 r., unnumbered pages; ibid., Protokół nr 38 z posiedzenia Komitetu Wykonawczego RB PKO odbytego 21 V 1970 r., unnumbered pages.

804 AAN, GUC, sign. 12/45, Informacja obrazująca zagadnienie przywozu w obrocie pozaplanowym samochodów osobowych i dostawczych, [1971], unnumbered pages.

from an English Rover and treated like a Western car set one back as much as $3,530, increased from the previous price of $2,760.

Sales results for the first half of the year showed that the new pricing policy was only partially effective. In the case of Big Fiats, there was a significant increase in sales, but with imported cars, sales practically stopped. The comparison of the number of cars sold before and after the introduction of the new prices is interesting. It should be noted that all car purchase contracts concluded before the Government Praesidium's decision of March 10 and finalised after that date still followed the old prices. During this time, PEKAO sold a total of 389 Western cars, while in the period from May 9 to September 30—only 23, which meant a huge decline in foreign currency earnings that could not be made up for even by the constantly growing sales of the Fiat 125p. At the same time, inventories of cars that found no buyers were growing. Due to the aforementioned problems with parking space for cars, the bank tried to sell them on the internal market. Finally, at the end of July 1970, the Ministry of Finance decided to remove the unfortunate point from the Government Praesidium's decision.

Returning to the Big Fiat for a moment, it bears emphasising that this sudden increase in sales was not just the result of the reduction in price. During the same meeting of March 10, 1970, the Government Praesidium also decided to increase the customs duties on passenger cars imported from abroad. Since 1968, there were three custom duty levels, depending on the engine capacity, as well as on whether the importer disposed of the car within three years of its importation and if a member of their family had paid those rates within the previous five years—otherwise the fee doubled. In the case of a first payment, the duty was set at 30 zlotys (for a vehicle with an engine displacement of up to 1,000 cm^3), 40 zlotys (1,000–1,600 cm^3) and 50 zlotys (over 1,600 cm^3) per kilogramme.[805] The new rate introduced in 1970 was unified and raised to the value of 150 zlotys per kilogramme.[806] This increase was very noticeable—in the worst-case scenario, a person importing a car from abroad had to pay customs duties five times as high. At the same time, customs duty exemptions, previously quite common, were completely abolished. While in the years 1962–1969, the value of customs payments

---

805 Dz. U. 1968, no. 25, pos. 169.
806 Dz. U. 1970, no. 5 pos. 37.

due amounted to over 923 million zlotys, the actual duties totalled only 424 million zlotys.[807]

Ultimately, the new customs tariffs were introduced on March 14 and significantly slowed the importation of passenger cars. Stefan Kisielewski noted this fact in his diary thusly: "The customs duty on cars imported from abroad has been increased threefold. This is a brutal blow to various [polish] engineers [working] abroad, who starve themselves to save up for a car. Indeed, our authorities really know how to discourage people."[808] In 1969, Poles imported 6,129 cars into the country, and during the following year, only 2,374. Interestingly, in the same period, the number of commercial vehicles being imported, for which the customs duty remained unchanged (20 zlotys per kg of vehicle), increased significantly. Many enterprising Poles took advantage of this fact and imported various types of vans into the country, which could be adapted for use as passenger cars and were eligible for lower import fees. Before the authorities became aware of this practice and introduced supplementary customs regulations, 487 delivery vehicles were imported into Poland during the third and fourth quarter of 1970, while in all of 1969, only 59 such vehicles were imported.[809]

In turn, the idea that people who bought a new car second-hand should pay above the official price stemmed from the desire to curb the practice of reselling new vehicles immediately after purchase. To that end, the authorities asked Bank PEKAO to increase the price of Big Fiats sold as part of internal exports. However, the bank's representatives responded that the use of two different car prices—depending on whether the buyer purchased the vehicle for his own use or for further sale—"is neither possible nor justified." The bank could in no way influence this type of transaction, because both parties made payments in foreign currencies and under the same conditions.

807 It should be emphasised that most customs duty exemptions applied to resettled people who, when returning to Poland, brought their belongings with them, very often including cars. In total, during this period, the returnees brought in over 10,000 cars, and the duty exemptions amounted to 405 million zlotys; AAN, GUC, sign. 12/45, Zestawienie samochodów osobowych sprowadzonych w obrocie pozaplanowym przez obywateli polskich z zagranicy w latach 1962–1969, [1970], unnumbered pages.

808 S. Kisielewski, *Dzienniki*, Warszawa 2001, p. 391.

809 AAN, GUC, sign. 12/45, Informacja obrazująca zagadnienie przywozu w obrocie pozaplanowym samochodów osobowych i dostawczych, [1971], unnumbered pages.

According to the bank, it was only possible to introduce a tax on the acquisition of property rights.[810]

4.3 "It was worth saving six grand": the general savings bank (*powszechna kasa oszczędności*)

In the first quarter of 1957, anyone who wanted to own a car gained a new opportunity to fulfil their desire: the General Savings Bank(Powszechna Kasa Oszczedności PKO) introduced a special type of savings books. Deposits could be made in any amount, bore no interest, but once every quarter, account owners could take part in a lottery draw for a passenger car. The rules were clear: only accounts of 6,000 zloty or more counted (the money could be deposited all at once or in 6 or 12 instalments), and for every thousand savings books, there was one bonus in the form of a car. The lucky ones whose book numbers were drawn kept all of their money: they could withdraw it or leave it in the account and take part in subsequent draws.[811]

The idea of a bonus in the form of a car, and later a motorcycle or a moped, turned out to be very successful. While PKO reports from 1956 state that "the distribution of the savings books is insufficient," a year later, at the end of 1957, a sudden increase was noted, mainly involving values that were rewarded with vehicles.[812] Almost 80,000 "car" savings books were registered, amassing 521 million zlotys, and 32,000 "motorcycle" accounts for a total amount of almost 125 million zlotys. For comparison, in the same year, Poles opened 3,100 housing books, mandatory, state-controlled savings scheme to eventually receive a subsidised cooperative apartment, collecting 15.7 million on their accounts (see Table 11).[813]

---

810 Ibid., sign. 12/45, Notatka w sprawie cen i trybu sprzedaży samochodów "Fiat 125p" w eksporcie wewnętrznym w Banku PKO, Warszawa, February 7, 1970, unnumbered pages.

811 "Nowe samochody dla posiadaczy książeczek PKO," *Motor* 1957, no. 13, p. 4.

812 AAN, Powszechna Kasa Oszczędności (hereafter: PKO), sign. 7/6, Sprawozdanie z działalności PKO w 1955 r., pp. 7–8.

813 Ibid., sign. 14/8, Sprawozdanie z działalności Powszechnej Kasy Oszczędności w roku 1957, p. 52.

Figure 4. Cars drawn during a savings campaign at Powszechna Kasa Oszczędności (PKO Bank), 1958, National Digital Archives, Zbyszko Siemaszko, 3/51/0/6.2/65

The first draw took place in July 1957, and seven cars were available to win: four Warszawas, two Wartburgs, and one IFA.[814] A *Kronika Filmowa* newsreel crew was present; the voice of actor Andrzej Łapicki described the event thusly: "The chance is 1 in 1,000, probably better than in Totek [Totalizator

814 "Nowe samochody dla posiadaczy książeczek," p. 4.

Sportowy] or Syrenka [lottery]. … Maybe fortune smiles at you for once in your life…."[815] In total, fifty-one cars were drawn in the first year. In subsequent years, the number of winning accounts increased. By the end of the 1950s, half a thousand lucky ones could count on a new car, as well as a motorcycle or moped. In total, between 1957 and 1969, Poles obtained almost 25,000 cars in this way, along with 8,100 motorcycles and 1,600 mopeds.

Table 11. Number of PKO bonuses and their value in the years 1957–1969

Year	Cars		Motorcycles		Mopeds	
	Number	Value in thousands of zl.	Number	Value in thousands of zl.	Number	Value in thousands of zl.
1957	51	3.422	72	507	-	-
1958	230	18.758	619	4.354	-	-
1959	333	29.962	786	5.502	-	-
1960	529	47.694	856	5.992	-	-
1961	786	70.805	927	6.489	-	-
1962	1.049	94.916	867	6.069	164	817
1963	1.441	130.104	834	5.838	228	1.141
1964	1.981	179.318	764	5.348	248	1.124
1965	2.489	224.243	670	4.690	236	1.062
1966	2.969	267.692	552	3.864	213	958
1967	3.589	323.172	466	3.262	201	905
1968	4.343	390.955	387	2.712	190	855
1969	5.077	457.122	329	2.632	182	819
Total	24.867	2.238.163	8.129	57.259	1.662	7.681

Source: AAN, PKO, sign. 14/15, Sprawozdanie z działalności Powszechnej Kasy Oszczędności za rok 1965, pp. 36–37; ibid., Sprawozdanie z działalności Powszechnej Kasy Oszczędności za rok 1967, pp. 256–257; ibid., Sprawozdanie z działalności Powszechnej Kasy Oszczędności za rok 1968, pp. 386–387; ibid., sign. 14/16, Sprawozdanie z działalności Powszechnej Kasy Oszczędności za rok 1969, pp. 45–46.

One of the lucky winners in 1964 was Stanisław Lem, who won a Warszawa. However, the writer did not intend to keep his prize; having owned a car for several years already, he had no interest in the vehicle from Żerań. In a

815 "Witaj szczęście," *Polska Kronika Filmowa* (hereafter: PKF) 57/46 A, 1957.

letter to dramatist Sławomir Mrożek, Lem wrote: "[W]e will definitely sell it along with the Wartburg, and whatever these two cars bring we will spend on something big."[816] Ultimately, having sold his cars, he bought a new Fiat 1800, which at that time cost 190,000 zlotys, though the transaction did not go particularly smoothly.[817] Selling a car was a very common practice at that time, especially for people who already owned a car and treated the PKO savings book as a chance to earn money in the value of the price of a new car.

Figure 5. Passenger cars gathered at the Ministry of Finance parking lot as the main prizes in the Powszechna Kasa Oszczędności lottery, 1958, National Digital Archives, Zbyszko Siemaszko, 3/51/0/6.2/65

---

816 S. Lem and S. Mrożek, *Listy 1956–1978*, Kraków 2011, p. 322.
817 Ibid., p. 384.

Practically from the beginning of its existence, this form of acquiring a car raised objections, although it should be noted that most of the critics were those who were unlucky in the draw. Doubts were raised about the fact that the accounts earned no interest, that the amount of the obligatory deposit changed (an increase from 6,000 to 9,000 zlotys), and that the number and values of the cars being drawn were not even. The author of an anonymous letter sent to *Trybuna Ludu* asked rhetorically: "How can we trust such an institution as the PKO is today?"[818] Some also questioned the draw itself, which—as reported in anonymous letters addressed to the Office of Letters and Complaints of the State Council and other entities—created "the possibility of abuse."[819]

However, these concerns were few. In the years 1960–1970, Poles deposited a total of 530,6 billion zlotys in PKO, of which 15.4% was in "car" savings books (see Table 12). The value of car-prize deposits increased every year: in 1960 it was 2,2 billion zlotys, in 1970—over 20,9 billion zlotys.

Table 12. PKO savings deposits in the years 1960–1970 and their structure

Year	Deposits in million zl.		Share of Deposits in PKO savings books, in %		
	Total	including: PKO	Cars	High interest rate	Housing
1960	19.088	14.307	11.7	6.1	2.2
1961	22.560	16.384	13.8	8.9	1.9
1962	29.653	21.506	15.3	11.4	1.3
1963	39.258	28.649	15.8	13.6	1.2
1964	48.117	35.016	16.4	16.3	1.5
1965	58.300	42.256	16.2	18.8	3.7
1966	71.424	51.951	15.8	21.3	5.2
1967	86.225	63.021	15.8	24.2	6.0
1968	99.416	73.412	15.8	25.8	7.0

818 AAN, KC PZPR, sign. 237/XXVII-23, Biuletyn nr 60/228, Warszawa, October 23,1957, pp. 159–160.

819 Ibid., Kancelaria Rady Państwa (hereafter: KRP), sign. 63/6, Wykazy anonimów, które wpłynęły do KRP od 1 I 1958 do 21 I 1958 r., p. 179. It is worth noting that similar allegations were made regarding the drawings of the popular Totolotek with cars as a reward; ibid., p. 84 (I would like to thank Dr Ewelina Szpak for pointing these documents out to me).

Year	Deposits in million zl.		Share of Deposits in PKO savings books, in %		
	Total	including: PKO	Cars	High interest rate	Housing
1969	115.352	86.890	16.2	27.0	7.5
1970	128.460	97.226	16.3	28.6	8.3

Source: Z. Krasiński, Czynniki ekonomiczno-społeczne rozwoju motoryzacji indywidualnej w Polsce w świetle badań ankietowych, Poznań 1972, p. 26.

It is very likely that some of these savings were deposited on car bonus accounts when the savers had "free money," for example an amount intended for the purchase of furniture that depended on the date of receipt of an apartment. On such occasions, "car" accounts were opened in hopes of a stroke of luck, and the money withdrawn as soon as the bonus was won. Such activities were observed in 1972,[820] but it can be assumed with a high degree of certainty that this had happened before.

4.4 Privileged groups

On October 1, 1955, I sent a letter asking to be allowed to purchase a voucher for an IFA passenger car and giving my reasons. However, the answer I received from the Office of the Council of Ministers—Bureau of Complaints ... indicates that my letter was misdirected and misunderstood. The car I am applying for will not be intended for private use, but for social purposes. In my parish in the Western Territories, there are 4 production cooperatives [and] 8 state farms, and the farmers and workers employed there use my services. In addition, I commute to 3 churches and 4 primary schools, which are several kilometers away from each other. Having a car would help greatly with the commute, and the time that working people waste sending horses for me and driving me back could be used for the good of the general economy. Since they say in the press and on the radio that in People's Poland, citizen can already purchase a car (and when I was in Warsaw as part of the Reconstruction of the Capital, I myself saw an IFA used by private people), your negative answer leads me to believe that my request was rejected because I am a priest.

The quote above is from a letter by priest Czesław Łaszyński. Despite his efforts, he did not succeed in his attempt to purchase an East German IFA.

820 AAN, PKO, sign. 14/19, Sprawozdanie Powszechnej Kasy Oszczędności [z] 1972 r., pp. 24–26.

An note on the letter states that the priest had a "negative attitude towards social change" because he criticised some of the actions by the authorities in his sermons. Moreover, "Father Łaszyński is not involved in the movement of progressive priests.[821] He opposes progressive priests … priests like Łaszyński do not deserve to be granted easier access to a car at a time when many progressive priests are themselves unable to buy one because almost no cars are sold to them privately."[822]

Another common example comes from the memoirs of Jerzy Putrament. In 1953, the writer became the owner of his own Warszawa: "In the fall, I was allowed to buy a Warszawa, still assembled from parts made in Moscow. The price was fabulous: less than twenty-five thousand zlotys! There were several such private Warszawas throughout Poland—other than me, Jakubowska, Kruczkowski and Tuwim were also allowed to buy them. At the time, private cars were marked with the letter 'H' and were such a rarity in Warsaw that every time I visited gas station, a crowd would gather like for a Jaguar or a Ferrari today."[823]

Leopold Tyrmand noted in his diary:

> Mine is a life without comfort. I live badly, the organization of sustenance from day to day is an affront to the very idea of civilization; I stand in line for bread, I clean. I am deprived of the amenities and privileges that are commonplace in democratic countries for a man of my age and earning potential. I suspect that a journalist who has something to contribute doesn't have to get along over there without an apartment or house, car, travel abroad—in other words, without the accessories of life that are rather elementary and undoubtedly not the most important, yet helpful in seeking the purpose of one's existence on a higher plane.[824]

These three different stories have a common denominator: a car, or more precisely, the desire to own one. For the authorities, the unknown priest

---

[821] Progressive priests (in Polish: księża patrioci) were group of Catholic clergy in Poland who actively collaborated with the Communist regime, they were granted with many privileges.

[822] *Listy do pierwszych sekretarzy KC PZPR*, ed. J. Stępień, Warszawa 1994, pp. 125–126.

[823] J. Putrament, *Pół wieku. Literaci*, Warszawa 1970, pp. 200–201.

[824] L. Tyrmand, *Diary 1954*, Evanston 2014, p. 53.

Łaszyński was someone who did not deserve his own car because of his views. Jerzy Putrament, a literary darling of the communist regime, bought his car at a time when those in the highest political circles were seriously considering a total ban on the ownership of private vehicles. So, Putrament had a right to feel exceptionally appreciated. In turn, Leopold Tyrmand—almost the complete opposite of Putrament—dreamed about a car, but because the communist authorities did not appreciate him, he had to put his dream on hold.[825]

The authorities were well aware of the power of such dreams. The society, in turn, was aware of the conditions that had to be met—the concessions that had to be made—to satisfy the desire to own a car.[826] In the USSR, the division between the communist avant-garde and the rest of the society was clear, and one of its markers was access to luxury goods, including, perhaps above all, private automobiles. High-ranking party officials, Stakhanovites, and famous writers provided living proof that things inside the country were going in the right direction on the road to communism. The vast majority who were deprived of such honours received the promise that sometime in the indefinite future, that which was currently available only to the chosen few would become available to everyone.[827] Only the aforementioned change of power allowed ordinary citizens of the USSR to come closer to realising their dreams of having a car.

---

825 Tyrmand only managed to drive his dream car on the streets of Warsaw after the success of his novel *Zły*. It was a Wartburg, which he bought with a voucher received from Józef Cyrankiewicz. In fact, Tyrmand had arranged it himself by personally calling the Prime Minister, who, realising he had Tyrmand on the line, reportedly said: "You're calling about the car voucher." Mariusz Urbanek also claims that Cyrankiewicz had "read *Zły* and liked it. so he gave [Tyrmand] the voucher"; M. Urbanek, *Zły Tyrmand*, Warszawa 2007, pp. 43, 86, 108.

826 In his diary, Leopold Tyrmand recalled the following conversation: "I ran into Biliński today … . 'You stopped being a European,' he accused me, 'when you gave up ambition.' He then explained what he meant by ambition: 'I mean, that a man of your talents shouldn't even have a car or house yet, at your age!' I asked him if he knows what the price is, in Poland as in Czechoslovakia, of a car and a house for a man my age. He said: 'That you ask such questions proves you have stopped being a European'"; L. Tyrmand, *Diary 1954*, pp. 170–171.

827 L. Gatejel, "Appealing for a Car," p. 123.

Meanwhile, in East Germany, individual motorisation had continued to develop along the lines of the Nazi concept, which mandated universal access to affordable cars. Even though, in the first decade after the war, Walter Ulbricht, leader of East Germany, decided to adopt the Soviet model, allocating vehicles for the most important members of the administration and workers who distinguished themselves in labour competitions, the situation changed in the mid-1950s. The West German example of the success of the popular Beetle made a strong impact on East Germans, who were keenly interested in events beyond the western border. They were increasingly demanding their own cars. The start of production of the Wartburg and Trabant, which propelled the annual growth of the car fleet to 21%, turned East Germany into the fastest motorising country of the Eastern Bloc.[828]

It has already been mentioned that in the postwar period, it was made quite clear who in Poland could count on special treatment from the authorities in terms of access to cars. Aside from activists, academics, and members of the intelligentsia,[829] this list included leading representatives of the working men: shock workers and workplace innovators (*racjonalizatorzy*). However, the latter received little support in this regard. For example, in the first half of the 1950s, the Ministry of Railways and the Ministry of Shipping (Ministerstwo Żeglugi, MŻ) submitted a request to the Economic Committee of the Council of Ministers, which dealt with the distribution of vehicles, to allocate a certain number of cars to leading railway workers and seamen. Unfortunately, it is not known exactly how many and what kind of cars were requested, but they were probably not numerous—most likely several dozen vehicles at most, because in the following years, the MŻ received nine East German IFAs (in 1955) and ten Warszawas (in 1956).[830] In subsequent years, leading workers were rewarded with cars on the occasion of industry holidays, but

---

828 Ibid., p. 131.

829 See, for example, AAN, URM KT, sign. 6/229, Notatka służbowa—dot. projektu uchwały Prezydium Rządu w sprawie nabywania przez pracowników nauki samochodów osobowych i motocykli, Warszawa, August 27, 1954, pp. 219–220.

830 AAN, KERM, sign. 6/249, Uwagi do załącznika nr 3 [from the Advisory Team to the Ministry of the Railways and the Advisory Team of the Ministry of Shipping], March 2, 1953, p. 44.

even then, there were few rewards.[831] Therefore, of all the privileged groups, workers were the least privileged. It was definitely easier to gain access to a car for representatives of the broadly understood intelligentsia or writers and actors, who were especially favoured by the authorities, although, of course, there were some exceptions.

When, at the end of the 1950s, the first instalment of the novel *Czar twoich kółek* (The Charm of Your Wheels) was published in the weekly *Przekrój*, its author, Marian Eile (writing under the pseudonym "Salami Kożerski"), compiled a list of people and professions privileged by the authorities. The list included several dozen well-known figures. along with the types of cars they owned. The list included writers, stage performers, academics, journalists, lawyers, and famous athletes—and even the 1957 Miss Polonia, Alicja Bobrowska. The vast majority of people on the list drove foreign cars.[832] In any case, Salami Kożerski's attempts to obtain his own car ultimately ended in success with the purchase of a small "Bikini Boy" Fiat 600 (so-called due to the association with the youth subculture *bikiniarze*, a group of young, mostly male, urban youth who expressed a cultural rebellion against the monotony and official doctrine of the Communist regime of the fifties and sixties in Poland through their clothing, interests, and behaviour). *Czar twoich kółek* itself, which revealed various absurdities of the Polish reality of the 1950s and 1960s, was intended to be published in entirety by the Iskry Publishing House, a fact that was announced after the last instalment appeared in *Przekrój*. However, the book was never released. Andrzej Klominek noted accurately: "*Czar twoich kółek* was a huge success and, to be fair, it did arouse an unhealthy, consumerist appetite for cars in many thousands of readers." Therefore, both the novel and *Przekrój* found themselves in hot water, which ultimately led to the novel's publication being suspended.[833]

In the following decade, the situation of privileged groups remained practically unchanged. In its editorial surveys, the weekly *Motor* usually cited statements made by famous people: academics, writers, and singers. Ordinary car users appeared in the periodical in such a role only sporadically.

---

831 Ibid., Rozdzielnik samochodów osobowych przeznaczonych dla osób prywatnych. Załącznik nr 3 [1956], pp. 66–67.

832 S. Kożerski and P. Rojek, "Czar twoich kółek," *Przekrój* 1959, no. p. 34.

833 A. Klominek, *Życie w* Przekroju, Warszawa 1995, p. 138.

The many readers of the weekly, which had a circulation of over 120,000, with very few returns (numbering in single-digit percentage points), may have been rather ambivalent about this issue.[834] On the one hand, *Motor* described various means of gaining a passenger car, although it must be said that it assessed the chances of success realistically (that is, as being low). On the other, the articles could have aroused (and probably did arouse) the feeling that cars are available to a very limited group of people, often famous people, usually those with the so-called access. This led to a pathological situation in which car owners were immediately treated with suspicion.[835] This attitude toward car owners is endemic within complaints addressed to the highest state authorities. Virtually every time the terms "profiteer" or "black market" appeared in such a letter, a private car was also mentioned.[836] The official propaganda added fuel to this fire, as well, by using the car as an object whose acquisition—or rather, the acquisition of sufficient funds to purchase it—necessitated a degree of illegal activity.[837]

The fact that one owned a car made others jealous. Unless the person who had their own car belonged to the privileged groups, they were treated with suspicion. For example, a pharmacist in the country complained: "In small towns, they believe that the owner of a car is a class enemy."[838] There were cases where the purchase of a car even excluded the buyer from the local, usually non-motorised community. Sometimes, a newly purchased car was deliberately destroyed or the buyer was omitted when workplace bonuses or prizes were distributed.[839] was Stefan Kisielewski observed a similar climate of distrust a few years later, noting in his diary: "It's telling: the closer to

---

834 AAN, KC PZPR, sign. XIX-224, Motor, 1958, pp. 1–4.

835 Por. L. Tyrmand, *Diary 1954*, p. 259.

836 Por. AAN, KC PZPR, sign. 237/XXVII-23, Biuletyn nr 42/210, Warszawa, August 16, 1957, pp. 15–16; ibid., sign. 237/XXXII-9, Dziedziny życia gospodarczego, w których obserwujemy szczególne nasilenie nadużyć, [1957], p. 22.

837 An illustrated supplement to *Życie Warszawy* featured a photograph of a number of passenger cars with a striking caption: "Eight thousand former SS-men (*every fourth in his own car* [italics mine—HW]) drove down to the minor township of Kariburg on the Main and went so far as to demand the payment of pensions to the families of their departed brothers in arms"; *Życie Warszawy. Dodatek ilustrowany*, August 25, 1957, p. 3.

838 A. K. Wróblewski, "Zawsze umiera kto inny," *Polityka* 1966, no. 44, p. 3.

839 Ibid.

Warsaw you get, the more the population dislikes the car, or rather the guy that rides it. Meanwhile, in Podhale, they like the motorist, because they don't care about money—they would only like to have it."[840] It seems that Kisielewski perfectly captured the very important factor that accounted for this reluctance. Owning a car in Poland in the 1950s and 1960s meant being able to afford it, and therefore having an income above the Polish average.

4.5 Miners

Upper Silesia was a very important region on Poland's automotive map. On the one hand, almost from the beginning of the People's Republic of Poland, coal miners were given special treatment by the authorities compared to other professional groups.[841] In terms of the number of passenger cars, the Katowice voivodeship took second place in the country, behind only Warsaw, a fact that was strongly emphasised by Upper Silesians.[842] On the other hand, this region also occupied a prominent place on the map of black market trade in cars, or, to be more precise, in car vouchers.

One way in which the special treatment manifested itself in was through easier access to attractive products. For instance, cars—or the possibility of acquiring them—were among the of awards one could receive for outstanding results in labour competition. In 1952, the cover of one issue of the weekly *Motor* featured a picksman from the Niwka mine named Szczepan Blaut, who achieved the annual coal mining norm sixfold in the first two months of 1952. As a reward, he received an allocation for an IFA.[843] The weekly photographed him carefully selecting his vehicle. This story was a visible sign that hard work allowed workers to fulfil the dream of owning their own vehicle.

However, not all miners were so lucky. Letters sent to the highest authorities include many complaints about irregularities in the distribution of vehicles intended for miners. For example, Stanisław C., a miner who worked for many years in the Ludwik coal mine in Zabrze, wrote to the State Council

840 S. Kisielewski, *Dzienniki*, p. 402.

841 See: L. Gatejel, "Appealing for a Car," p. 136.

842 AAN, KC PZPR, sign. 237/XXV-28, Biuletyn nr 12/301, Listy na różne tematy, Warszawa, September 18, 1959, p. 114.

843 *Motor* 1952, no. 32, p. 1.

in early 1958 that "people who have no connection with the workplace drive cars, and me, a miner, am left with dust or snow after that are left once they drive their cars over the road." Although he was a leading worker ("My work was top quality—I gave my country hundreds of tons of coal above the norm"), he was passed over in the distribution of cars, while at the same time—he complained—all engineers and technicians received one. Moreover, the director of the mine was trading in new cars, selling a new IFA (acquired for 18,000 zlotys) for 74,000 zlotys and a Wartburg (which he supposedly bought for 40,000 zlotys) for 135,000 zlotys. When Stanisław C. complained about the allocations for a car that, in his opinion, was due to him, he was called a "saboteur" and forced to change his workplace. In the Miechowice mine, the situation repeated itself: Stanisław C. continued to be ignored in the distribution of cars.[844]

Miners often sold the vouchers and vehicles received from the authorities. Journalists at *Motor* even conducted an investigation of sorts when it turned out that in 1952, a very high number of advertisements for the sale of motorcycles appeared in Upper Silesia. Their findings confirmed their suspicions: Jawa motorbikes were being sold mainly by leading workers at the mines. The journalists were fairly plain in their commentary: "It often turned out that the motorcycles ended up in the hands of speculators and kulaks .... A 'Jawa' as a capital investment for a rich peasant is really a bit too much."[845]

---

844 AAN, KC PZPR, sign. 237/XXV-25, Biuletyn nr 18/263, Warszawa, March 21, 1958 r., p. 174.

845 R. Frister, "Sprzedam nową Jawę," *Motor* 1952, no. 19, p. 3. In the 1960s, under a trade agreement with Italy, scooters of the extremely popular Lambretta brand were sent to Poland in exchange for coal. Miners who were given the opportunity to buy them, but who preferred to ride motorcycles and were happy to resell their Lambrettas, often to artists, among whom scooters of this brand were considered iconic. In this way, Wojciech Plewiński, a photographer cooperating with the weekly *Przekrój*, became an owner of two such scooter. Jan Morek, who cooperated with the Polonia publishing house and the Polish Interpress Agency, recalled: "If you had a Lambretta scooter and rode around Nowy Świat, you were the absolute pinnacle of a playboy in the Polish People's Republic.—Oh, here's another airline bag, foreign airlines...—They rode those scooters from Hybrydy to the Old Town and back again. Several times an hour. Sometimes, they went alone and came back with a girl..."; Ł. Modelski, Fotobiografia PRL. Opowieści reporterów, Kraków 2013, p. 41–42, 77.

In 1955, in consultation with the Ministry of Internal Trade, the Ministry of Mines introduced a bonus campaign for coal allocation buyouts called "Action Z." Miners who sold their allocation to the state received vouchers enabling them to purchase attractive household goods (washing machines, refrigerators), personal goods (cameras, watches), but also vehicles: bicycles, motorcycles, and cars. Initially, the campaign covered only miners, but in subsequent years, it was extended to employees of the steel and energy industries.[846] During the campaign's first two and a half years, miners "sold" a total of over 713,000 tons of coal, which constituted just over 13% of all coal allowances for that period. Goods earmarked for voucher sale were distributed through special stores. There was a specific "coal" conversion rate; for example, a miner could obtain a voucher for a motorcycle for 7 tons of coal from his allowance, and for a car for 25 tons. Problems began when it turned out that the vouchers that permitted purchases in a special store were anonymous, so any bearer, even a non-miner, could purchase the selected product. Speculative trade in vouchers began almost immediately. Prices were quite high: for a voucher for 5 tons of coal, sellers would demand between 100 and 300 zlotys per ton. The voucher for the purchase of a car commanded the highest price—sellers demanded up to 500 zlotys per ton of coal, which means that the potential vehicle buyer had to pay over 12,000 zlotys—an amount almost equivalent to the average annual earnings at the time—just for the opportunity to purchase a car. As the Ministry of Internal Trade warned, the introduction of vouchers for attractive goods tied to the sale of allowances resulted in an excessive concentration of these goods in one region of the country (Upper Silesia), which resulted in shortages in other parts of the country.[847]

The irregularities that affected "Action Z" came to the attention of the prosecutors. During an investigation conducted by the prosecutor's office

846 Archiwum Instytutu Pamięci Narodowej (hereafter: AIPN), sign. Ka 00150/1969, Streszczenie sprawy operacyjnego sprawdzenia krypt. "Odprysk" nr 11053/II, Sosnowiec, October 18, 1975, p. 39.

847 Moreover, with the development of "Action Z" in Upper Silesia, an increase in the number of people collecting coal from heaps was observed. This could mean that some of the miners who sold their coal shares had obtained it in this way; AAN, KC PZPR, sign. 237/XXXI-236, Notatka w sprawie skupu deputatów węglowych i funduszu dewizowego w górnictwie węglowym, [1957], pp. 25–26.

for the Katowice voivodeship, it was discovered that high-ranking officials took part in abuses in the distribution of attractive goods, primarily cars: Władysław Wróblewski, chief assistant for "Action Z" under the Minister of Mining and Energy; the general director of the Central Mining Supply Board in Katowice, together with his deputies; and the most important officials at the Ministry of Mining and Energy, including deputy ministers. Wróblewski himself had been travelling to Western European countries (France, Belgium, the Netherlands, England, and West Germany) since the mid-1950s to explore the potential for buying used passenger cars for miners.[848] The shadow of suspicion also fell on the minister, Franciszek Waniołka. The prosecutors established that employees of the general plenipotentiary's department were conducting an organised voucher speculation campaign. When the Ministry of State Control became interested in the irregularities in Upper Silesia and decided that it was illegal for people who were not miners to use the vouchers to purchase attractive goods, Deputy Minister Ludwik Salamon and director of the Organisational and Legal Department of the ministry, Jan Zimoch, gave retroactive effect to the minister's order no. 56 of July 27, 1957, thus legalising all purchases made up to that time, even by unauthorised persons. Incidentally, both Salamon and Zimoch had purchased cars as part of "Action Z" (Zimoch even bought two), even though they were not entitled to do so. In addition, both of them paid for the cars in instalments. Deputy ministers (Edward Grabowski, Franciszek Jopek, Eugeniusz Zadrzyński, and Wacław Królikowski) also bought cars this way, as did Director of the Administrative and Economic Board Jerzy Gałkowski, Director of the Staff Department Józef Siekański, and Director of the Office of the Council of Ministers Sylwester Nowotny. Some of them were also accused of falsifying voucher applications. The aforementioned Waniołka reportedly agreed to the sale of the vehicles acquired by Grabowski and Nowotny as part of "Action Z," even though they were not entitled to make such a purchase, and also allowed them and other senior officials to pay in instalments. This, in turn, was inconsistent with the resolution of the Government Praesidium of January 28, 1956.[849] The sentences in this case were rather high: Wróblewski was sentenced to

848 AIPN, sign. BU 1532/406, Ministerstwo Spraw Wewnętrznych Biuro Paszportów Zagranicznych, Warszawa, May 1957, p. 23.

849 AAN, KC PZPR, sign. 237/XXV-281, Notatka, January 14, 1958, pp. 131–136.

eight years under article 286, paragraphs 1 and 2 of the Penal Code; Olech Biliński and Janusz Weychan were sentenced to five and six years.[850] Jerzy Kurcyusz, who was arrested in the fall of 1957 on charges of writing an order enabling the trade in car vouchers, was cleared of the charges on December 24 and released from custody Ministry officials who purchased cars illegally faced no major consequences.

The introduction of the so-called foreign currency fund in the coal industry in November 1956 gave rise to slightly different problems. Each ton of coal extracted above the planned target was rewarded with 5 roubles. The amounts collected were to be administered by workers' councils. By order of the Prime Minister dated January 22, 1957, funds obtained in this way were to be used for the purchase of equipment that was primarily intended to improve work safety in mines. The remaining money was to be allocated for the acquisition of means of transporting employees to their workplace and for the development of private construction projects by the miners, as well as other purposes. However, in practice, the council used almost 95% of the money to purchase attractive goods (mainly motorcycles and cars, but also television sets and watches), which were then distributed among the crew. During the last two months of the fourth quarter of 1956, thirty-seven coal mines received 648,000 roubles through the fund. One of them, the Ludwik mine, allocated 47,000 for the purchase of cars.[851] It was found that in the coal industry in general, a total of 321 passenger cars and 1,949 motorcycles were purchased with the roubles, for a total value of over 3 million roubles, which represented half of the money collected in the foreign currency fund.[852] The method of division caused protests, since councils distributed acquired

850 AIPN, Ka, sign. 0162/701, Streszczenie materiałów archiwalnych b. więźnia Wróblewskiego Władysława, znajdujących się w OPW nr 1 w Siemianowicach, p. 17.

851 "Dewizy za ponadplanowy węgiel na zakup zagranicznych towarów," *Trybuna Ludu*, March 5, 1957, p. 1.

852 In this way, the Workers' Council of the "Sosnowiec" mine purchased 13 cars, 18 motorcycles, and 715 watches for a crew that numbered over 3,000 people. Similarly, in the "Czeladź" mine, where 3,500 people worked, thirteen cars, 45 motorcycles, and 10 mopeds were purchased for funds collected in the foreign currency fund; AAN, KC PZPR, sign. 237/XXXI-236, Notatka w sprawie skupu deputatów węglowych i funduszu dewizowego w górnictwie węglowym, [1957], pp. 25–26.

products among their members, the members of works councils, or mine supervision boards.[853]

The idea of liquidating the fund due to these abuses was floated at a meeting of the committee for heavy industry at the Central Committee of the PZPR. However, as one committee member noted, establishing the fund was a "political step" and its closure could be very badly received by the miners. The majority of those gathered were in favour of maintaining the fund, including Minister of Heavy Industry Kiejstut Żemajtis, along with the likes of Adam Wang. Franciszek Waniołka, then-Minister of Economy and Energy, participated in the meeting and ordered a tightening of the system by which funds were supposed to be expended for buses for transporting mine workers, equipment for factory aid stations, medical equipment, and medicines.[854]

4.6 A "trading fleet"[855]: maritime imports (1957)

In early December 1956, the editors of the biweekly *Ster* published a letter sent by the crew of the steamship *Gliwice*. It concerned the fact that Polish seamen could purchase used passenger cars in Western European countries and bring them back home on board of their ship. The letter argued: "Cars imported by sailors are generally better than many private cars and taxis driving on our roads. … For this purpose, we set aside the foreign currency we earn literally cent by cent, denying ourselves any entertainment abroad for months and limiting our families' household budgets to a minimum." However, the problem was the customs duty of 10 zlotys per kilogram of imported goods (it should be noted that this rate was already called prohibitive among proponents of

853 Ibid., p. 26.

854 Ibid., Protokół z posiedzenia Komisji ds. Przemysłu Ciężkiego przy KC PZPR, które się odbyło 12 X 1957 r., pp. 12–15.

855 The term used in the title of this subchapter was used during a meeting of a special party-government commission of the Central Committee of the PZPR, appointed to investigate the situation of Polish sailors, to whom such a name rightly belonged in the years 1956–1957, in the opinion of the broad public; AAN, KC PZPR, sign. 237/XXXI-248, Wnioski Komisji Partyjno-Rządowej powołanej do zbadania niektórych zagadnień dotyczących załóg pływających na statkach Polskiej Marynarki Handlowej, [–1958], p. 1.

motorisation).[856] In the case of a car that usually weighed several hundred kilograms or more, the entire operation (assuming a car price of US $50 to US $200) became unprofitable. Additionally, the amount of duty did not account for the age or technical condition of the car.[857]

in order to meet the expectations of the seamen, probably not only from the *Gliwice*, Director of Polish Ocean Lines (PLO) Jan Woźniakiewicz issued a circular in January 1957, in which he exempted sailors under his authority from paying freight for importing one passenger car from abroad every three years on PLO ships. He probably did not expect that in this way, he was giving several thousand Poles access to the Western European used car market, and his employees an additional injection of cash.[858]

Antwerp was a common stop on ship routes in the West, not only for Polish ships because, for several months every year, this Belgian city turned into the European centre for trade in used cars. Most of the cars were worn-down Cadillacs, Chevrolets Deluxe, Bedfords, or Studebakers.[859] The price of a car in Antwerp ranged from US $150 to US $200. A Polish sailor with the so-called currency bonus (*dodatek dewizowy*, a foreign currency allowance) on top of the basic salary, or even with some American currency earned through smuggling, could afford such a car. Later, he could either drive it himself or sell it on the private market, often at a profit of several dozen percent thanks to the black market price of the dollar.[860] It is worth emphasising that only seamen who sailed on Western European routes had the opportunity to engage in "maritime import." Crews whose voyages led, for example, to the Far East, and whose ships did not reach ports mentioned above, were practically deprived of such opportunities, which must have caused an unhealthy jealousy.

Very quickly, Scandinavian competition emerged in the form of a Finnish ship owner who offered cars for as little as US $40.[861] It should also be noted that the seamen did not buy and carry home only beat-up used cars. In the

856 "Sejm polskiej motoryzacji," p. 8.
857 "Chcemy przywozić samochody ale nam nie utrudniajcie," *Ster* 1956, no. 23, p. 1.
858 O. Budrewicz, "Belgia samochodami płynąca," *Przekrój* 1957, no. 612, pp. 8–9.
859 "Rozszerza się import marynarski," *Ster* 1957, no. 2, p. 2.
860 O. Budrewicz, "Belgia samochodami płynąca."
861 P. Proch, "Na temat Wybrzeża," *Ster* 1957, no. 11, p. 2.

Polish press, one finds pictures of members of Polish maritime crews driving on the streets of Polish coastal cities in shiny Oldsmobiles, Rolls-Royces, or Plymouths.[862] It was therefore only a matter of time before Polish authorities became interested in the issue of cars imported by sailors, or rather the lack of customs duties on them. It was calculated that by the end of June 1957, losses from unpaid duties amounted to approximately US $20,000. The Polish shipowner also incurred certain unspecified costs due to changes in routes for particular ships, which often adapted their plans to the current offer of Western European car dealers or specific orders from Poland. Half a year after Woźniakiewicz's instruction went into force, the Ministry of Shipping charged all seamen with back taxes, while also changing the customs tariff. In the case of donated cars, as of September 1, 1957, the customs duty was to be 50 zlotys per kg, which meant a fivefold increase.[863] It is therefore not surprising that the last days of August were quite busy for customs officers, because everyone wanted to bring goods into Poland, mainly cars, before the new tariff came into effect.[864]

The new customs duties caused a major stir. In May 1957, participants in an automotive survey conducted by the *Motoryzacja* monthly viewed the importation of used cars into Poland as a huge opportunity to motorise the society, especially when domestic production was unable to meet the rapidly growing demand for cars. One person even called for officials to "engage

---

862 (K), "Zamiast przemytu dewiz zorganizowana sprzedaż samochodów," *Ster* 1957, no. 13, p. 3.

863 W. Tobis, "Samochód—wróg publiczny nr 1. W świetle nowej taryfy celnej," *Motor* 1957, no. 35, p. 3.

864 W. J. T., "Za pięć dwunasta. Jutro nowa taryfa celna," *Motor* 1957, no. 37, p. 3. In 1960, the rate for 1 kg of car weight was reduced to 40 zlotys (Dz. U. 1960, no. 43, pos. 262), but the regulation of the Ministry of Health of July 18, 1968 introduced three customs duties dependent on the engine displacement. For cars with an engine displacement of up to 1,000 cm^3, the price was 30 zlotys per kg; over 1,000 cm^3 but under 1,600 cm^3—40 zlotys; and for cars with engines over 1,600 cm^3—50 zlotys. However, these rates only applied if the person importing the car agreed not to sell, donate, or exchange the vehicle within three years, and no one from their immediate family paid the same customs rate within five years. If these conditions were not met, the fees per kilogram increased to 60, 80, and 100 zlotys, respectively (Dz. U. 1968, no. 25, pos. 169). In 1970, the customs duty for passenger cars was unified; from then on, it amounted to 150 zlotys per 1 kg of vehicle weight; Dz. U. 1970, no. 5 pos. 37.

in contact with the Polish-American Council and organise a shipment to Poland—perhaps as gifts—instead of the usual 'old cloths'—surplus cars, the less fashionable ones, which American companies sell for a few dollar bills. These would be wonderful cars compared to the ones currently in use in Poland."[865] Photos of Western European and American passenger car graveyards, which appeared quite regularly in the press as proof of the imminent end of motorisation driven primarily by the profit motive of corporations taking advantage of the unthinking pursuit of Western fashions, evoked completely different sentiments. In 1965, even an automotive journalist would cry out: "Oh, if only our talented craftsmen, mechanics, tinsmiths, and painters were allowed on that little lot! At least half of the dead cars would come to life after a few weeks of work, and under the Poniatowski Bridge in Warsaw, where the car market, which will be discussed later, was situated, some of them would command a price Of way over 100,000 zlotys!"[866] It is easy to imagine that similar feelings were shared in the second half of the 1950s, especially when the possibility of importing such vehicles into the country was almost completely blocked.

The aforementioned Aleksander Rostocki believed that the new rates threatened to completely stop the private importation of cars, especially vehicles transferred to Poland as gifts from relatives. At the same time, however, he noted that the increased customs duty would effectively stop imports by seamen, which over time had simply become a speculative car trade. By way of conclusion, he noted bitterly:

> We will not obtain the few thousand cars that we could have received as gifts. … I do not understand why there must be one customs rate for all cars. … To me, one thing is certain: those who did it [i.e., import cars privately] were not interested in the development of motorisation in Poland. They think of a car just as a luxury, an object of speculation, the attribute of an embezzler, a means of drainage, a symbol of capitalism, the cause of all evil.[867]

---

865 "Ankieta Motoryzacji. Sprawy motoryzacji i transportu drogowego," *Motoryzacja* 1957, no. 5, p. 122.

866 A. Dąbrowski, "Gebrauchtwagen czyli handel używanymi samochodami," *Motor* 1965, no. 24, p. 6.

867 A. Rostocki, "Niecelna polityka celna," *Motor* 1957, no. 38, p. 3.

Another writer opined: "If we tolerate such things as a '*totek*', 'totolotek', and other such business [i.e. state-run lotteries], there is no point in knocking down that other kind of lucky star for the few fortunate ones."[868]

The issue of increased customs duties and maritime imports was also raised in the *Po Prostu* weekly. In the article "Uwaga: automobilizacja. Żerań w niebezpieczeństwie" (Caution! Automobilisation: Żerań under threat), the weekly commented with its characteristic, biting irony on the recent decisions of the authorities, seeing them as a simple means of increasing car prices on the free market.[869] The issue in which the article was supposed to appear, however, was confiscated by the censors and never saw the light of day.

It is difficult to estimate how many passenger cars were imported by the crews of Polish ships as part of maritime imports. Sailors continued to import cars throughout 1956. The *Motor* weekly reported that approximately 600 vehicles were imported through this channel, mainly American cars: Pontiacs, Fords, and Dodges.[870] The situation is further complicated by the fact that data from customs offices at particular ports do not refer specifically to cars that came into Poland in this way. The head of the Gdynia customs office, Tadeusz Wilczek, said at the end of March 1957 that since the beginning of the year, several hundred cars had passed through his unit.[871] Even if not all of those cars came in as maritime imports, this was still a considerable number, and it is very likely that it increased further by the middle of the year. Tomasz Szczerbicki estimates that in total, several thousand passenger cars on Polish roads came to Poland as part of maritime imports.[872] It seems that these estimates are close to reality.

4.7 The market of dreams and scams

As a Warsaw correspondent wrote in the summer 1956 issue of *Motoryzacja*: "A fellow car enthusiast who recently returned from a few weeks in the Soviet

---

868 J. Bujniewicz, "Czy może być lepiej?" *Motoryzacja* 1957, no. 7, p. 183.

869 AAN, KC PZPR, sign. 37/XIX-234, Wyjątki z skonfiskowanego prowokacyjnego numeru "Po Prostu" [1957] pp. 27–28.

870 "Czekając na konkrety," *Motor* 1957, no. 23, p. 5.

871 [hs], "Dziś rozmawiany: Z naczelnikiem Urzędu Celnego w Gdyni p. Tadeuszem Wilczkiem," *Ster* 1957, no. 10, p. 3.

872 T. Szczerbicki, *Samochody w PRL*, p. 96.

Union told me an interesting fact that could perhaps be applied here." This "fact" was indeed interesting: in some Soviet cities, there were streets and squares that held "a kind of an open-air market where they sold passenger cars." People who wanted to sell or buy a car met there. Direct contact between the sellers and the buyers offered the latter an opportunity to see and test a car on site. The correspondent, hiding behind the initials "Z.H.," thought that the Soviet practice could also work in Poland, especially "in larger automotive centres such as Warsaw, Stalinogród [Katowice] or the Tri-city [Gdańsk, Gdynia, and Sopot]." The only thing that remained was to choose the right time and place for such a market. Z.H. suggested Sundays between 11 am and 2 pm around Warsaw's Teatralny Square. This location was supported by a rather mundane, but important aspect within a Warsaw in the process of being rebuilt: "the vastness of the area recently cleared of rubble."[873]

It is unknowable what fate would have befallen Polish motorisation had it not been for Z.H.'s short note in *Motoryzacja*. Perhaps, sooner or later, a group of people who were determined to sell or buy a passenger car would have met somewhere in Warsaw. The fact is, however, that this report about the beginnings of car markets in the USSR could have given the green light to all potential buyers and sellers. It was, after all, in the same year that "several amateur sellers and buyers of cars, scooters, and motorcycles" first gathered at Plac Defilad in front of the Palace of Culture and Science in the centre of Warsaw. The choice of place was not accidental: they parked their vehicles near the guarded parking lot of the Polish Automobile Club, having previously announced in the press their intention to sell cars.[874] Soon enough, Wróblewski notes, the increasingly popular car markets began to annoy the city authorities, who did not want to have one of Warsaw's most representative places become a bazaar straight out of the capitalist system.[875]

873 Z. H., "Na polskim 'rynku' samochodowym," *Motoryzacja* 1956, no. 8, p. 280.
874 S. Szelichowski, "Niedzielny targ przed Pałacem Kultury," *Motor* 1963, no. 38, p. 3.
875 A. K. Wróblewski, *Polska na kółkach*, p. 84.

Figure 6. Car market at Dzika Street, Warsaw, 1969, National Digital Archives, Grażyna Rutkowska, 3/40/0/14/150

The first such spot was the Powiśle area, and in particular, 3 Maja Boulevard under the Poniatowski Bridge. However, within a few years, the number of sellers increased so much that the area was unable to accommodate all those interested, who often came to the capital from places far away, even by hundreds of kilometres. Thus began the Warsaw car market's journey around the capital, the first stop being Dzika Street in the Muranów district. Wróblewski mentions how local residents provided the crowds attending the market with "tea, stew, tripe, and everything necessary for real car trading."[876] Soon, however, even that area became too crowded. In the 1970s, Sunday car trade was pushed from on location to another, further and further from the centre of the capital, out of Malownicza Street (in the Okęcie district) to finally land near the airport in Bemowo.[877] Soon, car markets appeared in other Polish cities: in Szczecin, on Kopernika Street (already in the late 1950s); in 1963 in Kraków; somewhat later in Łódź, first at the corner of Nawrot and Wodna Streets, and then in a parking lot at Barlickiego Square; in Katowice, at Gliwicka Street; and in the Oliwa district of Gdańsk.[878] The Tri-city car market was unique in that, by 1969, Motozbyt opened a modern showroom and service centre right next to it, selling new Syrenas and Fiats.[879] In the following decade, Lublin also earned its own car market, the vehicles being traded in the Podzamcze district.

The emergence of car markets was received with great interest and high expectations. For many residents of Warsaw, and later those of other regions of Poland, especially when "incurably obsessed with motoring," a stroll through a square where cars were presented for sale was the highlight of every Sunday. It was a place for motorists to meet and exchange opinions.[880] Janusz Rolicki wrote in *Kultura*: "A river of curious people, craving smoke, exhaust fumes, looking under hoods, testing belts, kicking the tires, smacking their lips; entire families eager for motorisation."[881] For most, it was the only opportunity to commune with an inaccessible good. It is no accident that one *Kronika Filmowa* newsreel describes the car market thusly: "Motorisation, passions, business, fulfilled and unfulfilled hopes—all under the Poniatowski Bridge."[882]

---

876 Ibid., p. 83.
877 Ibid., p. 39.
878 mW, "Giełda notuje," *Motor* 1959, no. 20, p. 11; E. Niedźwiecka, *Łódź w PRL-u. Opowieść o życiu miasta 1945–1980*, Łódź 2011, p. 71.
879 bg, "Zapomniana oliwska giełda samochodowa," Trojmiasto.pl, 13 July 2016, http://historia.trojmiasto.pl/Zapomniana-oliwska-gielda-samochodowa-n103581.html (accessed: January 20, 2017).
880 P. Ambroziewicz, "Co dalej giełdo?" *Prawo i Życie* 1970, no. 3, p. 5.
881 J. Rolicki, "Salon automobilowy na Dzikiej," *Kultura* 1968, no. 22, p. 5.
882 "Giełda pod mostem," PKF 1964, 64/41B.

Almost from the very beginning, the *Motor* weekly tried to act as steward of the car markets. In 1963, it began an article series entitled *"Do wyboru, do koloru"* (literally: *You can choose in any colour you like*—it was irony), discussing the selection of vehicles available at car markets.[883] Ideas were also floated about having PZMot experts control the technical condition of the cars. *Motor* itself published a series of articles with advice on the purchase of a private car. The conclusion was not cheerful: the author warned readers that they could not always count on sellers being honest.[884]

"A market of dreams and scams"—this is how the Sunday car trade at Dzika Street was described in the early 1970s. Car prices rose very quickly, as did the demand for used cars, which could be bought without an allocation or a wait period of several years. One needed only to show up at the car market with enough cash. The selection was huge because at the time, the markets offered a very wide array of car makes and models from all over the world. In early 1964, a person with 15,000–25,000 zlotys could leave the market in a Chevrolet Fleetmaster, a KdF military all-terrain vehicle, a Mercedes 170 V, or a BMW 340, which was imported into Poland in 1952–1953. However, the latter car was almost completely devoid of technical support, and the difficult to manage two-carburetor engine made it unpopular among buyers. Prewar cars were even cheaper, going for around 10,000 zlotys, while "those most clapped out" were sold for between 2,000–5,000 zlotys. Prices for Polish cars varied depending on age. The cheapest one you could buy were Syrenas from a few years back, which in 1964 cost 18,000–25,000 zlotys. New cars usually sold for roughly the equivalent of official prices, although here, too, there were slight fluctuations in both directions, especially in the case of cars from the PKO lottery, which lost several percent off the official price. A two-year-old Warszawa, depending on its condition, cost approximately 80,000 zlotys, and a Syrena cost 50,000 zlotys. Imported cars were definitely the most expensive: new units usually sold for above the official prices. For example, while the official price at Motozbyt for a new Škoda 1000 MB was 95,000 zlotys, its price at the Warsaw car market in 1966 was 100,000–110,000 zlotys.

---

883 The first article in this series appeared in December 1963: "Do wyboru, do koloru," *Motor* 1963, no. 49, p. 1.

884 T. Sobiecki, "Jak kupować używany samochód?" *Motor* 1964, no. 1, p. 5.

An analysis of car market classifieds from the 1960s clearly shows that there was a group of makes and models that enjoyed a strong position on the market, whose prices did not experience significant fluctuations. Most often, these were cars of German brands: Volkswagen, Mercedes, but also Wartburg and Trabant. Volgas and Peugeots were also among the strong brands. This was reflected in their popularity. They were also treated as a relatively safe capital investment. Car markets reacted strongly to what the official market was offering. When the announcement came about the introduction of a new model (either Polish or foreign), the prices of older models dropped almost immediately. This was the case with Warszawas when sedan versions (without the characteristic hump) appeared on the market. The 203 and 204 models almost completely stopped the sales of older versions of this car on the car markets. A similar situation occurred with subsequent versions of the Syrena. Car prices were also influenced by the availability of spare parts. The price of more or less new P-70 s continued to decrease because potential buyers were discouraged by problems with purchasing plastic body components. In turn, the older IFA, although structurally similar to the P-70, maintained relatively high prices due to the adequate (or, as *Motor* put it, "truly excellent") supply of spare parts. On the one hand, the simplicity of the design of Polish cars was a curse, but on the other, it was often a blessing, especially in the event of a breakdown. As one *Motor* writer argued, "every POM and even a village blacksmith knows this car well. Let's not be afraid of old Warszawas, especially since they are getting cheaper…."[885]

The possibility of easily earning a profit of several, or even several dozen, percent on the sale of a new car made fewer and fewer sellers honest. One common practice was to purchase a car in poor technical condition and then "upgrade" it using home-made methods (sawdust in the gearbox to dampen the grinding of a faulty transmission, mustard in the radiator to seal leakages), and then sell it almost immediately at a considerable profit. Cars with unclear

885 "Do wyboru, do koloru," *Motor* 1964, no. 1, p. 4; "Do wyboru, do koloru," *Motor* 1964, no. 26 p. 4; "Do wyboru, do koloru. Kupujemy FSO-Warszawę," *Motor* 1964, no. 33, p. 4; "Do wyboru, do koloru. Jubileuszowe konfrontacje," *Motor* 1965, no. 1, p. 1; "Do wyboru, do koloru. Warszawy i Syreny," *Motor* 1965, no. 44, p. 4; "Wiosenna panorama rynkowa. Do wyboru, do koloru," *Motor* 1966, no. 14, p. 1.

histories were traded daily. The car market was full of organised gangs of touts and false buyers who pushed up prices.[886]

At the same time, ordinary people were offended by sellers who offered brand new cars straight from the factory. The problem was not only the price, which was often higher than the official one, but also doubts about the fair allocation of cars. In theory, cars were supposed to go to the most needy, but in reality, this was not always the case. Unsurprisingly, this found expression in letters to the *Motor* weekly, one of which states:

> If the cars received through allocation are sold on the open market at a high mark-up, who approves the allocations at the Trade Department of the Warsaw National Council? A similar, equally troublesome question concerns foreign cars. As we know from the "Do wyboru do koloru" column in *Motor*, the price of a new Fiat 600 is 83,000 zlotys. I wonder where I can buy a new Fiat for this money? Recently, at the car market in Warsaw, I talked to a certain gentleman in a responsible position who wanted to sell a new Fiat 600 for 125,000 zlotys.[887]

A decade later, in *Polityka*, Wróblewski described the reality of the car market with his typical irony:

> The car market was the go-to place for worn-out cars and for those whose owners had outgrown them, and for those that were still too big for them because the cost was too high—and even those bought due to great business needs. In the application, the owner-candidate argued that a car was absolutely necessary to perform his official duties. How strange that he was able to work on foot until now. A few days or weeks after the purchase, he could be seen at the car market, selling his new purchase for 30,000 or even 50,000 zlotys more.[888]

---

886 P. Ambroziewicz, "Co dalej giełdo?" p. 5.

887 "Głosy i odgłosy," *Motor* 1964, no. 33, p. 2.

888 A. K. Wróblewski, "Śmierć giełdy," *Polityka* 1977, no. 29, p. 1. In the discussion that followed Wróblewski's article, one reader from Bydgoszcz expressed a very interesting opinion, very accurately diagnosing the reality of the time: "We have double prices wherever supply does not meet demand: express prices for cars, survey prices in convenience stores, apartments in owner cooperatives earlier than in tenants' cooperatives; and where there is no other, higher price, there immediately appear speculation, swindle, double-dealing, etc. Therefore, whether the car markets will 'die', as you predict, or remain alive depends on the ratio of supply to demand, because the law of value has no regard for social justice"; *Polityka* 1977, no. 33, p. 8.

In this situation, the recurring questions about how to replace this form of car trading were greeted with great interest, although without much hope for a change for the better. This was the case with the proposal to replace car markets with state-run second-hand stores. Car prices in them were to be determined by appraisers. In the case of new cars from allocations, the maximum price was to be the official sale price. The very idea of doing away with the seller's profit, which often amounted to several dozen percent, would have elicited pitiful smiles among the public. It was justifiably predicted that after the introduction of this form of sales, private trade would move to the classified ads in newspapers.[889] In the USSR, in the early 1970s, people were allowed to buy used cars at state-run dealerships. However, a handling fee of several percent was added to the price of the cars sold there. Although the prices of second-hand cars—after adding various additional costs—were lower than those of vehicles sold in private transactions, this form of trade was not very popular.[890] Perhaps the decisive factor here was the generally poor selection of cars offered.

In virtually all Eastern Bloc countries, the sale of cars outside of official channels was extremely popular, in spite of the risk of legal sanction. In East Germany, trading in used cars by private individuals was treated as speculation and could be punished by up to eight years in prison. However, the threat did not stop East Germans from engaging in this type of trade. The transactions were conducted in a very peculiar way: the potential seller left the car with the window slightly open at one of the parking lots that used for illegal or semi-legal car sales in East Berlin. They placed a piece of paper on the driver's seat with the price cited for their vehicle. The person interested in the car dropped their counter-offer with contact details through the opening.[891] It is worth mentioning that East German decision-makers repeatedly tried to stop this private trade in used cars. As in Poland, they imposed a three-year pause during which one could not sell a car, as well as an obligation to resell used vehicles through state institutions. However,

889 P. Ambroziewicz, "Co dalej giełdo?" p. 5.
890 L. H. Siegelbaum, *Cars for Comrades*, p. 240.
891 J. Zatlin, *Currency of Socialism: Money and Political Culture in East Germany*, Cambridge 2007, p. 231.

these actions had little effect because, as official statistics showed, only 20% of the cars were sold using state channels.[892]

Let us, however, return to Poland. Another proposed solution to the anarchy of the car markets was to involve Motozbyt in the transactions, supervising them and providing the services of an appraiser. However, Motozbyt did not want to take on such a role because, in part because it would be tasked with providing the space for the conduct of these activities; it lacked such a space.[893] There was also a concern that an unsatisfactory opinion from an appraiser about a specific car (i.e. quoting too low a price) would lead the appraiser to be pressured or bribed to change their mind. It also quickly transpired that Motozbyt itself employed the same practices that were widely criticised in the case of car markets—while purchasing and selling used cars, it earned exactly the kind of money market traders did.[894]

These ideas were never implemented, and car markets survive in Poland to this day. They successfully resisted all attempts at change for a very mundane reason: they were the only place where a person with enough cash could really purchase virtually any model of car or motorcycle. Of course, there were some regional differences, but they were well known to those looking for specific makes and models. People who wanted to buy, for example, a West German Opel, or the extremely popular Ford Taunus, produced in Cologne, knew they would have to travel to Upper Silesia, where access to these cars was easier due to the privileges enjoyed by miners. In Kraków, one could buy a Mercedes with relative ease, because that was where they went from Vienna as part of internal imports. In turn, all foreign brands offered by PEKAO, such as Renault or NSU, were sold in the Podhale, where—as one commentator observed—"foreign currency [was] relatively plentiful." The short distance between the Polish coast and Scandinavia meant that those who wanted to buy a Volvo travelled to the north of the country.[895]

---

[892] Ibid., p. 233.

[893] A. K. Wróblewski writes, however, that ultimately, during the period when the car exchange was located in Warsaw's Bemowo district, anyone who paid an entry fee could benefit from a free inspection of the condition of the car by experts from Polmozbyt. Moreover, everyone who concluded purchase or sale agreements through Polmozbyt paid a lower duty; *idem*, *Polska na kółkach*, pp. 90–91.

[894] P. Ambroziewicz, "Co dalej giełdo?" p. 7.

[895] Ibid.

Fans of American brands, brought to Poland by sailors as part of maritime imports, also went there.

4.8 State used cars

Another way to acquire a vehicle was through the purchase of an official car surplussed by a state institution. As already mentioned, this possibility first appeared in the late 1940s, when officials introduced the distinction between "typical" and "non-typical" cars. In the first half of the 1950s, the state automobile fleet was gradually modernised, although not without resistance: old cars were being discarded and put up for sale. They could be purchased through the Headquarters of the Transport Cooperative of the Central Office of Trade in Automotive Equipment but only by other state offices, institutions, or entities of the socialised economy, if they did not have enough vehicles to perform their tasks.[896] Individuals could only buy passenger cars and motorcycles qualified as "group II" (vehicles requiring repair) or, in exceptional cases, group III (vehicles intended to be scrapped).[897] In the case of group III, MTDiL had to approve each sale. Priority was given to shock workers, workplace *racjonalizatorzy* (innovators) and those whose profession justified the use of a car. That list was quite long: state employees and workers in socialised enterprises (if their position, nature of their work, or their living conditions mandated ownership of a vehicle, in particular because of the need to constantly travel to the workplace in the absence of appropriate public transport); doctors, writers, publicists, journalists, artists, and other freelance workers with driving licences; and persons using horse-drawn wagons and taxis to provide public transportation services. Applications by individuals interested in purchasing a car had to be supported by a statement

---

896 MP 1951, no. A-21, poz. 254; AAN, MTDiL, sign. 165, Instrukcja Ministra Transportu Drogowego i lotniczego z 17 IX 1951 r., unnumbered pages.

897 Cars and motorcycles from automotive inventories were divided into three groups. Group I were new vehicles; group II were vehicles "capable of working after repair"; and group III were vehicles intended for scrap. A similar classification was introduced for components, accessories, and spare parts for motor vehicles: group I were "checked, new"; group II were "checked, used, suitable for use"; and group III were "unchecked new and used components and parts; used, suitable for regeneration, repair, rework"; MP 1951, no. A-11, pos. 163.

from the management at their workplace or an industry association. They were forwarded to the road transport departments of the praesidiums of provincial national councils, which processed the applications and issued opinions. Those who managed to purchase a car could not resell it without the consent of the relevant road transport department. However, if such a transaction took place, the vehicle could not be re-registered and accepted for use.[898] In 1954, "active motor sportsmen" were also given the opportunity to purchase state-owned cars. The procedure for granting purchase permits was also slightly changed. PZMot was included in the process, considering individual applications together with the road transportation departments of the praesidiums of provincial national councils. Consent to the purchase meant issuing a sales order, which expired after twenty days. After that date, the car could not be purchased.[899]

Each of the orders cited here included a list of brands intended for sale. In 1950, these were Citroëns (models 11L, 11BL, and 15), Fiats (various versions of the 1100 model), Pobedas, Škodas (1101 and 1102), Jeeps, and Chevrolets (Fleetmaster and Deluxe).[900] In 1953, the list expanded to almost twenty different makes and models, including Warszawas, BMWs (model 340), DKWs (F8 and F9), Tatras, Hillmans, and Rovers. In addition, "all official cars with an engine displacement above 3.0 litres produced since 1948" were also slated for sale.[901] Car prices were set by order of the chairman of the State Commission for Economic Planning dated January 16, 1951, and depended on the group to which the vehicle was classified. Prices were the highest with vehicles from group I (between 2,100 and 7,700 zlotys), but in practice, they were not available to individual buyers. Group II passenger cars could cost from 600 to 1,200 zlotys, while those from group III received a flat-rate valuation of 30 zlotys per vehicle.[902] In many cases, cars that were intended

---

898 MP 1952, no. A-45, pos. 638.

899 MP 1954, no. A-24, pos. 397.

900 MP 1950, no. A-123, pos. 1528, addendum.

901 MP 1953, no. A-28, pos. 337, addendum. In early 1954, Hillman and Rover were struck out from this list; MP 1954, no. A-5, pos. 154.

902 MP 1951, no. A-11, pos. 163.

for state officials and socialised economic entities were bought by private persons, evading the rules of the sale.[903]

At the end of 1956, an MTDiL order introduced the possibility of sale of excess passenger cars by units of state administration without the involvement of middlemen. The selling price was the retail list price of a new car reduced depending on the degree of wear and tear. Purchase priority was given to people whose conditions or type of work justified the need for a vehicle the most. It should be noted that the new order eliminated privileged professions, as well as the status of shock worker or innovator. Only Warszawas and imported cars with an engine displacement greater than 1,000 cm^3 and registered after January 1, 1953 (unless their mileage exceeded 150,000 km) were excluded from this form of sale. These vehicles were to be transferred to another entity that had vacancies in its fleet.[904] In accordance with the determination made by the State Price Commission, the price of such a car depended on the degree of its wear and tear and on its engine displacement, and should be within the range of 25,000 to 32,000 zlotys. Thus, the provisions of 1952 and 1954 were no longer valid.

Another change took place in May 1957, when the Ministry of Culture mandated that the sale of redundant vehicles was to be carried out by auction. Individuals could place their bids, but only if they had presented certificates from the road transport department of the praesidium of the provincial national council or the national council of a city separate from the voivodeship, depending on their place of residence, which confirmed the need for a vehicle justified by their economic or professional activity. As before, Warszawas and imported cars with a displacement of more than 1,000 cm^3 and a mileage of less than 150,000 km were not available for bids.[905]

The opportunity to buy a used state-owned car was very tempting. In the years 1954–1955, more than 1,200 applications were submitted to the road transport department of the Praesidium of the National Council of

---

903 AAN, URM KT, sign. 6/228, [Pismo w sprawie sprzedaży nietypowych samochodów osobowych, pochodzących z upłynnienia remanentów], Warszawa, 27 VII 1954 r., pp. 17–19.

904 MP 1956, no. 106, pos. 1244.

905 MP 1957, no. 56, pos. 353.

Warsaw, though only ten cars were intended for sale in 1954.[906] However, the purchase of such a vehicle, especially when it did not require too much expense on repairs, gave its buyer a chance to earn a significant amount of money. While the purchase price of a used "second-rate" car from a state institution was several thousand zlotys, its value on the free market was several times higher—and there were plenty of buyers. It is no wonder that these cars were much sought after and rarely did they reach beyond the circle of employees of state institutions. As one member of the Warsaw branch of the PZPR explained: "members of the secretariat of the Warsaw Committee assumed that, if these cars are intended for use for private initiative, it would be better if the comrades bought them."[907] They, in turn, often resold the cars at a significant profit.

As one *Motor* journalist wrote at the end of 1956: "Obtaining a voucher for such a vehicle is a complicated process. Apparently, there were shenanigans and fraud resulting from the purchase of a car for 4,000 zlotys that was worth 30,000–40,000 zlotys. ... During the last three years, I submitted 12 applications to all institutions that had some influence on the allocation process .... I even have some connections in these institutions, but I did not receive a voucher."[908]

* * *

The fact that Poles eagerly bought cars offered through official sales channels did not surprise decision-makers.[909] According to the research conducted by the Institute of Domestic Trade (Instytut Handlu Wewnętrznego IHW), the state unit that conducted scientific research forecasting consumer demand and analysing consumption patterns, on the structure of national income and the population's capacity to spend on specific consumption and industrial purposes, at the end of the 1950s, the Polish internal market was able

---

906 gp, "Samochód II kategorii," *Motor* 1956, no. 8, p. 4.
907 Quoted in B. Brzostek, "Szewroletariat," *Mówią Wieki* 2013, no. 5, pp. 54–55.
908 K. Wilczyński, "Rok 'Nijaki'," p. 4.
909 This opinion applies primarily to buyers who paid in Polish zlotys. As shown in the section on internal exports, a customer who was willing to pay for a new car in dollars could be much more selective.

to absorb 34,000 passenger cars annually. This forecast covered the years 1960–1965; this number was to double in the next five-year plan, and in the first half of the 1970s, it would reach 100,000.[910]

The ruling elite eagerly took advantage of this rush for privately owned four wheels, which helped regulate the amount of cash on the market. When the need arose to remove an excess, they only needed to announce the sale of an additional pool of passenger cars. If these happened to be of Western make, the scheme was almost bound to succeed. This was the case in 1957, when Motoimport, at the request of MHZ, decided to import several thousand units of the popular Fiat 600. The situation was unique in that this time, the usual technical inspection of vehicles intended for importation was abandoned. Apart from the aforementioned need to siphon cash from the market, this was due to preferential credit conditions granted to the Poles (the value of the transaction was over US $1.7 million, and the loan was granted for 4 years, with repayment scheduled to begin after 18 months), as well as the fact that this model enjoyed a fairly good reputation for driving quality and technical advancement. A report from the transaction states: "There could be no serious doubts as to the quality of these cars given the make itself. Moreover, two years of experience had proven the correctness of the selection of the make and model of cars in this transaction." Perhaps it was also important that, as a kind of bonus, Fiat added a few 600 s to the deal, which went directly to Motoimport employees.[911]

To return for a moment to the IHW, it is worth emphasising that the capacity of the internal market for cars that they forecast did not fully materialise. Although in the years 1960–1965, the number of passenger cars increased by over 124,000 (for an average annual increase of 20,600) and continued to rise

---

910 AAN, MK, sign. II/2, Protokół nr 1 z plenarnego zebrania Rady Motoryzacyjnej 9 I 1959 r., pp. 88–89.

911 AAN, MHZ, sign. 4/508 Sprawozdanie komisji powołanej zarządzeniem nr 13 Dyrektora Centrali "Motoimport" z 14 XI 1958 r., Warszawa, 24 I 1959 r., unnumbered pages.; ibid., sign. 4/512, Notatka dla Kierownika Zespołu Inspektorów Resortowych [...], Warszawa, 19 XII 1957 r., unnumbered pages. As Zdzisław Rurarz recalls, the company from Turin followed the same playbook in the 1970s, when it tried to convince members of Edward Gierek's administration to licence the Fiat 126p. At the time, several units of the model 137 were supposedly handed over to particular figures; Z. Rurarz, *Byłem doradcą Gierka*, Chicago–Toronto–Warszawa 1990, p. 114.

at a higher pace over the course of the next five years (39,700 per year), the assumed figures were not achieved (34,000 and 70,000 cars per year, respectively). Why? Was the state to blame for not providing enough vehicles? Or was it because the people simply could not afford to buy cars?

The state was certainly unable to meet the demand for cars. During the period in question, the supply of cars never came close to the amounts mentioned in the IHW report. The Polish automotive industry produced a total of 350,182 passenger cars in the years 1960–1970, of which 109,892 were exported. In other words, approximately 240,000 new cars were directed to the internal market. In reality, this number was even smaller, because some of the Warszawas produced for the Polish market went to state offices and institutions. Therefore, we can assume that, on average, approximately 20,000 cars manufactured in FSO every year were intended for domestic buyers. At the same time, in Czechoslovakia, where yearly production reached 90,000 units, over 63,000 of the new cars were intended for sale to private users. It should be noted, however, that these high results were achieved thanks to favourable data from the second half of the decade, when as many as 71,000 passenger cars of the 120,000 produced in Czechoslovakia reached private users.[912]

What the state could not provide, the people obtained through other channels. A survey conducted among the readers of *Motor* in 1960 showed that only 30% of car purchases were made through Motozbyt, and a half of the total were concluded between private persons. Consequently, only 35% of transactions concerned new cars.[913] Official data on production and state imports clearly showed that access to new cars through state channels was very limited. At the end of the 1960s, those who wanted to buy a Polish car in this way—a Syrena or a Warszawa (by the time, already treated as supplementary to a fleet consisting generally of Big Fiats)—had to wait two or four years, respectively, for their vehicle.[914]

---

912 M. Kousal, "Podstawowe zagadnienia rozwoju motoryzacji indywidualnej w Czechosłowacji," *Motoryzacja* 1986, no. 2, p. 33.

913 "Krajowa ankieta motoryzacyjnego 'Instytutu Gallupa'," *Motor* 1960, no. 11, p. 3.

914 AAN, GUC, sign. 12/45, Założenia protekcyjnej polityki celnej i cenowej w stosunku do eksportu i sprzedaży na rynku wewnętrznym samochodów marki "Polski Fiat," unnumbered pages.

Travelling through Poland in 1967, Carmen Laforet—one of the most esteemed Spanish intellectuals and novelists of the twentieth century—observed: "Poles have a great need for comfort and improved living conditions."[915] It seems that this sentence perfectly captures the state of the Polish society in the 1960s. In this "need for comfort" and the process of "improving living conditions," a personal car played a major role. As economist Zdzisław Krasiński once wrote: "A car purchase is driven by a host of emotions" though he added that the income level was decisive in this context. While in the case of the thousands of smaller items, the purchase was primarily determined by the buyer's emotions, with the particular good embodied in the car, what mattered most was "money, income, and price." Only after crossing a certain income level could one decide to buy one's own car.[916]

It is a question worth asking: were Poles able to afford their own car? The affirmative answer, supported by statistical data showing an increase in the number of cars in private hands, requires clarification. As had been noted in 1957, given an average salary of 1,580 zlotys, it was almost impossible to accumulate the savings necessary to purchase a car at a price of 65,000–115,000 zlotys. The few who could afford it had legal earnings several times above the average wage, or belonged to "all kinds of warriors of the economic underground, the organisers of major illegal schemes involving trade and speculation." The rest usually had to use up family savings, often organising schemes of their own, "arranging among those involved how the passenger car would be shared and how its high price would be covered."[917] Even the cheapest new car on the market, a Mikrus, cost several dozen monthly salaries. All potential buyers of their own four wheels had to save money for their dream vehicle "through enormous sacrifices made at the expense of normal existence." As one resident of Zawiercie in south Poland complained in a letter to the Polish Radio: "[I]n our conditions, to become the owner of a Mikrus, you have to spend 30 months, or almost three years, earning 1,700 zlotys a month, stop eating, stop wearing clothes, and never spend money

915 C. Laforet, *Za żelazną kurtyną. Podróż do Polski w 1967 r.*, Warszawa 2013, p. 112.

916 *Rynek samochodowy*, ed. Z. Krasiński, Warszawa 1980, pp. 66–68. Cf. H. Lefebvre, *Everyday Life in the Modern World*, Bloomsbury 2016, p. 87.

917 J. Bujniewicz, "Czy może być lepiej?" p. 182.

on anything else."[918] It is, therefore, not surprising that *Szpilki* very often published drawings depicting car owners wearing torn clothes and worn-out shoes, such as the one by Zbigniew Lengren from a 1961 issue of the magazine.

Figure 7. Zbigniew Lengren, „Właściciel wozu"

In 1967, a married couple from Krotoszyn wrote a letter to Władysław Gomułka, describing the trials and tribulations of a future car owner:

> Since 1963, my husband and I have been saving, putting aside one of our salaries into a PKO book to be able to eventually buy the car we have dreamed of for so many years. What we are facing is a disappointment. ... This application [for a car] may not be approved for another five years and nothing is certain yet. Dear Wiesław! This disappointment has affected me primarily. We denied ourselves everything, all the entertainments and vacations that each of us deserves, in order to put aside these savings and buy this car, and then our dreams came crashing down. In our car, we wanted to travel through our country, which we have to admit we do not

918 Archiwum Dokumentacji i Zbiorów Programowych Polskiego Radia i Telewizji (hereafter: ADPPRiT), sign. 1050/29, Biuletyn nr 85 w sprawie samochodów Mikrus produkcji WSK—Mielec, 23 XI 1959 r., unnumbered pages.

know well yet. So, I am asking you, Dear Comrade Wiesław, for help in completing the allocation of this car. We're talking about a "Škoda 1000 MB."[919]

According to PKO data on total household savings, in 1960, only 0.3% of households not involved in agriculture—approximately 14,000—that were eligible to purchase a car had accumulated funds equal to the price of the cheapest model (approximately 60,000 zlotys). By the middle of the decade, this percentage increased to 3.5% (180,000 households); in the early 1970s, it was already approximately 10%, corresponding to 583,000 families.[920]

According to very interesting data on saving goals collected by the Central Statistical Office (GUS) in 1967, only 5.8% of households that saved with PKO did so with the intention of buying a car (see Table 13). Moreover, among the families of blue-collar workers, this percentage was even smaller (2.1%). Meanwhile, owning a car was the goal for 10% of white-collar households; in mixed families, the rate was 6.7%. Polish families were much more likely to save money to buy clothes, furniture, or other durable goods.[921]

Table 13. Saving goals indicated by households according to socio-professional groups and household size

Main Savings Goal	Households			
	Together	Type of Work		Mixed
		Physical	White collar	
Including:				
Clothing	14.2	14.4	13.8	14.9
Furniture	10.0	8.5	11.2	11.7
Automobile	5.8	2.1	10.3	6.7
Other	8.6	8.2	8.1	10.8

(Continued)

919 AAN, KC PZPR, sign. XI/1055, Krotoszyn, 25 IX 1967 r., pp. 25–26.

920 Z. Krasiński, *Czynniki ekonomiczno-społeczne*, p. 28.

921 Research on saving goals conducted by the Institute of Commodity Economics at the Poznań University of Economics showed that people who saved enough money to buy a car cared more about obtaining a cooperative apartment, building a single-family house, furnishing their homes, as well as also travelling; Z. Krasiński, *Czynniki ekonomiczno-społeczne*, pp. 28–29.

Table 13. *(Continued)*

Main Savings Goal	Households				
	Together	Type of Work			Mixed
		Physical	White collar		
	Households by Number of People				
Including:	1	2	3	4	5 or more
Clothing	15.0	13.5	12.3	14.8	16.9
Furniture	5.9	11.5	10.5	10.5	9.0
Automobile	1.8	5.6	7.6	6.8	4.4
Motorcycle, scooter	0.7	0.8	1.2	2.8	0.3
Other	3.7	10.2	9.6	9.7	7.0

Source: Z. Krasiński, Czynniki społeczno-ekonomiczne, p. 28.

Examining the budgets of Polish families in the mid-1960s, Andrzej Tymowski noticed that money for a car often came from "extraordinary" income ("inheritance," lottery winnings), or from savings accumulated on "car" savings books, or from the sale of dollars earned during, for example, "a long delegation to a 'hard currency' country." In his opinion, however, a household in which two adults were working (and the husband earned at least 5,000 zlotys) "can purchase one [a car] without particular difficulty, of course if they do not support a very large family and if they 'tighten their belts' a bit."[922] In 1966, when the results of these studies were published, the average monthly salary in socialised industry was 2,200 zlotys. Even engineers and industrial technical workers earning above the national average received salaries below the amount cited by Tymowski. Their average gross wages in the same year amounted to just over 3,400 zlotys.[923] Meanwhile, as the

922 A. Tymowski, "Cztery kółka a budżet domowy," *Życie Gospodarcze* 1966, no. 2, p. 3. See also M. Kula, *Mimo wszystko bliżej Paryża niż Moskwy. Książka o Francji, PRL i o nas, historykach*, Warszawa 2010, p. 152ff. It is worth recalling the words of Lesław Łowczyński from 1957, quoted above, for whom the minimum monthly earnings that allowed for the purchase and maintenance of a car were 5,500 zlotys; L. Łowczyński, "Samochodzik czy samochód popularny dla świata pracy," pp. 70–71.

923 *Mały Rocznik Statystyczny* Motoryzacji 1968, part 2, p. 12 (appendix to *Motoryzacja. Pismo transportu drogowego* 24 [1968], no. 2).

aforementioned study by Krasiński's team showed, it was not until 1973 that the nominal income of 5,000 zlotys, and 7,000 zlotys in 1979, became "a threshold marking the beginning of stronger interests directed towards owning a car."[924] As one diarist concluded: "A car … is a very expensive joke."[925]

Instalment sales were a great help for people who were unable to pay for a new car in cash. In the 1960s, an average of just over 20% of cars were sold this way each year, though this value varied significantly between individual years. The most cars—as much as 32.4%—were sold on credit in 1964, and the least—only 9%—in 1970.[926] As journalist Feliks Bąbol noted, using the services of the state enterprise called the Public Instalment Service (Obsługa Ratalnej Sprzedaży ORS) allowed even workers earning just 1,500–2,000 zlotys a month to purchase their own car (see Table 14).[927]

Table 14. Loans granted to the public by PKO in the years 1960–1970

Year	Total	Including for purchase of		Share of Loans		
		Cars	Motorcycles and mopeds	For cars	For motorcycles and mopeds	In total car sales
	In Millions of zlotys			In interest to total loans		
1960	4.930	330	356	6.7	7.2	25.5
1961	5.173	462	391	8.9	7.6	28.9
1962	5.765	584	419	10.1	7.3	23.1
1963	6.394	617	567	9.7	8.9	28.0
1964	6.593	675	439	10.2	6.6	32.4
1965	7.316	783	347	10.7	4.7	24.4
1966	8.904	866	264	9.7	3.0	25.8
1967	7.754	580	409	7.5	5.3	17.9
1968	7.326	425	251	5.8	3.4	11.6
1969	7.533	605	175	8.0	2.3	13.2
1970	8.658	455	395	5.3	4.6	9.0

Source: Z. Krasiński, Czynniki społeczno-ekonomiczne, p. 29.

924 *Rynek samochodowy*, p. 68.

925 "Marzula," "Myślę wciąż o Marion," in: *Życie bez fikcji. Dzienniki*, ed. S. Adamczyk, Warszawa 1976, p. 50.

926 In France in the late 1960s, more than half of families surveyed on the degree of habituation to cars had bought their own car on credit; M. Roche, "Samochód," p. 286.

927 F. Bąbol, "Nie ma ucieczki przed motoryzacją," *Odgłosy* 1964/1965, no. 51/1, p. 5.

One example was Łódź, where, in 1964 alone, the ORS granted loans for this purpose in the amount of 59 million zlotys, which was almost 10% of all car loans granted at that time.[928] In the years 1960–1970, Poles borrowed 6,382,000 zlotys for this purpose, which was just over 8.3% of the total value of loans granted during the period; the most came in 1966, when the value of loans granted by ORS amounted to 866 million zlotys. Almost every year, at least 8% of the value of all new loans was intended for the purchase of a car or motorcycle.[929] Nevertheless, as Krasiński's research shows, only 15.9% of car owners in the early 1970s financed their purchase using a loan. Systematic saving was definitely the most popular method, indicated by over 66% of repondents.[930] This was undoubtedly determined, again, by the price of a new car and therefore, the value of monthly instalments. In a letter to her family, sociologist Nina Assorodobraj-Kula mentioned plans to buy a new Škoda together with Jadwiga Strzelecka and Jan Strzelecki: "Janek [Strzelecki] will pay what's due in cash, and we will earn and save on installments."[931] This reality is perfectly summarised by responses to a *Polityka* survey about motorisation. Many of those who decided to participate in the survey had to save for a few years, and even for more than a decade ("this was the goal of my life, finally realised," "I got the car virus and I still have it").[932]

Therefore, the answer to the question who could afford a car in Poland at that time is, certainly not everyone, and those who could afford their own

928 Ibid.; J. J. Szczepański also bought his first car through ORS: *idem*, *Dziennik 1964–1972*, Kraków 2013, pp. 100–101.

929 A worker employed as a foreman noticed a rather interesting and non-obvious aspect of instalment purchases—namely, the fact that the obligation to pay specific amounts every month required a stable income at an appropriate level: "ORS has helped us, foremen, more than the seven decrees on discipline did. Whoever wants to have something—looks for an ORS. Then, he does what's necessary to pay the instalments, no backtalk. This is the best thing they have come up with, because it is human nature that when you've gotten used to something better, you'll get stuck in to keep what you have. Now, the best workers are those who bought motorcycles or furniture on instalments, or anything whatsoever. They never slip up"; A. Jędrzejczak, "Sąd nad posiadaczem," in: *Młodzi stąd. Reportaże 1950–1965*, ed. A. Pawłowska and J. Feliksiak, Warszawa 1966, p. 378.

930 Z. Krasiński, *Czynniki społeczno-ekonomiczne*, "Tabela syntetyczna II."

931 M. Kula, *Mimo wszystko bliżej Paryża niż Moskwy*, p. 154.

932 A. K. Wróblewski, "Polska Samochodowa," *Polityka* 1966, no. 40, pp. 1 and 8.

four wheels were limited in their choices, whether they bought from the state or from private individuals. Andrzej Tymowski, quoted above, demonstrated that in the mid-1960s, the annual income of households owning a car was 65% higher than the national average.[933] Zdzisław Krasiński emphasised that in 1971, owning a car was still the privilege of the elite (only 5% of households), available only to a narrow group of people, primarily from larger cities, who worked in technical professions and had a higher education.[934] The results of *Polityka*'s automotive survey from the mid-1960s support this claim. Based on the responses, it is clear that the development of individual motorisation involved a very limited part of the society—primarily engineers, doctors, economists, and military officers aged 30–40, often young married couples with one or two children (if—it should be noted—both parents worked). In his commentary, Andrzej Krzysztof Wróblewski rightly notes that "the wave of motorisation has not yet reached new professional circles, but is instead passing through those that have been buying cars for several years and where a car is not an extraordinary rarity."[935] The survey *Social diversification of opinions on the material situation* (*Społeczne zróżnicowanie ocen sytuacji materialnej*) conducted in 1968 by the Center for Public Opinion Research and Programme Studies, confirmed the capabilities of Poles in this area. When asked about the most needed items, 19.6% of people employed in specialised named the car in the first place, and among officials, 8.6% named it in the second place. Among both skilled and unskilled labourers, owning a car did not in the top five, giving way to such items as a refrigerator, television set, washing machine, sewing machine, or motorcycle.[936]

Unfortunately, we do not have complete data on the geographical diversity of car owners. The Central Statistical Office has only began publishing this type of data in 1960. However, its data allow us to draw certain general conclusions.

---

933 A. Tymowski, "Cztery kółka a budżet domowy," p. 3.

934 Z. Krasiński, *Czynniki społeczno-ekonomiczne*, p. 9. In the USSR in the early 1980s, 58% of car owners were white-collar workers, 35% were blue-collar workers; L. H. Siegelbaum, *Cars for Comrades*, p. 241.

935 A. K. Wróblewski, "Zawsze umiera kto inny," p. 3.

936 K. Zagórski, *Społeczne zróżnicowanie ocen sytuacji materialnej (Wstępne wyniki badania pt. "Jak nam się żyje?")*, Warszawa 1969, p. 18.

Table 15. Number of passenger cars by voivodeship in 1960–1970

Voivodeship	1960		1965		1966		1967		1968		1969		1970	
	Together	Private	Together	Private	Together	Private	Together	Private	Together	Private	Together	Private	Together	Private
Warsaw (city)	15.668	10.869	35.473	29.980	40.238	34.352	40.056	40.314	49.855	44.894	55.059	50.037	60.400	50.500
Kraków (city)	5.978	4.854	10.355	9.109	11.818	10.583	13.928	12.706	15.958	14.797	17.279	16.133	18.600	17.600
Łódź (city)	5.040	4.130	11.428	10.095	13.297	11.813	14.649	13.300	15.753	14.617	17.350	16.149	19.600	18.500
Poznań (city)	5.092	4.169	10.690	9.532	12.873	11.726	14.678	13.557	16.832	15.699	19.004	18.090	21.600	20.600
Wrocław (city)	4.807	3.936	9.330	8.447	10.024	9.084	11.388	10.445	13.242	12.341	14.922	14.157	16.800	16.100
Białostockie	1.988	1.261	4.472	3.599	5.411	4.489	6.324	5.383	7.739	6.806	9.097	8.238	11.000	10.100
Bydgoskie	5.685	4.307	11.347	9.785	13.877	12.198	16.069	14.385	18.522	16.869	21.291	19.802	24.100	22.700
Gdańskie	7.067	5.524	13.750	11.891	15.801	14.095	18.229	16.479	21.631	19.952	23.890	22.505	28.100	26.900
Katowickie	17.864	15.253	33.080	29.725	42.149	39.058	46.602	43.302	51.111	47.935	56.518	53.591	65.100	62.700
Kieleckie	3.344	2.385	6.651	5.560	8.148	6.998	9.467	8.320	10.794	9.664	12.751	11.711	14.300	13.300
Koszalińskie	2.547	1.660	4.762	4.007	5.872	5.042	6.644	5.831	7.853	7.064	9.125	8.334	10.200	9.500
Krakowskie	4.634	3.935	9.417	8.634	10.528	9.658	11.949	11.087	13.494	12.683	15.596	14.842	18.100	17.300
Lubelskie	3.492	2.294	7.748	6.416	8.760	7.370	10.042	8.731	11.152	9.974	12.869	11.787	14.600	13.600
Łódzkie	3.368	2.761	6.804	6.096	8.338	7.597	9.997	9.257	11.515	10.839	13.388	12.783	15.300	14.600
Olsztyńskie	2.843	2.068	6.305	5.438	7.563	6.610	9.031	8.123	10.161	9.260	11.678	10.866	12.800	12.000
Opolskie	2.969	2.276	7.138	6.219	8.308	7.361	9.787	8.847	11.063	10.200	12.730	11.943	14.300	13.500

Voivodeship	1960		1965		1966		1967		1968		1969		1970	
	Together	Pri-vate	Together	Private	Together	Private	Together	Private	Together	Private	Together	Private	Together	Private
Poznańskie	5.684	4.696	13.282	12.190	15.551	14.385	18.463	17.292	21.455	20.314	24.630	23.559	26.900	25.800
Rzeszowskie	3.076	2.072	6.134	4.998	7.243	6.014	8.267	7.022	9.539	8.351	11.253	10.115	13.300	12.200
Szczecińskie	3.242	2.186	7.118	6.937	8.258	6.979	9.635	8.459	10.760	9.723	12.414	11.482	14.700	13.800
Warszawskie	4.846	4.076	12.143	11.249	14.435	13.478	17.540	16.618	20.427	19.508	23.257	22.411	27.000	26.100
Wrocławskie	5.687	4.410	12.840	11.501	14.803	13.417	16.403	15.106	18.231	17.041	20.261	19.165	22.800	21.800
Zielonogór-skie	2.436	1.674	5.204	4.400	6.095	5.263	6.745	5.915	7.481	6691	8469	7.889	9.800	9.200
Total	117.357	90.796	245.471	214.908	289.390	257.570	325.893	300.479	374.568	345.222	422.831	395.589	479.400	448.400

Source: Rocznik Statystyczny 1967, p. 317; Rocznik Statystyczny 1968, p. 304; Rocznik Statystyczny 1969, p. 308; Rocznik Statystyczny 1970, p. 305; Rocznik Statystyczny 1971, p. 358.

It is clear that the city of Warsaw and the Warsaw Voivodeship (see Table 15) were the unchallenged leaders here, concentrating (on average) over 18% of all passenger cars in the years 1966–1970. Even Upper Silesia, supposedly favoured by the authorities in this respect, was unable to compete with the capital city or its voivodeship. In Warsaw itself, there were only slightly fewer passenger cars than in the entire Katowice Voivodeship. Meanwhile, the number of passenger cars was the lowest in the voivodeships with capitals in Białystok, Koszalin, Zielona Góra, Rzeszów, and Olsztyn. In 1966, according to data from the transportation departments of the local WRNs, a total of 27,400 cars were in private hands in those voivodeships, which is fewer than in Warsaw alone. In subsequent years, this disparity remained practically unchanged.

However, the situation was completely different in terms of the annual percentage increase in the number of private cars. In Warsaw, it was 10% on average; in the Gdańsk voivodeship—17.5%; and in the Katowice voivodeship—15%. Meanwhile, in the least motorised voivodeships, the increase was 17%. Moreover, in Białystok and Rzeszów, this increase was the highest in the entire country—over 19%—while the average for the country was 14.8%. Therefore, it is evident that in the second half of the 1960s, it was these regions of Poland that had motorised the most, although at the same time, in absolute numbers, the number of cars found there was much lower than in Warsaw or the Katowice voivodeship, where in 1970 alone, the number of cars increased by 9,109, whereas in the Białystok region, it increased by 5,611 units in the entire period 1966–1970. Therefore, it was in the richer regions of Poland (mainly separated cities and specific voivodeships, such as *Katowickie* or *Gdańskie*) that the vast majority of private cars was concentrated. In the poorer regions (Lesser Poland, Podkarpacie, but also parts of Lower Silesia), it was not until the late 1970s that an acceleration in the motorisation of the society could be observed, although to an extent incomparable to the rest of the country.[937]

---

937 In Western Europe, as well, most passenger cars were concentrated in cities. In France in 1968, according to census data, most cars (53.9%) were owned by residents of towns with a population of 20,000 to 50,000. In cities with over 200,000 inhabitants, there were definitely fewer cars (49%). Paris was interesting in this respect, where less than half of the inhabitants (44.9%) had a car. There was also a high saturation of cars in rural communes—51.2%; M Roche, "Samochód," p. 283.

It is not without reason that in his answer to Warsaw residents during a pre-election meeting Władysław Gomułka noted: "A car is not yet an article of common use in our country and there is probably no need to sell it at a small, 5% or 10% profit. The buyers are a relatively small group of people with high earnings."[938] In other words, it was the strict rationing of cars through official state sales channels (official allocations and prepayment lists) and the relatively high prices that constituted a significant obstacle to meeting the huge demand for vehicles within the Polish society.[939]

938 "Polityka zgodna z interesami niżej zarabiających grup ludności," *Motor* 1969, no. 22, p. 2.
939 K. J. Mórawski, *Syrena*, p. 58.

Everyday Worries

There were two keywords in the economic realities of the People's Republic of Poland. The first we might call official, and it was: plan. The second, unofficial one, was: shortage. Introduced into the discourse by Hungarian economist János Kornai, the concept of a shortage economy reflects like few others the realities of countries located east of the Iron Curtain.

In the conditions of a centrally directed economy, where the word "plan" was ever-present, shortage affected everything, including matters of motorisation. There were shortages of spare parts, service stations, fuel, roads, and, finally, cars. Motorised Poles, left without state support, had to adapt very quickly to the realities of shortage, which meant that the ultimate dream was to have a car that broke down relatively rarely and for which spare parts were relatively easy to find.

In 1969, *Szpilki* published an epigram entitled "To an automobilist" ("Do automobilisty"):

> There was one whose income didn't go too far
> With holes in his trousers, still he bought a car
> Once inside, he found he could never go out
>
> Cause a bare backside won't earn you much clout
> So he died in his box; here's a lesson for us:
> Trousers work better for cov'ring your ass!
> Hark! Automobilist, please keep this in mind:
> A car, yes! But trousers first, for your behind.[940]

[940] A. Nowicki, "Do automobilisty," *Szpilki* 1968, no. 17, p. 6.

Poles were indeed willing to sacrifice a lot just to finally be able to get behind the wheel of the four wheels they dreamed of. However, this was usually just the beginning. Car maintenance was quickly becoming one of the most significant expenses. In the budgets of motorised households of non-manual workers, the costs associated with operating a car occupied third place, after food and clothing. So, where did the money necessary for refuelling and servicing the car come from? Andrzej Tymowski noticed that households that had a car most often gave up some of their food needs—they ate meat and cold cuts less often, and even abandoned restaurant meals. Next, came the expenses on new home furnishings, on transportation, culture, sports, and alcohol and tobacco.[941]

It is a difficult, and perhaps even impossible, task to attempt a hierarchy of particular shortages in the automotive market. Each of them affected the everyday use of the car. For this reason, the order in which the everyday problems of motorised (and unmotorised) Poles are discussed is completely random. However, first one should take a look at the condition of Polish roads and the passenger cars that drove on them.

5.1 Transportation museum

Wróblewski, who has already been quoted many times above, described the Polish motorisation as a "transportation museum":

> We imported several thousand of used vehicles through relatives, sailors, and more or less direct routes. Most of them are old cars that have enriched our automotive resources with a multitude of makes and models …, these cars are run without any warranty, with no possibility of purchasing parts if something breaks down. … At every step, there is chaos, neglect, disregard. Petrol, service stations, repair workshops, wolf traps in the roads, road markings… … It is an open secret that our low-octane petrol ruins car engines, shortening their life by half.[942]

---

941 A. Tymowski, "Cztery kółka a budżet domowy," p. 3.

942 A. K. Wróblewski, "Chleb i sól nie wystarczą. Dziewiczy los motoryzacji," *Życie Warszawy*, August 23, 1957, p. 6.

Although the above was written at the beginning of Władysław Gomułka's rule, it seems to be an ideal description of what the subsequent decade or so of Gomułka's reign would have in store.

Is it possible to determine, at least approximately, what kinds of cars Poles were driving? Was Wróblewski's claim about Poland as a "transportation museum" justified? Undoubtedly yes, although first it is worth taking a look at the statistical data on the number of cars that rode on Polish roads in the first quarter century after the end of World War Two.

It should be emphasised from the start that the first data provided by the Central Statistical Office (Główny Urząd StatytycznyGUS) regarding the number of passenger cars in Poland referred to the years 1949 and 1950. After that, there was a five-year break, because the GUS yearbook was not published until 1955, which is also when data on the number of passenger cars owned by private persons were first published. From that moment on, information on this subject was published systematically.

In 1955, of the 40,300 cars of this type, just over half (20,500) belonged to private owners. In subsequent years, this percentage increased. In 1970, the number of passenger cars amounted to 479,400 units, of which 426,900 were in private hands, constituting 89% of all such cars in Poland. Compared to 1955, this meant a more than twentyfold increase in the number of cars owned by private individuals. However, in the quarter century discussed here, the first ten years deserve particular attention. In that period, between 1955 and 1965, the number of passenger cars increased sixfold (to 245,500), but the truly dramatic increase (over tenfold) that has never been seen before in the history of Polish automobilism, concerned private cars.[943]

Unfortunately, it is impossible to say with certainty what makes and models were on Polish roads in the 1950s and early 1960s. Based on findings from the previous chapters, we can assume that the shape of the passenger car fleet at the beginning of the 1950s did not differ significantly from that at the end of the 1940s. State imports simply did not reach private recipients.

---

943 For comparison: under Edward Gierek, a time of a real boom in the production of the popular car, the indicators were better in absolute numbers, but compared to the Gomułka period, the results were not as impressive. Compared to 1970, the number of passenger cars, altogether and privately owned, increased only fivefold. It is worth noting, however, that the percentage of the latter increased significantly, to over 97%.

Therefore, they were largely used cars, often with prewar or wartime origins, derived from UNRRA deliveries, surplus purchases, and repossession. These cars were very problematic to use: they consumed fuel, broke down frequently, and had an obvious shortage of spare parts necessary for repairs. At the same time, as a result of the introduction of the division into typical and non-typical vehicles, the multitude of different marks and vehicles was, to some degree, eliminated.[944]

Taking a closer look at the available statistics, one can easily see that the number of passenger cars between 1950 and 1955 remained practically unchanged, and even decreased slightly, probably because many cars were unsuitable for further use due to their technical condition. At that time, the number of new automobiles being imported was quite low and could not fill the space left by withdrawn vehicles, and the very limited domestic production (of the Warszawa) was unable to meet those needs. It was estimated that given the condition of the state automobile fleet, which amounted to 25,000 cars in 1951, and assuming a five-year period of use per vehicle, maintaining the then-current size of the fleet required the addition of 5,000 cars per year. Meanwhile, the supply plan for 1952 included only 1,300 vehicles for the administration and state enterprises with. This meant that the period of use had to be extended to 19 years. The situation would improve slightly in subsequent years (in 1953, 1,700 cars were expected to be delivered, reducing the periods of use to 14 years), but it was still just a drop in the ocean of needs. Moreover, shortages in technical resources and an inadequate supply of spare parts meant that the period of use was extended by an additional 30%.[945]

The first official data on the purchase of passenger cars come from 1956, when 694 automobiles were imported. For comparison, in 1938 it was over 4,300 cars. In subsequent years, however, the value of Polish automotive imports increased significantly. In 1957, of the almost 62,000 passenger cars, over 40,000 remained in private hands. Among the automobiles owned by socialised institutions, the most numerous were Škodas (approximately 5,000) and Warszawas (4,700). In total, they constituted almost half of all "state" cars. Other brands were much less common. There were 1,400 Fiats, 750

---

944 J. Ender, "Co zrobić z samochodami po-UNRRO-wskimi?" *Motor* 1958, no. 22, p. 3.
945 AAN, PKPG, sign. 378, Notatka w sprawie ilości i stanu samochodów osobowych, Warszawa, [July 1952], pp. 24–25.

Pobedas, 600 Citroëns, 650 Chevrolets, and 400 East German DKWs (the abbreviation was jokingly developed as "*dykta, klej, woda*"—plywood, glue, water—in reference to the poor quality of the bodywork). Taken together, these brands accounted for almost 65% of state passenger cars. The remaining 7,500 cars came from over 70 different brands. We can therefore assume that some (or perhaps even most) of them were represented by single specimens. The situation was further complicated by the fact that these statistics did not include either models or subtypes. Evidently, over a decade of attempts to standardise the state automobile fleet had led to nothing.

Things did not look so bleak compared to privately owned passenger cars. Here, the variety of brands was much greater: private users drove automobiles produced by 113 different companies. The most popular were DKW and IFA, whose number was estimated at 3,500. The next places were taken by Mercedes and Warszawa (2,000 units each), Wartburg (1,200 units), Fiat (600 units), BMW (300 units), and Citroën (240 units). However, these accounted for less than 16% of all passenger cars in private hands. The remaining 34,400 came from over a hundred different brands (here, too, the statistics did not specify models and types). As a result, Polish road traffic in the late 1950s could be a dizzying sight, even if only the brands riding on roads across the nation are taken into account. Additionally, Poles drove—unsurprisingly, given political and economic conditions—automobiles whose average age was one of the highest in Europe: around 15 years, compared to around 4 years for the rest of the continent. The fact that Polish drivers continued to use such a huge number of makes, models, and types meant that maintaining them in service required great effort. As journalist Olgierd Budrewicz put it, "[t]he notorious shortage of spare parts forced automobile owners to make completely original design modifications. Many older cars are true Michurin crossbreeds, with only the outside resemblance to their factory prototypes."[946]

At the beginning of the 1960s, the share of particular brands in the automobile fleet began to slowly change. Old, prewar cars were disposed of and replaced by cars of Polish production, as well as imports, mainly from other countries of the Eastern Bloc. Questionnaires that the editors of *Motor* prepared for the readers provide an interesting material for analysis for this

---

[946] Ibid.

period. With some exaggeration, they called them surveys, but even if the respondents did not meet the requirements of a representative sample, it is still an important source, the analysis of which allows us to reconstruct to a certain degree the share of car brands used by Poles in the period in question. Among the most popular types of cars, the "survey" from 1960 names: Syrena, Warszawa, Škoda (model 440, i.e. the popular Spartak), Moskvitch, Fiat 600, and the P-70. These makes and models were indicated by 61% of readers. It is worth noting the appearance of the Żerań-produced Syrena on the list, as well as imported Fiats and Moskvitches. Among the remaining, less frequently mentioned automobiles, the most numerous were: DKW, Opel, Fiat (mainly model 1100), older Škoda models (1101 and 1102), Mercedes (170 V) and Citroëns (11BL).[947] Two issues are worth emphasising here. First, the latter group included cars that were designated as "typical" in the late 1940s. Second, the infamous, fearsome Citroën Légère, the basic vehicle of the Ministry of Public Security, also appeared there.[948] Therefore, the path these cars took into private hands probably led from the state fleet.

In 1965, *Motor* published another study. This time, results showed a fairly clear favourite among domestic car owners. Over 15% of those who answered the survey had a Syrena. Further places were taken by: Škoda (6.4%), Wartburg (5.5%), Trabant (3.4%), Moskvitch (2.7%), and Warszawa (1.8%). Only 1% of respondents indicated that they owned the smallest Polish automobile, the Mikrus.[949]

Survey research conducted by Zdzisław Krasiński's team from Poznań in the early 1970s showed a similar trend—a clear supremacy of Polish automobiles among the public.[950] More than half of city residents (54.1%) drove

---

947 "Krajowa ankieta motoryzacyjnego 'Instytutu Gallupa'," p. 3.

948 See: L. H. Siegelbaum, *Cars for Comrades*, p. 201.

949 L. Rejewski, "Dlaczego kupują?" *Motor* 1965, no. 51/52, p. 2.

950 When constructing the sample, the territory of Poland was divided into three sections: 1) the most affluent section, represented by independent voivodeship capitals; 2) the moderately affluent section, which included seven voivodeships; and 3) the least economically developed group (also seven voivodeships). Three voivodeships were excluded from the research: *zielonogórskie* and *koszalińskie*, which were considered intermediate cases, and *szczecińskie*, for organisational reasons. During the research, changes were introduced: the share of surveys from the most affluent regions was reduced in comparison to those from the less developed regions. The reason was "the

cars manufactured in Żerań. Most of them were Syrenas, then Big Fiats and Warszawas. Further down the list were foreign small-engine cars: Trabants and Zastavas. Subsequent places were taken by Škodas, Moskvitches, and Wartburgs. Only 9% of respondents indicated "other," which usually meant Western brands. The Syrena was the undisputed leader in rural areas, where it was indicated by over 34% of respondents; 25% owned a Warszawa and 9.1%, a Moskvitch, while the next positions were taken by Škodas, "small-engine cars," Big Fiats, Wartburgs, and "others."[951] The research on car ownership in Poland conducted by Krasiński's team reveals one more interesting factor. A significant percentage of owners of "cheap" car brands (Syrena, Trabant, Zastava) had purchased their vehicle within the previous 7–8 years, which means it was probably their first car. For owners of more expensive models (Big Fiat, Warszawa, Western cars), the vehicle was likely pre-owned.[952]

Unfortunately, it is very difficult to obtain specific figures on the ownership of individual makes by Poles. While information on the number of automobiles produced in Poland is still easily available (e.g. through official FSO statistics), foreign vehicles present great difficulties, especially for the 1950s and early 1960s. Vehicles were registered in the transport departments of the provincial national councils, but their registries have proven difficult to access. GUS did not collect such detailed statistics. Moreover, it should be noted that information on the number of private passenger cars began to appear in the "Statistical Yearbooks" (*Rocznik statystyczny*) only in the mid-1960s.

It is much easier for the 1960s. For the period from 1962, there are very detailed statistics regarding foreign makes that were imported into Poland through so-called unaccounted-for trade, that is, privately. The lists prepared annually by the Central Customs Office shed a bit more light on the automobile fleet that Poles had at their disposal.

Starting in 1962 until 1970, over 27,000 vehicles were brought in from abroad as unaccounted-for imports (see Table 16). While in 1962, there were just over a thousand such vehicles, in the following years, this number systematically increased. Poles brought in the most units, as many as 6,198,

---

unwillingness to provide answers by respondents living in large voivoideship capitals, especially Warsaw"; Z. Krasiński, *Czynniki ekonomiczno-społeczne*, pp. 10–11.

951 Ibid., p. 98.

952 Ibid.

in 1969. However, in 1970, there was a significant decline: only slightly over 2,300 vehicles were privately imported into Poland, which was a direct result of the change in customs duties imposed on automobiles.

Table 16. Unaccounted-for importation of passenger cars in the years 1962–1970

Year	1962	1963	1964	1965	1966	1967	1968	1969	1970	Łącznie
Imports	1.100	1.075	1.536	2.319	2.866	5.061	5.587	6.198	2.374	27.116

Source: AAN, GUC, sign. 25/140, Kompendium Statystyczne Administracji Celnej 1946–1970, pp. 63–64.

The geographical distribution of imports is also very interesting. Apparently, passenger cars produced in West Germany already had the strongest position on the market at that time. Over the course of nine years, Poles brought over 17,000 of them. The most popular brands were: Volkswagen, Opel, Ford, and Mercedes (see Table 17).

Table 17. Unaccounted-for importation of passenger cars, according to make, in the years 1962–1970

Make	1962	1963	1964	1965	1966	1967	1968	1969	1970	Total
Volkswagen	188	214	298	638	1.035	1.571	2.042	2.160	572	8.718
Opel	136	154	215	328	410	655	470	320	132	2.820
Ford	109	89	221	413	364	632	548	656	222	3.254
Mercedes	51	58	73	138	167	324	306	300	159	1.576
DKW	7	13	12	23	22	30	37	46	5	195
BMW	2	5	6	14	37	133	139	140	43	519
NSU	-	-	1	5	11	34	74	120	32	277
Total West Germany	493	533	826	1.559	2.046	3.379	3.616	3.742	1.165	17.359
Simca	226	161	139	135	131	142	110	120	39	1.203
Peugeot	61	86	118	126	144	162	127	167	102	1.093
Renault	55	73	84	108	126	199	125	163	61	994
Citroën	12	8	11	16	17	25	34	35	26	184
Total France	354	328	352	385	418	528	396	485	228	3.474
Austin	2	9	8	23	32	35	47	50	69	275
Morris	4	5	9	23	18	30	41	40	42	212
Hillman	4	3	3	6	11	13	21	50	23	134

Make	1962	1963	1964	1965	1966	1967	1968	1969	1970	Total
Triumph	3	1	5	6	9	13	18	14	4	73
Vauxhall	3	2	3	4	4	5	7	14	7	49
Total Great Britain	16	20	28	62	74	96	134	168	145	743
Fiat/Italy	65	87	126	205	288	438	629	710	237	2.785
Volvo	2	1	9	28	44	173	184	137	84	662
Saab	1	-	-	2	7	13	11	20	2	56
Total Sweden	3	1	9	30	51	186	195	157	86	718
Chevrolet/USA	7	10	11	20	14	21	23	11	10	127
Moskvitch	69	78	75	141	205	193	309	420	178	1.668
Volga	9	30	28	25	36	42	78	120	76	444
Zaporożec	3	7	2	8	8	-	-	-	-	28
Total USSR	81	115	105	174	249	235	387	540	254	2.140
Wartburg	3	9	13	30	18	41	46	150	79	389
Trabant	6	7	11	20	14	1	3	24	5	91
Total East Germany	9	16	24	50	32	42	49	174	84	480
Škoda/ Czechoslovakia	15	13	24	25	18	22	39	100	50	306
Others	14	17	15	22	33	114	119	111	115	560

Source: AAN, GUC, sign. 25/140, Kompendium Statystyczne Administracji Celnej 1946–1970, p. 12.

Imports from other countries did not reach such impressive levels. During the period in question, 3,400 vehicles were imported from France—Simcas, Peugeots, Renaults, and Citroëns; from Italy came 2,700 Fiats; and from the USSR, 2,100 Moskvitches, Zaporozhets, and Volgas. It should be noted that private importers favoured vehicles produced in East Germany and in Czechoslovakia (480 and 306 units, respectively) less than those from Sweden (718 Saabs and Volvos) or Great Britain (734 Austins, Morrises, and others).[953]

The statistics for planned imports looked completely different. During the sixteen years between 1956 and 1970, Poland purchased over 157,000 foreign

953 See: AAN, Główny Urząd Ceł (hereafter: GUC), sign. 25/141, *Kompendium Statystyczne Administracji Celnej 1956–1974*, Warszawa 1975, pp. 129–130.

vehicles, of which over 131,000 were from other countries of the bloc. The largest number, over 55,000, came from East Germany; 39,000 from the Soviet Union; and 33,000 from Czechoslovakia (see Table 18).

Table 18. Official importation of passenger cars from communist countries in the years 1956–1970

Year	USSR	East Germany	Czechoslovakia	Total
1956	–	–	–	1.694
1957	255	1.155	555	5.416
1958	2.223	1.993	3.351	7.699
1959	2.985	715	2.065	5.871
1960	2.556	1.072	2.069	5.824
1961	2.149	1.504	3.165	7.146
1962	4.323	5.877	3.017	13.804
1963	2.409	5.213	2.983	10.833
1964	2.869	3.453	47	6.775
1965	2.935	10.173	2.222	21.905
1966	3.612	4.538	829	13.724
1967	2.838	4.318	1.824	16.236
1968	3.676	3.997	2.192	11.627
1969	2.835	4.048	4.583	12.900
1970	3.666	7.461	3.659	16.492
Total	39.331	55.579	32.546	157.946

Source: Rocznik Statystyczny 1963, p. 320; Rocznik Statystyczny 1965, p. 343; Rocznik Statystyczny 1971, p. 422.

Unfortunately, we do not have data that could show continuously the scale of official importation from capitalist countries. It is only possible to collect data for the late 1960s (see Table 19). The volume of import for the years 1967–1969 definitely confirms the primacy of official imports within the bloc. In that period, over 34,000 vehicles were purchased in countries belonging to the socialist camp. The most, over 12,000, came to Poland from East Germany. The USSR (9,300) and Czechoslovakia (8,500) were also important sources of imports. At the same time, just over 6,000 vehicles came to Poland from capitalist countries, mainly from France (2,595 units), Italy (1,947 units), and West Germany (just over a thousand units).

Table 19. Planned importation of passenger cars, 1967–1969

Year	Total	Import													
		Communist Countries						Capitalist Countries							
	[3+9]	Total	USSR	Czecho-slovakia	East Ger-many	Roma-nia	Yugo-slavia	Total	France	West Ger-many	Italy	Eng-land	Swe-den	Spain	Austria
1	2	3	4	5	6	7	8	9	10	11	12	13	14	15	16
1967	16.236	12.856	2.838	1.824	4.318	10	3.866	3.380	1.413	717	1.128	117	5		
1968	10.603	9.871	3.676	2.192	3.997	4	2	1.742	732	303	567	136		3	1
1969	12.840	11.905	2.835	4.583	4.048	457	2	935	450	226	252	2	2		3
Razem	39.679	34.632	9.349	8.599	12.363	471	3.870	6.057	2.595	1.246	1.947	255	7	3	4

Source: AAN, GUC, sign. 25/140, Kompendium statystyczne administracji celnej 1946–1970, p. 33.

As can be seen, the directions of both official and private imports complemented each other perfectly. If Poles could not buy an automobile produced, for example, in West Germany, they took matters into their own hands. In turn, very limited private imports from socialist countries were probably caused by "sufficient" access to cars produced there through official state channels.

The increasing number of vehicles and people authorised to drive them raises questions about the condition of roads in Poland. In 1960, the density index was 33.6 km/100 km^2, while five years later, it reached 37 km/100 km^2. However, almost a quarter of the roads retained unimproved surfaces, covered with gravel and cobblestones, unfavourable for automobile traffic. In the early 1970s, the density index rose to as high as 41.9 km/100 km^2. Compared to 1955, there were over 31,700 kilometres of new hard-surface roads.[954] However, the 1960s brought significant improvement in the type of surface. In 1960, there were 34,400 km of so-called improved hard-surface roads (covered with bricks, clinker, concrete, stone-concrete slabs, and bitumen), while in 1970, that value already passed 76,000 km. However, very large regional differences could still be observed (see Table 20). The situation was the worst in eastern regions of the country. The Lubelskie and Białostockie voivodeships had less than 30 km of hard-surface roads per 100 km^2 of area, while the Katowickie, Opolskie and Wrocławskie voivodeships had more than 50 km per 100 km^2. In comparison, the Krakowskie Voivodeship represented a particularly positive example, with a density index of 55.1 km/100 km^2, which placed it at the forefront of the country.

---

954 *Rocznik Statystyczny* 1971, p. 351.

Table 20. Roads with a hard surface in specific voivodeships in 1960 and 1970 (in km)

Voivodeship	Total				Total			
	In absolute numbers	Per 100 km²	About the surface		In absolute numbers	per 100 km²	About the surface	
			Improved	Unimproved			Improved	Unimproved
	1960				1970			
Poland overall	104.439	33.6	34.484	69.915	130.432	41.9	76.139	54.293
Białostockie	4.862	21.0	1.329	3.533	6.779	29.3	2.090	3.870
Bydgoskie	6.377	30.7	2.109	4.268	8.598	41.2	5.613	2.985
Gdańskie	4.398	40.0	1.630	2.759	4.803	43.5	3.030	1.773
Katowickie	3.977	41.8	1.921	2.056	4.966	52.0	3.531	1.435
Kieleckie	5.720	29.4	1.818	3.902	9.454	48.5	3.835	5.619
Koszalińskie	6.737	37.5	2.380	4.357	6.932	38.3	4.925	2.007
Krakowskie	5.681	37.0	1.480	4.201	8.456	55.1	4.451	4.005
Lubelskie	4.196	16.9	1.765	2.431	6.846	27.5	4.705	2.141
Łódzkie	6.269	36.7	1.516	4.753	8.457	49.5	3.517	4.940
Olsztyńskie	7.698	36.7	3.098	4.600	7.887	37.4	5.501	2.386
Opolskie	4.975	52.3	2.288	2.687	5.162	54.0	3.941	1.221
Poznańskie	10.481	39.2	2.663	7.818	11.937	44.5	6.549	5.388
Rzeszowskie	4.676	25.1	1.442	3.234	7.263	39.0	3.627	3.636
Szczecińskie	4.577	35.1	1.922	2.655	5.090	39.9	2.925	2.165
Warszawskie	7.496	25.5	2.923	4.573	11.224	38.2	5.884	5.340
Wrocławskie	10.689	56.8	4.176	6.513	10.794	57.1	7.345	3.449
Zielonogórskie	5.639	38.9	2.601	3.038	5.784	39.7	3.851	1.933

Source: Rocznik Statystyczny 1961, p. 241; Rocznik Statystyczny 1971, p. 351.

5.2 SAMs

> Dearest fellows!... I am overjoyed
> To share with you that at this time
> I finished building my newest toy
> The cheapest car—the SAM. So cheap!
> Simply a dream come true
> For those whose wages don't come through[955]

Poles wanted to drive their own cars. This is an indisputable fact. When in 1957, *Motor* conducted a survey among its readers entitled "What kind of car would I like to buy," it proved that Poles were willing to sacrifice a great deal just to be able to buy their own car. To the question, "How much can you save in three years to buy your own micro-car ... ?" 23.5% of respondents chose the value of 12,000 zlotys; 34.2%—24,000 zlotys; 22.4%—36,000 zlotys; and 19.9% pointed to 48,000 zlotys. Taking into account the average monthly earnings at that time (1,279 zlotys), this meant that Poles were prepared to make many concessions when it came to motoring, often at the expense of other pleasures. Respondents were also willing to give up better performance for a lower price. In turn, when asked: "Which of these can you do yourself: assembly, painting, or upholstery?" one reader replied: "Give us the engine and tires, we will do the rest ourselves."[956] As it turned out, these were prophetic words. In the 1950s, individually constructed vehicles were an interesting aspect of emerging individual motorisation. At that time, especially in the first half of the decade, it was often the only way to obtain the desired vehicle. Among the supporters of this idea was PZMot, under whose auspices the first competition of self-built cars was organised in 1953.

From the very beginning of its existence, the *Horyzonty Techniki* monthly was highly involved in helping home-grown designers, publishing technical articles that were intended to facilitate the construction of their own vehicles. It was there that the series entitled "Building a car" was published, authored by Witold Rychter. Three articles described step-by-step the construction

---

955 M. Załucki, "Sami dojdziemy," *Szpilki* 1960, no. 38, p. 6.
956 "Wyniki ankiety: Jaki samochodzik chciałbym kupić?" *Motor* 1957, no. 48, pp. 3–4.

of a simple car, which was named "Hortek" in honour of the magazine.[957] Amateur carmakers eagerly shared their experiences in building cars on their own with other readers.[958] Some of their works were truly interesting and had many ingenious solutions, such as the anti-theft protection in a Hortek built by a resident of Szczecin, who placed a button under the driver's seat that activated a sound signal turned off by a hidden switch.[959]

In 1958, Adam Słodowy published a book entitled *Budowa samochodu amatorskiego* (Construction of an amateur car), in which he guided do-it-yourself enthusiasts through the stages of building their own four-wheeled, and occasionally three-wheeled vehicle. In the text, he argued that, in fact, anyone could build a car, even people without "special skills or advanced knowledge of construction." The advantage was undoubtedly significantly lower costs; Słodowy maintained that the cost of materials used for construction, assembly work being done by oneself, would not exceed 15–20%, and in the case of a simplified design, even 10% of the cost of a factory car. One inconvenience was the time that one had to devote to building the car, which could even take several months in the worst case, although "working systematically, every day outside working hours, 4–6 hours a day, you can build a car or a micro-car over the few winter months." It should be added that the resulting car "is even more attractive because it is not mass produced."[960]

The idea of constructing one's own vehicle was strongly promoted by *Motor*. Beginning in October 1952, the weekly published a column entitled "Do you want to have your own car," which explained the principles of vehicle construction, and in subsequent issues, it included photos and descriptions of the more interesting constructions made by the readers.[961] From that moment on, these cars became known by the moniker "SAM", short for "Amateur Car of the *Motor* Weekly" ("*Samochód Amatorski Tygodnika 'Motor'*"). As had been the case with *Horyzonty Techniki*, *Motor* published articles explaining the principles of construction of this type of a car. In 1959, together with

957 W. Rychter, "Budujemy samochodzik," *Horyzonty Techniki* 1949, no. 10, pp. 441–443; ibid., no. 11, pp. 490–494, 505–505, and 528–532.

958 See, for example: *Horyzonty Techniki* 1952, no. 2, pp. 90–91; ibid., no. 3, p. 139.

959 *Horyzonty Techniki* 1952, no. 7/8, p. 368.

960 A. Słodowy, *Budowa samochodu amatorskiego*, Warszawa 1958, pp. 5 and 8.

961 "Czy chcesz mieć własny samochód?" *Motor* 1952, no. 25, p. 5; J. Olczyk, "Sam na trzech kółkach. 'Cyklop'," *Motor* 1952, no. 29, p. 9.

Przekrój and Wydawnictwa Komunikacyjne, *Motor* announced a competition for the best SAM.[962] The plan was to award four constructors in total: one for the best two-wheeled vehicle (cash prize of 3,000 zlotys); one for a sports motorcycle (6,000 zlotys); one for a sports car (6,000 zlotys); and one for an unconventional solution (4,000 zlotys).[963] Around 200 vehicles entered the competition, of which 65 qualified for the next stage. The final took place on June 28 at Plac Defilad in Warsaw. The winner in the most prestigious category of SAM car was a vehicle constructed by two residents of Warsaw named Moldenhauer and Gawron. The award, sponsored by the Automotive Service of the MON, was a GAZ 67.[964] Among the winners was also the famous Rak: a SAM racing car which successfully took part in Polish track championships in the racing and sports car category, and which raced in Budapest during the International Grand Prix, where it competed with factory BMWs and Škodas.[965] The event ended with a parade of participants in the competition, which, despite unfavourable weather conditions (rain), was attended by throngs of interested Varsovians. The competition for the best SAM was warmly received by editors of *Horyzonty Techniki*, who saw it as an opportunity to find out what self-built cars looked like at the end of the 1950s, ten years after the first Horteks.[966] Among the vehicles invited to the competition finals were some whose external appearance did not differ much from the micro-cars popular in Western Europe at that time. However, most SAMs were fairly primitive designs, largely dependent on the availability of individual components.

Although it was clear that the promotion of constructing SAMs would in no way solve the problem of the motorisation of the Polish society, it was widely viewed as an opportunity to at least partially fulfil the dream of having one's own car, thus far realised only by a slim minority.[967] Various circles demanded that the state "make life a little easier" for private car

---

962 *Motor* 1959, no. 11, p. 3; *Przekrój* 1959, no. 727, p. 4. Already in 1957, the Kraków weekly extensively reported on the Western European fashion for micro-cars; see, for example: GK, "Auto-skuter czyli radość na kółkach," *Przekrój* 1957, no. 617, p. 20.

963 "6000 piechotą nie chodzi," *Motor* 1959, no. 17, p. 10.

964 "I ogólnopolski konkurs SAM-ów," *Motor* 1959, no. 228, pp. 8–9.

965 M. Kieta, "SAM-y bardzo przyjemny nałóg," *Przekrój* 1959, no. 744, pp. 6–7.

966 Z. Perzyński, "SAM na cenzurowanym," *Horyzonty Techniki* 1959, no. 9, p. 403.

967 Ibid., p. 407.

designers, for instance, by providing them with technical documentation of ready-made design solutions, as well as by enabling them to purchase basic elements: engines, gearboxes, clutches, etc. It was suggested that repositories of equipment destined for scrap, some of which was suitable for re-use, could provide them. The idea was taken up by the editors of *Motoryzacja*, who even suggested that the Automotive Industry Design Office develop and widely disseminate technical documentation of several basic types of SAMs. Meanwhile, state industry and cooperatives would take provide the basic elements necessary for this individual production. "Neither of these is impossible," *Motoryzacja* argued.[968]

Years later, Adam Słodowy recalled his own adventure with a SAM. It all began with an undamaged car headlight found in a scrap yard in 1946. After a few months, the engineer was already driving his own SAM, equipped with a single-cylinder, two-stroke engine from an East German DKW, capable of bringing the vehicle up to 40 km/h. The experiences he accumulated while building his own car resulted in the aforementioned guide. Despite a high print run, the first edition of the book sold out in the blink of an eye, and a year later, in 1959, a second edition was published.[969]

SAMs enjoyed a relatively long life. Even at the end of the 1960s, advertisements appeared in which the designers of these vehicles offered various types of components and parts for sale or exchange.[970]

5.3 The ruling class behind the wheel

In the USSR, a passer-by could guess with a high degree of certainty who the passenger of a car was based just on the make. Volgas, Chaikas, and the

---

968 "Ankieta Motoryzacji," p. 123.

969 In addition to the book mentioned here, Adam Słodowy wrote several other highly popular automotive titles: *Samochód bez tajemnic* (Warszawa 1966); *Jeżdżę samochodem Skoda 1000 MB* (Warszawa 1967); *Skoda 1000 MB, 1100 MB, 100, 110: technika jazdy, obsługa i usprawnienia* (Warszawa 1969); *Sam obsługuję samochód* (Warszawa 1969); *Usprawniam własny samochód* (Warszawa 1971). However, the biggest bestseller on this subject was the *Podręcznik kierowcy amatora* (Amateur driver's handbook), first published in 1952, which went through six editions, reaching over a quarter million copies.

970 See, for example: "Giełda przyjaciół," *Motor* 1969, no. 1, p. 11.

bulky ZIL limousines were assigned to specific functions and positions in the party apparatus and the state. Produced at the Likhachov plant, ZIL cars served only the most important people in the state. Meanwhile, Volgas and Chaikas were intended for the lower strata of the party nomenklatura. In turn, ordinary citizens drove Zaporozhets and Moskvitch cars. In communist Albania, a practically unmotorised country, the most important people in the country were given Mercedes cars, ministers drove Peugeots, and directors of various socialist institutions rode in Fiats 125p starting in the 1970s. Thus, the attempt to turn the car into just a means of transport and deprive it of all signs of social distinction, which was communist rulers' intention, came to nothing.[971]

The situation was similar in Poland. Back in the late 1970s, specific car makes and models were assigned to particular social groups. Engineers and members of the "free professions" most often drove cars of the class of a Big Fiat. In turn, workers and farmers usually made do with smaller, and therefore cheaper Syrenas or Fiats 126p.[972] One can well risk the assumption that the same was true of the preceding decade, except that instead of Fiat 126p, workers and farmers moved around primarily on motorcycles.

However, since the end of the 1940s, it was primarily members of the party apparatus or those in higher positions at various types of state institutions who constituted the core group among users of passenger cars. When the situation, began to change after 1956 and ordinary people gained increasing access to cars, members of the *nomenklatura,* that is the individuals who were appointed to the most crucial, strategic posts across the state apparatus, the economy, remained a privileged class. In virtually all countries of the Eastern Bloc, one of the most important privileges enjoyed by political and party elites was access to luxury goods, especially cars—as Lewis H. Siegelbaum describes it, "one of the most 'deficit' of commodities."[973] The parts of East Berlin where major state institutions were located came to be called "Volvograd" after the Swedish brand of cars popular among East German party activists.[974]

---

971 L. Gatejel, "The Common Heritage of the Socialist Car Culture," p. 147; B. Brzostek, "Szewroletariat," pp. 54–55.

972 *Rynek motoryzacyjny*, ed. Z. Krasiński, Warszawa 1980, p. 113.

973 L. H. Siegelbaum, *Cars for Comrades*, pp. 173, 204–205.

974 L. Gatejel, "The Common Heritage," p. 148.

In Poland, the official class was called the "Chevroletariat" (after the Chevrolet Fleetmaster cars popular in the 1940s and 1950s, the most striking vehicles of the state fleet). Karol Modzelewski recalled that his father's ministerial office came with the right to official cars with a chauffeur.[975] As a member of the Politburo of the PZPR, Roman Zambrowski had at his disposal a Chevrolet Impala and a Mercedes, and could also use on of several armoured ZIS cars.[976] Artur Starewicz recalled that the Mercedes cars used by Polish officials were referred to as "second Mercedesses." The "first" ones were at the disposal of the most important officials, and after reaching a certain mileage, they were handed over to lower-level officials.[977]

Figure 8. Western European cars in front of the Hotel Europejski, Warsaw, 1969, National Digital Archives, Grażyna Rutkowska, 3/40/0/5/53

975 K. Modzelewski, *Zajeździmy kobyłę historii. Wyznania poobijanego jeźdźca*, Warszawa 2013, pp. 67–68.

976 M. Szumiłło, *Roman Zambrowski 1909–1977*, Warszawa 2014, pp. 306–307. Cf. L. Tyrmand, *Dziennik 1954. Wersja oryginalna*, Warszawa 1999, p. 154.

977 Artur Starewicz's report for Jane Curry. I would like to thank Michał Przeperski for sharing this source.

However, the title of the greatest car enthusiast among Poland's ruling elite belonged to Józef Cyrankiewicz, the "eternal premier." According to Eleonora Syzdak and Bogdan Syzdak, "he loved fast driving. He was a reckless, but really wonderful driver." Cyrankiewicz's excellent skills in this area were also confirmed by the chauffeurs who drove other members of highest stratum of power in Poland. The Prime Minister usually drove himself; he did not allow his security to drive him around. He would often escape them as a joke, picking up hitchhikers along the way (most often women). When he crossed the speed limit and was stopped by the traffic police, he was often unrecognised and paid the fines. Mercedes was a brand he would always prefer, and it is commonly believed that he lobbied for the purchase of cars from the German manufacturer for Polish officials. Along with Artur Starewicz, Adam Rapacki, and Maria Rutkiewicz (Starewicz's wife), he was the first to test the East-West Route (Trasa WZ, The Six-Year Plan's key road investment, linking right-bank Warsaw with the left-bank districts across the Vistula) before its official opening. It is worth adding that all four of them travelled in Starewicz's small Fiat 500.[978] It is important to emphasise that the Polish communists did not share in the splendour—"automotive" or otherwise—with which Leonid Brezhnev, Josip Broz Tito, and Nicolae Ceaușescu surrounded themselves.[979]

When the London émigré press launched a vociferous attack in 1955 against the enormous lack of restraint among party officials in terms of access to cars and the extent to which they used them, one *Motor* journalist commented: "The claim that private cars belong to members of ... the 'communist elite' defies the laws of logic. After all, this 'communist elite'—in normal language—those in positions of responsibility, have official cars .... Why would they still need private cars?"[980] It is fair to say that that journalist was right, even if only partially. It would be more accurate (given the number of private cars in the mid-1950s) to say that few members of the political apparatus had

---

[978] E. Syzdak and B. Syzdak, *Zanim zostanie zapomniany*, Warszawa 1996, p. 242; Artura Starewicz's report for Jane Curry.

[979] Leonid Brezhnev had a dozen luxury cars of foreign brands in his private garage. They included, among others, a Rolls-Royce, a Cadillac, and a Mercedes; L. H. Siegelbaum, *Cars for Comrades*, p. 241; I. Berend, *Central and Eastern Europe 1944–1993: Detour from the periphery to the periphery*, Cambridge 1996, p. 45.

[980] T. Domaniewski, "Dziewięć bujd na resorach," *Motor* 1956, no. 1, p. 4.

their own cars, and most of those who were entitled to official vehicles used them freely, also for private matters.

The unrestrained use of state-owned cars was a major charge directed against the authorities both in the 1950s (as already mentioned) and in the following decade, but the problem was not specific to Poland. In virtually all Eastern Bloc countries, official cars became de facto private vehicles. Disciplinary actions were taken often in each of those states, but they usually yielded no results. The Hungarian case has been the subject of some research; after the events of 1956, particularly great significance was attached in that country to breaking with the common practices of the party apparatus of the Rákosi era, including the use of official cars for private matters. In early 1957, significant restrictions were put in place on, for example, the mileage of official cars, and all costs resulting from using them for private purposes were to be covered by the users. That these changes were grossly ineffective can be seen from statistics on expenses on official cars: in 1958, 16 out of 18 committees (equivalent to voivodeships) exceeded the annual budget for this purpose. Moreover, party oversight bodies stated in their reports that the cars were being used in an uneconomic and uncoordinated manner, and most of the costs resulting from private use (incidentally, very frequent) were not covered by the party officials. They usually attempted to hide such use by falsifying travel documents (for example, vehicle logs or fuel bills).[981]

The Polish case was not very distinct from those of other Eastern European countries. In an anonymous letter to the Polish Radio from 1951, a concerned employee of the Central School of the State Machine Centres and Production Cooperatives in the Ursynów district of Warsaw wrote: "The institution grants a delegation allowance for a chauffeur who takes the director's family home for the holidays from Konstancin to Wyszków through Radzymin and back in an official car … . The Secretary of the school, P[…] Ryszard, also drove an official car through Skierniewice to Łowicz and back … in private matters—with the consent of director B[…]. In addition, director B[…] puts the car from 6.30 to 10.30 am at the disposal of his wife, who is not an employee of our institution."[982]

981 For more on this subject, see G. Péteri, "Alternative modernity?," p. 49ff.

982 AAN, KC PZPR, sign. 237/XXV-4, Wyjątki z listów, nr 4, Warszawa, 31 V 1951 r., p. 40.

At a time when almost every minute of downtime at work was converted into tons of coal or steel unproduced, some also started to look at the use of official cars in this way. Writing in *Motoryzacja*, in a reality where it was commonly understood that chauffeurs of official cars made money on the side by illegally trading fuel or giving rides to other people, Jan Bujniewicz reflected:

> When walking around the city during or after working hours, one sees rows of well-parked official cars, in front of the buildings of ministries, central management offices, or the seats of social organisations and trade unions, waiting to whisk away directors or employees of various institutions to deal with urgent business matters. There is apparent movement in these columns of cars during working hours—some leave, others arrive, but only in exceptional cases do the lines of waiting vehicles shrink to a few cars, and they soon form again into a large line of shiny machines. Such scenes, which last for hours, are a major sight in many prominent places in Warsaw. ... Should we not consider when and who will take the trouble to calculate how many high-value cars that could be used for urgent economic and administrative needs are permanently immobilised in Warsaw in this way?[983]

It was common knowledge that chauffeurs of official cars made money on the side by illegally trading fuel or giving rides to other people.

After October 1956, attempts were made to stop these abuses, but they were usually unsuccessful. Władysław Gomułka tried to eliminate these practices, which put the regime in a bad light, through frequent savings campaigns and inspections, but his efforts brought little results. In 1963, Wróblewski wrote that while only "the most impudent" drivers of official cars sold petrol and car parts, "everyone smuggles passengers": "Truth be told, one can hardly demand that the elementary sense of economics not rebel when a car stands idle for hours. ... A passenger who is in a hurry doesn't care who he pays the 15 zlotys to."[984]

---

983 J. Bujniewicz, "Samochód służbowy czy taksówka (artykuł dyskusyjny)," *Motoryzacja* 1955, no. 7, pp. 216–217.

984 AKW, "Cień za kierownicą," *Polityka* 1963, no. 49, p. 2.

Figure 9. Cars parked in front of the Sejm building, Warsaw, 1956, National Digital Archives, Zbyszko Siemaszko, 3/51/0/2.1/27

At the end of 1967, the number of official cars in Poland exceeded 27,000. Almost 10% of them were in Warsaw. The Ministries of Construction (311), Health and Care (219), and Machinery and Industry (158) had the most. Looking for savings within the political administration, officials decided to recalculate the number of car access privileges. Two acts—resolution no. 219 of the Council of Ministers from December 1967 and order of February 1968 of the Ministry of Transportation—were intended to improve the management of official passenger cars. Wherever the need for a car could not be justified, access to the car was revoked. However, where it was retained, a financial limit of 100,000 zlotys per year was introduced for the maintenance of cars and drivers and the purchase of fuel. The impact of these actions was quite significant: 4,500 car privileges were removed, as many as 1,580 in the capital alone. At the same time, a resolution passed in December 1967 made it easier to purchase cars for use as official vehicles. Directors, managers, and presidents of various institutions, as well as people practicing the professions of agronomist, veterinarian, or inspector, could now expect the process of purchasing a vehicle (in an instalment plan with the PKO) to be expedited. For the use of these cars for official purposes, they received an equivalent of 2.3 zlotys per km, though the car's maximum monthly mileage could not exceed 1,000 km.[985]

In the late 1960s and early 1970s, attempts to find savings in this area were also made in Romania and the USSR. Members of the Romanian *nomenklatura* were encouraged to buy Dacias produced in Mioveni, which they would also use as official cars, and to that end, the state agreed to provide fuel and servicing for free. However, this solution turned out to be unacceptable, because officials were afraid that the ordinary Dacia would reduce their status, putting them on an equal footing with ordinary citizens, who increasingly drove cars of this make. An identical situation took place in the USSR, where the proposal that the *nomenklatura* exchange its worn-out, fuel-hungry limousines (Pobedas and Volgas, still commonly used in the 1950s and early 1960s) for Zhigulis and Moskvitches was met with loud criticism from its members, especially older ones.[986]

5.4 "For god's sake, think it through": accidents, safety, legislation

As motorisation advanced, victims of the car began to outnumber those of the railways or horse-carts. Automobile accidents were among the top ten causes of death in the United States in the late 1920s. In France, automobiles overtook horse-drawn carriages as the leading cause of road fatalities in 1924. More than four decades later, in its report from fifteen developing countries,

985 B. W. Olszewska, "Operacja Limit," *Polityka* 1969, no. 42, p. 5.

986 L. Gatejel, "Appealing for a Car," pp. 134–135.

the World Health Organisation showed that 17% of all deaths were the result of incidents involving cars. More people died only from enteritis.[987]

A survey on road safety conducted by the Center for Public Opinion and Program Studies (Ośrodek Badania Opinii Publicznej i Studiów Programowych OBOPiSP) in 1970 showed that only a quarter of respondents felt safe on city streets; two-thirds of respondents claimed to have the thought that they might be in an accident before going on the road.[988] In August 1946, Witold Rychter wrote in *Motoryzacja*: "I have recently driven a few thousand kilometres around Poland, but I cursed and annoyed myself enough for more than ten thousand kilometers."[989] Driving on Polish roads right after the war was certainly not an easy task. Even apart from damaged road surfaces and the small number of available cars, the scale of problems faced by drivers was immense.

A delegation of Czech and Slovak writers visiting Poland were delighted with what they found: the incredible pace of reconstruction, which continued even at night; the wonderful Kraków, filled with horse-drawn carriages. The only thing that scared them was the habits of Polish drivers. To our southern neighbours, it clearly resembled the way Russians drove on local roads in the immediate postwar period. Poles drove the same way: they moved quickly, ignoring regulations, riding in the middle of the road and passing other vehicles both on the right and on the left. This was true especially of Warsaw.[990] An almost identical observation can be found in the memoirs of Marian Sękowski, who began work as a driver for the State Motor Transport

987 J. Foreman-Peck, "Death on the Roads: Changing National Responses to Motor Accidents," in: *The Economic and Social Effects of the Spread of Motor Vehicles*, ed. T. Barker, London 1987, pp. 264–290.

988 S. Szostkiewicz, *Bezpieczeństwo na drogach publicznych (Wstępny raport z badań)*, Warszawa 1970, p. 3; *idem*, "Bezpieczeństwo na drogach publicznych w opinii społecznej," in: *Problemy bezpieczeństwa ruchu drogowego. Konferencja naukowo-techniczna*, Warszawa 1971, p. 524.

989 W. Rychter, "Precz z drogowym bałaganem!" *Motoryzacja* 1946, no. 1, p. 12.

990 A. C. Nor [Josef Kaván], *Cesta do Polska*, Praha 1947, p. 93ff. Interestingly, just after hostilities ended, in early June 1945, the commander of the garrison of Warsaw, Col. Józef Sokólski, wrote: "The safety conditions of the movement of motor vehicles within the capital city of Warsaw in the period from June 1 to the present day have improved significantly because not a single disaster was registered during that time"; AAN, URM, sign. 5/39, Rozkaz nr 17, Warszawa, 9 VI 1945 r., p. 54.

Company right after the war. Driving conditions were very difficult: "Military drivers, who drove mostly under the influence of alcohol, followed no regulations, and they drove massive military trucks. You had to move out of their way. Having the national flag on your bumper was no protection against collision."[991] This was echoed by Maciej Bernhardt, who also drew attention to the Soviet kings of the road.[992] In his diary, Leopold Tyrmand described the behaviour of chauffeurs of state officials:

> [I]ncreased traffic of limousines of party dignitaries, among which rush, rumbling dully, armored limousines of the highest Politburo notables. These huge, black Škodas are the terror of Warsaw drivers. The power of their engine is equal to the power of a tank. They rush down Nowy Świat, completely disregarding the rules of the road. This is how the cars of gangster bosses used to drive through the streets of Chicago during their rule over that city, just as heavy with protective armor that cannot be penetrated by an automatic machine gun.[993]

A reading of the daily press from that period only confirms the belief that this was the norm. Here are just some of the titles of articles that appeared within less than two weeks in June 1946: "Anarchy on the streets of Warsaw"; "A disturbing increase in accidents"; "A car rolls over on Marszałkowska Street"; "Numerous car accidents are the fault of drivers and chauffeurs"; and "Do not exceed the speed limit."[994] As one author rightly noted, "accident reports do not include collisions on [non-urban] roads due to insufficient communication with urban centers. Things are probably even worse on [these] roads."[995] A year later, at an inter-party meeting of the PPR and PPS, the issue of car accidents and road traffic was on the agenda. As in June 1946, the first summer months of 1947 were full of serious collisions, often with fatal consequences. As an analysis carried out at the meeting indicated, the main problem—apart from "such objective causes as the poor condition of the automobile fleet [and] the lack of an appropriate number of regulatory

991 M. Sękowski, *Pamiętnik warszawskiego taksówkarza*, Warszawa 1985, p. 408.

992 M. Bernhardt, *Z Miodowej na Bracką. Opowieść powstańca warszawskiego*, part 2, Kraków 2012, p. 54.

993 L. Tyrmand, *Dziennik 1954*, p. 247.

994 *Rzeczpospolita*, 12, 17, 22 i June 30, 1946.

995 T. G., "Wolna trybuna. Jak karać piratów drogowych," *Motoryzacja* 1946, no. 1, p. 16.

devices in cities"—was "drinking and widespread non-compliance with traffic regulations among drivers."[996] Rychter made similar observations: "I am afraid," he wrote, "that road traffic, which is developing at a dizzying pace, will be thrown completely out of whack and once that happens, in a year's time, only someone hungry for thrills or suicidal will want to be on the road." The young and therefore inexperienced drivers posed a particular threat; Rychter called them "brats" on wheels who think the road was built only for them and have no time for anyone or anything, least of all the state-owned car they are driving."[997]

Various control bodies were tasked with supervising road traffic. As mentioned by Rychter, these included the Citizens' Militia, Main Road Inspection, the military, and ad hoc special inspection teams. For the most part, the inspectors checked the documents of both the car and the driver. The technical condition of the car, and even the driver's sobriety were checked much less often, which was probably due to the limitations of knowledge of the inspectors.[998] At the meeting of the PPR and PPS on road safety mentioned above, it was proposed that all policemen be trained in traffic rules and equipped with means of transport.[999] Especially the first two or three postwar years were exceptional in this respect, because the troubled Polish provinces were still particularly dangerous for car users. Due to the limitations of the fleet, each car was worth its weight in gold. Vehicles were frequently confiscated under the pretext of a routine inspection. This was done by "various civil, military, and public security authorities, in short—organisations with weapons in their possession." There were cases in which cars became the loot of the so-called forest bands: "Cars were increasingly hijacked into the surrounding forests, where tyres were taken off and engines were dismantled and then sold to the local population," where they probably served as power generators. Such situations were recorded by a resident of the then-district

996 AAN, KC PPR, sign. 295/XI-81 (mf 2315/15), Wytyczne międzypartyjnej narady PPR i PPS w sprawie walki z wypadkami samochodowymi z 31 VII 1947 r., p. 158.

997 W. Rychter, "Precz z drogowym bałaganem," p. 13.

998 Ibid., pp. 12–13.

999 AAN, KC PZPR, sign. 295/XI-81 (mf 2315/15), Wytyczne międzypartyjnej narady PPR i PPS, p. 159.

of Radom.[1000] Cars were oftentimes taken by Soviet soldiers.[1001] In May 1947, the Central Board of the Textile Industry complained that its DKW had been removed by an unidentified office. As it turned out, this case had been going on since 1945, but despite continuous correspondence, it was still not known who actually took the car.[1002]

The increase in the number of cars on the road and the resulting intensification of traffic further worsened the already difficult situation on the roads. An article published in *Motoryzacja* in 1955 states: "Strongly-built trucks and buses behave differently in street traffic, especially at intersections, than light passenger cars or vans. They tend to barge in, especially buses. … Horse carts ride one after the other, and the drivers either sleep on their carts or chatter carelessly at the top or bottom of a long line of vehicles. … However, individual drivers 'barge in', as the drivers put it, regardless of the arrangement of other vehicles at the given moment."[1003] A journalist at *Więź* described Poland's road reality in the early 1960s thusly: "Our drivers are pirates, murderers, and drunkards, and it is always them and only them who are to blame. The wheels crush innocent victims, underage children, weak women and old men—in a word, 'normal people', that is, pedestrians. There is almost always a monster behind the wheel."[1004] In turn, a *Motor* reader wrote in a letter to the editor: "I do about 2,000 kilometers a month. I drive in constant fear because of the enormous danger lurking at every step or metre of road. … [D]rivers go about drunk, … do not obey the rules, … drive with total recklessness."[1005] One can conclude that the above descriptions reflect the realities on the road at that time quite well.

1000 J. Boniecki, "Pierwsze dziesięciolecie, Plon konkursu pamiętnikarskiego Moje trzydziestolecie," Wojewódzka Biblioteka Publiczna w Kielcach, sign. Ręk. 138/16, p. 7.
1001 Ibid.
1002 Ibid., [Informacja], Warszawa, 19 V 1947 r., unnumbered pages.
1003 Z. Hiller, "Ruch uliczny widziany oczami kierowcy," *Motoryzacja* 1955, no. 6, p. 178.
1004 J. Wit, "Pod czterema kółkami…," *Więź* 1961, no. 4, p. 148 (quoted in B. Brzostek, *Za progiem. Codzienność w przestrzeni publicznej Warszawy lat 1955–1970*, Warszawa 2007, p. 328).
1005 "Nie skutki lecz przyczyny," *Motor* 1966, no. 46, p. 2.

Figure 10. Intersection of Nowy Świat Street and Jerozolimskie Avenue, Warsaw, 1955, National Digital Archives, Zbyszko Siemaszko, 3/51/0/12.5/597

In the 1950s and 1960s, Polish roads presented an interesting and unique image compared to Europe. For example, Bohdan Tomaszewski mentions that, in addition to motor vehicles, there were various other "unnatural obstacles on the roads": wagons, cows, children playing football, flocks of geese, cyclists and motorcyclists going in circles "who, moreover, often ride 'doped up' on Sunday evenings," chickens and dogs, and pedestrians.[1006]

1006 B. Tomaszewski, "Pani w zielonym kapeluszu," *Kultura* 1965, no. 29, p. 11.

Beyond motor vehicles, both four- and two-wheeled, horse-cart played an important part.[1007] In 1972, their number was estimated at 2 million, while there were only 1.3 million four-wheeled vehicles, only 656,000 of which were passenger cars.[1008] In the first half of 1963, 3,158 horse-drivers were fined in Łódź, while the number of officially registered horse carts in the Transport Department of the Praesidium of the local Municipal National Council amounted to just over half thousand. This meant that each of them was fined at least once a month.[1009]

In early 1956, Rychter wrote that "automobile accidents are multiplying at an alarming rate," and in subsequent years, the situation became even worse.[1010] Between 1955 and 1970, 18,500 people died in 187,799 accidents, and over 170,000 were injured (see Table 21). In 1970, the State Insurance Company (PZU) paid out over 1 billion zlotys from compulsory motor insurances and voluntary motor insurances for damage resulting from road accidents, while in 1967 this amount was 678.4 million zlotys.[1011]

1007 See: B. Brzostek, *Za progiem*, pp. 320–321.

1008 AAN, KC PZPR, sign. XI/898, Informacja o stanie bezpieczeństwa ruchu drogowego w 1972 roku, maj 1973 r., p. 46.

1009 "Kodeks drogowy w oczach społeczeństwa," *Zagadnienia Karno-Administracyjne* 1963, no. 4/5, p. 120.

1010 W. Rychter, "Analiza wypadków jako podstawa do akcji zapobiegawczej," *Motoryzacja* 1956, no. 2, p. 36.

1011 Third-party liability insurance for motor vehicle owners was compulsory at the time in most countries on both sides of the Iron Curtain. The form it took varied. In some countries, the obligation was imposed on all car owners, while in others, it applied only to those engaged in the commercial transport of goods and passengers. In the USA in the late 1960s, only three states (Massachusetts, New York, and North Carolina) required third-party liability insurance for private owners of passenger cars. Another form involved paying an appropriate amount of money as a deposit in the event of a road accident; AAN, Komisja Planowania przy Radzie Ministrów (hereafter: KPpRM), sign. 41/17, Uzasadnienie projektu rozporządzenia Rady Ministrów w sprawie obowiązkowych ubezpieczeń następstw nieszczęśliwych wypadków i odpowiedzialności cywilnej z ruchu pojazdów mechanicznych, Warszawa, [July 1958], unnumbered pages.; M. B., "Ubezpieczenie pojazdów samochodowych w USA," *Wiadomości Ubezpieczeniowe* 1968, no. 12, p. 21. In postwar Poland, compulsory civil liability insurance for means of transport was introduced on January 1, 1962, when the regulation of the Council of Ministers on this matter came into force (Dz. U. 1961, no. 55, pos. 307). Previously, people who carried out licenced commercial transport of goods and passengers had to have an insurance of this kind, while others could

Table 21 Number of accidents in the years 1955–1970

Year	Accidents	Killed	Injured
1955	11.205	1.481	6.165
1956	16.132	1.621	9.484
1957	16.651	1.875	11.134
1958	20.574	1.769	13.441
1959	22.858	1.963	17.786
1960	27.642	2.009	21.254
1961	23.986	2.525	22.703
1962	24.059	2.253	22.207
1963	23.540	2.354	22.580
1964	21.937	2.313	20.798
1965	22.505	2.475	20.700
1966	24.987	2.741	23.283
1967	29.825	2.997	27.290

(Continued)

acquire it if they wished: in 1961, approximately 100,000 drivers had the insurance. At that time, the premium for a car capable of transporting 3 to 5 people was 972 zlotys per year. Army and militia vehicles were excluded from the compulsory third-party liability insurance. It is worth noting that the Act of March 28, 1952 on state insurance provided for compulsory civil liability insurance for means of transportation. It was anticipated that it would be introduced by a regulation of the Council of Ministers, which, however, never materialised; Dz. U. 1951, no. 4, pos. 26; "Jak kalkulowano wysokość składek ubezpieczeniowych," *Motor* 1962, no. 12, p. 10; C. Mikołajczyk, "W sprawie obowiązkowego ubezpieczenia w komunikacji," *Wiadomości Ubezpieczeniowe* 1957, no. 5, pp. 10–15. As of 1961, third-party liability and accident insurance rates depended on vehicle size. For the smallest vehicles (up to two passengers and 499 cm^3 engine displacement) the annual premium was 550 zlotys; for medium-sized vehicles (3–5 passengers), it was 750 zlotys; and for the largest vehicles (over 5 passengers), as much as 900 zlotys. The annual fee was due in January. However, in 1962, this turned out to be extremely problematic, because many people who had voluntarily bought a third-party liability insurance in previous years hoped that some of the unused premiums would be credited to their new insurance. This did not happen until the Ministry of Finance determined that part of the money would be returned; "Składki ubezpieczeniowe," *Motor* 1961, no. 53, p. 11; K. Goździewski, "Ubezpieczeni contra PZU czy odwrotnie?" *Motor* 1962, no. 8, p. 4. The cost of the optional comprehensive cover insurance differed depending on the engine displacement—from 500 zlotys to 3,500 zlotys; J. Flisek, "Dlaczego auto-casco nie jest popularne," *Motor* 1963, no. 48, p. 3; H. Piotrowski, "Ocena stanu bezpieczeństwa drogowego w Polsce w latach 1964–1970," in: *Problemy bezpieczeństwa ruchu drogowego*, p. 14.

Table 21. *(Continued)*

Year	Accidents	Killed	Injured
1968	32.137	3.424	29.442
1969	36.532	3.418	34.917
1970	41.813	3.446	34.398
Total	187.799	18.501	170.030

Source: "Na miłość boską—Zastanówcie się!" Motor 1957, no. 14, p. 4; Z.S., "SOS naszych dróg. Co 30 minut—wypadek, co 5 godzin ginie człowiek," Motor 1958, no. 15, p. 4; W. Płaza, "Wypadki drogowe w Polsce w roku 1959," Motor 1960, no. 12, p. 10; A. Rostocki, "Motoryzacja w liczbach. Sami nie wiemy co posiadamy," Motor 1962, no. 1, p. 3; "Wypadki w 1961 r.," Motor 1962, no. 9, p. 11; B. Sosień, "Smutny bilans jednego roku," Motor 1964, no. 7, p. 3; (KG), "Więcej pojazdów—mniej wypadków. Stan bezpieczeństwa ruchu drogowego w latach 1961–1964," Motor 1965, no. 28, p. 3.

The year 1961 was particularly tragic. In that year, for every 10,000 motor vehicles, there were 192 accidents, resulting in over 20 fatalities—a sad record for the period between the end of World War II and the end of 1970. Early in the next decade, that indicator, although still high, never came close to reaching the 1961 level (see Table 22).

Table 22. Number of accidents and their victims (killed and injured) per 10,000 motor vehicles in the years 1961–1970

Year	Per 10.000 motor vehicles					
	Number of accidents		Number killed		Number injured	
	total	1961=100	total	1961=100	total	1961=100
1961	192.4	100	20.3	100	182.1	100
1962	170.5	88.7	16.1	79.3	157.1	86.2
1963	139.3	72.5	14.3	70.4	133.6	73.3
1964	117.0	60.7	12.3	60.6	111.0	61.0
1965	111.6	58.0	12.3	60.6	102.6	56.2
1966	112.9	59.7	12.4	61.0	105.2	57.7
1967	126.4	65.7	12.7	62.5	115.6	63.4
1968	127.4	66.3	13.6	67.0	116.7	64.0
1969	136.9	71.1	12.8	63.0	119.6	65.6
1970	146.8	74.6	12.1	59.2	120.8	66.4

Source: M. Kotula, "Dane liczbowe dotyczące stanu bezpieczeństwa ruchu drogowego w Polsce w latach 1961–1970," in: Problemy bezpieczeństwa ruchu drogowego. Konferencja naukowo-techniczna, Warszawa 1971, p. 561.

Poland led Europe in terms of the number of accidents per 1,000 motor vehicles. While in 1965, this indicator reached a value of 10.8 in Poland, in Western European countries, it was several times lower. For example, in West Germany, the rate was 1.2; in Austria, 1.3; in France, 1.0; and in Denmark, 0.9.[1012] Another, more reliable indicator—the number of people killed per 100 million kilometres travelled—also placed Poland among the worst in Europe; in the years 1966–1969, it averaged 15. At the same time, Spain recorded about fourteen deaths per 100 million kilometres, while in West Germany the value was as low as 8, in Great Britain—just 4, and in the USA—3. The reason for this state of affairs was certainly the many years of familiarity with motorisation in Western societies. Poland, like Spain, began to motorise relatively late, and the inhabitants of both countries were only just learning to live around two- and four-wheeled motor vehicles. Interestingly, in 1966, this indicator was higher in Spain than in Poland; however, while it systematically decreased in the following years in Franco's Spain, it increased in People's Poland.[1013]

The most common types of accidents were collisions between vehicles and with pedestrians. In the years 1961–1970, they accounted for over 60% of all road incidents (see Table 23).

Table 23. Accidents by type (1961–1970)

Year	Accidents total	Vehicle collisions		Hitting an obstacle		Hitting a pedestrian		Hitting an animal		Other	
		Total	%	Total	%	Total	%	Total	%	Total	%
1961	23.986	7.332	30.7	3.199	13.3	7.359	30.8	293	1.0	5.803	24.2
1962	24.059	7.242	30.0	2.964	12.3	7.211	30.0	242	1.2	6.400	26.5
1963	23.540	7.100	30.2	2.808	12.0	7.509	32.0	171	1.0	5.952	25.0
1964	21.937	6.795	31.0	2.503	11.4	7.151	32.6	139	0.8	5.349	24.2
1965	22.505	7.134	31.7	2.582	11.5	7.567	33.6	140	0.8	5.082	22.4
1966	24.987	7.707	31.0	2.618	10.5	8.985	36.0	188	0.5	5.489	22.0
1967	29.825	9.501	31.9	3.026	10.1	10.784	36.0	214	0.7	6.300	21.1

(Continued)

[1012] S. Dąbrowska, "Wypadki drogowe w latach 1965–1985," *Wiadomości Statystyczne* 1987, no. 3, p. 24.

[1013] M. Kotula, "Dane liczbowe dotyczące stanu bezpieczeństwa ruchu drogowego w Polsce w latach 1961–1970," in: *Problemy bezpieczeństwa ruchu drogowego*, p. 581.

Table 23. *(Continued)*

Year	Accidents total	Vehicle collisions		Hitting an obstacle		Hitting a pedestrian		Hitting an animal		Other	
		Total	%	Total	%	Total	%	Total	%	Total	%
1968	32.137	10.156	31.5	3.280	10.2	11.384	35.5	188	0.5	7.129	22.3
1969	36.532	12.305	33.8	3.687	10.1	12.012	33.0	241	0.4	8.287	22.7
1970	41.813	14.963	35.4	4.323	10.4	13.488	32.2	248	0.6	8.791	21.4

Source: own calculations based on M. Kotula, "Dane liczbowe dotyczące stanu bezpieczeństwa," p. 575.

Most of the victims died in accidents caused by motorcyclists and truck drivers. The former were responsible for 43.3% all fatalities in the years 1961–1970. The latter, in turn, enjoyed a particularly bad reputation.[1014] Drivers who abused alcohol and who worked long hours behind the wheel caused the death of over 4,100 people in the years 1961–1970 (see Table 24). Truck drivers were frequently satirised in the pages of *Szpilki*. Zbigniew Ziomecki showed them as bloodthirsty road menaces and Juliusz Puchalski as suppliers of innocent souls to Heaven.

Table 24. Perpetrators of fatal accidents 1961–1970

Year	Fatalities in accidents caused by drivers by vehicle type								
	bus	cars		motor-cycles	tractors	trams	bicycles	horse-drawn wagons	others
		trucks	passeger						
1961	48	375	186	1.004	117	17	152	72	18
1962	56	345	212	828	95	9	120	51	19
1963	52	329	206	872	71	12	144	72	16
1964	67	324	227	749	58	11	140	72	6
1965	74	355	232	741	84	11	120	43	11
1966	66	366	287	748	84	6	166	48	6
1967	79	439	320	731	88	27	190	51	14
1968	81	504	384	877	107	14	243	76	17
1969	117	584	404	750	105	9	251	79	5
1970	90	485	404	720	109	15	290	86	16

Source: M. Kotula, "Dane liczbowe dotyczące stanu bezpieczeństwa," p. 574.

1014 B. Brzostek, *Za progiem*, p. 321.

rys. Zbigniew Ziomecki
SZOFER W SAMOCHODZIE — RÓWNY WOJEWODZIE

rys. Juliusz Puchalski
— Szoferzy ciężarówek wejściem dla dostawców!...

Figure 11. (a) Zbigniew Ziomecki, „Szofer w samochodzie równy wojewodzie". (b) Juliusz Puchalski, „Niebo"

The "drunken base" of the PKS located on Ziemowita Street in Warsaw was described many times in contemporary press accounts.[1015] Moreover, according to the inhabitants of the capital, car depots and their surroundings (for example, on Radzymińska Street, where the Municipal Retail Trade had its depot) were particularly dangerous when it came to road accidents. Varsovians had an equally gloomy perspective on Świerczewskiego Street.[1016] Statistical data on road accidents and where they took place confirms that in cities, where traffic intensity was much higher than elsewhere, collisions occurred twice or even three times more often than in non-urban areas (see Table 25).

Table 25. Road accidents in and outside cities (1961–1970)

Year	Accidents on open roads					Accidents in cities and housing settlements						
	inter-provincial		other roads		%	provincial		district level		other		%
	total	%	total	%		total	%	total	%	total	%	
1961	2.352	10.4	5.405	22.6	33.0	5.985	25.0	4.848	20.2	5.396	21.8	67.0
1962	1.757	7.3	4.119	17.1	24.4	7.210	30.1	5.066	21.0	5.907	24.5	75.6
1963	1.495	6.4	3.942	16.7	23.1	7.080	30.1	5.041	21.4	5.982	25.4	76.9
1964	1.473	6.7	3.740	17.1	23.8	6.921	31.6	4.416	20.0	5.387	24.6	76.2
1965	1.681	7.5	3.973	17.6	25.1	7.232	32.2	4.213	18.7	5.406	24.0	74.9
1966	1.856	7.5	4.379	17.5	25.0	7.866	31.5	5.120	20.5	5.766	23.0	75.0
1967	2.228	7.4	5.096	17.1	24.5	9.920	33.2	6.011	20.1	6.570	22.2	75.5
1968	2.452	7.6	5.743	17.9	25.5	10.324	32.2	6.469	20.1	7.149	22.2	74.5
1969	3.002	8.2	6.539	17.9	26.1	11.874	32.5	7.237	19.8	7.880	21.6	73.9
1970	3.397	8.1	7.243	17.6	25.7	13.972	31.0	8.243	20.7	9.003	21.6	74.3

Source: M. Kotula, "Dane liczbowe dotyczące stanu bezpieczeństwa," p. 563.

It is, therefore, not surprising that, while travelling from Warsaw to Kraków in 1957, Jerzy Zawieyski noted in his diary: "In the afternoon, we left for Kraków by car. … The road to Kraków was empty. We passed at most five passenger cars and a few trucks. … We arrived in Kraków at 9 pm—that is, after five hours of driving with a half-hour rest in Kielce."[1017] A few years later,

---

1015 T. Stępień, "Śmierć czyha na ulicach," *Trybuna Wolności* 1955, no. 39, p. 4.

1016 Ibid.

1017 J. Zawieyski, *Dzienniki*, vol. 1: *Wybór z lat 1955–1959*, ed. A. Knyt with M. Czoch, Warszawa 2011, p. 378.

in 1961, when he had just returned from Paris, he wrote: "[I]t seems that the streets are empty, people are poorly and shabbily dressed, and there is no car traffic."[1018] A similar observation was made by Stefan "Kisiel" Kisielewski in a column for *Tygodnik Powszechny* after travelling with Leopold Tyrmand in his new Fiat from Warsaw to Gdańsk: "An idyllic, heavenly landscape, emptiness, silence—a car appears maybe once every half hour. It's an incomprehensible sight for a foreigner, and a disturbing one for a Pole."[1019] However, the situation changed as years passed, and soon, Stanisław Lem was writing about the increased car traffic, especially on the more popular routes: "[T]he road is empty outside the main routes …, but in five, six, seven years, things are going to be tighter. Even today, you can sense this on some routes, and when you drive, for example, to Krynica or Zakopane, the smell of exhaust is suitably suffocating."[1020]

Figure 12. The Wrocław-Zgorzelec highway, 1969, National Digital Archives, Zbyszko Siemaszko, 3/51/0/6.13/91

1018 *Idem*, *Dzienniki*, vol. 2: *Wybór z lat 1960–1969*, ed. A. Knyt with M. Czoch, Warszawa 2012, p. 111.

1019 Kisiel [Stefan Kisielewski], "Samochody, samochody," *Tygodnik Powszechny* 1958, no. 35, p. 3.

1020 S. Lem and S. Mrożek, *Listy 1956–1978*, trans. T. Lem and R. Niziołek, Kraków 2011, p. 460. At the same time, however, the writer's son Tomasz, who rode with his father in a Fiat around Kliny (where the Lems lived) in Kraków as a small child, recalled: "I don't remember ever passing another car"; T. Lem, *Awantury na tle powszechnego ciążenia*, Kraków 2009, pp. 58–59. See: L. H. Siegelbaum, *Car for Comrades*, p. 212.

The main causes of accidents in the 1960s included: drunk driving, excessive speed, illegal passing, and failure to comply with right-of-way rules (see Table 26). Throughout the decade, the share of driver errors ranged between 61.6% and 74.5%. Pedestrians were much less likely to be responsible for accidents (between 21.6% and 29%). In their case, the main type of error leading to an accident was violent incursion onto the road.

Table 26. Causes of road accidents in Poland 1961–1970

Year	Pedestrian errors				Driver errors														Vehicle technical deficiencies		Participation in accidents in %		
	Total		Incursions onto the road		Total		Type of error														Pedes-trian errors	Driver errors	Techni-cal defi-ciencies
							Drunk driving		Excessive speed		Illegal passing		Loss of control		Failure to yield		Other[a]						
		1961=100		%		1961=100		%		%		%		%		%		%		1961=100			
1961	5.163	100	1.921	37.2	17.474	100	4.019	23.0	2.855	16.3	2.710	15.5	1.028	5.9	1.501	8.6	250	1.4	748	100	73.0	21.6	3.14
1962	5.152	99.8	2.068	40.2	17.986	102.9	3.604	20.0	2.840	15.8	1.576	8.7	1.387	7.7	2.761	15.3	275	1.5	641	85.7	74.5	21.4	2.8
1963	5.532	107.2	1.832	33.0	17.084	97.8	3.315	19.5	2.512	14.7	1.501	8.8	1.388	8.2	2.738	16.1	196	1.1	640	85.7	72.5	23.5	2.7
1964	5.552	107.5	1.804	32.4	15.562	89.0	2.747	17.7	2.350	15.2	1.400	9.0	1.217	7.8	2.774	17.8	191	1.2	649	86.8	71.0	25.3	2.96
1965	5.934	114.9	2.419	40.8	15.577	89.2	2.416	15.5	2.375	15.4	1.493	9.6	1.393	8.9	2.806	18.0	194	1.2	712	95.2	69.2	26.4	3.16
1966	7.213	140.2	3.088	42.8	16.600	95.0	2.694	16.2	2.390	14.4	1.600	9.6	1.193	7.2	3.263	19.7	251	1.7	802	107.0	66.7	29.0	3.21
1967	8.536	165.3	3.900	45.7	19.967	114.8	2.813	14.1	2.979	14.9	1.902	9.5	1.329	6.7	4.064	20.5	278	1.4	1.015	135.6	67.0	28.6	3.4
1968	8.721	169.0	4.110	47.2	21.634	123.8	3.047	14.2	3.444	16.0	1.938	9.0	1.572	7.3	4.187	19.4	292	1.3	1.111	148.5	66.0	27.2	3.45
1969	9.392	182.0	4.325	46.2	25.409	145.3	3.076	12.1	3.820	15.1	2.343	9.2	2.004	7.9	5.133	20.2	346	1.4	1.300	174.0	69.6	25.7	3.56
1970	10.704	205.0	4.943	46.2	25.744	147.2	3.223	12.5	4.414	17.2	2.569	9.9	2.449	9.5	5.757	22.4	327	2.1	1.447	194.0	61.6	24.8	3.46

[a] *"Other" included, among others, accidents resulting from lack of experience.*

Source: own calculations based on: M. Kotula, "Dane liczbowe dotyczące stanu bezpieczeństwa," p. 567.

In the second half of the 1950s and early 1960s, drunk road users were a real menace. In 1953, drivers "under the influence" caused 14.8% of all accidents; a year later, the share increased to 16.7%.[1021] In 1959, drunk road users (motor vehicle drivers, motorcyclists, pedestrians, and horse-drivers who often drove unlit carts[1022]) were responsible for approximately 15% of all accidents, while in 1961, their share reached a high of 23%. In the following years, it decreased, giving way first to excessive speed,[1023] and later to failure to yield the right of way, which from the mid-1960s was the primary cause of approximately 20% of accidents caused by drivers. At the same time, however, the percentage of fatalities resulting from accidents caused by drunk drivers remained at a very high level (approximately 25%). Tightening regulations[1024] and campaigns designed to raise awareness of the dangers of combining alcohol use with driving did not help. In April 1955, the Citizens' Militia carried out a test: drivers suspected of driving under the influence of alcohol were asked to blow into a tube with a special chemical substance that changed colour if the driver

---

1021 J. Wojciechowski, "Wyniki walki o bezpieczeństwo w ruchu drogowym w trzech kwartałach 1954 r.," *Motoryzacja* 1955, no. 1, p. 3.

1022 At the end of 1956, at a meeting of the Transportation Commission of the Provincial National Council in Kielce, the issue of road safety in the Kielce voivodeship was raised. One of the topics was the inspection of horse carts. As the commission members noted, at some point MO officers responsible for inspections stopped checking whether horse-drawn vehicles were equipped with lamps and reflectors. The reason was the unavailability on the market of the necessary quantities of reflective glasses and lanterns for that purpose. Archiwum Państwowe w Kielcach (hereafter: APK), Prezydium Wojewódzkiej Rady Narodowej w Kielcach (hereafter: PWRN Kielce), sign. 5, Wyciąg z notatki nr 11/56 z posiedzenia Komisji Komunikacyjnej WRN, odbytego 20 XII 1956 r., p. 1.

1023 Until the end of 1960, the prewar speed limit of 40 km/h was still in force in built-up areas. The speed limit was increased to 50 km/h by regulation of ministers of transportation, internal affairs, and national defence published on December 2, 1960. In some cases, at the request of the relevant praesidium of the national council, the Minister of Transportation could increase the speed limit to 60 km/h; Dz. U. 1960, no. 55, pos. 319.

1024 In 1957, the Ministry of Transportation issued a regulation under which "a driver found to be under the influence of alcohol, even if it is for the first time, will lose his driving licence for a period of from 3 months to 1 year. Confiscation of the driving licence will take place even if the driver has committed no road traffic offence and his vehicle had no technical defects. … In addition, observation of detained drivers will take place at the drunk tank even when no one is on duty"; "Uwaga Kierowcy," *Motor* 1957, no. 42, p. 6.

had drunk at least a glass of vodka. Over the course of a day, twenty drunk drivers were detained. News about this experiment spread like wildfire, and over the following month, the police failed to arrest a single drunk driver. "So what," Tadeusz Stępień despondently concluded, "if to this day, the Citizens' Militia has not been equipped with this tool. Because apparently … there is no legal basis for having a suspect blow" into the tube.[1025] From 1961 to 1967, 186,000 people were sentenced for drunk driving. Among them was a man who, having stolen a fire truck, killed one person and seriously injured another, as well as a PKS bus driver who drove erratically through city streets and ran into a group of people, killing two.[1026] In 1966 alone, out of 30,430 convicted drivers, as many as 6,446 were repeat offenders. A year later, that number increased to 6,758, even as the total number of convicted drivers decreased (to 28,164). Men were clearly in the lead, constituting an absolute majority. In 1967, only sixty-nine women were convicted of driving under the influence of alcohol.[1027] Therefore, it is not surprising that policemen would react with joy when chancing upon a sober driver. A drawing by Juliusz Puchalski depicting such a scene was published in 1964 in *Szpilki*.

Figure 13. Juliusz Puchalski, „Mamy trzeźwego! Natychmiast zawiadomić prasę!"

1025 T. Stępień, "Śmierć czyha na ulicach."

1026 AAN, Prokuratura Generalna (hereafter: PG), sign. 1/13, Informacja o sprawach, które w roku 1966 skierowane zostały przez Prokuraturę do sądów, z wnioskiem o rozpoznanie w trybie doraźnym, Warszawa, 31 I 1967 r., p. 135.

1027 *Mały Rocznik Statystyczny Motoryzacji* 1968, part 4, p. 31.

For a long time, attitudes toward people who drank while driving were more than lenient. It was commonly believed that small doses of alcohol were harmless.[1028] In a letter to the editor, one *Motor* reader recalled his experience of a driving course:

> When I was finishing the car and motor course eleven years ago, the instructor told us that a small amount of alcohol (for example, a glass [of vodka]) is not harmful to the driver and only speeds up the reflexes, gives him courage. You just have to be careful not to drink too much, because then the driver will be drunk and that is dangerous. I didn't have a thorough enough knowledge of this issue at that time, so I was a little worried, because I didn't like vodka or drink it, and therefore I wouldn't be a good driver of a motor vehicle.[1029]

When in 1966, militia officers who inspected the vehicles of a construction company did not content themselves with finding technical faults and detained three drivers who were found to be "in a condition indicating abuse" the director interceded on behalf of his employees, asking that harsh consequences be withheld "because the schedule is tight, construction is a priority, and there aren't many drivers in the area."[1030] Despite repeated appeals against the sale of alcohol to drivers in bars, restaurants, or hotels, they could still easily obtain it.[1031] This was confirmed by a provocation carried out in 1964 in the Poznań Voivodeship, during which militiamen and officers of the Volunteer Reserves of the Citizen's Militia (Ochotnicza Rezerwa Milicji Obywatelskiej ORMO), wearing motorcycle helmets, gloves, and glasses, bought beer without any problems in half of the thirty-one places they inspected.[1032]

The data on the age and gender of road accident victims is very interesting.[1033] Statistical information on road accidents that took place in 1955–1966 on the streets of Poznań was used for research conducted by the Department

---

1028 X. Gliszczyńska and A. Witoszek, "Wpływ alkoholu na pracę kierowców," *Motoryzacja* 1956, no. 4, p. 107.

1029 "Ostrzegać na kursie," *Motor* 1965, no. 6, p. 2.

1030 W. Bryx, "Kontrola społeczna musi zacząć działać," *Motor* 1966, no. 43, p. 1; See also: J. Wojciechowski, "Wyniki walki o bezpieczeństwo," pp. 4–5.

1031 "Może wprowadzić zakaz sprzedaży?" *Motor* 1962, no. 48, p. 11.

1032 "Przeczytaliśmy dla was. Pożyteczna inicjatywa," *Motor* 1964, no. 35, p. 2.

1033 In the mid-1980s in the USA, car accidents were the leading cause of death among people of pre-retirement age. The average age of road accident victims was 27, while for

of Forensic Medicine of the Medical University of Poznań. The statistics show that more than twice as many men than women died in accidents. Moreover, the greatest number of fatal victims were between the ages of 11 and 20 (18.3%) and 21 and 30 (17.6%). If we add to this total the 11.8% of victims who were under the age of eleven, it turns out that in Poznań, people under the age of thirty accounted for over 47% of all fatalities in road accidents, and one in every four were children.[1034]

Figure 14. Car accident at the intersection of Madalińskiego and Łowicka streets, Warsaw, 1957, National Digital Archives, Zbyszko Siemaszko, 3/51/0/6.21/207

heart disease, it was 76 and for cancer, 68; L. S. Robertson, "Motor Vehicle Injuries," *Public Health Reports* 100 (1985), no. 6, p. 580.

1034 W. Koska, "Wiek i płeć a wypadki drogowe," *Polski Tygodnik Lekarski* 1970, no. 7, pp. 272–273.

The data for the entire country are slightly different. In the years 1961–1970, out of 28,000 accidents, fatalities under the age of fourteen accounted for 13%, and those aged 15–24, for 15%. In the case of the youngest victims, the vast majority were pedestrians—as many as 3,511 out of 3,876, or over 90%. Even if this percentage decreased over the decade (in 1961, it was 89%, and in 1970, it fell to 78%), these were still alarming figures. At the same time, the decade also saw an increase in the share of the oldest road users in fatal accidents. While in 1961, they constituted 5.1% victims, by the end of the 1960s, that value more than doubled, to 10.7%. As in the case of children, the majority of the victims were pedestrians—over the decade, this ratio increased from 75% to 80%. As far as the gender of the victims, men died in road accidents more often than women. Between 1961 and 1969, on average, one woman was killed for every four men: the total number of fatalities was 19,408 men and 5,188 women. However, considering only accidents involving pedestrians, the number of fatalities (as well as injuries) is practically the same. The warped proportions are certainly due to the significantly higher percentage of men among the drivers, which made them much more exposed to accidents.[1035]

The analysis of the number of road incidents by days of the week is interesting. The "most dangerous" days were those adjacent to a day off from work. Most accidents took place on Saturdays and Mondays. Interestingly, in 1975, a change occurred, and the largest number of fatalities was recorded on Fridays, Saturdays, and Mondays. The most likely reason for this state of affairs was the introduction of twelve off-work Saturdays.[1036] In turn, accidents on Sundays, although not very numerous, were most likely to be fatal. Often caused by the so-called Sunday drivers, who drove only occasionally, these accidents were much more dangerous and had much more serious consequences. A sad tradition also developed around common name days and paydays, when accidents came to occur more frequently, usually caused by road users under the influence of alcohol.

After 1956, Polish roads were among the most dangerous in Europe. A WHO report published in the mid-1960s placed Poland first on the list of countries with the highest number of fatal road accidents. Pedestrians were particularly exposed to danger. While the global average of fatal accidents

---

1035 M. Kotula, "Dane liczbowe," pp. 569–570.

1036 J. Polony, *Wypadki drogowe. Problematyka kryminalistyczna*, Warszawa 1978, p. 17.

with pedestrian involvement was 33%, this percentage was significantly higher in Poland.[1037] In the Netherlands, almost 2,479 people died in 55,000 accidents in the mid-1960s. In the same period, a similar number of deaths in road accidents was recorded in Poland (2,475), but only in 22,500 accidents. The Dutch fatality rate (4.5%) was still slightly higher than the average for all countries of the European Economic Community. In 1965, a total of 1,148,343 accidents were recorded in the EEC countries, with 50,163 fatalities (4.3%). Meanwhile, in the same period, this percentage reached almost 11% in Poland. In 1970, this rate increased within the EEC, reaching 4.8%. In the early 1970s in Poland, it reached 8.2%. Returning to the example of the Netherlands, however, a significant disparity should be noted. Although the number of both accidents (58,883) and fatalities (3,181) increased in the Netherlands, when compared to Polish data (41,813 and 3,446, respectively), the contrast illustrates the distance between Polish and European standards. However, the same disparity also existed in comparison to Central and Eastern European countries. In East Germany in 1965, there were 98,121 accidents, in which 1,730 people died, and in 1970—52,207 and 2,139, respectively.[1038] In Czechoslovakia in 1960, there were 1,682 fatalities, and in 1967, 1,818.[1039]

Unfortunately, those dramatic figures were a characteristic feature of a country at an early stage of motorisation. Similar statistics were recorded in almost all countries—the difference was mainly in the time of their recording. Poland began to motorise a decade, or even several decades later than most of the other European countries; in addition, motorcycles played a much greater role in Poland than elsewhere.[1040] It is, therefore, not surprising that

1037 A. Zgorzelska, "Dorosnąć do motoryzacji. Nowy Kodeks Drogowy," *Kierunki* 1968, no. 42, pp. 1 and 9.

1038 This large difference between the number of accidents in 1965 and 1970 resulted a change in the data collection methodology. As of 1967, the East German statistical office classified events in which material losses exceeded 300 marks as "road accidents"; *Statistisches Jahrbuch der Deutschen Demokratischen Republik* 1970, p. 249, http://www.digizeitschriften.de/download/PPN514402644_1971/PPN514402644_1971___log63.pdf (accessed: June 14, 2017).

1039 *Rocznik Statystyki Międzynarodowej* 1970, p. 268.

1040 J. Foreman-Peck, "Death on the Roads," p. 264; S. Dąbrowska, "Wypadki drogowe w latach 1965–1985," p. 25.

the number of road accidents decreased in most Western European countries in the 1960s and 1970s, while in Poland it remained consistently very high.[1041]

The large number of fatalities was undoubtedly due to the failure to apply basic safety measures, such as seat belts or, in the case of motorcyclists, helmets.[1042] In Western countries, seat belts began to be serially installed in cars at the turn of the 1960s. In the USA, the first GMC cars equipped with this protection were produced as early as 1952. Ford, in turn, offered its customers an entire safety package starting in 1956. For US $9, the buyer received a car equipped with, among other things, seat belts and a rear view mirror. However, it quickly became apparent that the buyers cared primarily to pay the lowest possible price for the car. Therefore, accessories that increased the level of safety inside the car were not very popular—only 20% of all cars

1041 A striking example of how the degree of motorisation affected the degree of road safety is the case of East Germany and West Germany. The unification of the two German states brought a dramatic change in the number of accidents. Although the level of motorisation in East Germany stood out positively among other countries of the socialist bloc, the events of 1990 and the opportunity to purchase previously heavily rationed goods resulted in a 40% increase in the number of new cars and the distance travelled by them within two years. At the same time, however, the number of road accidents quadrupled. Statistics show that there was a particularly dramatic increase in accidents involving young people (18–20 years old)—this rate increased elevenfold; A. Saupe, "Human Security and the Challenge of Automobile and Road Traffic Safety: A Cultural Historical Perspective," *Historical Social Research / Historische Sozialforschung* 2010, vol. 35, no. 4 (134), p. 105.

1042 In a survey conducted by *Motor*, one of the questions concerned the need for motorcyclists to use helmets. Only 62% were in favour of wearing them while riding. One reader called wearing a helmet a "torment," especially during warm months, when "instead of exposing your face to the sun's rays, you will have to put your head in a 'pot'." At the end of his letter, he appealed to the editors "to protect us, as far as possible, from the obligation to wear helmets"; W. Bryx, "W hełmie czy bez?" *Motor* 1960, no. 17, p. 3. Perhaps the poor workmanship of the protective helmets played a part. This was the subject of another letter sent to *Motor*. A reader who used a helmet manufactured by the Kaliskie Zakłady Tworzyw Sztucznych complained that it was heavy, poorly made, and too tight. Its unrefined design, especially the faulty "drain profile of air streams" caused great discomfort while driving. As it soon became clear, motorcyclists in Poland did not have much choice, because the product of the Kalisz factory was the only one that met Polish safety standards in force as of January 1, 1962. In 1963, it was estimated that 300,000 motorcyclists were using helmets, while the number of registered motorcycles at that time was 1,180,000.

sold by Ford had them.[1043] In Europe, Porsche and Mercedes-Benz were the first to offer seat belts in cars, introducing them in 1957. In the same year, Swedish engineer Nils Bohlin invented three-point seat belts, which Volvo began installing in its cars in 1959. By 1961, over 70% of all cars produced by the Swedish company were equipped with them.[1044] In the USA, the National Traffic and Motor Vehicle Safety Act was passed in 1966, requiring that drivers and passengers use seat belts, and from 1968 on, all cars manufactured by the American car industry were to be equipped with them.[1045] In Poland, the obligation to use seat belts was not introduced until 1983, but it only applied to the front seats of cars and on roads outside built-up areas. In

1043 R. Volti, *Cars & Culture: The Life Story of a Technology*, Baltimore 2004, pp. 96–97. It is worth mentioning that at the end of the 1920s, some automotive companies refrained from updating their designs with elements that could improve the safety of drivers and passengers for fear of rising production costs and declining car sales. This was the case with the president of GMC, Alfred Sloan, who personally blocked the idea of serial assembly of so-called safe windows in cars; ibid., p. 116. Other innovations that are now standard equipment in cars, such as airbags, were also approached with great caution by customers, mainly due to their high price. When in 1973, customers who wanted to buy Oldsmobiles, Buicks, or Cadillacs were offered airbags at prices ranging from US $181 to US $300, the vast majority of them refused. Only 20% of buyers decided to accept the proposal, while GMC estimated 50,000 potential buyers. It was only in the 1990s that airbags started becoming more and more common in cars. In 1992, more than half of all passenger cars sold in the USA were equipped with them, and three years later, virtually all of them were; ibid., p. 118.

1044 A. Saupe, "Human Security," p. 109.

1045 J. Foreman-Peck, "Death on the Roads," p. 283. A major change in thinking about car safety came with the publication of Ralph Nader's *Unsafe at Any Speed: The Designed-In Dangers of the American Automobile* (New York 1965). Nader was a staff attorney for the automotive safety subcommittee of the US Senate. In the book, he discussed the Chevrolet Corvair—a car that was supposed to be the American answer to the wave of European small cars, but due to design errors, unfortunately became dangerous for drivers, passengers, and other road users. In the conclusion, Nader stated that the entire American industry, fearing loss of profits, remained indifferent, and sometimes even hostile, to any changes that improved the safety of motorists. Nader's book was so impactful that it caused a sharp decline in sales of the Corvair, which was ultimately discontinued in 1969; R. Volti, *Cars & Culture*, pp. 116–117; J. J. Fink, *The Automobile Age*, London 1990, pp. 288, 290–293; J. P. Bardou, J. J. Chanaron, P. Fridenson, and J. M. Laux, *The Automobile Revolution: The Impact of an Industry*, Chapel Hill 1982, pp. 286–287; A. Zieliński, *Rozwój koncepcji samochodu osobowego w XX wieku*, Warszawa 2005, p. 207.

turn, motorcyclists were not required to wear a helmet until February 1, 1964. Initially, the rule only applied to users of vehicles with an engine displacement above 170 cm^3 and outside of built-up areas. After half a year, it was extended to two-wheeled vehicles with engines over 140 cm^3, regardless of the terrain. From September 1, 1964, users of vehicles with smaller engines also had to wear helmets, but this obligation applied depending on the place where the vehicle was registered.[1046]

The example of the 1950s and 1960s clearly shows that Polish drivers were quite reluctant and reserved towards these innovations. Some even suggested that driving with fastened seat belts was much more dangerous: "My friend managed to get out of the [burning] car at the last moment and extinguish his burning clothes. I wonder what would have happened if he had been entangled in seat belts?" An unfastened seat belt was also said to have saved a driver who fell with his car into the Wrocław city moat: "I personally am a supporter of the Russian proverb: the slower you go, the farther you will go. I don't exceed 65 km[/h] even on highways."[1047] For most Polish drivers, the problem of road safety was not directly related to the use of seat belts, but to the general improvement of driving habits: "I have never felt the need to have seat belts. I cannot afford to drive riskily and damage the vehicle! ... Is this why we have to pay tribute in the form of seat belts and the numerous fines for not wearing them (I get out of the car a dozen times in cities along the route, sometimes every few metres)? What has been done in the meantime to ensure road safety? What are the plans in this area? Put on your seat belt and pay the fine?"[1048] Another driver noted the problem with access to seat belts and associated it with the shortage of spare parts: "It is hardly surprising that Motozbyt is not concerned about the sale and popularisation of seat belts, since it has so many other weak areas in its commercial activities."[1049] Seat belts were not easy to obtain at all.

According to Błażej Brzostek, "[t]he chaos on the streets was eagerly attributed to the 'national' tendency of Poles to disobey authorities and disregard

---

1046 MP 1963, no. 97, pos. 462; 1964, no. 4, pos. 227.
1047 "Protestuję," *Motor* 1966, no. 45, p. 2.
1048 "Nie skutki lecz przyczyny," *Motor* 1966, no. 46, p. 2.
1049 "Może najpierw części?" *Motor* 1966, no. 45, p. 2.

the law."[1050] As I have already tried to show here, no one among road users was blameless. "*K'sobiści*" (concerned only with their own interests), "leftists" and "centrists" (driving cars on the left side or down the middle of the road) were the royalty, and pedestrians walked into the streets "exaggeratedly" to cross to the other side.[1051] Drivers divided the latter into several categories: "try-to-run-me-down," "I-will-fit-through-here," and "I-will-make-it." However, according to *Motor*, "the most dangerous type is the indecisive ones who hesitate until the last moment and finally throw themselves under the wheels." One driver, whose hobby turned out to be game hunting, even claimed: "It would be good if we could simply cull the passers-by."[1052] "*Lechickie narowy*"—Putrament's term for disobedience toward the authorities and disregard for the law (literally meaning "Lechite frivolities")—were said to characterise the "Polish driving school."[1053] Stanisław Lem described Warsaw drivers who failed to adhere to the basic rules of the road thusly: "There is a lot of traffic, rather wild, they pass you on the right, as well as the left."[1054]

It is worth devoting some space to this very issue—the legal regulations in force on the roads and the people who were supposed to ensure compliance with the law. As already mentioned, until the early 1960s, vehicle traffic in Poland was guided mostly by regulations dating back to the Second Polish Republic. Calls for change emerged in the mid-1950s because the legal situation where road traffic regulations and some of the necessary rules for safety and order on the roads remained uncodified demanded one. In light of the ever-increasing number of vehicles on Polish roads, the need for uniform regulations became urgent.[1055]

Nevertheless, the legal regulations from the prewar period, although amended several times in the second half of the 1940s, throughout the 1950s, and into the early 1960s, were only superseded on by an act on safety and order

---

1050 B. Brzostek, *Za progiem*, p. 334.

1051 See, for example: J. Putrament, *Pół wieku. Literaci*, Warszawa 1970, p. 200.

1052 W. Tobis, "Rzecz o przechodniach i kierowcach czyli 'człek człekowi wilkiem' (albo jeszcze czymś gorszym)," *Motor* 1962, no. 21, p. 16.

1053 B. Brzostek, *Za progiem*, p. 334; M. Kwiatkowski, "Polska szkoła jazdy?" *Motor* no. 34, p. 1.

1054 S. Lem and S. Mrożek, *Listy*, p. 363.

1055 E. Olechnowicz, "Założenia kodyfikacji przepisów ruchu drogowego," *Motoryzacja* 1955, no. 10, p. 296.

on public roads dated November 27, 1961.[1056] On October 1, 1962, a common order by the Minister of Transportation and the Minister of Internal Affairs regarding traffic on public roads was issued, concerning the implementation of the provisions of the November act. The new code organised, collected, and specified previously applied customs and rules of road traffic. The regulations were fully adapted to the Geneva Convention on Road Traffic and the Protocol on Road Signs of 1949, as well as the European Agreement of 1950.[1057] The MO conducted widely attended meetings throughout the country, explaining the most important changes that came into force in October 1962. A total of approximately 25,000 such meetings took place. PZMot also joined in the effort of promoting the new code, as did the National Defense League, which, conducted a series of meetings and training sessions for over half a million drivers, cyclists, and other road users during the first two years of the new regulations being in force.[1058]

However, it quickly transpired that this popularity was due in part to the fact that the book edition of the new code quickly disappeared from bookstore shelves, becoming a real rarity.[1059] In the Rzeszów Voivodeship, Dom Książki only had 9,600 copies, while the number of people interested in buying the volume exceeded that value several times over. When asked for his opinion on the new rules for using the roads, Ryszard Skała, a motoring journalist from the Lower Silesian *Słowo Polskie*, strongly criticised the manner of their introduction: "First it was adopted, and then popularised insufficiently broadly, and finally it was ruled that, although it is in force from April 1, we will only need to abide by it when all road users become familiar with the related provisions and regulations." As a result, instead of issuing tickets, MO officers had to look the other way when they witnessed offences. This led to "the most wrongful belief that the highway code is so

[1056] Basic concepts were codified (for example: *road*, *vehicle*, and *driver*), general rules of traffic, safety, and traffic organisation on roads were discussed, and issues of road traffic control and safety surveillance were also raised; Dz. U. 1961, no. 53, pos. 295.

[1057] Poland joined the Geneva Convention on September 25, 1958 (Dz. U. 1958, no. 54, pos. 321), and the European agreement in May 1959; Dz. U. 1959, no. 51, pos. 324.

[1058] J. Wojciechowski, "Bezpieczeństwo ruchu drogowego," pp. 160–161.

[1059] In 1966, one reader of *Polityka* wrote to its editors on this matter: "It is amazing that at a time when you can't find the road code on bookstore shelves, the massive *Kalendarz Motoryzacyjny* has seen print"; "Listy do redakcji," *Polityka* 1966, no. 51, p. 1.

mild and forgiving that not only is there no need to follow it, but it is not even worth familiarising yourself with its contents."[1060]

The fairly widespread criticism of the new regulations prompted the very swift introduction of an amendment in July 1968.[1061] That was when the order from the Minister of Transportation and the Minister of Internal Affairs regarding traffic on public roads was published.[1062] The need to change the code after only five years was explained, in part, by the accruing of "different experiences indicating a need for changes in regulations and a clearer and more precise approach to the norms of social coexistence on the road." Additionally, the new code included provisions adapted to the new World Convention on Road Traffic and the Convention on Road Signs and Signals, which were being prepared at that time. The most important changes included the collection into one paragraph and slight modification of guidelines for how drivers should approach marked pedestrian crossings, the more precise formulation and expansion of guidelines regarding the manoeuvring of motor vehicle along with some definitions, as well as the adaptation of the Polish system of road signs and signals to the international system.[1063]

Unfortunately, once again, insufficient preparation for the moment when the new regulations would come into force evoked strong criticism. Writing for *Kierunki*, Jerzy Milewski observed that "almost everyone who has anything to do with these matters."[1064] Drivers criticised the increased protection given to pedestrians (who now gained right of way at designated crossings), while pedestrians, as Jerzy Flisak perfectly illustrated in *Szpilki*, criticised the lack of respect for their rights on the road that drivers showed them.[1065] The

---

1060 "Kodeks karny w oczach społeczeństwa," *Zagadnienia karno-administracyjne* 1963, no. 4/5, p. 113.

1061 A. Zgorzelska, "Dorosnąć do motoryzacji," p. 1.

1062 Dz. U. 1968, no. 27, pos. 183.

1063 In the case of signs, the changes consisted in modifying the appearance of some and introducing new ones; Z. Drexler, "Nowy kodeks drogowy," *Motoryzacja* 1968, no. 10, pp. 252–255.

1064 J. Milewski, "Parę westchnień niepraworządnych," *Kierunki* 1968, no. 42, p. 9.

1065 "Kodeks nie zwalnia od myślenia, *Motor* 1968, no. 39, p. 1; "Zmiany w Kodeksie Drogowym," *Motor* 1968, no. 42, pp. 3 and 11. Criticism of the new solutions can also be found in other sources; see, for example, J. Zając, "Pieszy podmiotem przestępstwa drogowego," *Służba MO* 1970, no. 2, pp. 187–188.

changed appearance of certain road signs and signals raised concerns because, it was noted, for drivers to become used to the changes might take time.[1066]

Figure 15. Jerzy Flisak, „Nie mogę się przyzwyczaić!"

Ensuring road safety was primarily the purview of the MO, first through road traffic sections at provincial MO headquarters, and then through the Road Traffic Inspectorate at the MO Main Headquarters, established in January 1962, replaced in 1965 by the Road Traffic Control Department—the popular *drogówka* (traffic police).[1067] In addition, there were groups for safety and order on public roads of the ORMO and community inspectors

---

[1066] J. Milewski, "Parę westchnień niepraworządnych," p. 9.

[1067] T. Krupa and D. Oleander, "'Drogówka' jako jedna z pierwszych służb milicyjnych w powojennej Warszawie," *Bezpieczeństwo i Administracja. Zeszyty Naukowe Wydziału Bezpieczeństwa Narodowego Akademii Obrony Narodowej* 2015, no. 1, p. 24; Z.

of road traffic inspectors involved directly with the ORMO.[1068] The *drogówka*, accounting for approximately 10% of all MO officers, was additionally supported by the Youth Traffic Service, an organisation which numbered 135,000 members in 1965.

In the second half of the 1960s, the number of officers employed at the Road Traffic Control Department increased by a further 16.5%, which enabled the department to create structures at the district level. However, practically from the beginning—the establishment of the Road Traffic Section[1069]—traffic police relied primarily on motorcycles, while passenger cars (mainly Warszawas, a negligible number of Syrenas, and later Big Fiats) were only supplementary. This meant that in the late autumn, winter, and early spring months, inspections were only carried out to a very limited extent. Vehicle shortages accompanied policemen practically throughout the period in question. Toward the end of 1956, during a meeting of the Transportation Commission of the Provincial National Council in Kielce, its representatives complained that due to the lack of cars, the officers keeping order on the roads were forced to work ... on foot, because the few available motorcycles were not suitable for use in winter conditions.[1070]

In the second half of the 1960s, traffic officers handed out an average of 170,000 applications for penalties (of up to 4,500 zlotys) to penal-administrative committees and imposed approximately 2 million zlotys in fines (of up to 100 zlotys) for traffic offences. They accounted for 40% of all applications for penalties and over 80% all fines imposed by the MO. The vast majority went to drivers, who received 45.5% of the applications and 69.3% of the citations.[1071] Lower ranks were occupied by cyclists (27% of applications, but

---

Jakubowski, *Milicja Obywatelska 1944–1948*, Warszawa 1988, pp. 134–136; A. Misiuk, *Historia Policji w Polsce. Od X wieku do współczesności*, Warszawa 2008, p. 184.

1068 "Zawsze na posterunku," *Motor* 1965, no. 41, p. 1; A. Misiuk, *Historia Policji w Polsce*, p. 184; J. Pytel, *Ochotnicza Rezerwa Milicji Obywatelskiej (1946–1989)*, Warszawa 2009, pp. 208–209.

1069 Zenon Jakubowski writes that in the initial period, there was a shortage of motorcycles, and patrols in the field often had to use public transport: PKS buses and trains; *idem*, *Milicja Obywatelska*, p. 135.

1070 APK, PWRN Kielce, sign. 5, Wyciąg z notatki nr 11/56 z posiedzenia Komisji komunikacyjnej WRN, odbytego 20 XII 1956 r., p. 1.

1071 It is, therefore, not surprising that drivers were among the most willing to question the correctness of the ticketing procedure in general; see M. C. Niedzialek,

only 7.9% of fines), pedestrians (17.1% and 16.1%, respectively) and horse-drivers (10.5% and 6.7%, respectively). Another form of penalty took the shape of cards with information about offences committed by road users, which were sent to their workplaces (in the case of professional drivers) or schools (in the case of students). Such correspondence amounted to 150,000 letters per year. Participants in a survey on road safety conducted by the *Polityka* weekly in 1969 offered assessment of the work of the traffic police. Most respondents demanded more patrols on the roads—specifically, motorised patrols, because "the current style of standing by the side of the road and waving the lollipop" (a lollipop-shaped traffic baton) was far from effective. It was noted that MO officers were much more likely to be found "where get tickets, not where you get in an accident." One driver complained: "The militiamen punish first, and when asked why, they answer, I will always find something." At the same time, most respondents would accept far-reaching restrictions on their freedom in exchange for increased safety. One wrote: "The police are very demanding, but that's a good thing"; another added that "in 95% of the cases where I had to pay a fine, [the militiamen] were right."[1072]

In addition to road traffic control and crime prevention,[1073] the traffic officers engage in various kinds of deterrence. One of them was an operation code-named *Jutrzenka* (Dawn), organised together with ORMO in 1962. Its aim was to force drivers to turn on their dipped headlights immediately after dusk, which was among the provisions of the highway code. It was not commonly done at the time, for a number of reasons.[1074] One of them was very mundane; according to *Motor*, "[e]veryone knows that Warszawas and Syrenas leave the factory floor with lights set incorrectly and there is no use adjusting them afterwards. However, if you're stubborn and lower the

---

"Działalność MO w opinii pracowników poznańskich zakładów pracy," in: *Milicja Obywatelska a społeczeństwo (Synteza i reinterpretacja badań z lat 1967–1983)*, Warszawa 1984, pp. 204–206.

1072 A. K. Wróblewski, "Zawsze umiera kto inny," p. 3.

1073 For more on this subject, see T. Krupa, "Działalność propagandowo-profilaktyczna Milicji Obywatelskiej na rzecz bezpieczeństwa w ruchu drogowym," *Bezpieczeństwo i Administracja. Zeszyty Naukowe Wydziału Bezpieczeństwa Narodowego Akademii Obrony Narodowej*" 2015, no. 3, pp. 87–102.

1074 "Operacja 'Jutrzenka'—znaczy więcej światła dla miast," *Motor* 1962, no. 48, p. 9.

headlights to drive around the city without annoying other drivers, you will automatically shorten their range. So, it's a design defect."[1075]

In the summer of 1964, a woman from Warsaw went on holiday to Mielno with her husband in her Wartburg. As they left Koszalin, a lollipop swung out of a Simca that was passing them, stopping the woman driver. The rest of the story is presented in a letter the woman sent to *Motor*:

> There was an inspection, but not like any other. The polite gentleman in civilian clothes apologised for stopping me and gave me an accounting of the mistakes I made while driving through the city.… I also learned that I had driven the Wartburg correctly through 12 difficult situations, which is why I received a beautiful, colourful car washing sponge and a postcard with a view of Koszalin as a gift. On the back of the postcard was the inscription: "For respectful driving in Koszalin, August 1964." … I was so happy. My husband is proud of me.[1076]

The stop was probably conducted by a member of the Community Inspectors of Road Traffic. Established in 1963 by order of the Chief Commander of the Militia, the organisation brought together representatives of many professions, including popular writers, actors, and singers of the period, such as Jarema Stępowski, Tadeusz Fijewski, Stanisław Mikulski, Mieczysław Fogg, and Henryk Kotarski. After passing a specialised exam, community inspectors gained the prerogative to stop any vehicle that violated the regulations on safety and orderliness on public roads. Their equipment included a badge with the inscription "Community Inspector of Road Traffic," a police shield, a signal flashlight, a sobriety tester with a protocol form for registering use, and penalty application forms. At the end of 1966, there were already 230 groups of community traffic inspectors with a total membership of almost 9,000. They operated in conjunction with around 20,000 members of the ORMO, who were not authorised to conduct traffic stops.[1077] Four years later, 44,000 ORMO members and 21,100 community inspectors were policing road traffic.[1078] As reported in *Motor*, in the first three quarters of 1964 alone, "civilians with lollipops in their lapels" completed 12,000 hours of service,

---

[1075] E. Gąsiorek, "'Jutrzenka' bez jutra," *Motor* 1964, no. 50, p. 4.
[1076] "Pożyteczna inicjatywa," *Motor* 1964, no. 38, p. 2.
[1077] J. Pytel, *Ochotnicza Rezerwa Milicji Obywatelskiej*, pp. 209–210.
[1078] H. Piotrowski, Ocena stanu bezpieczeństwa drogowego…, p. 16.

detained thirty-three drunk drivers, and suspended eighty-six registration certificates for cars with technical defects, while also recovering three stolen vehicles.[1079]

In Poland under Władysław Gomułka, theft of private cars was not a particularly significant social or criminal problem, even if compared to road crimes, which accounted for an average of 12.4% of all crimes in the years 1966–1970, taking third place behind thefts of private property and thefts of public property, but above arson and burglary of public and private facilities.[1080] Meanwhile, among crimes covered under article 257 of the Penal Code—that is, theft of private property—the misappropriation of cars accounted for slightly more than 1% in 1968–1969.[1081] Even if this practice gained momentum as the number of cars in private hands increased, it still constituted only a fraction of crime. At the turn of the 1960s, between 1958 and 1962, the Citizens' Militia initiated investigations into 1,004 cases of private car theft. Investigations were successful in 664 cases.[1082] In turn, in the years 1967–1969, 2,951 thefts were recorded, of which 1,302 happened in 1969 alone.[1083] A large percentage of the resulting cases, over 55%, were successful. The number of misappropriated cars was the largest in Warsaw: 204 in 1968 (91 were found), and 347 the following year (204 were found). Interestingly, most of the perpetrators were under 21 years old. They were mainly men who were often familiar with the design of the vehicles due to

---

1079 I. Golik, "Koledzy-kierowcy z 'lizakami'," *Motor* 1964, no. 42, p. 1.

1080 AAN, PG, sign. 5/212, Statystyka przestępstw w latach 1966–1970, Warszawa 1971, p. 3.

1081 Ibid., sign. 5/217, Biuletyn Statystyczny MO. Przestępczość oraz wyniki pracy organów Milicji i Prokuratury, grudzień 1969 r., p. 9.

1082 R. Ciesielski and S. Rybicki, "Kradzieże pojazdów samochodowych," *Służba MO* 1963, no. 2, p. 277.

1083 For comparison, it is worth noting that in 1970 alone, in the West German state of Rhineland-Westphalia, 1,534 cars were not recovered. Throughout the Federal Republic of Germany, annual losses in this respect were estimated at 30 million marks. The MO closely monitored the growing problem of car theft in Western Europe, bearing in mind the fact that sooner or later it would also achieve similar proportions in Poland. See H. Baneck and G. Holzenbecher, "Złodzieje samochodów działający pod szyldem specjalnej firmy obrotu volkswagenami," *Biuletyn Informacyjny. Ośrodek Informacji Naukowo-Technicznej Zakładu Kryminalistyki KGMO* 1972, no. 3 (7), pp. 75–78.

their profession or studies at technical schools. One of the car thief rings that were dismantled in the capital, for example, consisted of students from an automotive school. In turn, in Poznań, one detained group consisted of a car mechanic, a locksmithing student, and students of an automotive school and a telecommunications school.[1084] One Warsaw gang, composed of people aged 16 to 23, stole as many as twenty cars in the last two months of 1956.[1085]

Most often, the cars were stolen for parts, which were then traded. In many cases, the MO found the cars with some of the most valuable components missing or in a state of complete destruction.[1086] In particular, the practice of destroying cars or defacing company emblems caused headaches for owners of the vehicles. Author Maria Dąbrowska noted in her diary on April 7, 1958 that "unfortunately, in Poland you cannot leave your car on a dirt road without risking that the tires will be removed, or that the windows will be broken and the blankets stolen, not to mention the theft of everything on the outside."[1087] Warszawas were definitely the most likely to be misappropriated. During the first quarter of 1966, out of ninety-five cars stolen throughout the country, twenty of them came from the Żerań factory. The particular popularity of the model among thieves was due to the lack of quality security measures and, perhaps more importantly, the ease of selling individual parts. The most common recipients of stolen parts were taxi drivers and owners of certain private car repair shops.[1088] However, sometimes the theft was committed just to use the car for … a joyride.[1089] One victim of this kind of theft was an employee of the public television company who noticed that her car was missing from the parking lot near her workplace. Despite immediately reporting the theft to law enforcement authorities, the car could not be found. After a few days, it "found itself"—parked in the same place from which it

1084 R. Ciesielski and S. Rybicki, "Kradzieże pojazdów samochodowych," pp. 278–279.

1085 B. Brzostek, *Za progiem*, p. 330, note 219.

1086 A. Kondracki, "Kradzieże samochodów i motocykli," *Służba MO* 1967, no. 2, p. 257.

1087 M. Dąbrowska, *Dzienniki powojenne 1955–1959*, Warszawa 1996, pp. 291–292.

1088 S. Kubiak, "Czy można zapobiegać kradzieżom samochodów?" *Motor* 1967, no. 13, p. 1.

1089 There were also other reasons, such as in one case in Łódź, where a stolen Warszawa was reportedly used first as a means of transport that the thieves (aged 18 to 21) used to reach the Kampinos Forest, and then as … a place to sleep overnight; E. Merz, "Młodociani złodzieje samochodów," *Motoryzacja* 1962, no. 7/8, p. 211.

had disappeared, "clean, washed, and in perfect order." Inside was a letter from the thieves: "The tank is full, a minor defect in the car has been fixed. We apologise for the inconvenience and thank you very much."[1090]

5.5 "Being a lightweight product, petrol, evaporates easily"

As Piotr Grabarczyk claimed in a 1963 issue of the Katowice weekly *Poglądy*: "Every Pole wants to drive a car, so petrol is starting to become as important in his budget as bread, milk, and clothing."[1091] However, while the first part of the sentence can be accepted without much reservation, what follows requires commentary. At the time of publication of the issue of the weekly, there were just over 188,000 passenger cars on Polish roads, over 80% of which belonged to private owners. Even if the significant number of privately owned two-wheeled vehicles (1,168,000) is added to this number, access to petrol remains a concern for a rather narrow slice of the Polish society at the time.[1092] None of this, however, changes the fact that for "every motorised Pole," keeping their vehicle fuelled was an important matter.[1093] In his book about the black market in communist Poland, Jerzy Kochanowski correctly characterises the petrol issue, stating that "the socialist shortage economy made it difficult, on the one hand, to obtain a car, while on the other, making it extremely easy to provide it with fuel using informal channels."[1094] The fact that the state, "whose nationalised economy was characterised by enormous waste and absurd regulations and standards, often necessitating abuses," exercised monopoly over the distribution of goods such as fuel, made it relatively easy to obtain illegal access to petrol.[1095]

The problem of unofficial trade in fuel emerged almost concurrently with the decision by the authorities to promote individual motorisation. Petrol

---

1090 E. Merz, "Łowcy samochodów," *Motoryzacja* 1962, no. 4, p. 106.

1091 P. Grabarczyk, "Uwaga benzyna," *Poglądy* 1963, no. 12, p. 4.

1092 A. M. Restecki, "Zrealizowane oczekiwania. Miliony samochodów osobowych w r. 1975," *Motor* 1966, no. 30, p. 3.

1093 A. Tymowski, "Cztery kółka a budżet domowy," p. 3.

1094 J. Kochanowski, *Tylnymi drzwiami. "Czarny rynek" w Polsce 1944–1989*, Warszawa 2010, p. 234.

1095 Ibid.; cf. A. K. Wróblewski, "Wytrych," *Polityka* 1966, no. 42, p. 7.

was a highly scarce commodity, and in the face of economic difficulties and huge demand owed to industrialisation, it was often worth its weight in gold. In the first postwar years, officials considered the introduction of rationing, and for a moment it was even in force, but fears prevailed that restrictions on the sale of petrol would lead black market practices to develop; thus, officials attempted to limit consumption, for instance through legislation, including restrictions on the registration of private vehicles and their mileage.[1096] At the same time, efforts were made to seal the state's fuel tanks in every possible way.

At the beginning of the second quarter of 1949, at the request of the Praesidium of the Council of Ministers, the Ministry of the Treasury sent a draft circular to the Ministry of Transportation, calling on officials to take a closer look at fuel management in state institutions and identify any irregularities. The frequency with which owners of vehicles used in commercial transport (such as taxis) purchased petrol at Central Office of Petroleum Products (CPN) stations, along with what was characterised as confidential information, suggested that some of the petrol consumed by these cars could have come from illegal trade. There could only be one source of these "uncontrolled leaks": employees of state offices, enterprises, and institutions. Given that the standards for fuel consumption for motor vehicles were established by a separate regulation (dated January 27, 1948), and each fuel purchase had to be carefully documented with invoices issued by the CPN, detecting excessive consumption of petrol would seem very easy. If an inspection of distance travelled, which the tax office conducted for the purpose of calculating taxes, showed that the inspected entity consumed more petrol than was indicated in the accounts and standards, suspicions arose that the petrol could have been purchased illegally. If the inspection indicated the opposite situation—lower consumption and no surplus fuel—it would be taken as a

1096 At the turn of 1957, a temporary restriction on fuel distribution was introduced. This was tied to the political situation in Hungary, as a result of which transport routes through Romania and Hungary were closed. Owners of private cars could receive a maximum of 30 litres of fuel. From March 1, 1957, these restrictions were suspended due to unplanned oil deliveries from the USSR and the reopening of the Hungarian route; (p), "Jak z benzyną?" *Motor* 1957, no. 2, p. 3; "Wniosek o zniesienie z dniem 1 marca br. ograniczeń benzynowych," *Trybuna Ludu*, February 17, 1957, p. 1; P. Grabarczyk, "Uwaga benzyna," p. 4.

sign of illegal sale of petrol.[1097] However, in its opinion on the draft for the new circular, the Automotive Department of the Ministry of Transportation strongly criticised the project proposed by the Ministry of Treasury. Firstly, attention was drawn to the fact that the consumption standards published in the "Journal of Tariffs and Standards" permitted deviations in the use of fuel depending on operating conditions. Cars could burn more fuel depending on the state of the road, location, use of trailers, etc. Moreover, the difference could reach up to 60% of the norm. Another issue was the fact that many enterprises reported significantly exceeded consumption standards (often even by 100%) and far-reaching fuel savings up to 30% in some cases at the same time. The final conclusion was that the amount of fuel expended cannot be the basis for calculating the mileage of vehicles, and the only reliable method should be checking mileometers.[1098] Yet, this did not end the matter. The initiator of the planned circular, a representative of the Praesidium of the Council of Ministers, joined the discussion to defend his position while explaining that decisive steps had to be taken to tighten the methods of fuel distribution by the CPN. One solution was to introduce "CPN petrol receipts," presenting "an approximate amount of petrol that should be used in relation to the given number of kilometres." All vehicle owners were to keep such a book, which would be used to record every transaction and whose absence would make the purchase of fuel impossible.[1099] Nonetheless, the Ministry of Transportation did not abandon the use of fuel consumption as the basis for calculating the number of kilometres travelled, especially since, as officials indicated, most private cars did not have a mileage counter.[1100]

In the face of vocal opposition to some of the ministry's ideas from administration employees, fuel rationing returned once again; as it later turned out, it had been a part of the government's plans throughout the first half of the 1950s. While at the beginning of the decade, the government was prevented from introducing rationing by the fear of a return of black market trade in

---

1097 AAN, URM, sign. 16/237, Okólnik w sprawie kontroli należytego udokumentowania zakupu benzyny do pojazdów mechanicznych [projekt], kwiecień 1949 r., p. 32; ibid., Notatka służbowa dla Dyrektora Ob. Wieczorka Janusza, p. 35.

1098 Ibid., Udokumentowanie zakupu paliw do poj. mech., Warszawa, 17 VI 1949 r., p. 34.

1099 Ibid., Notatka służbowa, p. 35–36.

1100 Ibid., Udokumentowanie zakupu benzyny do pojazdów mechanicznych, Warszawa, 4 VII 1949 r., p. 37.

fuel, the process was already very advanced in 1952 to introduce restrictions on the distribution of petrol. At that time, one department of the PKPG initiated a series of consultations with the Ministry of Road Transport and Aviation and the CPN to discuss the possibilities, advisability, and mode of introducing rationing. A special commission was even established, consisting of PKPG members, tasked with defining the rules for restrictions on fuel distribution and fuel consumption standards for vehicles, as well as for rewarding the most fuel-efficient drivers. The plan was to generate a 5% fuel profit in 1952 compared to the previous year.[1101] However, the condition of the automobile fleet of the state institutions was a problem. Some institutions had modest resources in this area and were therefore unable to use their fuel allocations. Others had the opposite problem: intensive use of vehicles required larger amounts of petrol, which was in short supply. Throughout the discussions, it proved impossible to develop an outline of the organisational structure for the distribution of fuel cards and coupons. Thus, it was determined—as in previous years—that restrictions on fuel sales could result in a return to black market practices, the conclusion being that petrol rationing would be used only as a "final recourse."

Nonetheless, officials also decided to prepare for a time when an urgent need for rationing might arise, one organised around one of four potential principles.[1102] The first was the assumption that the amount of fuel being distributed would be tied to the type of vehicle; the second one, that it would depend on the vehicle and its user; the third assumed a centralised distribution tied to the users depending on the period covered by the allocation; and the fourth based distribution on the specific tasks of the individual users. Each of these principles had its pros and cons, but in the case of the first two, the conclusion was that, if introduced, they would prevent neither black market practices nor hoarding by individual users. Centralised distribution, in turn, required the creation of a separate apparatus responsible for distribution, but officials claimed that it was a "more appropriate solution than the two previously mentioned," without offering any justification. All "unsocialised" carriers, apart from taxis and horse-drawn carriages, would submit a quarterly

1101 AAN, PKPG, sign. 2, Protokół z posiedzenia Kolegium PKPG w dniu 13 X 1951 r. w sprawie bilansów materiałowych na r. 1952, pp. 178–179.

1102 Ibid., sign. 5282, Notatka służbowa, 25 IV 1952 r., unnumbered pages.

requirement for fuel demand. Private vehicle users, on the other hand, would receive monthly certificates for specific amounts of fuel from district offices or city councils, depending on the types of cars they owned, fuel consumption standards, and the permitted monthly mileage. Moreover, owners of private vehicles were to keep vehicle inspection books recording all of their trips, where each refuelling visit at a CPN station would be marked.[1103]

Ultimately, it was decided to introduce accurate records of fuel sold in the form of the so-called petrol checks, which, however, very quickly became an object of black market trading, their value comparable, as described years later, "with bills from the National Bank of Poland, suitable for use as currency in lower-quality inns, in card games, etc."[1104] Another idea to reduce the consumption of fuel—especially by state-owned cars, which were its main users at the time—was to modernise the state automobile fleet. In the first half of the 1950s, from the moment FSO started producing Warszawas, these cars became the basic vehicle for state officials. However, despite quite good driving characteristics, these cars were gas guzzlers, burning on average a dozen or so litres per 100 kilometres. While using the Warszawas for longer trips could make financial sense, short routes were very expensive. Therefore, it was proposed that state offices be provided with small-engine Škodas or DKWs, or that the purchase of heavy motorcycles from BMW or JAWA be considered.[1105] However, in the face of the increase in the number of cars in private hands at the turn of the 1960s, along with the aforementioned indolence of the state in this respect, the illegal fuel market became a highly important part of the grey zone.[1106]

1103 Ibid.

1104 B. W. Olszewska and H. Jezierski, "Benzyna," *Polityka* 1965, no. 20, p. 1.

1105 AAN, PKPG, sign. 378, Notatka w sprawie ilości i stanu samochodów osobowych, Warszawa, [lipiec 1952 r.], p. 24–25.

1106 J. Kochanowski states that in 1956 fuel crimes were not yet a significant problem. The analysis of illegal practices in state transport showed that the value of stolen gasoline was estimated at 70 million zlotys, which was far behind the thefts of transported goods (200 million zlotys), tools (170 million zlotys) or the transport of the so-called "heads" (170 million zlotys); J. Kochanowski, Tylnymi drzwiami…, p. 236.

How many Poles were driving on "hot" petrol?[1107] The aforementioned Grabarczyk performed a simple calculation, using the example of Upper Silesia. It was a peculiar region because the level of motorisation of its inhabitants was above the Polish average. Of the 170,000 motor vehicles registered in the region in 1963, 140,000 were in private hands, over 100,000 of which were motorcycles. The remaining 40,000 were passenger cars, mostly small-engine vehicles, often so-called Sunday cars, that is driven only. A thousand taxis and luggage cars completed the fleet. Given the consumption standards, private vehicles should have consumed approximately 25% of the petrol throughout the region. Meanwhile Sundays, over the course of several years, average annual consumption remained much lower: in 1959 it reached only 9.8%, and a year later, 15.9%. In subsequent years, it remained at a similar level (19.1% and 16.9%), never reaching the aforementioned value.[1108] This meant that each year, the missing percentages, or rather octanes, came from state tanks.

It is no coincidence that the lowest fuel consumption level was achieved in 1959. This was the year of the greatest scandals related to the illegal petrol trade in Upper Silesia. In 1960, several hundred drivers and several dozen gas station managers were taken to court in just one case. By forging petrol receipts, they directed a stream of illegal fuel worth nearly 2 million zlotys to the black market. One quarter of this amount was reportedly misappropriated by the manager of a gas station from the Bogucice district of Katowice.[1109] In the following years, more such scandals were uncovered, including in Praszka in the Łódź Voivodeship, where local station employees issued fictitious bills to the tune of 900,000 zlotys, and on the coast, in Gdańsk and Lębork, where the misappropriation amounted to 700,000 zlotys.[1110]

Estimates for the entire country say that in 1965 private vehicles consumed 284,500 tons of fuel, not even half of which was distributed through gas stations. Without risking a major error, it can be assumed that the rest came from state sources.[1111] It was estimated that the resulting annual losses to the

---

1107 The term commonly used for illegal goods in Polish at the time was literally "left" (lewy, lewa, lewe), taking from the well-established association of the left-hand side as evil, treacherous, or ominous (in contrast to "right," prawy/prawa/prawe).

1108 P. Grabarczyk, "Uwaga benzyna," p. 4.

1109 Ibid., pp. 5 and 12.

1110 J. Kochanowski, *Tylnymi drzwiami*, p. 238.

1111 Ibid., p. 236.

state amounted to half a billion zlotys on average.[1112] Attempts were made to counteract this practice. The coordinated action of the MO against abuses in fuel management, undertaken in the second half of 1963, turned out to be very fruitful. By the end of June 1965, as a result of almost three hundred investigations, 1,210 people were subjected to prosecution, of which 349 were CPN employees and 861 managers of state-owned transport companies. Losses as a result of fraud were estimated at over 19 million zlotys.[1113] Despite these successes, illegal trade in fuel continued in full swing.

In 1965, together with the Ministry of Transportation and the General Headquarters of the Citizens' Militia, CPN conducted research to determine the amount of petrol consumed by private vehicles, which was intended to help determine how much fuel was purchased illegally by private customers. The survey covered almost 26,000 vehicles from all voivodeships. The result of the study was alarming. Comparison of the survey results and PZU data with an analysis of market sales of liquid fuels in the years 1963–1967 yielded the finding that the average annual sale of illegal fuel amounted to approximately 170,000 tons, to a total value of 702 million zlotys.[1114]

As can be seen, the people closest to the state fuel reserves, led by transport and gas station workers, although in some cases representatives of the local administration also became involved.[1115] Generally, all methods of illegally obtaining fuel took advantage of the imperfect calculation of fuel consumption standards by state transport and the lack of reliable controls. Only in winter, drivers of transport companies could burn several percent more fuel due to weather conditions. In turn, riding in difficult terrain justified the burning of twice the standard amount. By exploiting this system, a frugal driver could save significant surpluses of petrol, which he could then sell illegally, usually to private car users, whether with the help of station employees or alone, draining the fuel straight from the tank with a rubber hose into a canister.[1116]

1112 B. W. Olszewska and H. Jezierski, "Benzyna," p. 1.

1113 D. Jarosz and M. Pasztor, *Afera mięsna: fakty i konteksty*, Toruń 2004, p. 133.

1114 J. Dałek, "Wykrywanie przestępstw w gospodarce materiałami pędnymi," *Służba MO* 1968, no. 2, p. 216.

1115 AAN, KC PZPR, sign. 237/XXXII-9, Dziedziny życia gospodarczego, w których obserwujemy szczególne nasilenie nadużyć, 1957 r., p. 11.

1116 P. Grabarczyk, "Uwaga benzyna," p. 12.

Drivers transporting so-called general cargo and bulk goods used the "block method," in which the total shipment travel was reduced while a "friendly" distributor recorded a higher total in the vehicle book. For example, a driver of a state-owned truck was assigned to transport a specific amount of coal, which—according to standards—would require ten trips, but in reality, the driver only took three trips with an overloaded trailer. This required the use of wooden blocks to support the vehicle's springs to prevent them from breaking. At short distances (for example, from the centre of Warsaw to its Praga district), a driver who knew the fuel consumption standards could save 50 litres of fuel: instead of 280 km, he would ride only 84 km.[1117] Of course, this raises the question about the devices used to mark the mileage. Drivers of state-owned cars had achieved near-perfection in falsifying mileage and tampering with odometers, and their ingenuity in this regard knew no limits. As Jerzy Kochanowski determined, in 1964 alone, out of 20,000 cars checked for this kind of abuse, a third either had no odometers or had ones that were damaged.[1118] In turn, gas station staff often used the so-called "bubble" method. The managers of a station that had accrued a surplus would agree with a supplier that everything above what could fit in the station's tanks would be put in cans, which would then go to private car owners. Very soon, it became an open secret that the arrival of a tanker at a gas station meant that fuel could be bought, in spite of the sign informing consumers that the station was closed for a delivery.[1119]

A kind of network was created, in which suppliers (drivers, gas station staff), intermediaries (employees of CPN and transport companies who legalised the "flow [of fuel] from the socialised sector to the private sector"),[1120] and recipients (usually private car users) all played equally important roles.[1121] Everyone derived tangible financial benefits from it: both suppliers and

1117 B. W. Olszewska and H. Jezierski, "Benzyna," p. 4.

1118 J. Kochanowski, *Tylnymi drzwiami*, p. 237.

1119 B. W. Olszewska and H. Jezierski, "Benzyna," p. 4.

1120 Ibid., p. 4.

1121 J. Kochanowski writes that "in institutions where fuel management rules were strictly observed, there were crew protests, and drivers left their jobs, looking for more liberal bosses" (*idem*, *Tylnymi drzwiami*, p. 236). In sporadic cases, as P. Grabowski relates, bodily harm or beatings could even be threatened. In one road work company in Upper Silesia, employees wanted to throw their manager into a pot of hot asphalt

intermediaries earned tidy sums, while buyers not only saved money, but also gained relatively easy access to fuel. It was probably this last factor that determined the popularity of "hot" petrol.

Even a glance at the number of gas stations operating in the period in question shows that in some regions of the country, the process of refuelling an automobile required a great deal of time and effort. Immediately after World War II, there were only a few dozen stations within the new borders of Poland. The first gas stations in postwar Poland were built in larger cities—Warsaw, Kraków, Katowice, Łódź, Poznań, Wrocław, and Gdańsk. Then came time for other voivodeship capitals and major district capitals. Usually, the location of a gas station was tied to the more important transportation routes. By the end of 1945, 26 stations were established, the next year, 159, and in 1947, twice as many. By the end of 1955, drivers could refuel at 679 CPN points in Poland, and five years later. at 760. By the early 1960s, drivers could use any of a thousand stations. Over the course of that decade, the increase was not as great: by the end of Władysław Gomułka's era, there were 1,100 gas stations in Poland (see Table 27). Since 1963, fuel could also be purchased at the so-called garage stations, which were usually located next to larger enterprises. Toward the end of the 1960s, drivers could also refuel their cars at stations belonging to PKS, Motozbyt, and PZMot. In 1968, there were thirty-nine of them in total.[1122]

Table 27. Gas stations in Poland (1945–1970)

Year	Number of stations	
	Public	Garage
1945	26	-
1946	159	-
1947	317	-
1948	332	-
1949	383	-
1950	415	-
1951	453	-
1952	538	-

because he refused to sign forged work reports; P. Grabowski, "Uwaga benzyna," p. 4.

1122 A. Rostocki and W. Wieniawski, *Motoryzacja w liczbach 1969*, Warszawa 1970, p. 266.

Year	Number of stations	
	Public	Garage
1953	620	-
1954	662	-
1955	679	-
1956	697	-
1957	702	-
1958	707	-
1959	760	-
1960	1.005	-
1961	1.039	-
1962	1.077	-
1963	1.075	1.154
1964	1.085	1.336
1965	1.082	1.552
1966	1.079	2.000
1967	1.083	2.302
1968	1.085	3.076
1969	1.092	3.981
1970	1.100	4.805

Source: A. Rostocki, W. Wieniawski, Motoryzacja w liczbach 1969, Warszawa 1970, p. 266; A. Rostocki, W. Wieniawski, Motoryzacja w liczbach 1973–1976, Warszawa 1977, p. 160.

Once again, car users in the most motorised voivodeships were in a privileged position, as most gas stations were located there. In early 1968, Warsaw itself had forty-six stations—although before 1939, it had twice as many.[1123] In 1969, the Warsaw, Katowice, Wrocław, and Poznań voivodeships had a total of 390 stations, which made up more than a third of all domestic fuel sales points. At the same time, the Rzeszów, Koszalin and Białystok voivodeships each had only forty-seven stations.

In 1962, before the start of the holiday season, the *Motor* weekly published an aid for drivers in the form of a map of the CPN station network, including information about the opening hours of individual points.[1124] The data contained in the map seems not to have been very up to date for 1962,

1123 W. Śmiałkowski, "Kłopoty motoryzacyjne," *Stolica* 1968, no. [January 7, 1968].
1124 "Prezent dla kierowców," *Motor* 1962, no. 19, pp. 8–9.

because—judging from the cited number of stations—it most likely came from the second half of the 1950s and was only updated on the basis of materials provided to the editorial office directly by CPN. Nevertheless, the data showed that out of 700 stations, only 35 were open 24 hours a day, while 128 were open from 6 am to 10 pm, and the majority were open from 8 am to 2 pm. The editorial comment was quite pointed: "So, pleasant journeys—without the ballast of fuel canisters ... ... Of course, the last comment refers to drivers with strong nerves and an optimistic mood. For the less courageous drivers, we recommend carrying 5 liters of fuel ... ."[1125]

In March of the same year, *Motor* reprinted several pieces of advice for British motorists intending to visit Poland in the near future, published by one of British daily, one of which concerned fuel. It was recommended to carry a reserve of fuel in a jerry can, as attempts to buy petrol at stations could be very troublesome. It was difficult, first of all, to "find a petrol pump" and second, "to find one that is working." Third, "there could be additional complications just when filling the tank." As is evident, a driver who set out for Poland had to be ready for many surprises.[1126]

The publication of the aforementioned gas station map in *Motor* prompted an increased number of letters addressed to the editorial office by readers who tried to obtain fuel following the magazine's recommendations. One of them, travelling to Warsaw via Gostynin, Gąbin, and Sochaczew, only found a station whose working hours corresponded to the information published in the weekly in Sochaczew. Everywhere else, clerks refused to sell him fuel, explaining that they never worked within the hours given in the newspaper.[1127] There were also common complaints about the refusal to sell petrol just before closing time.[1128] Buying petrol on Sundays and holidays was very problematic.[1129] Queues in front of those stations that were open were practically the norm.[1130]

1125 Ibid., p. 9.
1126 AaZ, "POLAND," *Motor* 1962, no. 9, p. 11.
1127 "Samowola stacji CPN," *Motor* 1962, no. 23, p. 11.
1128 "Prośby nie odniosły skutku," *Motor* 1962, no. 5, p. 11.
1129 "Nigdy w niedzielę. CPN nie lubi świąt," *Motor* 1962, no. 28, p. 2.
1130 "Czy CPN nie zauważa kolejki?" *Motor* 1965, no. 33, p. 4.

In 1965, the number of gas stations increased to 1,080. However, only sixty were open 24 hours a day, and the vast majority (760) only 6–7 hours a day. As a result, Poland in the mid-1960s could be considered a "fuel desert," and the advice to bring along a canister with a few litres of petrol was absolutely justified. It was calculated that an unlucky driver might need to ride for several hundred kilometres before "finding an open gas station on a Polish road in the afternoon, let alone in the evening."[1131] At the end of the decade, the situation improved significantly: of 1,100 gas stations, 198 were open 24 hours a day, and at 894 stations fuel was sold for sixteen hours per day.[1132] It is worth emphasising that CPN estimated in 1965 that the actual needs were at the level of 1,400 gas stations. Meanwhile, plans called for the construction of only 100 new stations by the end of the decade. As statistical data shows, even this was not achieved. However, the hours of operation of individual facilities were slowly extended. In 1966, over 100 of them were open 24 hours a day, though the number of those open for 16 hours a day increased significantly: from 261 in 1965 to 890 in 1966.[1133] This was undoubtedly related to the transfer of some stations to the so-called commission sales system. Stanisław Bursztyński, deputy commercial director of CPN, explained this decision thusly: "When the wage depends on the amount of fuel sold, the station staff will certainly decide to extend working hours, if necessary, to organise additional shifts … . It will make it worthwhile to clean the car window and inflate the tyres for free."[1134]

As can be seen, the change would also affect the quality of service at the stations, which had so far been inconsistent. This can be clearly seen in letters sent by desperate drivers to the editorial office of *Motor*. It was very common for customers to be treated unequally by the station staff, who divided them into "friends" and "strangers."[1135] The additional services mentioned by Bursztyński, such as washing windows or inflating tyres, were rare. One

---

1131 K. Szelestowska, "Aby nie było benzynowej pustki," *Motor* 1965, no. 36, p. 1.

1132 A. Rostocki and W. Wieniawski, *Motoryzacja w liczbach 1973–1976*, Warszawa 1977, p. 162.

1133 S. Kubiak, "CPN zapowiada radykalną poprawę," *Motor* 1966, no. 11, p. 3.

1134 B. Koperski, "Czy koniec kłopotów z kupnem benzyny?" *Motor* 1965, no. 3, p. 3.

1135 "To nam się nie podoba—Stacja CPN. Ale jaka?" *Motor* 1961, no. 35, p. 10.

highly illustrative example was a station whose employees received a chamois for cleaning the windows, but—as a later inspection showed—"the CPN staff proudly declared that they were saving the skins—a deficit item, after all—and that they clean car windows only for foreign customers, who pay in dollars."[1136] Letters sent to *Motor* include another interesting example. One reader found station employees reluctant to fill the tank completely without knowing the exact amount of petrol to be pumped into the tank. The reason was the station's outdated equipment in the form of old pumps and dispensers that were not equipped with metres, retained because the staff preferred not to bother with calculating fees for unusual amounts of fuel. After all, it was more convenient to do it in "round" amounts.[1137]

The introduction of the commission sales system at CPN stations actually improved the quality of service.[1138] While in 1965, only 21 stations operated under the new rules, by the following year, there were 346 of them.[1139] More and more stations were open 24 hours a day and on weekends. It was noted that "finally [at CPN stations] the driver is treated like a customer, and not like a intruder." However, services such as tyre inflation still remained a problem. CPN issued a special recommendation on this matter, imposing an obligation on station staff to perform this service free of charge. Over half a thousand stations were to receive air compressors for that purpose.[1140]

Station locations, opening hours and service quality are only one side of the coin. The other side involved equally important matters of the availability, price, and quality of the fuel sold there. In mid-1965, drivers using CPN stations could choose from three types of petrol: ethanol 70 ("red"), ethanol 80 ("blue") and ethanol 87 ("yellow"). The most popular one, sold at all stations, was the one with the lowest octane number—"red." In 1965, "yellow" was distributed by only 10% of all stations, and "blue"—by 35%. In practice, this meant that drivers had relatively easy access only to 70-octane petrol,

---

1136 "Bez komentarzy," *Motor* 1965, no. 38, p. 4.

1137 "Biurokracja w CPN," *Motor* 1965, no. 38, p. 2.

1138 A. K. Wróblewski, "Wytrych," *Polityka* 1966, no. 42, p. 7.

1139 S. Kubiak, "CPN zapowiada radykalna poprawę," p. 3.

1140 B. Koperski, "Gorzej i lepiej. Przed motoryzacyjnym szczytem," *Motor* 1966, no. 21, p. 1.

which was clearly the worst quality. Even cars of domestic production, which at that time did not represent a high technical level, had engines adapted to at least 75 octane fuel. Filling them with the popular "blue" fuel drastically shortened their lifespan: the engine overheated more often, its components wore out faster, and the crank system suffered damage.[1141] When asked about the reasons for the distribution of particular types of fuel at their stations, the CPN management explained this fact by citing low interest among buyers in better, and therefore more expensive gasoline. Stations were supplied based on demand, which—as it turned out—often depended on the season. For example, there was a visible decrease in passenger car traffic in the winter months, which translated into much less traffic at gas stations. Even in Warsaw, the city with the highest motorisation in Poland, fuel sales in the winter of 1965–1966 were approximately 50% lower compared to the summer period. It is therefore not surprising that these months were considered the "driest" of the year.[1142] However, the distribution of low-quality fuel was determined primarily by fuel costs.

At that time, Poland also had some of the highest petrol prices in Europe.[1143] Czechs and Slovaks, for example, paid less—2.1 and 2.4 Czech koruna for a litre of fuel in 1965, depending on type. This meant that, given an average monthly salary of 1,493 korunas, they could afford over 600 litres of petrol. In East Germany, average monthly earnings could buy approximately 400 litres of fuel, while in Poland, average earners were only able to afford 210 litres of 70-octane or 155 litres of 87-octane petrol.[1144] The price to octane

---

1141 B. W. Olszewska and H. Jezierski, "Benzyna," p. 1; W. Tabencki, "Na tropie parujących złotówek. Benzyna ale jaka?" *Motor* 1965, no. 40, p. 3.

1142 (g), "Czy tylko w stolicy? Sezonowe kłopoty CPN," *Motor* 1966, no. 7, p. 2.

1143 "Jakie paliwa?" *Motor* 1966, no. 16, p. 4.

1144 *Statistisches Jahrbuch der Deutschen Demokratischen Republik* 1966, p. 200, https://www.digizeitschriften.de/dms/img/?PID=PPN514402644_1966|log33&physid=phys230#navi (accessed: February 20, 2017). This relationship was much more unfavourable if we take into account Western European countries. In Sweden, the average monthly salary could buy over 700 litres of fuel in the mid-1960s, while in France, it could buy over 900 litres; *Statistik Årsbok för Sverigie* 1965, p. 228, http://www.scb.se/Grupp/Hitta_statistik/Historisk_statistik/_Dokument/Statistiskproc.20årsbokproc.201914-2001/Statistiskproc.20arsbokproc.20forproc.20Sverigeproc.201965.pdf (accessed:

ratio was equally unfavourable. In Czechoslovakia, as the octane number increased by 13.5%, the price rose by 14%; in Romania, these values reached 28% and 37%, respectively; and in Hungary, 21% and 37%, respectively. In Poland, however, a 14% increase in the octane number was accompanied by a price increase of 25%. Thus, in 1965, a litre of the popular "red" petrol cost 4.8 zlotys, a litre of "blue", 6 zlotys, and a litre of "yellow", 6.5 zlotys.[1145] In Western European countries, these proportions were much lower. In England, as octane number increased by 12.5%, the price rose by 7%. For example, the price of a gallon (4.5 litres) of 80-octane petrol was 42 pence; of 90-octane petrol, 45 pence; and of the best, 100-octane petrol, 48 pence. In West Germany, an octane number increase of 7% resulted in an 11% price increase, while in Sweden, the values were 8% and 3.7%, respectively. It should be added that practically all of Western Europe used high-octane gasoline, usually at the 86–90 octane level.[1146]

Meanwhile, on the black market, prices were usually halved, because the cost of a litre of petrol for state entities was set at 2.4 zlotys.[1147] It is also worth emphasising that state institutions, which were the main consumers of the product at that time, were largely responsible for the demand for specific types of fuel. However, the economic calculation was key here, too: in order to reduce the costs of operating the cars, "red" gasoline was the primary choice, and it also accounted for most of the black market transactions. The types of fuels sold by CPN changed in mid-1966, when the previously established petrol ratings were replaced by new ones: with an octane number of 75 (dyed blue) and 94 (dyed yellow). The price per litre increased to 5 zlotys and 6.5 zlotys, respectively.[1148] The popular yellow-coloured petrol would appear at almost 500 gas stations by the end of the year.

February 20, 2017); Ch. Baudelot and A. Lebeaupin, "Les salaries de 1950 à 1975," *Economie et statistique* 1979, vol. 113, no. 1, p. 17.

1145 B. W. Olszewska and H. Jezierski, "Benzyna," p. 1.

1146 "Jakie paliwa?"

1147 P. Lipka, "Czy zwłoka słuszna?" *Motor* 1957, no. 38, p. 3.

1148 SK, "Spełniono dwa postulaty. Jeździmy na lepszej benzynie," *Motor* 1966, no. 33, p. 1.

What, then, would make up a perfect gas station? Stanisław Dygat, who took part in the annual driver survey organised by *Motor*, saw it this way:

> I once dreamed that I was driving to Kraków and, while leaving Warsaw, I saw something that must have seemed fantastic even in my dream: a wonderful gas station equipped with a service station, with a kind staff and a manager who cared if the customer is satisfied, a luxury cafe with a jukebox, and the general atmosphere that makes you congratulate yourself on being a motorised person. But the strangest thing about this dream was that when I pinched myself to wake up, it turned out that it was not a dream, but a completely real edifice in the town of Janki, near Warsaw.[1149]

Figure 16. CPN petrol station in Janki near Warsaw, late 1950s / early 1960s, National Digital Archives, Zbyszko Siemaszko, 3/51/0/6.20/166

The improvement in service quality and fuel availability at CPN stations discussed a few paragraphs earlier did not last long. The 1967 holiday season put paid to the promises. Drivers who wanted to inflate their tyres or add water to the radiator while refuelling still faced huge difficulties. Most stations lacked

1149 "Motoryzacja i ja," *Motor* 1962, no. 50/51, p. 3.

air compressors, which was explained by market shortages. There was also a shortage of distilled water, a result of difficulties in finding suitable glass containers. However, the main complaint concerned problems with purchasing fuel. In a letter to *Motor*, one Varsovian wrote: "At the market square in Płońsk on Sunday, July 22 of this year, at 7 pm, there was a crowd of cars of tourists foreign and domestic. Everyone was looking for petrol because all stations from Ostróda to Płońsk were closed (about 150 km). Stations on the route from Grudziądz to Płońsk (ok 165 km) were likewise closed."[1150] The market in Płońsk quickly filled up with helpful drivers who eagerly offered to sell fuel, although at a rather prohibitive price—200 zlotys per canister!

5.6 "I dream of a warszawa for which there are parts and also mechanics"[1151]—technical service stations

The above-mentioned survey conducted among the readers of the *Motor* weekly, in addition to asking about makes and models, also included a question about the degree to which drivers were satisfied with their cars. According to the survey, owners of Fiats, French Simcas and East German P-70 s were the most satisfied. Everyone who drove such cars on a daily basis considered them to be really good and worth recommending. Slightly worse results (88 and 84%, respectively) were achieved by Moskvitches and Warszawas. Syrenas were clearly the worst in this regard; only 70% of Syrena owners expressed satisfaction with their car.[1152] No doubt, owners' low or high level of satisfaction with their car was determined by the quality of the technical service.

In the case of some car makes, usually produced in other countries of the Eastern Bloc, their unreliability and low quality were proverbial. *Motor* published a letter to the editor in which a reader performed a very simple calculation: "In November—117 units, in December—145 units, in January—171 units, in total—487 units. Monthly average—162 units. … [T]his is the number of Warszawas repaired under warranty by one regional

---

[1150] B. Koperski, "Stacja benzynowa to nie urząd," *Motor* 1967, no. 35, p. 3; cf. O. Czeniewicz, "Na szlaku wielkiej posuchy," *Motor* 1967, no. 36, p. 3.

[1151] S. Lem and S. Mrożek, *Listy*, p. 49.

[1152] "Krajowa ankieta motoryzacyjnego 'Instytutu Gallupa'."

service station. Counting all twelve regional stations, it can be assumed that 23,328 'Warszawas' were repaired under warranty over the course of the year. If FSO produces 13,000 Warszawa per year, these numbers suggest that, after leaving the factory floor, each car of this brand must be repaired twice."[1153] Of course, this does not reflect the actual data on the car's failure rate, but it illustrates the general opinion on it, inspired by the serious financial outlay buyers were often forced to bear. Cars of Polish production, especially Syrenas, lost value almost immediately after leaving Motozbyt. They were definitely not among the favourites in the used car market. New units that were offered second-hand often carried prices reduced by 5–15% from the factory price.[1154] The same was true at the car markets, where in 1965, for example, new Syrenas were offered for 62,000–65,000 zlotys (the following year, even 60,000), and the cars still did not find buyers.[1155] An even greater drop in value applied to used cars. A one-year-old Syrena cost 10,000–18,000 zlotys less, and each subsequent year meant an additional drop of 5,000–10,000 zlotys. Generally, this make was seen as one of the so-called weaker cars, which were not particularly popular on the used car market.[1156] However, if a buyer intended to buy a Syrena, journalists suggested purchasing an older model, whose value on the used car market at the end of 1964 was approximately 18,000–25,000 zlotys, while warning that such a car would require an immediate expense (of "at least 10,000 zlotys") for repairs.[1157]

It is, therefore, not surprising that buyers sometimes discussed their purchase in a rather ambiguous tone, suggesting trouble rather than satisfaction. This is the sentiment behind a sentence in one diary which reads: "I contracted a Trabant."[1158] Jan Józef Szczepański described his Syrena in similar terms: "An inflow of money. Film, radio. We make investments. Today, I opened a

---

1153 "List czytelnika 'Motoru' do Kontrolerów Technicznych FSO," *Motor* 1960, no. 9, p. 15.

1154 T. Szczerbicki, *Syrena*, p. 162.

1155 "Do wyboru, do koloru. Warszawy i Syreny," p. 4; "Wiosenna panorama rynkowa. Do wyboru, do koloru," p. 1.

1156 "Do wyboru, do koloru. Jubileuszowe konfrontacje," p. 1.

1157 "Do wyboru, do koloru. Dziś FSO-Syrena," *Motor* 1964, no. 37, p. 4.

1158 "'Lech'," in: *Pamiętniki pokolenia. Prace nadesłane na Wielki Konkurs Wspomnień pod nazwą "Rośliśmy z Polską Ludową" ogłoszony przez ZG ZMS, ZG ZMW Instytut Filozofii i Socjologii PAN, P.W. "Iskry" i "Sztandar Młodych,"* Warszawa 1966, p. 141.

car savings book at PKO. Nonsense, of course. Odds of 1 in a 1,000. But if you win—that's where problems begin."[1159] The writer ultimately did not win the car in the draw. However, two years later, in 1964, he decided to buy a Syrena in instalments through Motozbyt. After several months—a relatively short wait—and having completed many formalities, in which he was aided by his friend Stanisław Lem, acting as guarantor, Szczepański managed to secure the car.[1160] Again, like a few years earlier, he did not seem to show any enthusiasm, treating the car as a necessity: "The day before yesterday, I picked up the Syrena. After fifteen minutes, it turned out that it had a gearbox defect (incorrectly installed cable). The car is still there, in the yard, by the window. I don't even want to look at it."[1161] However, this was only the beginning of the writer's struggles with the car. Less than a week after collecting the car from Motozbyt, he wrote in his diary: "The ordeal with the car continues," probably not expecting that constant breakdowns of his Syrena would become an important subject of his daily observations.[1162] After a few years, on February 13, 1967, he wrote: "Today, I sold the Syrena"—and it is hard not to see this as a sigh of relief.[1163]

Even a functional new car did not guarantee trouble-free driving, as discovered by Stanisław Lem, who bought a new Fiat 1800 in 1964 with the proceeds from the sale of the Warszawa he had won through PKO. There was little choice because the Motozbyt in Warsaw only had one Fiat in stock, so dirty that "its color became visible only yesterday, after a thorough washing; it is white." On the way back to Kraków, it turned out that there was no oil in the engine. The writer had to hitch a ride to Grójec, where he managed to arrange for his Fiat to be towed and bought the oil. However, the other car also broke down. He only managed to reach the car he had left by the side of the road with the help of a taxi. As it later turned out, the whole mess was caused by a loose oil filter. Interestingly, the Multi-Branch Service Cooperative

---

1159 J. J. Szczepański, *Dziennik*, vol. 2: *1957–1963*, Kraków 2011, p. 448.
1160 S. Lem and S. Mrożek, *Listy*, p. 299.
1161 J. J. Szczepański, *Dziennik*, vol. 3: *1964–1972*, Kraków 2013, p. 47.
1162 Ibid., pp. 47–48.
1163 Ibid., p. 199.

for Craft Car Repair in Grójec, which helped Lem, did not bill him. As a thank you, the writer later sent them copies of his books.[1164]

Vehicle servicing was carried out by Technical Automobile Service stations, which performed warranty inspections, as well as regular and major repairs of cars and motorcycles.[1165] Almost throughout the period in question, there was great variation in the availability of automotive services in different regions of the country. In 1962, there were 69 TOS stations in Poland, among which were fifteen regional stations (in voivodeship capitals), 44 field stations, 9 roadside stations, and 1 seasonal station.[1166] This was not enough for the rapidly growing number of cars and motorcycles on Polish roads. Two years later, before the start of the holiday season, there were over 600 service stations in total, including fifty-one "own facilities," forty-four technical emergency vehicles, and five mobile stations. "Don't expect to be dazzled," commented one participant in a conference chaired by Deputy Minister of Transportation Walenty Szablewski, reflecting on these numbers.[1167] Gaps in the state service network had to be filled by private workshops. As the previously cited survey from 1960 shows, almost 60% of readers were able to repair basic faults in their own vehicles by themselves, while 12% required help from TOS. At the end of 1968, the TOS network comprised seventy-nine stations (see Table 28). Independent workshops were also maintained by local industry (69), Motozbyt (28), and PZMot (33), and CPN (12). The majority, as many as 2,091, were workshops run by private craftspeople, but these only dealt with minor repairs. There were few large stations where a full car service could be performed, and almost all of them belonged to the TOS network. Almost a third of all repairs were carried out there.

1164 S. Lem and S. Mrożek, *Listy*, p. 385.

1165 "TOS się rozwija," *Motor* 1955, no. 41, p. 6.

1166 K. Goździewski, "Lotne pogotowie techniczne—konieczność chwili," *Motor* 1962, no. 20, p. 3.

1167 W. Babski, "Usługi motoryzacyjne w nadchodzącym sezonie," *Motor* 1965, no. 24, p. 1.

Table 28. Number of facilities in the public network of car service stations (as of December 31, 1968)

Branch	Total	Number of facilities in the network			Outside of the network	percent share of processing capacity
		G	P	D		
TOS	79	16	42	18	3	28.0
Local industry	69	-	20	39	10	6.3
Motozbyt	28	-	3	23	2	2.3
CPN	12	-	-	10	2	0.2
PZMot	33	-	7	26	-	3.8
Craft shops	2.091	-	-	1.065	1.026	29.0
Other	536	1	46	285	204	29.9
Total	2.848	17	118	1.466	1.247	100.0

G—large stations in the main network of service stations—full service
P—medium-size stations in the basic network—limited service
D—small stations in the ad hoc network—uncomplicated repairs and simple service
Source: A. Rostocki and W. Wieniawski, Motoryzacja w liczbach 1969, p. 285.

In the early 1970s, there were just over 3,000 facilities throughout the country providing automotive services, for an average of 173 cars per workshop (see Table 29). The situation in this respect was definitely best in the independent cities and voivodeships of Bydgoszcz, Koszalin, Szczecin, and Kielce. There were several reasons for this. One was a relatively small automobile fleet, as in the case of the Kielce voivodeship, were the ratio was 164 cars per workshop. Another was a relatively well-developed material and technical base for automotive services in relation to the number of passenger cars, as in the Szczecin and Bydgoszcz voivodeships. The third factor that promoted relatively easy access to service stations was the number of workers employed in automotive services. In this aspect, the Koszalin and Bydgoszcz voivodeships excelled.[1168]

[1168] *Warunki techniczno-organizacyjne obsługi samochodów osobowych w opinii użytkowników samochodów oraz właścicieli prywatnych warsztatów naprawczych w świetle badań ankietowych*, Poznań 1973, p. 39.

Table 29. Number of registered private passenger cars, service facilities, and workers employed therein, and the value of repair, renovation, and maintenance services on passenger cars in 1971, by voivodeship

Voivodeship	Number of cars		Value of services		Number of service facilities		Employees		
								number	
	Units in thousands	Structure in %	Zlotys in thousands	Share in %	Units	Number of cars per facility	people	Cars per employee	Employees per facility
Total	528.900	100	995.056	100	3.049	173	9.621	55	3.2
City of Warsaw	63.800	12.1	153.992	15.5	218	293	1.064	60	4.9
Kraków city	19.100	3.6	41.186	4.1	58	329	323	59	5.6
Łódź city	20.400	3.9	49.241	4.9	102	200	404	50	4.0
Poznań city	23.300	4.4	49.024	4.9	87	268	406	57	4.7
Wrocław city	18.200	3.4	40.532	4.1	66	276	344	53	5.2
Białostockie	12.400	2.3	16.734	1.7	9.3	133	180	69	1.9
Bydgoskie	27.500	5.2	58.271	5.9	197	140	596	46	3.0
Gdańskie	30.500	5.8	53.890	5.4	139	219	511	60	3.7
Katowickie	71.700	13.5	128.585	12.9	415	173	1.346	53	3.2
Kieleckie	16.600	3.1	35.271	3.5	101	164	325	51	3.2
Koszalińskie	11.600	2.2	28.413	2.9	90	129	304	38	3.4
Krakowskie	20.400	3.9	27.167	2.8	114	179	320	64	2.8
Lubelskie	16.100	3.0	26.225	2.6	107	150	275	58	2.6
Łódzkie	17.400	3.3	22.391	2.3	126	138	294	59	2.3
Olsztyńskie	13.800	2.6	23.362	2.3	90	153	215	64	2.4

(Continued)

Table 29. *(Continued)*

Voivodeship	Number of cars		Value of services		Number of service facilities		Employees		
								number	
	Units in thousands	Structure in %	Zlotys in thousands	Share in %	Units	Number of cars per facility	people	Cars per employee	Employees per facility
Opolskie	16.200	3.1	22.142	2.2	121	134	314	52	2.6
Poznańskie	31.600	6.0	49.585	5.0	225	140	638	49	2.8
Rzeszowskie	15.300	2.9	20.759	2.1	114	134	261	59	2.3
Szczecińskie	15.800	3.0	32.969	3.3	97	163	278	57	2.9
Warszawskie	30.100	5.7	56.859	5.7	218	138	555	54	2.5
Wrocławskie	25.900	4.9	40.344	4.1	183	141	489	53	2.7
Zielonogórskie	11.200	2.1	18.103	1.8	88	127	179	63	2.0

Source: Warunki techniczno-organizacyjne obsługi samochodów osobowych w opinii użytkowników samochodów oraz właścicieli prywatnych warsztatów naprawczych w świetle badań ankietowych, Poznań 1973, p. 40.

At the same time, in the field of automotive services, although the socialised sector accounted for a smaller number of facilities (only 28% of the total) and fewer employees (30.8% of all employees in automotive services), it carried out over 44% of the global value of services. This could be due to the better technical equipment at these facilities and greater capacity to mechanise repair, renovation, and maintenance processes.[1169] The obligation to perform warranty repairs and inspections in state-owned entities certainly also played a part.

Not only the number of state-owned service stations, but also the quality of their work left much to be desired, as *Motor* readers often reported in letters to the editor. For example, one resident of Kujawy complained about the TOS in Włocławek, which kept his MZ motorcycle waiting for repair for almost half a year.[1170] In turn, one *Motor* article described the Factory Service Station at FSO as "not at all worse than other service and repair workshop"—it was "just the same."[1171] "There is one device for dynamic wheel balancing on the entire Gdańsk coastal region," wrote a resident of Sopot in a letter to *Polityka* in 1966, having found himself stuck in a queue of car owners waiting for repairs in front of the local TOS since dawn. The entire operation took over seven hours: "During this time, 4 employees … 'serviced' 6 cars, including mine, performing some basic operations, without even dismantling the carburetor in any of the cars."[1172] When the MHW carried out an internal inspection of the Motozbyt branch located at 36 Stalingradzka Street in Warsaw in April 1965, it was discovered that the staff who carried out quality inspections of new cars—both those manufactured in Żerań and imported—did not have the basic tools necessary to conduct them. As stated in the post-inspection report, of the twenty-three measuring instruments with which quality control units were supposed to be supplied according to regulations, the Warsaw office did not have a single one. The same was true of tools for measuring battery voltage or checking galvanic coatings or

1169 Ibid., pp. 38–39.
1170 "Między TOS-em a Motozbytem," *Motor* 1964, no. 9, p. 2.
1171 "Papierowe gwarancje. Ściśle tajne," *Motor* 1965, no. 33, p. 11; cf. "Zupa z żółwia," *Motor* 1955, no. 13, p. 3.
1172 "Polska samochodowa," *Polityka* 1966, no. 50, p. 6.

tyre pressure.[1173] A statistical study on satisfaction with automotive services conducted in 1970 showed that only slightly more than half of all customers left the workshops satisfied with the quality of the service provided. It was even worse when it came to timeliness and price: here, only 29.5% were satisfied.[1174] In a letter to Stanisław Lem, Sławomir Mrożek described the work of the mechanics repairing his car after a minor accident: "The car is still not ready; a month has passed already before the mechanics began to stand by and scratch their heads, lazily leaning their elbows on the body and chatting in a friendly manner."[1175]

It is thus not surprising that any deviations from this norm were carefully recorded by the weekly. An article from 1962 discusses the newly opened Auto Service Motozbyt station at 1. Armii Avenue in Warsaw. Small, but perfectly equipped with state-of-the-art tools representing "the cream of domestic production in this field," it was reportedly "an example worthy of imitation in all respects."[1176] *Motor* also described the TOS station on Omulewska Street in Warsaw, which had undergone a serious metamorphosis. In spite of previous criticism, the magazine reported with great joy the appearance of "signs of improvement": "Have you ever been to a diagnostic station? No? Go to the one on Omulewska Street. There you will find a station at the European level, so clean that everyone who enters starts looking for the doormat, which, of course, has been provided."[1177] An owner of a Warszawa (which, "as we know, has many faults") spoke in equally warm terms about one TOS station in Toruń, "surprised by the friendly attitude of the director and all employees towards the client."[1178]

1173 AAN, Ministerstwo Handlu Wewnętrznego (hereafter: MHW), sign. 18/7, Protokół kontroli nr 16/65, Warszawa, 7 IV 1965 r., unnumbered pages.

1174 "Usługi dla ludności w ocenie mieszkańców," *Badania Korespondentów Miejskich* 1970, no. 2, p. XXVII.

1175 S. Lem and S. Mrożek, *Listy*, p. 42.

1176 "Auto Service Motozbyt, Warszawa Al. I Armii," *Motor* 1962, no. 8, p. 10.

1177 T. S., "Pierwsze jaskółki poprawy," *Motor* 1962, no. 36, p. 10.

1178 "Z książki życzeń i zażaleń," *Motor* 1962, no. 45, p. 11.

Figure 17. Car Service Station at 27 Omulewska Street, Warsaw, 1955, National Digital Archives, Zbyszko Siemaszko, 3/51/0/6.20/164

Trying to remedy the insufficiencies of state technical resources, decision-makers tried to modify the organisation of the network to avoid leaving drivers without help in case of problems during the hottest season. They attempted, for example, to create a network of stations and workshops along main travel routes and around tourist destinations and resorts. *Motor* first published news about this initiative, and then carried out an inspection, the results of which were later published. It turned out that the Koszalin voivodeship was the best in terms of technical assistance for motorists. One of the conveniences it offered was that the opening hours of particular stations and workshops overlapped across 24 hours. Stations in the Szczecin voivodeship received an equally positive assessment, and earned additional plaudits for preparing information boards in four languages. The Kraków voivodeship also focused on efficient service and provided information in German (although "the quality of the writings" is no cause for pride"). In other voivodeships, the things did not go as smoothly. This was particularly the case in Warsaw, which "has a lot of workshops and private stations, and the voivodeship is mostly empty," while "socialized facilities are becoming mired in competition and lack clarity over what to focus on, especially in the case of mobile service stations."[1179]

The problems with TOS were not the result of a lack of training or even an inappropriate attitude towards the customers, although these certainly had an impact on the overall assessment of their performance. One unsolved problem during the period in question turned out to be the lack of spare parts and consumables.[1180] In 1962, the automotive industry produced spare parts to a value of 1.2 billion zlotys, which was only a drop in the ocean of needs.[1181] During the first fifteen years after World War II, the sales of spare parts reached the value of 9.7 billion zlotys, and in the years 1961–1965, of 1 billion zlotys in excess of that.[1182] The Automotive Industry Association (Zjednoczenie Przemysłu Motoryzacyjnego, ZPM), took over from Motozbyt the task of balancing needs in this area. Pursuant to resolution no. 280 of the Council of Ministers, ZPM was also responsible for "production programming," taking into account the demand resulting from the use of vehicles in the country and "conducting the sales policy" of these products.[1183] However, there were recurring problems, and it was very difficult, and sometimes simply impossible, to solve them.

Early in the second half of the 1950s, shortages of spare parts were blamed on "communication difficulties" between Motozbyt and the Central Automotive Production Board (CZPS) and the plants subordinated to it. It was noted that FSO did not sign a contract for the supply of parts for 1955 until May of that year. However, plants cooperating with the factory at Żerań did not comply with the requirements of the contracts for the parts they supplied, producing arbitrary quantities (usually below demand) of random components. An inspection showed that certain manufacturers "were not

---

1179 W. Babski, "Czy lepiej z usługami," *Motor* 1965, no. 32, p. 1.

1180 "TOS stations, which should represent the interests of the user and manufacturer, are unable to fulfil their obligations. They do not have the full range of necessary parts"; M. Kras, "Gwarancja… na papierze," *Motor* 1962, no. 2, p. 11.

1181 "Produkujemy coraz więcej pojazdów. Osiągnięcia przemysłu motoryzacyjnego," *Motor* 1962, no. 52, p. 3.

1182 (sz), "20 lat Motozbytu," *Motor* 1966, no. 23, p. 1.

1183 AAN, Stowarzyszenie Inżynierów i Techników Motoryzacji (hereafter: SIiTM), sign. 2/7, Roman Pijanowski, Organizacja zbytu części zamiennych i pojazdów samochodowych, unnumbered pages.

encouraged by the [CZPS] regarding the proper implementation of the plan for the production and supply of spare parts for 'Motozbyt' and were not adequately supervised in the management of the supply."[1184] In addition, it was discovered that large-scale trade in spare parts intended for Motozbyt was taking place in the inspected plants. The parts were sold to both cooperative and state institutions. One example is the Apparatus and Lighting Plant in Warsaw, which sold parts, mainly lamps, worth 2.5 million zlotys over eleven months of 1955. The inspection's conclusions were not optimistic: "Plants currently produce motor vehicles without providing them with the most necessary consumable spare parts."[1185]

The cooperative nature of production in the automotive industry made it especially difficult to coordinate between the multiple manufacturers responsible for the production of parts. On the other hand, the obligation imposed on the industry (not only automotive) to fully sate the demand for spare parts for the manufactured equipment raised the question of who was to supply these parts: in the case of passenger cars, was it supposed to be FSO or its cooperators? This lack of precise guidelines was one of the reasons for the complaint that the Hungarian government filed with Motoimport regarding automotive equipment imported from Poland. It transpired that the trade agreement signed with the Hungarian People's Republic assumed the delivery of spare parts for vehicles exported to Hungary in 1966, to a value of almost 2.5 million roubles. Meanwhile, by the end of November, Poland was only able to fulfil some of its obligations, sending to Hungary components worth just over 1.5 million roubles.[1186] This was explained by problems with the factories producing the parts: "Countless demands on our part intervening at different levels of the industry did not have the right effect, mainly due to shortcomings in the cooperation between the final manufacturer and its numerous cooperators."[1187] The trade attaché at the Hungarian embassy even

---

1184 Ibid., Centralny Zarząd Produkcji Samochodów (hereafter: CZPS), Ministerstwo Kontroli Państwowej Zespół Kontroli Państwowej Przemysłu "S", Warszawa, [January 30, 1956], pp. 3–6.

1185 Ibid., p. 6.

1186 AAN, Ministerstwo Handlu Zagranicznego, sign. 2/4, [Informacja], Warszawa, 15 XII 1966 r., unnumbered pages.

1187 Ibid., Informacja—odpowiedź CHZ Motoimport dot. współpracy pomiędzy CHZ Motoimport a CHZ Mogürt, Warszawa, 11 V 1966 r., unnumbered pages.

threatened to suspend the importation of Polish cars if the problem of spare parts was not resolved quickly enough.

The year 1965 yielded some data. That year, the automotive industry produced the following quantities of spare parts for domestically produced cars: for the Warszawa, 30% of the value of vehicles produced; for Star trucks—70%; and for Syrenas—6%. Noting the fact that the value of parts produced for cars belonging primarily to the state fleet was much higher than that of those for a car intended for private use, one can clearly see what the priorities were. At the same time, however, attention was drawn to the fact of very large disparities in the demand for spare parts between public and private users. In the latter case, demand planning could be based on technical standards, which was not possible in the case of state-owned cars. This supposedly reflected the low degree of vehicle use and a disrespectful attitude towards state property—which does not change the fact that, even if decision-makers found it easier to define the production volume of spare parts for private users in this way, that volume remained insufficient for the end users.

This can be seen, for example, in letters sent to *Motor*. According to readers, the availability of spare parts was dramatically low. One owner of a Warszawa wrote: "Starting from turn signal bulbs, through all kinds of seals and shock absorbers, and ending with fenders—everything is practically unattainable."[1188] Another user of the same make of car had a similar problem: "I bought a new Warszawa 204, one of the main—and very naive—arguments being the expected ease of purchasing spare parts for a domestic car. The second day after the purchase, the rear plastic lamp holders were stolen. I was astonished to find that obtaining these plastic frames is completely impossible in Warsaw."[1189] Syrena drivers also wrote letters in a similar tone.[1190]

1188 W. Jeżewski, "Opony do Warszaw, czyli historia jakich wiele," *Motor* 1964, no. 30, p. 3.

1189 "Aż się wierzyć nie chce," *Motor* 1965, no. 32, p. 2. Cf. "Giełda pod mostem," PKF 64/41B, 1964.

1190 "Dlaczego nie ma części do Syren?" *Motor* 1965, no. 25, p. 2; "Czy nie ma części do skuterów OSA?" *Motor* 1965, no. 24, p. 2.

In its forecast for the second half of 1966, *Motor* offered no hope for any improvement in this:

> Currently, there is a shortage of almost 40% of parts for the Škoda 1000 MB. Therefore, there are serious problems with warranty service for cars of this make that have been sold. … [T]hose who want to buy a Škoda or Wartburg end up buying Syrenas, because we know that, whichever car you buy, you will find… NO PARTS [upper case in original—HW]. Parts are not available in sufficient quantity for the following cars: Škoda, Zastava, Moskvitch, and, despite assurances from salespeople, also for Wartburgs and Trabants. If you have to wait several weeks for a minor element, then given the strict mileage limits required for warranty inspections, all you can do is simply lock the car down.[1191]

One of the most sought-after automotive products were tyres. Tyre shortages were particularly noticeable on the spare parts market. Despite the existence of factories in Dębica and Poznań, the demand for tyres remained great. In 1965, both plants announced plans to produce over 400,000 vehicle tyres, while according to the Ministry of Trade, as many as 600,000 were needed. Thus, even the planned importation of 65,000 tyres would not suffice. *Motor* reported that, "[d]espite the imposition of a modicum of order (sign-ups for a list of allocations and requests being fulfilled in the order in which they were submitted), there may be a shortage of tyres for passenger cars."[1192] Certain remedial measures on the part of the domestic industry led to a slight improvement the following year (a total of over 619,000 tyres were delivered, including 200,000 through import), but irregular deliveries still caused issues.[1193] In their letters, many readers complained about problems with vehicle tyres—not only unavailability, but also poor quality. "Potato slippers"—as tyres produced in Poland were commonly called—did not enjoy a good reputation, and claims that products from the Dębica plant worked perfectly in tropical conditions (a reference to the destinations of export of Stars, Nysas, and Żuks) inspired only irritation.[1194]

[1191] B. Koperski, "Gorzej i lepiej" (emphasis in original—H. W.).

[1192] "Opon wciąż zbyt mało," *Motor* 1965, no. 15, p. 3.

[1193] S. Kubiak, "Nieco lepiej z ogumieniem," *Motor* 1966, no. 8, p. 1.

[1194] "Jedno pytanie," *Motor* 1964, no. 14, p. 2; S. Kubiak, "Nieco lepiej"; see also "A jednak prawdziwe," *Motor* 1966, no. 22, p. 2.

It was not only that the domestic spare parts industry did not meet the needs, but the volume of imports was also insufficient. When the scale of import of vehicles from abroad increased, it immediately resulted in a shortage of parts.[1195] According to a survey from 1960, 80% of readers had this problem. In these conditions, the owners of two Polish makes—Warszawas and Syrenas—fared comparatively better, with only 57% and 90% of owners, respectively, complaining about the lack of parts.[1196] "Importing cars without importing an appropriate number of spare parts from abroad is an obvious absurdity," argued one participant in a conference on the activities of Motozbyt, organised in early 1964 by Deputy Prime Minister Eugeniusz Szyr.[1197] Nevertheless, the problem was truly serious and affected a huge number of users of imported cars—indeed, according to some sources, nearly all of them.[1198] When Bank PEKAO decided to import several dozen British Triumph Herald cars in September 1961, as internal exports, it decided to meet the needs of potential buyers and requested that Motozbyt "secure" access to spare parts for this model. Motozbyt demanded that an appropriate amount of foreign currency be transferred for this purpose, 3% of the value of the entire transaction and a subsequent limit of 10%. Ultimately, the plan fell through because the council of the bank rejected Motozbyt's demands.[1199] Perhaps this was also the reason why Triumphs were not very popular among PEKAO customers: of the sixty-four cars that were imported in 1961, only half were sold. In a statement printed in *Motor*, the director of the Warsaw district TOS complained about the excessive variety of imports, which was reportedly causing shortages of components for foreign cars. The way out of this impasse was to limit importation to the most reliable makes and to "widely promote cars of domestic makes in all possible ways (PKO, instalment and direct sales of 'Warszawas' and 'Syrenas')."[1200]

1195 "Około 50 000 motocykli…," *Motor* 1956, no. 46, p. 6.
1196 "Krajowa ankieta motoryzacyjnego 'Instytutu Gallupa'."
1197 AAN, URM, sign. 62/8, Protokół nr GS-1/63 z konferencji w sprawie omówienia sytuacji w zakresie rynku motoryzacyjnego w Polsce, [January 4, 1963], p. 204.
1198 "Krajowa ankieta motoryzacyjnego 'Instytutu Gallupa'."
1199 Archiwum Centralne Banku Pekao SA (hereafter: AC PEKAO), sign. 163, Protokół nr 90 z posiedzenia Komitetu Wykonawczego RB PKO odbytego 21 IX 1961 r., unnumbered pages.
1200 J. Lech, "Czy potrzeba tyle marek pojazdów?" *Motor* 1963, no. 19, p. 3.

Spare part shortages were often the subject of discussion among the most important people in Poland. There were various ideas about how resolving the stalemate, even very bizarre ones, such as the announcement by Deputy Minister of Heavy Industry Antoni Czechowicz that at the turn of the 1960s, "the improvement of the situation [on the spare parts market] will be facilitated by the recently decided reduction in the planned production of vehicles" by approximately 1,500 units in total, mainly passenger cars (Warszawa and Syrenas).[1201]

Sobiesław Zasada's triumphs in national and international car rallies made him one of the most popular Polish sportspeople of his day. In a vote for the best sportsperson in Poland organised by *Przegląd Sportowy*, he took first place in 1967. This resulted in, among other things, an avalanche of correspondence from his fans. In addition to letters congratulating him on his successes and requesting an autograph, there were also pleas for help in obtaining parts for both cars and motorcycles.[1202] It is almost certain that Zasada was unable to fulfil these requests. They probably never even reached him. Nevertheless, people who had contacts abroad were in a privileged situation in terms of access to spare parts. When Jan Szczepański was looking for parts for a motorcycle, he asked his aunt Maria Kuncewiczowa, who travelled often in Western Europe, to bring the missing components along on her way back.[1203] Stanisław Lem wrote to Sławomir Mrożek, residing in Italy, asking for the purchase of a radial shaft seal that was unavailable in Poland, a new ignition switch, an oil filter, and suspension elements for his Fiat.[1204]

Lacking access to parts, expert mechanics, and car repair shops, private owners of vehicles often had to take matters into their own hands. In the case of Polish cars (especially Syrenas), their simple design allowed for self-service of most breakdowns. It is also not surprising that guides on self-repairs as well as articles describing the process of repairs step-by-step were very popular with readers. In his analysis of the car market in East Germany, Eli Rubin notes that, due to insufficient access to the service network, Trabant drivers had to

1201 AAN, Ministerstwo Komunikacji, sign. II/2, Protokół nr 9/P z posiedzenia Prezydium Rady Motoryzacyjnej odbytego 24 XI 1959 r., p. 501.

1202 "Listy do Sobiesława Zasady," *Motor* 1968, no. 51/52, p. 11.

1203 J. J. Szczepański, *Dziennik*, vol. 3, p. 344.

1204 S. Lem and S. Mrożek, *Listy*, pp. 421, 486, and 601.

be familiar with the individual mechanisms and components of their cars, or at least to know someone who had such knowledge. The detailed manual supplied with the car from Zwickau was undoubtedly helpful; Rubin calls it a de facto textbook on automotive engineering.[1205] Meanwhile, the manuals supplied with Polish cars looked completely different. As one Syrena owner suggested in 1962,

> [i]t must be objectively admitted that the abbreviated user manual that the owner of the car receives with it is truly unworthy of the name of a manual, given that it has serious shortcomings (it says nothing about headlight adjustment and explains only very vaguely how to adjust the gears, and don't get me started on the quality of the paper and printing). The manual for the "Wawel 2" television set is printed on better quality paper, and the drawings are clear and large. It would seem that an item such as a car (seven times more expensive than a TV set) deserves a better manual.[1206]

Oftentimes, manuals were not included with the car, which sparked outrage because, as another owner of a Syrena wrote, "[t]here is no need to prove that, for myself and many others, the manual is of primary importance."[1207]

Around the end of the 1950s, *Motor* calculated the daily cost of operation of a passenger car per 1 km of travel. Involving many different car models, both domestic (Warszawa, Syrena) and foreign (Simca, Fiat, Renault, Škoda, and Volga), the comparison showed that, depending on distance travelled per year, the cost ranged from 1.13 to 2.35 zlotys. Cheapest was the Polish Mikrus, and the most expensive was the Warszawa.[1208] Three years later, *Motor* repeated the study, this time focusing exclusively on the Warszawa produced in Żerań, and carefully detailed all expenses. Taking fixed costs (obligatory fees, depreciation, etc.) and variable costs (fuel, oil and tyre consumption, as well as technical service) into account, the cost of one kilometre (given an annual mileage of 24,000 km) amounted to 2.06 zlotys.[1209] The calculations carried out by the weekly's editorial team were met with great criticism from

---

1205 E. Rubin, "Understanding a Car in the Context of a System. Trabants, Marzahn, and East German Socialism," in: *The Socialist Car*, pp. 129–130.
1206 "Drobne oszczędności," *Motor* 1962, no. 1, p. 11.
1207 "Będą instrukcje," *Motor* 1962, no. 18, p. 11.
1208 "Ile kosztuje eksploatacja samochodu?" *Motor* 1959, no. 10, pp. 4–5.
1209 "Ile cię kosztuje samochód rocznie," *Motor* 1962, no. 4, p. 4.

the readers. Doubts were raised primarily by the annual mileage, which drivers believed was rather high. The journalists explained that they based their calculations on the average mileage of a car used by a person in a profession that required the use of a car: "We did not account for the so-called 'Sunday drivers', believing that they are not the majority in Poland."[1210] New calculations, based on the suggested average annual mileage of 5,000 km, gave an increased cost of 3.32 zlotys per kilometre.[1211] It seems that the "corrected" calculations were closer to the truth, although the annual mileage remains questionable. According to Zdzisław Krasiński, in 1960, cars in Poland travelled on average approximately 7,000 km per year, and this number did not exceed 10,000 kilometres until the mid-1970s, which was still much lower than in the first version of the calculations.[1212]

However, regardless of the frequency and intensity with which a car was used, the expenses related to its purchase and maintenance were a significant part of a household budget, as already mentioned. Another relevant aspect was durability; as noted, in countries that were undergoing motorisation, cars were typically kept in running order as long as possible, and the average age of a car exceeded a decade. It was different in countries at an advanced stage of motorisation: there, the period of use was significantly shortened, amounting to only eight years.[1213] In a volume discussing the Polish society at the threshold of the transformation in 1989, Hanna Bojar wrote that owning a car was a matter of prestige and a symbol of advancement, and the fact that it might be practical faded into the background. Purchasing a car required many sacrifices, and the considerable expense involved in its use meant that it was only driven occasionally.[1214] It seems that this observation about the 1980s can be applied to earlier decades.

1210 "W odpowiedzi czytelnikom—Ile cię kosztuje samochód rocznie," *Motor* 1962, no. 7, p. 11.

1211 Ibid.

1212 Z. Krasiński, H. Mruk, and P. Rzepczyński, *Handel i usługi na tle rozwoju motoryzacji indywidualnej*, Warszawa 1977, Instytut Handlu Wewnętrznego i Usług, Biblioteka 153, p. 39; cf. M. Roche, "Samochód," p. 285.

1213 Z. Krasiński, H. Mruk, and P. Rzepczyński, *Handel i usługi*, p. 22.

1214 H. Bojar, "Rodzina i życie rodzinne," in: *Co nam zostało z tych lat… Społeczeństwo polskie u progu zmiany systemowej*, ed. M. Marody, Londyn 1991, p. 51.

In the second half of the 1960s, there was a significant increase in sales of automotive products. Per capita, sales increased by 35%. Greater increases were only recorded in the sales of furniture and ceramics and glassware—40% and 58%, respectively. At the beginning of the 1970s, turnover on the automotive products market doubled compared to 1960. This proved that the Polish society was becoming motorised, even if the technical level of the cars left much to be desired because, due to their age, mileage, and technical condition, most vehicles required frequent interventions by mechanics.[1215]

5.7 Seventy percent from 50 to 100 per 1,000: garages and parking lots

Poland's wartime destruction gave architects, planners, and urbanists a great deal of space in which to work. There was one paradigm—the Soviet paradigm, as an article from 1953 proclaims: "Socialist construction must keep the future in view, it must foresee the development and progress of the settlements. A socialist urban planner cannot be blind to the progress and the accurate lines of development of the city or district that he designs, he cannot fail to understand the importance of transport and connectedness."[1216] However, it quickly turned out that even if the paradigm was "clear and unambiguous," reality often—perhaps even almost always—diverged significantly from intentions.

Already in 1952, it was a commonly expressed opinion in various circles that planners had failed to properly address the matter of garages and parking lots. Critics cited the realities of the USSR, where plans for every new housing estate assigned space for fourteen passenger cars and twenty-eight motorcycles per 1,000 inhabitants. These indicators were presumed to be slightly lower for Poland (10 and 15, respectively). A housing estate of the type built at that time in Muranów (for approximately 40,000–45,000 inhabitants) had to account for at least 400 passenger cars and 600 motorcycles. Moreover, car garages were to be located within a five-minute walk. However, as Edward Laskus reported, the rebuilt districts were in fact almost completely devoid

1215 Z. Krasiński, H. Mruk, and P. Rzepczyński, *Handel i usługi*, pp. 39 and 56.

1216 W. Lesiak, "Urbaniści zapominają o garażach i postojach samochodów," *Motoryzacja* 1953, no. 3, p. 77.

of garages: "Even with the current number of cars, it is exceedingly difficult to find garages and parking spaces for them [while] the use of taxis for travel to and from a garage is too troublesome and economically nonsensical."[1217] Laskus opted not to lay all of the responsibility at the feet of the design workshops, which he thought were not to blame because the programme that defined the basic assumptions for their work did not contain sufficient data on garages, parking lots, and other automotive infrastructure. However, the Warsaw City Planning Office had also adopted the rule that 75% of cars in the city should have parking spaces and that the travel time between local garages and the apartments of their users should not exceed 8 minutes. The example of Western Europe and America—which, as Laskus noted, were full of forcibly built oddities such as underground garages, ground floors converted into parking places, or multi-story parking lots—illustrated the results of short-sightedness in urban planning.

The problem was real, and seemed to worsen with each new construction effort. In 1953, as the housing estates of Marszałkowska Dzielnica Mieszkaniowa (Marszałkowska Residential District, MDM), Muranów, Mokotów, Mirów, Młynów, and Koło were being built in Warsaw, those observing the builders noticed a rather disturbing fact. Even though the newly built housing estates "were designed and constructed on a scale unknown in pre-September [1939] Poland," no one seemed to remember about a somewhat important detail, "the absence of which is not felt yet, but may cause great difficulties for urban planners and architects in a few years," namely garages, which, even when they were erected, were "poorly designed, unwieldy things."[1218] Given the state of advancement of the construction works, it was still possible to make up for the oversights, but the matter of garages required immediate action because "when the housing estates are completed and the areas around them are developed, the difficulty will be much greater; it will then be possible to overcome only with the greatest effort and at the greatest expense."[1219] As it later turned out, these were prophetic words.

1217 E. Laskus, "Zagadnienie budownictwa samochodowego, a w szczególności garaży i parkingów w miastach," *Motoryzacja* 1954, no. 8, p. 233.

1218 F. Kawa, "O garażach trzeba pomyśleć," *Stolica. Tygodniowa kronika budowy Warszawy* 1953, no. 14, p. 6.

1219 Ibid.

Not only did the situation not improve; it worsened. Already in 1956, it was noticed that the roads built for horse carts were "narrow and unsuitable for automobile traffic." Large city centres were becoming more and more crowded, traffic was increasing, and it was becoming practically a miracle when one found a free space to park one of the still very few cars. "Even today, theoretically speaking, no car users can settle their affairs in institutions or shops located on the Nowy Świat." The urban density of the Warsaw city centre and the downtown area of Śródmieście also prevented the creation of new parking lots. The problem of garages being in newly built areas on both the right and the left bank of the Vistula—Praga II, Grochów, and WSM Żoliborz—returned once again: "Where are the garages, where is there even space for garages?" people asked rhetorically.[1220] Among those who commented in similar tones in *Motor* were writer Józef Prutkowski and pianist Barbara Hasse-Bukowska. When Prutkowski wanted to use his garage, he had to take a taxi because "there is not a single garage in the entire Mokotów area. No one planned for them."[1221] The fact that the situation was slowly changing from "rather bad" to "very bad" is evidenced by another symptomatic opinion: "[V]illa districts such as Saska Kępa, Żoliborz, and Mokotów have more garages than do the recently built large residential districts."[1222]

Certainly, much would improve with appropriate legislation to regulate access to garages and parking spaces in newly built housing estates. The first such regulations appeared at the turn of the 1960s. In May 1960, the Ministry of Municipal Economy (MGK) issued a crucial circular that organised the issue of garage construction from own funds of the populace. Previously, the Regulation of the Council of Ministers of July 25, 1958 on rents for commercial premises was in force, stipulating that payments for garage use were due regardless of whether the garage was built by the state or by a private person. The MGK circular brought a fundamental change: from now on, any person who built a garage (a so-called permanent garage, according to a design approved for the given housing estate) in an area indicated by the relevant Municipal Residential Buildings Authority would not pay rent for

---

1220 Z. Mróz, "Zagadnienia urbanistyczne a motoryzacja," *Motoryzacja* 1956, no. 2, pp. 30 and 32.

1221 "13 błyskawicznych wywiadów 'Motoru'," *Motor* 1956, no. 1, pp. 8–9.

1222 J. Michalak, "Nowoczesne garaże," *Przegląd Samochodowy* 1957, no. 9, p. 63.

a period of 5–10 years, only bearing the costs of use of the garage and of the surrounding space. The rate was to be set at 20% of the rental rate for a lease. After the expiry of the rent-free period, the fees specified in the July 1958 regulation would apply—from 5 to 9.25 zlotys per square metre of garage area, depending on the location.[1223] The Directorates for the Construction of Workers' Housing Estates (DBORs) were tasked with designating areas for the construction of garages, and ensuring that the needs of an area were taken into account in urban designs.[1224]

However, DBORs were not interested in designating garage spaces because, in their opinion, it was being done at the expense of space for the construction of residential buildings. Therefore, from the point of view of DBORs, garages were unnecessary and generated additional costs. In many cases, a designer who tried to force through the inclusion of garages in a construction plan encountered strong resistance from the higher-ups. Wiktor Bryx even claimed that the effort to obtain a permission to build a garage and visits with "county and district architects, ... national councils, in an attempt to gain the support of the administration of a house that had a piece of free yard that could serve as the foundation for a future garage" were comparable to a visit to the dentist. "Anyone who has never had such problems is unlikely to understand why owners of motor vehicles pursue so stubbornly any space for their vehicles."[1225] Even when the permission was obtained, it did not mean an end to the problems. In most cases, it triggered an avalanche of appeals, protests, and interventions by residents of nearby blocks who opposed the construction of a garage in their immediate vicinity. As Wiesław Śmiałkowski wrote in *Stolica*, "[i]t needs no explanation that all of this causes delays in the construction process, and often holds it up for many months." This was inevitable, "[u]nless someone from the block committee making the intervention received a car allocation."[1226]

1223 Dz. U. 1958, no. 50, pos. 245.

1224 The circular called on DBOR to indicate areas that were to be designated for garages on the sites of ongoing or completed construction of residential estates; B. Ryś, "Zielone światło dla budujących garaże," *Motor* 1960, no. 24, p. 3.

1225 W. Bryx, "Gdzie znaleźć garaż?" *Motor* 1960, no. 12, p. 11.

1226 W. Śmiałkowski, "Kłopoty motoryzacyjne (Garaże)," *Stolica* 1967, no. 53, p. 13.

An attempt was made to address the financial aspect of the issue in the Resolution no. 363 of the Council of Ministers published on September 13, 1961, which stipulated that only nurseries, kindergartens, shops, and service points would be financed from the funds and expenditures of the state housing construction entities. Garages were classified as municipal facilities and their construction was to be financed by the future user. In Warsaw alone, from 1963 to 1967, 8,800 garages were built according to these rules, but not in all districts. In some, such as Śródmieście, were subject to a total ban on their construction.[1227] Meanwhile, in 1966 and 1967 alone, the number of passenger cars registered in the capital increased by almost 6,000, to a total of over 40,000; a year later, that number reached 44,800.[1228]

At this point, it is worth devoting some space to statistics regarding garages and parking spaces. Determining their number is problematic because it has not been possible to find aggregate data covering the whole of Poland, and if any exist, they are fragmentary and often concern only a single year. For example, in 1956, there were over 23,000 garages in Poland for almost 70,500 garage spaces. However, only slightly over 50,000 were used for parking cars because some (2,800) were unsuitable for use due to their technical condition, while others served as granaries, chicken coops, and cellars.[1229] On average, there were just over four cars per garage space in the country, but there is significant geographical diversification to this data. The situation was best in the Zielona Góra and Gdańsk voivodeships, where there were 1.8 and 1.9 cars per parking space, respectively. Similar numbers were recorded in the Koszalin (2.5) and Szczecin (2.6) voivodeships. Elsewhere, the ratio was three or more cars per parking space. The situation was the worst in the Kraków voivodeship (8 cars per parking space). Warsaw placed second with just over seven cars per space. The statistics on the number of garages used for other purposes are also interesting. In the Wrocław voivodeship, no cars were parked

---

[1227] Ibid.

[1228] *Rocznik Statystyczny* 1967, p. 316; *Rocznik Statystyczny* 1968, p. 304; *Rocznik Statystyczny* 1969, p. 308. In 1967, there were a total of 19,100 parking spaces in Warsaw, in guarded and unguarded parking lots and lay-bys, along with so-called kerbside spaces; W. Śmiałkowski, "Motoryzacyjne kłopoty," *Stolica* 1967, no. 51/52, pp. 12–13.

[1229] Of the cited 23,000, 10,200 were in good condition, while the others were in average condition. Garages in poor condition were usually makeshift affairs, fit only for immediate demolition; "Batalia o garaże," *Motor* 1960, no. 39, pp. 3 and 11.

in 6,500 spaces; in the Zielona Góra voivodeship—1,900; in the Katowice voivodeship—1,500; in the Olsztyn voivodeship—1,200; and in the Opole voivodeship—1,100. The most efficient use of garages occurred in the Kielce and Łódź voivodeships, where only 213 and 214 spaces, respectively, were not occupied by cars. In comparison, Warsaw, with 552, looked rather poor.

In subsequent years, not only did the situation not improve—it worsened dramatically. In 1960, approximately 110,000 passenger cars and 600,000 motorcycles were registered in Poland, but there were only about 30,000 garages, of which a third were used contrary to their intended purpose—as workshops, warehouses, and various types of storage spaces. To make matters worse, even in places where this element of automotive infrastructure was theoretically possible to take care of at an early stage of planning and construction, it seemed to be completely ignored. This was the case even in the newly built city of Świdnik, where the garage question was completely ignored already during the construction of the first housing estates in this "motor city."[1230] As early as 1957, desperate residents were asking why "there will be no garages this year."[1231] Some kept their motorcycles in the laundry rooms or basements of their blocks, others even in their apartments.[1232] They built makeshift wooden booths for their cars in spaces between blocks, in green areas, and in parks. As a result, the city was "surrounded by a 'ring of garages' built in the wild."[1233] Most, however, were forced to park on the streets, exposing their vehicles (both cars and motorcycles) to the risk of damage by people irritated by such use of the roadsides. One resident of the city wrote to *Motor*, describing the intentional damage inflicted on several cars and motorcycles (scratched paint, slashed tyres) in a single night in September 1968.[1234]

1230 "Świdnickie garaże," *Motor* 1961, no. 7, p. 11.

1231 Archiwum Państwowe w Lublinie (hereafter: APL), Prezydium Miejskiej Rady Narodowej w Świdniku (hereafter: PMRN Świdnik), sign. 33, Protokół nr 2/57 z sesji Miejskiej Rady Narodowej w Świdniku odbytej 27 III 1957 r., unnumbered pages.

1232 Ibid., sign. 38, Protokół nr 1/ 1962 z I-szej Sesji Miejskiej Rady Narodowej w Świdniku odbytej 1 III 1962 r., unnumbered pages.

1233 Ibid., sign. 48, Protokół nr VII/3/70 z VII sesji Miejskiej Rady narodowej w Świdniku odbytej 25 V 1970 r., unnumbered pages.

1234 J. Pawłowski, "Polityka antygarażowa?" *Motor* 1968, no. 41, p. 2.

To improve the situation, the Chairman of the Urban Planning and Architecture Construction Committee issued Order no. 15, establishing guidelines for the design of housing estates in the first half of the 1960s. It imposed an obligation to foresee 15–20 garages and twice as many parking spaces for every thousand inhabitants of the planned housing estate. However, despite repeated attempts to design the estate in such a way that a garage would not increase the overall costs,[1235] it was still a drop in the ocean of needs. Notably, at the end of the 1950s, it was estimated that the planned cost of building garages and parking spaces for passenger cars would total 11 billion zlotys by 1980. Comparing this amount to costs of residential space, it would correspond to the construction of a city for 700,000 inhabitants.[1236] It is thus not surprising that at the time, no one except motor vehicle owners wanted garages and parking lots.

Further regulations concerning garages were introduced in 1966, when an ordinance of the Minister of Construction and the Building Materials Industry was published regarding the technical conditions of public buildings, including garages. According to the ordnance, garages were to be built of non-flammable materials and properly ventilated. They could either take the shape of free-standing buildings or be appended to other structures. In the case of detached garages, the minimum distance from the nearest building was to be 3 m from a wall without a window and 10 m from a wall with a window.[1237]

In November 1969, at the request of the Central Board of the Housing Construction Cooperative (CZSBM), a study was prepared under the title "Parking lots and garages in cooperative housing estates in a large city." Guidelines contained therein were adopted as binding by the CZSBM in early 1970. The number of necessary parking and garage spaces was to be determined based on the motorisation prognosis until 1985 developed by the Public Transport Project Office and subsequently approved by the

---

1235 For example, attempts were made to connect transformer stations with garages, to build garages on the ground floors of planned residential blocks, etc.

1236 W. Chlebowicz, "Uwagi ogólne o parkingach," *Miasto* 1959, no. 12, p. 30.

1237 AAN, Ministerstwo Budownictwa i Przemysłu Materiałów Budowlanych (hereafter: MBiPMB), sign. 3/78, Zarządzenie w sprawie warunków technicznych, jakim powinny odpowiadać obiekty budowlane budownictwa powszechnego, pp. 161–164.

Motorisation Council. It anticipated that in 1970, the number of passenger cars per thousand inhabitants would be 55; in the mid-1970s—90; and in 1980—150. Based on these numbers, it was assumed that there would be a need for parking and garage space for 80–90% of the volume anticipated in the hypothesis. Garage boxes were to be replaced over time by the so-called stacked facilities—local, multi-level parking lots with a maximum of four levels, capable of accommodating between 100 and 300 vehicles. Above all, they were supposed to be inexpensive, which is why it was decided that they would be unheated and completely devoid of ventilation devices. This simply meant no side walls. At the same time, in order to further reduce costs, the drivable surface in facilities of this kind was to be made of light materials that could be easily dismantled, which excluded the possibility of using them to park trucks. Interestingly, the recommendations included the note that designs of residential areas would not account for parking spaces for people who were not residents of the given estate. Thus, they would have to park their cars in parking spaces marked on residential streets.[1238]

The last important regulation was the new urban planning norm introduced in 1974. It changed the rules determining the density of housing estates. In terms of parking spaces and garages, it provided for one parking space for every two apartments, leaving open the possibility of building a second level, thus doubling the number of parking spaces.[1239]

Meanwhile, the reality of the 1960s was that illegal trade in garages was flourishing, and the rental market was also highly developed. People who unsuccessfully applied for a legal allocation were forced to pursue semi-legal ways of obtaining the parking space they wished to have for their car. The cost of purchasing a garage could reach 10,000 zlotys, while rent was several hundred zlotys per month. Taking into account, on the one hand, the limited number of garage spaces, and on the other, the constantly growing number of cars, it is no wonder that such offers, many of which appeared in classified

---

[1238] AAN, Centralny Związek Spółdzielni Budownictwa Mieszkaniowego w Warszawie (hereafter: CZSBM), sign. 9/14, Zalecenia Rady techniczno-Ekonomicznej CZSBM w sprawie zasad rozwiązywania problemów garażowania i parkowania w osiedlach mieszkaniowych w warunkach dużego miasta (pow. 100 tys. mk), Warszawa, 12 III 1970 r., unnumbered pages; ibid., Parkingi i garaże w osiedlu spółdzielczym w warunkach dużego miasta, Warszawa, listopad 1969 r., unnumbered pages.

[1239] I. Jacyna, "Samochód w mieście," *Życie Gospodarcze* 1980, no. 13, p. 7.

ads in the daily press, attracted interest very quickly. However, people who did not obtain a garage or simply could not afford one tried to seek justice from the highest authorities. In one such case, described in a letter to the Bureau of Complaints and Letters of the Office of the Council of Ministers, one person offering a garage in Warsaw assured officials that all formalities related to changing the accommodation allocation could be completed immediately. Ultimately, on the initiative of the Bureau and following an intervention of the Ministry of Municipal Economy, the allocation for the garage was withdrawn.[1240]

Every year, 600,000 m^2 of living space was delivered in Warsaw alone, approximately 80% of which came in the form of cooperative construction. The plan for the first half of the 1970s called for an annual average of 800,000 m^2, which meant that approximately 50,000 people moved into new housing estates. According to the guidelines, securing the parking needs of such an estate required the construction of 7,140 parking spaces per year, including 1,150 garages (assuming thirty-four garage spaces per 1,000 inhabitants, as per the recommendations of the chief architect of Warsaw). Plans for the years 1971–1975 were 33% higher. One report on access to parking spaces within the newly built parts of Warsaw noted: "Against these calculations, reporting data on the number of garage spaces built in all Warsaw housing estates in the years 1961–1969 must be very alarming." In under a decade, a total of 2,247 garages were built in all housing estates. In addition, the plan for 1969 assumed the construction of another 313. In total, almost 2,500 garages were planned. By way of conclusion, the authors of the report wrote:

> [I]t must be assumed that the issue of parking spaces for passenger cars in residential areas deserves its own place in the programme for the city (the way that schools do, for instance) and cannot be resolved by constructing smaller or larger buildings as "additions" to the proper substance of residential construction (the way a small garage or tool shed can still be an addition to a single-family house). Similarly, it would be impossible to solve the issue of primary schools by building one or two classrooms ad hoc as additions to a residential house. Today, every citizen knows that the issue of schools is a problem in itself that requires a comprehensive solution appropriate to demographic assumptions, etc. The issue of garages and parking lots

1240 AAN, URM, sign. 14/4, Sprawozdanie z działalności Biura Skarg i Listów w 1963 r., Warszawa, 21 I 1964 r., p. 74.

> on housing estates has now become such an independent item within residential construction. Failure to recognise it or postponement of appropriate solutions and decisions may result in a situation that is hopeless or will generate numerous irregularities.[1241]

However, in fact, all these attempts to regulate the garage problem failed, not so much because of legal chaos, but rather non-compliance with regulations and indolence of officials when issuing construction permits. Adding to this the objections and protests by residents (for example, in the form of letters sent to the authorities[1242]), one finds that Polish housing estates became a major battleground. Some of the blame lay with car owners who, unable to wait for a building permit, started the construction of "four walls and a roof" for their car on their own. A comment from 1975 sums the situation up aptly: "The authorities, concerned with the problem of building apartments, are trying to put off the issue of garages as long as possible. The other 83% of residents [who do not have their own car] come to their aid by protesting against the construction of garages."[1243]

* * *

Obtaining one's own vehicle was only the first step on the bumpy road of a car owner. Daily use, as discussed above, was often much more of a challenge. This is confirmed by studies conducted in the late 1980s by the Center for Public Opinion Research, the results of which can very likely be applied to the period a quarter of a century earlier, as well. In a survey entitled "How is life treating us?" a car is described as a luxury good, usually by people who did not have one. The situation changed dramatically when an automobile appeared in the household. Then, the problems and difficulties associated

---

1241 AAN, CZSBM, sign. 9/14, Parkingi i garaże w osiedlu spółdzielczym w warunkach dużego miasta, Warszawa, listopad 1969 r., p. 33.

1242 AAN, KC PZPR, sign. XXVII-36, Informacja, listopad 1961 r., pp. 14–25.

1243 J. Jakubowski, "Miejsce dla samochodu," *Czas* 1975, no. 3, p. 6. As L. H. Siegelbaum notes, most residents of housing estates who did not own cars opposed the construction of garages and designated parking spaces. Moreover, in complaints and letters addressed to the highest authorities, they often referred to motorists in terms that placed them outside of the socialist community; *idem*, *Cars for Comrades*, p. 232.

with its everyday use gradually stripped it of its magical charm, turning it into an ordinary utility item intended to make its owner's life easier. One began to notice the car's low quality, and the term "good car" became synonymous with a Western car.[1244] A bitter smile must have graced the lips of anyone who heard the popular joke about the Polish driver who enjoyed his car twice: first, when he bought it, and then, when he sold it. The period in between consisted of nothing but worry and trouble.[1245]

1244 M. Strzelecka, "Samochód—symbol dobrobytu (wynik sondażu Centrum Badania Opinii Społecznej)," *Przedsiębiorstwo i Rynek* 1988, no. 4 (19), pp. 35–37.

1245 J. Meissner, "Kupiłem używany samochód," *Przekrój* 1947, no. 13/14, p. 40. In a letter to Stanisław Lem, Sławomir Mrożek described his broken-down car in the following way: "So when I killed it [the car], I didn't regret it like a decent, normal owner would, like a father to the car. I rather felt a kind of hideous relief, vindictive satisfaction …"; S. Lem and S. Mrożek, *Listy*, p. 61.

Conclusion

What is a car? A car is a vehicle
that the working class uses
through its representatives.[1246]

The first long-term economic plans (1947–1949, 1950–1955) attempted to rebuild and then expand Poland's automotive industry based on the production of trucks, tractors, and machines. Although a contract was signed with Fiat for the production of a passenger car, the contract was terminated as a result of a political decision. Passenger cars (primarily Warszawas produced under a Soviet licence and limited imports from abroad) were to complement production and meet the needs of a very limited group of recipients: officials, representatives of selected professions, some accomplished leading workers and workplace *racjonalizatorzy* (innovators). In terms of motorisation, the period of Stalinism was associated with the primacy of public transport and increasing restrictions imposed on individual passenger car users. Through restrictive legislation, this group of vehicle users was brought down severely in number. As a result, in the mid-1950s, only 20,500 vehicles were in private hands.

The events of 1956 encouraged the society to increasingly demand improved living conditions, including access to cars. The new government, headed by Władysław Gomułka, fulfilled these demands only in part. Cars became available to buy and the production of passenger cars began inside the

1246 A. Dziurawiec, *Późny Gomułka, wczesny Gierek*, Warszawa 2009, p. 118.

country, but both the volume of the production and access to cars remained very limited. Motozbyt had new vehicles on sale, but obtaining a permission to purchase them was extremely difficult. Moreover, buyers of new cars could not sell them for several years. All of these factors had a major impact on the development of the private car market.

The new government's policy towards motorisation was pragmatic, as reflected in its instrumental treatment of the issue. The ruling elite seemed not to notice the positive sides of motorisation for the society, which only became apparent with the passage of time. The decisions of the central authorities were often aimed at achieving the fastest possible results in a short term or within several years. This was the case, for example, with the contract with Fiat for the production of the 125p model. When it became apparent in the early 1960s that the Polish car industry was producing obsolete models that were completely uncompetitive on foreign markets, the search for a way to improve export results began. A decision was thus made to enter into an agreement with the Italian company. From the very beginning, it was assumed that it would be a car intended for export. Thus, neither the experts, nor the general public (who wanted a small, affordable car) were satisfied. Even though officials promised that the foreign currency obtained through exports would be partially allocated to increase the importation of passenger cars for sale, these promises were never fulfilled.

The financial situation of most of the population did not allow Poles to buy or maintain an automobile. At the same time, the authorities did nothing to make it easier for Poles to gain access to their dream four-wheeled machine. Moreover, the prices of automotive products—cars, parts, but also fuel—were the highest in Poland out of all the countries of the Eastern Bloc. The opportunity to purchase to new cars, both Polish and imported, was also difficult (due to rationing). Despite this, Poles bought cars using various methods and channels. The number of private cars increased by over 432,000 over the course of fifteen years. Most often, cars were purchased in private transactions (from friends, family, classified ads, at car markets). Less often, purchases were made through official state channels (through Motozbyt or internal exports sold by PEKAO), frequently in instalments. Another way to obtain one's own vehicle was through the lottery tied to PKO's so-called car savings books, as well as through various types of lotteries in which the main prize was a passenger car.

The sale of new cars, both Polish and imported, for dollars by PEKAO, as part of the internal exports programme, is a perfect example of how the pockets of the Poles were being actively drained. While initially cars could only be bought by families living abroad for their relatives in Poland, as the popularity of this form of sale (and source of state profit) grew, people living in Poland were also allowed to buy cars for dollars. The only condition was that the price be actually paid in the currency. Thus, the considerable savings that the Poles had made were efficiently siphoned off.

Infrastructure development did not keep pace with the development of individual motorisation. Neither the network of gas stations nor that of service workshops was sufficient for the growing number of automobile users. Similarly, there were too few parking spaces and garages, which were constantly in short supply. During the period in question, Polish roads became one of the most dangerous in Europe. Poland led in fatal accidents, drunk drivers, and incidents caused by users of two-wheeled vehicles. It is clear that the rather late adoption of motorisation resulted in a lack of familiarity with automobiles and street traffic, the intensity of which increased in proportion to the number of vehicles.

Throughout the period in question, car thefts were not perceived as a significant social problem, even as their number was increasing. The detection rates of this type of crime, very often committed by people under twenty, was rather high. Most often, cars were stolen for parts.

* * *

Perhaps in order to avoid the accusation from the censors that he was promoting a lifestyle alien to the socialist system, in his article for *Przekrój* (cited above), Stanisław Lem wrote in the late 1950s that the burgeoning development of motorisation, which he was witnessing at that time, was not in its nature a "rigid and schematic copying of the West; here as well, there is a national style, and in catching up [to the West], we are following a Polish road—figuratively and literally."[1247] However, as Teresa Pałaszewska-Reindl noted, the Polish society was characterised by "high sensitivity and

[1247] S. Lem, "O polskiej drodze do motoryzacji," *Przekrój* 1957, no. 645, p. 20.

susceptibility to new trends in fashion, lifestyle, foreign innovations, etc.," and governed rather by "the mechanism of imitation of the international, and therefore the effect of demonstrative internationalism."[1248] In a letter to Czesław Miłosz, the author of *The Captive Mind* from January 14, 1964, Jerzy Giedroyc, the Editor-in-Chief of *Kultura* in Paris wrote in a similar vein: "I stubbornly claim that the only secret weapon America has is its lifestyle and wealth."[1249] Certainly, individual motorisation played a major part in this perspective. Available through various types of media (press, cinema, etc.), but also through private observation, the image of the motorised West had an impact on the social expectations of the Poles. During his scholarship to Harvard University, Szczepański wrote repeatedly about the fact that in the United States, owning a car was nothing unusual. Moreover, a car was no longer an indicator of social prestige: doctors and teachers, as well as workers could afford one.[1250]

In its attitude toward motorisation, the Polish society under Władysław Gomułka, but also before and after, did not differ much from the society that motorised the earliest and the most—the French society. As David Inglis notes, it took a relatively short time (between 1945 and the mid-1960s) for the private car to cease to be a product reserved for the upper social classes in France; instead, it became central for the lives of all classes, even though most French people did not own a car. This was a consequence of the enormous influence of mass media, which strongly promoted the development of motorisation.[1251] In Poland, although private cars were rarer than in France, private ownership of vehicles and their capabilities were perceived as being of the utmost importance, even by the youngest. In 1961, one issue of the biweekly *Płomyk* featured a drawing in which a boy pushed a wooden toy car with a girl seated inside, being observed by two other children, one of

---

[1248] T. Pałaszewska-Reindl, *Konsumpcja dóbr trwałego użytku w Polsce*, Warszawa 1966, p. 87.

[1249] Jerzy Giedroyc and Czesław Miłosz, *Listy 1964–1972*, ed. M. Kornat, Warszawa 2011, p. 6.

[1250] See, for example, entries dated July 7 and August 10, 1958 in: J. J. Szczepański, *Dzienniki*, vol. 2: *1957–1963*, Kraków 2011, p. 177.

[1251] D. Inglis, "Auto Couture: Thinking the Car in post-war France," *Theory, Culture & Society* 2004, vol. 21, no. 4–5, p. 201.

whom says to the other: "Ever since he's had a car, girls have been going crazy about him."[1252]

When the regime changed in Poland in 1956, motorisation was still waiting for an opening. Although there were more and more passenger cars in private hands, Władysław Gomułka's rule was not favourable for individual car owners. Despite a twelvefold increase in the number of cars between 1955 and 1970, at the end of that period, Poland was still in the distant forty-third place in the world in terms of the number of inhabitants per passenger car; the world average was 19.6, while in Poland, it was four times higher (77.2). Poland's position was equally unfavourable when compared to other countries within the socialist bloc; in this context, its position even worsened (see Table 30). While in 1960, Poland was third among Eastern Bloc countries in terms of the number of inhabitants per car (just behind Czechoslovakia and East Germany), by the beginning of the next decade it had dropped by two places, having been overtaken by Yugoslavia and Hungary, both of which had had a similar level of motorisation in 1960.[1253]

Table 30. Number of inhabitants per passenger car in Eastern Bloc countries in the 1960s and 1970s

Country	Number of inhabitants per car		
	January 1, 1960	January 1, 1970	Growth in percentage
East Germany	111.0	16.5	660.7
Czechoslovakia	77.1	19.2	401.6
Yugoslavia	339.2	36.2	934.4
Hungary	438.8	53.5	811.1
Poland	253.8	77.2	328.8
Bulgaria	841.1	111.0	761.4

(Continued)

1252 *Płomyk* 1961, no. 8, p. 250.

1253 The level of saturation with passenger cars in the country in 1970 corresponded to the level of motorisation in the USA in 1913 (81 inhabitants per car), Sweden in 1928 (65), France in 1925 (70), England in 1925 (63), Germany in 1936 (71) and Czechoslovakia in 1960 (77.1); AAN, KPRM, sign. 7489, *Kierunki polityki gospodarczej w zakresie kształtowania rynku samochodowego w Polsce w okresie 1973–1980*, Warszawa 1973, p. 8; *Rocznik Statystyczny* 1972, p. 677.

Table 30. *(Continued)*

Country	Number of inhabitants per car		
	January 1, 1960	January 1, 1970	Growth in percentage
USSR	-	132.0	-
Romania	1840.0	200.0	920.0
Albania	-	592.0	-

Source: AAN, KPpRM, sign. 7489, Kierunki polityki gospodarczej w zakresie kształtowania rynku samochodowego w Polsce w okresie 1973–1980, Warszawa 1973, p. 8.

* * *

In one of his drawings published in *Szpilki*, Szymon Kobyliński brilliantly captured the Polish desire for motorisation, which was still accessible only to a very limited number of people. As Stefan Kisielewski wrote in his diary: "A car is a dream—Gomułka is a loser for denying us universal motorisation-—it would technologise our society, and make it even more mixed and uniform, which is probably in line with the 'Polish raison d'état'."[1254] Aleksandra Zgorzelska echoed his sentiments:

> For many years, motorisation was disliked in our country, particular in its 'individual' form. There were rumblings that it was snobbery and luxury, and therefore something fundamentally un-socialist (why?). It was said that it was imported from a hostile system and supposedly narrowed the horizons of those possessed by its demonic powers, limited our native class consciousness—and as a result, no thought was given to the possibility of integrating it into the socialist model of consumption, no consideration for the fact that this individual motorisation is so greatly desired by the socialist society."[1255]

These two opinions perfectly reflect the realities of the period from the end of World War II to the end of 1970. In this period, motorisation in Poland was stuck between the pragmatism of the authorities and the expectations of the society; from this perspective, the era of Władysław Gomułka figures as a period of lost opportunity.

1254 S. Kisielewski, *Dzienniki*, Warszawa 2001, p. 256.
1255 A. Zgorzelska, "Samochód i my," *Kierunki* 1971, no. 5, p. 3.

Bibliography

Archiwum Akt NowychArchiwum dokumentacji PRL

Centralne Archiwum PEKAO SA

Archiwum Instytutu Pamięci Narodowej

Ośrodek dokumentacji i zbiorów programowych TVP

Archiwum Państwowe w Kielcach

Archiwum Polskiego Radia

„Badania korespondentów miejskich" 1970, nr 2

„Biuletyn Informacyjny", Ośrodek Informacji Naukowo-Technicznej Zakładu Kryminalistyki KG MO 1972, nr 3

„Czas" 1975, nr 3

„Drogownictwo" 1946, nr 1/2

„Dziennik Ustaw" 1946, nr 7; 1948 nr 27; 1960 nr 55

„Głos Ludu" 1948, nr 117; nr 131

„Horyzonty Techniki" 1949 nr 10; 1951 nr 2; 1952 nr 2, 7/8; 1954 nr 2, 8, 12; 1956 nr 9, nr 43, nr 104, nr 106; 1957 nr 12; 1

„Kierunki" 1968 nr 42; 1971 nr 5

„Kurier Polski" 1958 nr 72

„Mały Rocznik Statystyczny «Motoryzacji»" 1968

„Mały Rocznik Statystyczny" 1938

„Mały Rocznik Statystyczny" 1939

„Miasto" 1959 nr 12

„Monitor Polski" 1949 nr 59; 1950 nr 123; 1951 nr 11, nr 21; 1952 nr 46; 1953 nr 28; 1954 nr 5, nr 24; 1957 nr 56, nr 81, nr 98; 958 nr 31; 1959 nr 9; 1963 nr 38, nr 97; 1961 nr 334; 1968 nr 31; 1971 nr 36; 1974 nr 36; 1975 nr 36; 1977 nr 16

„Motor" 1955 nr 13, 41; 1957 nr 2, 38, 42; 1960 nr 9, 17; 1961 nr 35; 1962 nr 5, 9, 21, 23, 48; 1964 nr 35, 38, 47, 50; 1965 nr 6, 16, 38, 40, 41, 44; 1966 nr 7, 11, 21, 30, 33, 43, 45, 46; 1967 nr 13; 1968 nr 39, 42

„Motoryzacja" 1946 nr 1; 1947 nr 1, 2, 8; 1953 nr 3, 12; 1954 nr 1, 2, 8; 1955 nr 1, 6, 10; 1956 nr 1, 2, 3, 4, 8; 1957 nr 5, 7; 1958 nr 1; 1959 nr 5; 1962 nr 4, 7/8; 1963 nr 7/8; 1965 nr 11; 1966 nr 12; 1968 nr 10; 1986 nr 2

„Nowe Drogi", Organ teoretyczny i polityczny Komitetu Centralnego Polskiej Zjednoczonej Partii Robotniczej 1956 nr 10

„Odgłosy" 1959 nr 27; 1964/65 nr 51/1

„Płomyk" 1961 nr 8

„Polityka" 1962 nr 32; 1963 nr 49; 1965 nr 19, 20, 54; 1966 nr 40, 42, 44, 50, 51; 1968 nr 13; 1969 nr 3, 5, 42, 44; 1977 nr 29, 33

„Prawo i Życie" 1969 nr 12; 1970 nr 3

„Przedsiębiorstwo i Rynek" 1988 z. 4

„Przegląd Samochodowy" 1957 nr 9

„Przegląd Techniczny" 1959 nr 21

„Rada Robotnicza" 1960 nr 6

„Rocznik Statystyczny Transportu" 1967

„Rocznik Statystyczny" 1949–1971

„Rocznik Statystyki Międzynarodowej" 1970

„Statistik Årsbok för Sverigie" 1965 (http://www.scb.se/Grupp/Hitta_statistik/Historisk_statistik/_Dokument/Statistisk%20årsbok%201914-2001/Statistisk%20arsbok%20 for%20Sverige%201965.pdf)

„Statistisches Jahrbuch der Deutschen Demokratischen Republik" 1970 (http://www. digizeitschriften.de/download/PPN514402644_1971/PPN514402644_1971___log63. pdf [dostęp: 14 VI 2017])

„Statistisches Jahrbuch der Deutschen Demokratischen Republik" 1966 (https://www.digizeitschriften.de/dms/img/?PID=PPN514402644_1966|log33&physid=phys230#navi [dostęp: 20 II 2017])

„Ster" 1956 nr 23; 1957 nr 2, 10, 11, 13

„Stolica" 1953, nr 14; 1967 nr 51/52; 1968 nr 13

„Szpilki" 1968

„Świat" 1975 nr 41

„Technika Motoryzacyjna" 1953 nr 7; 1954 nr 10; 1956 nr 9, 11; 1957 nr 2, 12; 1958 nr 8

„Trybuna Wolności" 1955 nr 39

„Wiadomości Statystyczne" 1987 nr 23

„Wiadomości Ubezpieczeniowe" 1957, nr 5; 1968 nr 12;

„Wiedza i Życie" 1959 nr 10

„Zagadnienia Karno-Administracyjne" 1963 nr 4/5

„Życie Gospodarcze" 1948 nr 7; 1959 nr 35, 50; 1960 nr 11; 1961 nr 3; 1966 nr 2; 1968 nr 32; 1980 nr 13

Kompendium Statystyczne Administracji Celnej 1956–1974, Warszawa 1975

Rostocki A., Wieniawski W., *Motoryzacja w liczbach 1969*, Warszawa 1970

Polska Kronika Filmowa

M-20 Warszawa, PKF 47/51

Giełda pod mostem, PKF 64/41B

Boniecki J., *Pierwsze dziesięciolecie*, Plon konkursu pamiętnikarskiego *Moje trzydziestolecie*, Wojewódzka Biblioteka Publiczna w Kielcach, sygn. Ręk. 138/16

Relacja Artura Starewicza, Hoover Institution Archives, Jane L. Curry Collection, Box 9

www.encysol.pl/wiki/Jerzy_Kurcyusz (dostęp: 19 I 2017)

http://www.nowedrogi.pl/index.php?option=content&task=view&id=32&Itemid=93 (dostęp: 21 I 2011)

Augustynowicz A. F., *Walka o samochód w Polsce*, Warszawa 1934

Bernhardt M., *Z Miodowej na Bracką. Opowieść powstańca warszawskiego*, cz. 2, Kraków 2012

Dąbrowska M., *Dzienniki powojenne 1945–1949*, Warszawa 1997

FSO Syrena. Instrukcja obsługi, Warszawa 1960

Giedroyc J., Miłosz C., *Listy 1964–1972*, oprac. M. Kornat, Warszawa 2011

Humor z Polski. Dowcipy z lat 1948–2008, zebrała E. Rychlewska, Poznań 2008

II Zjazd Polskiej Zjednoczonej Partii Robotniczej. Stenogram. Warszawa, 10 III–19 III 1959 r., Warszawa 1959

Jastrun M., *Dziennik 1955–1981*, Kraków 2002

Kisielewski S., *Dzienniki*, Warszawa 2001

Laforet C., *Za żelazną kurtyną. Podróż do Polski w 1967 r.*, Warszawa 2013

Listy do pierwszych sekretarzy KC PZPR, oprac. J. Stępień, Warszawa 1994

Ludowa i socjalistyczna. Pamiętniki Polaków 1918–1978. Antologia pamiętnikarstwa polskiego, wybór i oprac. B. Gołębiowski, M. Grad, F. Jakubczak, Warszawa 1983

Modzelewski K., *Zajeździmy kobyłę historii. Wspomnienia poobijanego jeźdźca*, Warszawa 2013

Motoryzacja Polski w świetle opinii publicznej, cz. 1–2, Warszawa 1934

Nor A. C. [Josef Kaván], *Cesta do Polska*, Praha 1947

Nowakowski W. E., *Okruchy systemu*, „Karta" 2014, nr 76

Pamiętniki pokolenia. Prace nadesłane na Wielki Konkurs Wspomnień pod nazwą „Rośliśmy z Polską Ludową" ogłoszony przez ZG ZMS, ZG ZMW Instytut Filozofii i Socjologii PAN, P.W. „Iskry" i „Sztandar Młodych", Warszawa 1966

Prace Rady Motoryzacyjnej 1958–1964, Warszawa 1965

Putrament J., *Pół wieku. Literaci*, Warszawa 1970

Rakowski M., *Dzienniki polityczne 1967–1968*, Warszawa 1999

Rakowski M., *Dzienniki polityczne 1969–1971*, Warszawa 2001

Regulski J., *Blaski i cienie długiego życia*, Warszawa 1980

Różański H., *Śladem wspomnień i dokumentów (1943–1948)*, Warszawa 1987

Rurarz Z., *Byłem doradcą Gierka*, Chicago–Toronto–Warszawa 1990

Rychter W., *Moje dwa i cztery kółka*, Warszawa 1983

Sękowski M., *Pamiętnik warszawskiego taksówkarza*, Warszawa 1985

Słodowy A., *Budowa samochodu amatorskiego*, Warszawa 1958

Słodowy A., *Jeżdżę samochodem Skoda 1000 MB*, Warszawa 1967

Słodowy A., *Podręcznik kierowcy amatora*, Warszawa 1952

Słodowy A., *Sam obsługuję samochód*, Warszawa 1969

Słodowy A., *Samochód bez tajemnic*, Warszawa 1966

Słodowy A., *Samochód bez tajemnic*, Warszawa 1971

Słodowy A., *Skoda 1000 MB, 1100 MB, 100, 110: technika jazdy, obsługa i usprawnienia*, Warszawa 1969

Słodowy A., *Usprawniam własny samochód*, Warszawa 1971

Słownik biograficzny techników polskich, z. 6, red. nacz. Z. Skarzyński, Warszawa 1995

Szczepański J. J., *Dziennik*, t. 1: *1945–1956*, Kraków 2009; t. 2: *1957–1963*, Kraków 2011; t. 3: *1964–1972*, Kraków 2013

Tyrmand L., *Dziennik 1954. Wersja oryginalna*, Warszawa 1999

Zawieyski J., *Dzienniki*, t. 1: *Wybór z lat 1955–1959*, wybór i oprac. red. A. Knyt, współpr. M. Czoch, Warszawa 2011

Życie bez fikcji. Dzienniki, wybór, wstęp i oprac. S. Adamczyk, Warszawa 1976

Opracowania

Akhtar M., Humphries S., *The Fifties and Sixties. A Lifestyle Revolution*, Basingstoke and Oxford 2001

Automobilklub Polski 1909–2009. Monografia, red. B. Mierkowski, Warszawa 2009

Bardou J. P., Chanaron J. J., Fridenson P., Laux J. M., *The Automobile Revolution. The Impact of an Industry*, Chapel Hill 1982

Barthes R., *Mit i znak*, Warszawa 1970

Baudelot Ch., Lebeaupin A., *Les salaries de 1950 à 1975*, „Economie et statistique" 1979, vol. 113, no. 1

Baudrillard J., *Społeczeństwo konsumpcyjne. Jego mity i struktury*, Warszawa 2006

Berend I. T., *Central and Eastern Europe 1944–1993. Detour from the periphery to the periphery*, Cambridge 1996

Bojar H., *Rodzina i życie rodzinne*, w: *Co nam zostało z tych lat... Społeczeństwo polskie u progu zmiany systemowej*, red. M. Marody, Londyn 1991

Brzostek B., *Szewroletariat*, „Mówią Wieki" 2013, nr 5, s. 54–55

Brzostek B., *Za progiem. Codzienność w przestrzeni publicznej Warszawy lat 1955–1970*, Warszawa 2007

Bugowski R., *Polski Fiat jako „miejsce pamięci". Rola i obraz marki polskiej drugiej połowy XX wieku. Refleksje wokół koncepcji*, „Klio" 2011, nr 1, s. 123–140

Bukowski W., *Samochody PRL-u*, Łódź 2010

Burleigh M., *Trzecia Rzesza. Nowa historia*, Kraków 2010

Busch F., *Transportation in Postwar Germany*, „Annals of the American Academy of Political and Social Science" 1948, vol. 260 (November)

Ciesla B., *Difficult Relations. German Automobile Construction and the Economic Alliance in Eastern Europe, 1945–1990*, w: *Towards Mobility. Varieties of Automobilism in East and West*, ed. D. Schlinkert, M. Grieger, U. Gutzmann, Wolfsburg 2009

Krasiński Z., *Czynniki ekonomiczno-społeczne rozwoju motoryzacji indywidualnej w Polsce w świetle badań ankietowych*, Poznań 1972

Dłutek A., *Kooperacja polsko-włoska Fiat 126p: zakup licencji: opis przypadku*, Warszawa 1979

Duignam P., Gann L. H., *The Rebirth of the Democratic World 1945–1958*, Cambridge 1992

Dziurawiec A., *Późny Gomułka, wczesny Gierek*, Warszawa 2009

Fałkowski M., *Życie codzienne w samochodzie. Schematy interakcji i wzajemnego postrzegania się kierowców z perspektywy socjologii życia codziennego*, „Kultura i Społeczeństwo" 2010, t. 54, nr 1

Fava V., *The Elusive People's Car. Imagined Automobility and Productive Practices along the „Czechoslovak Road to Socialism" (1945–1968)*, w: *The Socialist Car. Automobility in the Eastern Bloc*, ed. L. H. Siegelbaum, New York 2011

Fava V., *The Socialist People's Car: Automobiles, Shortages, and Consent on the Czechoslovak Road to Mass Production (1918–1964)*, Amsterdam 2013

Fiat w Polsce (sprzedaż licencji), Warszawa 1980

Fink J. J., *The Automobile Age*, Cambridge–London 1988

Fitzpatrick S., *Życie codzienne pod rządami Stalina. Rosja radziecka w latach trzydziestych XX wieku*, Kraków 2012

Foreman-Peck J., *Death on the Roads: Changing National Responses to Motor Accidents*, w: *The Economic and Social Effects of the Spread of Motor Vehicles*, ed. T. Barker, London 1987

Friedrich S., *Autos bauen im Sozialismus. Arbeit und Organisationskultur in der Zwickauer Automobilindustrie nach 1945*, Leipzig 2008

Garbacz A., *Mikrus. Auto, któremu nie pozwolono dorosnąć*, Stalowa Wola 2011

Gatejel L., *Appealing for a Car: Consumption Policies and Entitlement in the USSR, the GDR, and Romania, 1950s–1980s*, „Slavic Review" 2016, vol. 75, no. 1 (Spring 2016)

Gatejel L., *The Common Heritage of the Socialist Car Culture*, w: *The Socialist Car. Automobility in the Eastern Bloc*, ed. L. H. Siegelbaum, New York 2011

Gatejel L., *Warten, hoffen und endlich fahren: Auto und Sozialismus in der Sowjetunion, in Rumänien und der DDR, 1956–1989/91*, Frankfurt am Main 2014

Gierowski J. A., *Historia Włoch*, Wrocław–Warszawa–Kraków 1999

Górski M., *Historia konstrukcji samochodów FSO. 1951–2011*, Warszawa 2013

Grandin G., *Fordlandia. Henry Ford i jego miasto-państwo w amazońskiej dżungli*, przeł. J.J. Górski, Warszawa 2012

Groniewski K., *Technika motoryzacyjna w Polsce międzywojennej*, Warszawa 1965

Gunn S., *People and the car: the expansion of automobility in urban Britain, 1955–1970*, „Social History" 38, 2013, no. 2

Hanasz W., *Engines of liberty. Cars and the Collapse of Communism in Eastern Europe. A personal essay*, http://www.cei.org/pdf/1755.pdf

Handel i usługi na tle rozwoju motoryzacji indywidualnej, Warszawa 1977

Heitmann J. A., *The automobile and American Life*, Jefferson 2009

J. M., *Zmotoryzujmy Polskę*, Warszawa 1939

Jarosz D., Pasztor M., *Afera mięsna: fakty i konteksty*, Toruń 2004

Jarosz D., Pasztor M., *Skazani na podległość. Z dziejów stosunków polsko-włoskich w latach 1945–1958*, Warszawa 2013

Jastrząb M., *Edukacja w zakresie bezpieczeństwa ruchu drogowego w polskich szkołach. Historia inercji instytucjonalnej*, w: *Na lądzie, w wodzie i w powietrzu... Z dziejów transportu i komunikacji na ziemiach polskich na przestrzeni wieków*, red. T. Głowiński, R. Klementowski, Wrocław 2014, s. 279–288

Jastrząb M., *Fiat's small cars for Polish mass motorisation: The Small Engine Car Factory in Bielsko-Biała and Tychy, 1971–1980*, „Journal of Transport History" 2017, vol. 38, no. 1

Jastrząb M., *Historia motoryzacji i przemysłu motoryzacyjnego. Stan i cele badań*, w: *Przegląd badań nad historią gospodarczą w XXI wieku*, red. R. Matera, A. Pieczewski, Łódź 2011, s. 161–173

Jastrząb M., J. *Wawrzyniak, Dwie nowoczesności polskiego przemysłu motoryzacyjnego: o rozwoju zależnym Fabryki Samochodów Osobowych*, „Acta Poloniae Historica" (w druku)

Jastrząb M., *Nadzór nad wielką inwestycją przemysłową: budowa Fabryki Samochodów Małolitrażowych i wdrożenie produkcji Fiata 126p*, w: *Z dziejów przemysłu na ziemiach polskich*, red. R. Klementowski, E. Kościk, Wrocław 2012, s. 113–122

Jastrząb M., *Socjalistyczna praworządność i egalitaryzm. Nadużycia władzy w epoce gierkowskiej i walka z nimi. Przykład talonów samochodowych*, w: *Społeczeństwo polskie w latach 1980–1989*, red. N. Jarska i J. Olaszek, Warszawa–Kraków 2015, s. 70–86

Jastrząb M., *The idea of developed socialist society and a private car* – tekst udostępniony przez Autora

Jastrząb M., *Zajazdy dla zmotoryzowanych w Polsce lat siedemdziesiątych*, „Przegląd Historyczny" 2013, nr 2, s. 325–348

Jaworska J., *Cywilizacja „Przekroju". Misja obyczajowa w magazynie ilustrowanym*, Warszawa 2008

Jędrzejczak A., *Sąd nad posiadaczem*, w: *Młodzi stąd. Reportaże 1950–1965*, wybór A. Pawłowska i J. Feliksiak, Warszawa 1966

Judt T., *Powojnie. Historia Europy od 1945*, Poznań 2008

Juźwik A., *Zagraniczna pomoc charytatywna dla dzieci i młodzieży w Polsce w latach 1945–1950*, „Polska 1944/45–1989. Studia i Materiały" 2013, nr 11

Kaliński J., *Historia gospodarcza XIX i XX w.*, Warszawa 2008

Kaliński J., Liberadzki B., *Transport w Polsce w latach 1918–1978. Zarys historii*, Warszawa 1986

Kaliński J., *Motoryzacja a infrastruktura drogowa w Polsce po 1918 r.*, w: *Na lądzie, w wodzie i w powietrzu… Z dziejów transportu i komunikacji na ziemiach polskich na przestrzeni wieków*, red. T. Głowiński, R. Klementowski, Wrocław 2014

Kaliński J., *Plan odbudowy gospodarczej 1947–1949*, Warszawa 1977

Kaliński J., *Polityka gospodarcza Polski w latach 1948–1955*, Warszawa 1987

Karpiński A., *PRL a uprzemysłowienie i urbanizacja Polski*, w: *Zrozumieć PRL*, red. W. Żółtkowski, Warszawa 2012

Keiller P., *Sexual Ambiguity and Automotive Engineering*, w: *Autopia. Cars and Culture*, ed. P. Wollen, J. Kerr, London 2002

Kirchberg P., *Plaste, Blech und Planwirtschaft. Die Geschichte des Automobilbaus in der DDR*, Berlin 2000

Klominek A., *Życie w „Przekroju"*, Warszawa 1995

Kochanowski J., *Rewolucja międzypaździernikowa. Polska 1956–1957*, Kraków 2017

Kochanowski J., *Tylnymi drzwiami. „Czarny rynek" w Polsce 1944–1989*, Warszawa 2010

Kochański A., *Jan Rustecki*, w: *Polski Słownik Biograficzny*, t. 33, 1991, z. 1

Komornicki T., *Przemiany mobilności codziennej Polaków na tle rozwoju motoryzacji*, Warszawa 2011

Konieczniak Z., *FSO. Fabryka Samochodów Osobowych 1951–1986*, Warszawa 1986

König W., *Volkswagen, Volksempfänger, Volksgemeinschaft. „Volksprodukte" im Dritten Reich: Vom Scheitern einer nationalsozialistischen Konsumgesellschaft*, Paderborn 2004

Korczyk H., *Janusz Regulski*, w: *Polski Słownik Biograficzny*, t. 30, 1987, z. 127

Koshar R., *Cars and Nations. Anglo-German Perspectives on Automobility between the World Wars*, „Theory, Culture & Society" 2004, vol. 21, no. 4/5

Kozieł K., *Prasa w latach 1944–1989*, w: *Prasa, radio i telewizja w Polsce. Zarys dziejów*, red. D. Grzelewska *et al.*, Warszawa 1999

Krupa Z., *Działalność propagandowo-profilaktyczna Milicji Obywatelskiej na rzecz bezpieczeństwa w ruchu drogowym*, „Bezpieczeństwo i Administracja. Zeszyty Naukowe Wydziału Bezpieczeństwa Narodowego Akademii Obrony Narodowej" 2015, nr 3

Kula M., *Mimo wszystko bliżej Paryża niż Moskwy. Książka o Francji, PRL i o nas, historykach*, Warszawa 2010

Kuroń J., Żakowski J., *PRL dla początkujących*, Wrocław 1995

Landau Z., Tomaszewski J., *Bank Polska Kasa Opieki SA*, Warszawa 1990

Landau Z., Tomaszewski J., *Zarys historii gospodarczej Polski 1918–1939*, Warszawa 1999

Lefebvre H., *Everyday Life in The Modern World*, New York 2016

Lem S., Mrożek S., *Listy 1956–1978*, tł. z ang. T. Lem, z fr. R. Niziołek, Kraków 2011

Leszczyński A., *Sprawy do załatwienia. Listy do „Po Prostu" 1955–1957*, Warszawa 2000

Lista G., *Futuryzm*, tłum. E. Gorządek, Warszawa 2002

Łuczak C., *Pod niemieckim jarzmem (Kraj Warty 1939–1945)*, Poznań 1996

Majewski M. W., *Poszukiwania złóż ropy naftowej i gazu w Polsce (1919–1939)*, „Annales Universitatis Pedagogicae Cracoviensis. Studia Historica" 2009, t. 8

Majewski M. W., *Powstanie przemysłu motoryzacyjnego w II Rzeczypospolitej 1919–1928*, w: *Z dziejów przemysłu przed 1945 rokiem*, red. J. Chumiński, M. Zawadka, Wrocław 2012

Majewski M. W., *Rozwój motoryzacji w Drugiej Rzeczypospolitej*, Kraków 2016

Makłowicz J., *Zmotoryzujmy Polskę*, Warszawa 1931

Marvick A., *The Sixties: cultural revolution in Britain, france, Italy and the United States, c. 1958–1974*, New York 1998

McShane C., *Down the Asphalt Path. The Automobile and the American City*, New York 1994

Mezer J. de, *Cywilizacja motocyklowa. Motoryzacja motocyklowa w Polsce 1945–1965*, Warszawa 2011

Miczka T., *Czas przyszły niedokonany. O włoskiej sztuce futurystycznej*, Katowice 1994

Milijkovic M., *Western Technology in Socialist Factory: the Formative Phase of the Yugoslav Automobile Industry, 1955–1962*, Cold War History Research Center at Corvinas University of Budapest, 2013, s. 6 (http://www.etd.ceu.hu/2013/miljkovic_marko.pdf [dostęp: 18 V 2016])

Miniuk A. I., *The Use of German Industrial and Scientific Technical Potential in the Development of the Soviet Motor Industry* w: *Towards Mobility*

Misiuk A., *Historia Policji w Polsce. Od X wieku do współczesności*, Warszawa 2008

Misztal S., *Branże wiodące stołecznego przemysłu w latach 1945–1976*, w: *Wielkie zakłady przemysłowe Warszawy*, red. J. Kazimierski *et al.*, Warszawa 1974

Modelski Ł., *Fotobiografia PRL. Opowieści reporterów*, Kraków 2013

Mórawski K. J., *Syrena. Samochód PRL-u*, Warszawa 2005

Morawski W., *Dzieje gospodarcze Polski*, Warszawa 2010

Nestorowicz M. W., *Sprawa drogowa w Polsce. Zagadnienie gospodarcze*, Warszawa 1924

Nestorowicz M. W., *Stan dróg kołowych Królestwa Polskiego*, Warszawa 1913

Nettleton N., *Driving towards Communist Consumerism. AvtoVAZ*, „Cahiers du monde ruse" 2006, vol. 47, no. 1–2, s. 131–151

Niedziałek M. C., *Działalność MO w opinii pracowników poznańskich zakładów pracy*, w: *Milicja Obywatelska a społeczeństwo (Synteza i reinterpretacja badań z lat 1967– 1983)*, red. S. Buczyński *et al.*, Warszawa 1984

Niedźwiecka E., *Łódź w PRL-u. Opowieść o życiu miasta 1945–1980*, Łódź 2011

Obyczaje polskie. Wiek XX w krótkich hasłach, red. M. Szpakowska, Warszawa 2008

Opowieść o FSO. Historia tej warszawskiej fabryki, red. prow. Z. Boniecki przy współpr. R. Gajewskiego, korekta i uzup. E. Pietrzak, Warszawa 2010

Pałaszewska-Reindl T., *Konsumpcja dóbr trwałego użytku w Polsce*, Warszawa 1966

Péteri G., *Alternative modernity? Everyday Practices of Elite Mobility in Communist Hungary, 1956–1980*, w: *The Socialist Car. Automobility in the Eastern Bloc*, ed. L. H. Siegelbaum, New York 2011

Płocica M., Winiarski B., *Mikrus MR-300. 3 lata produkcji, 50 lat historii*, Kraków 2011

Podbielski Z., *Polski Fiat 125p/FSO 125p*, Warszawa 2009

Pytel J., *Ochotnicza Rezerwa Milicji Obywatelskiej (1946–1989)*, Warszawa 2009

Pyter M., *Prawne zasady użytkowania pojazdów mechanicznych*, „Czasopismo Prawno-Historyczne" 2011, t. 63, z. 2

Reinhard W., *Życie po europejsku. Od czasów najdawniejszych do współczesności*, Warszawa 2009

Reinisch J., *„We shall Rebuild Anew a Powerful Nation". UNRRA, Internationalism and National Reconstruction in Poland*, „Journal of Contemporary History" 2008, t. 43, nr 3

Relich M., *Załamanie motoryzacji w Polsce na skutek tzw. demotoryzacji kraju w latach 1931–1935 i próby jej odbudowy w drugiej połowie lat 30. XX wieku*, w: *Na lądzie, w wodzie i w powietrzu… Z dziejów transportu i komunikacji na ziemiach polskich na przestrzeni wieków*, red. T. Głowiński, R. Klementowski, Wrocław 2014

Robertson L. S., *Motor Vehicle Injuries*, „Public Health Reports" 1985, vol. 100, no. 6

Roche M., *Samochód*, w: *Psychologia życia codziennego*, red. M. Reuchlin, tłum. z fr. Z. Zakrzewska, Warszawa 1983

Rostocki A., *Kochajmy stare gruchoty*, Warszawa 1977

Rostocki A., Tarczyński J., *Automobilizm w Warszawie do 1939 r.*, Warszawa 1988

Rummel A., *Polskie konstrukcje i licencje motoryzacyjne w latach 1922–1980*, Warszawa 1985

Rychter W., *Dzieje samochodu*, Warszawa 1979

Rynek motoryzacyjny, red. Z. Krasiński, Warszawa 1980,

Ryś B., *Rozwój polsko-jugosłowiańskich stosunków gospodarczych*, Łódź 1986

Sachs W., *For the Love of the Automobile. Looking Back into the History of Our Desires*, Oxford 1992

Salvadori R., *Sceny pierwotne*, w: *idem*, *Mitologia nowoczesności*, tłum. H. Kralowa, Warszawa 2004

Saupe A., *Human Security and the Challenge of Automobile and Road Traffic Safety: A Cultural Historical Perspective*, „Historical Social Research / Historische Sozialforschung" 2010, vol. 35, no. 4 (134)

Setright L. J. K., *Drive On! A Social History of the Motor Car*, London 2003

Siegelbaum L. H., *Cars for Comrades. The Life of the Soviet Automobile*, Cornell University Press 2008

Skobelski R., *Polityka PRL wobec państw socjalistycznych w latach 1956–1970. Współpraca napięcia konflikty*, Poznań 2010

Skodlarski J., *Zarys historii gospodarczej Polski do 1945 roku*, Warszawa–Łódź 1997

Socjologia codzienności, red. P. Sztompka, M. Boguni-Borowska, Kraków 2008

Sowiński P., *Wakacje w Polsce Ludowej: polityka władz i ruch turystyczny (1945–1989)*, Warszawa 2005

Sulima R., *Antropologia codzienności*, Kraków 2000

Syzdak E., Syzdak B., *Zanim zostanie zapomniany*, Warszawa 1996

Szarota T., *Okupowanej Warszawy dzień powszedni. Studium historyczne*, Warszawa 1988

Szarota T., *Życie codzienne w stolicach okupowanej Europy. Szkice historyczne. Kronika wydarzeń*, Warszawa 1995

Szczerbicki T., *Mercedes a sprawa polska*, Warszawa 2006

Szczerbicki T., *Samochody w PRL. Rzecz o motoryzacji i nie tylko…*, Warszawa 2010

Szczerbicki T., *Syrena*, Czerwonak 2016

Szelichowski S., *Dzieje polskiej motoryzacji*, Łódź 2012

Szostkiewicz S., *Bezpieczeństwo na drogach publicznych w opinii społecznej*, w: *Konferencja Naukowo-Techniczna pt. Problemy bezpieczeństwa ruchu drogowego, Warszawa, 5–6 maja 1971: materiały*, Warszawa 1971

Szostkiewicz S., *Przemiany w strukturze załogi Fabryki Samochodów Osobowych w latach 1956–1961*, Wrocław–Warszawa–Kraków 1965

Szumiłło M., *Roman Zambrowski 1909–1977*, Warszawa 2014

Tarczyński J., Jeleń W., *Początki polskiej motoryzacji. Samochody CWS*, Warszawa 1991

Tarczyński J., Szczerbicki T., *Samochody osobowe Polski Fiat 508 i 518*, Warszaw 2003

The Economic and Social Effects of the Spread of Motor Vehicles, ed. T. Barker, London 1987

Turnock D., *The East European Economy in Context. Communism and Transition*, London–New York 1997

Urbanek M., *Zły Tyrmand*, Warszawa 2007

Volti R., *Cars and Culture. The Life Story of a Technology*, Baltimore 2006

Wieczorkiewicz A., *Polska Jugosławia. Gospodarka współpraca*, Warszawa 1972

Wilk H., *Być kierowcą w PRL. Problemy zmotoryzowanych w świetle publikacji „Motoru" w latach 1955–1966*, „Polska 1944/45–1989. Studia i Materiały" 2011, t. 10, s. 223–262

Wilk H., *Od Sputnika do selenautów. Kosmiczny wyścig w świetle oficjalnej propagandy PRL (1957–1969)*, w: *Yesterday. Studia z historii najnowszej. Księga dedykowana prof. Jerzemu Eislerowi w 65. rocznicę urodzin*, red. J. Olaszek, A. Dudek, Ł. Kamiński *et al.*, Warszawa 2017

Wilk H., *Ministerstwo Motoryzacji czy Centralny Urząd Samochodowy? – polska motoryzacja na rozdrożu. Plany, możliwości, instytucje (1944–1948)*, „Pamięć i Sprawiedliwość" 2015, nr 1, s. 144–162

Wilk H., *„Nawet samochodów nie ma, zostały graty po Niemcach" – motoryzacyjny punkt startu – Polska 1944–1949*, „Polska 1944/45–1989. Studia i Materiały" 2013, t. 12, s. 301–330

Wilk H., *Próba modernizacji polskiego przemysłu maszynowego w drugiej połowie lat 60. Przypadek fiata 125p*, „Roczniki Dziejów Społecznych i Gospodarczych" 2016, t. 76, s. 411–438

Wilk H., *Stan motoryzacji w województwie kieleckim w latach 1945–1949*, „Świętokrzyskie Studia Archiwalno-Historyczne" 2016, t. 5, s. 321–350

Wilk H., *Wybrane aspekty rozwoju motoryzacji i jego wpływu na środowisko naturalne w powojennej Polsce*, w: *Od systemu żarowego do ekorozwoju. Ochrona i wykorzystanie zasobów środowiska naturalnego na ziemiach polskich – aspekt historyczny*, red. T. Głowiński, M. Zawadka, Wrocław 2016, s. 297–306

Wituch T., *Spór o Triest – wczesny epizod „zimnej wojny"*, „Dzieje Najnowsze" 1997, nr 2

Wójcik T., *Centralne Warsztaty Samochodowe w Warszawie w latach 1918–1928. Przyczynek do genezy polskiej motoryzacji*, „Przegląd Historyczno-Wojskowy" 2013, nr 2

Wójcik T., *Wybrane aspekty działalności wojska w rozwoju motoryzacji II Rzeczypospolitej*, w: *Z dziejów przemysłu przed 1945 rokiem*, red. J. Chumiński, M. Zawadzki, Wrocław 2012

Wolle S., *Wspaniały świat dyktatury. Codzienność i władza w NRD 1979–1989*, Warszawa 2003

Wróblewski A. K., *Polska na kółkach*, Warszawa 1989

Zatlin J. R., *The Currency of Socialism. Money and political culture in East Germany*, New York 2007

Zawistowski A., *Polska Ludowa. Wzrost podporządkowany doktrynie politycznej*, w: *Polskie osiągnięcia gospodarcze. perspektywa historyczna*, red. J. Kaliński, Warszawa 2010

Zieliński A., *Rozwój koncepcji samochodu osobowego w XX wieku*, Warszawa 2005

Index

Note: Page references followed by "n" indicates a single note number and "nn" indicates a range or series of note numbers on the cited page.

445

Polish Studies – Transdisciplinary Perspectives

Edited by Krzysztof Zajas and Jarosław Fazan

Vol. 1 Artur Płaczkiewicz: Miron Białoszewski: Radical Quest beyond Dualisms. 2012.

Vol. 2 Kinga Kosmala: Ryszard Kapuściński: Reportage and Ethics or Fading Tyranny of the Narrative. 2012.

Vol. 3 Michał Nowosielski: Polish Organisations in Germany. Their Present Status and Needs. 2012.

Vol. 4 Krzysztof Zajas: Absent Culture. The Case of Polish Livonia. 2013.

Vol. 5 Magdalena Sitarz: Literature as a Medium for Memory. The Universe of Sholem Asch's Novels. 2013.

Vol. 6 Barbara Przybyszewska-Jarmińska / Lech Sokół (eds.): Poland and Artistic Culture of Western Europe. 14th–20th Century. 2014.

Vol. 7 Katarzyna Fazan / Anna Róża Burzyńska / Marta Bryś (eds.): Tadeusz Kantor Today. Metamorphoses of Death, Memory and Presence. Translated by Anda MacBride. 2014.

Vol. 8 Andrzej Hejmej: Music in Literature. Perspectives of Interdisciplinary Comparative Literature. Translated by Lindsay Davidson. 2014.

Vol. 9 Grzegorz Niziołek: Warlikowski: Extra Ecclesiam. Translated by Soren Gauger. 2015.

Vol. 10 Ryszard Koziołek: Sienkiewicźs Bodies. Studies of Gender and Violence. Translated by David Malcolm. 2015.

Vol. 11 Wojciech Tygielski: Italians in Early Modern Poland. The Lost Opportunity for Modernization? Translated by Katarzyna Popowicz. 2015.

Vol. 12 Dariusz Jarosz / Maria Pasztor: Polish-French Relations, 1944-1989. Translated by Alex Shannon. 2015.

Vol. 13 Urszula Augustyniak: History of the Polish–Lithuanian Commonwealth. State – Society – Culture. 2015.

Vol. 14 Piotr Sobolczyk: Polish Queer Modernism. 2015.

Vol. 15 Jacek Soszyński / Agnieszka Chamera-Nowak (eds.): Book versus Power. Studies in the Relations between Politics and Culture in Polish History. Editorial assistance by Dan Embree. Translated by Jacek Soszyński 2015.

Vol. 16 Wojciech Kriegseisen: Between State and Church. Confessional Relations from Reformation to Enlightenment: Poland – Lithuania – Germany – Netherlands. Translated by Bartosz Wójcik and copy-edited by Alex Shannon. 2016.

Vol. 17 Urszula Sowina: Water, Towns and People. Polish Lands against a European Background until the Mid-16th Century. Translated by Justyna Woldańska. 2016.

Vol. 18 Grzegorz Krzywiec: Chauvinism, Polish Style. The Case of Roman Dmowski (Beginnings: 1886-1905). Translated by Jarosław Garliński. 2016.

Vol. 19 Andrzej Sakson: Von Memel bis Allenstein. Die heutigen Bewohner des ehemaligen Ostpreußens: Memelland, Kaliningrader Gebiet, Ermland und Masuren. Übersetzt von Marek Drewnowski. 2016.

Vol. 20 Antoni Mączak: Unequal Friendship. The Patron-Client Relationship in Historical Perspective. Translated by Alex Shannon. 2017.

Vol. 21 Olga Szmidt / Katarzyna Trzeciak (eds.): Face in Trouble – From Physiognomics to Facebook. Copy-edited by Soren Gauger. 2017.

Vol. 22 Alina Cala: Jew. The Eternal Enemy? The History of Antisemitism in Poland. 2019.

Vol. 23 Agata Brajerska-Mazur / Edyta Chlebowska (eds.): On Cyprian Norwid. Studies and Essays. Vol. 1: Syntheses. 2019.

Vol. 24 Beata Nowacka / Zygmunt Ziątek: Ryszard Kapuściński. Biographie d'un écrivain. 2019.

Vol. 25 Stanisław Bylina: Religiousness in the Late Middle Ages. Christianity and Traditional Culture in Central and Eastern Europe in the Fourteenth and Fifteenth Centuries. 2019.

Vol. 26 Igor Kąkolewski / Christian Lübke / Przemysław Urbańczyk (eds.): The Dawning of Christianity in Poland and across Central and Eastern Europe. History and the Politics of Memory. 2019.

Vol. 27 Bogumił Szady: The Geography of Religious and Confessional Structures in the Crown of the Polish Kingdom in the Second Half of the Eighteenth Century. 2019.

Vol. 28 Ewa Masłowska: Mediating the Otherworld in Polish Folklore. A Cognitive Linguistic Perspective. 2019.

Vol. 29 Adam Andrzej Kucharski: Placing Poland at the heart of Irishness. Irish political elites in relation to Poland and the Poles in the first half of the nineteenth century. 2020.

Vol. 30 Jolanta Sikorska-Kulesza: The Tolerated Evil. Prostitution in Poland of 19th Century. 2020.

Vol. 31 Żaneta Nalewajk: Leśmian Internationally: Contextual Relations. A Comparative Study. 2020.

Vol. 32 Anna Machcewicz: Civility in Uncivil Times. Kazimierz Moczarski's Quiet Battle for Truth, from the Polish Underground to Stalinist Prison. 2020.

Vol. 33 Bartosz Kaliski: Messengers of the Free Word. Paris – Prague – Warsaw, 1968–1971. 2020.

Vol. 34 Dorota Litwin-Lewandowska: For the Polish Raison d'État in Austria. Poles in the Political Life of Austria in the Dual Monarchy Period (1867-1818). 2020.

Vol. 35 Marek Kornat: Poland and the Origins of the Second World War. A Study in Diplomatic History (1938–1939). 2020.

Vol. 36 Barbara Klich-Kluczewska: Family, Taboo and Communism in Poland, 1956-1989. 2021.

Vol. 37 Agata Brajerska-Mazur / Edyta Chlebowska (eds.): On Cyprian Norwid. Studies and Essays. Vol. 2. Aspects. 2021.

Vol. 38 Justyna Straczuk: The Graveyard and the Table. The Catholic-Orthodox Borderland in Poland and Belarus. 2021.

Vol. 39 Marta Wojtkowska-Maksymik / Magdalena Zawisławska (eds.): Studies in Polish Language and Literature. 2022.

Vol. 40 Joanna Gierowska-Kałłaur: The Civic Management of Eastern Territories (1919–1920). The Reasons for the Failure of Piłsudski's Federation Idea. 2022.

Vol. 41 Agata Brajerska-Mazur / Edyta Chlebowska (eds.): On Cyprian Norwid. Studies and Essays. Vol. 3. Interpretations. 2022.

Vol. 42 Maciej Junkiert / Krzysztof Trybuś / Michael Düring / Rebekka Wilpert (eds.): Polen und Deutsche im Angesicht der revolutionären Umwälzungen. 2023.

Vol. 43 Agata Brajerska-Mazur / Edyta Chlebowska (eds.): On Cyprian Norwid. Studies and Essays. Vol. 4. Contexts. 2023.

Vol. 44 Magdalena Śniedziewska: Seventeenth-Century Dutch Painting and Modern Literature. 2024.

Vol. 45 Rafał Dobek: Louis Wolowski (1810-1876). Polish insurgent, French politician, Banker and Economist. 2024.

Vol. 46 Aleksandra Wójtowicz: The Staszic Palace as Affective Heterotopia: New Category of Spatial Description. 2024.

Vol. 47 Włodzimierz Bolecki: Modalities of Polish Modernism. 2025.

Vol. 48 Piotr Toczyski: Four Internet Studies in Global Ethics and Global Education. Focus on Poland. 2025.

Vol. 49 Roman Duda: A History of Polish Mathematics. A Cultural Perspective from Origins to Modernity. 2026.

Vol. 50 Hubert Wilk: Driving Towards Socialism: Society, Power, and Cars in Poland 1945-1970. 2026

www.peterlang.com